Contemporary Philosophy of Thought

Contemporary Philosophy

Each volume in this series provides a clear, comprehensive and up-to-date introduction to the main philosophical topics of contemporary debate. Written by leading philosophers, the volumes provide an ideal basis for university students and others who want an engaging and accessible account of the subject. While acting as an introduction, each volume offers and defends a distinct position in its own right.

Published Works

Contemporary Philosophy of Thought

Truth, World, Content

Michael Luntley

The right of Michael Luntley to be identified as Author of this work has been asserted in accordance with the Copyright, Designs and Patents Act 1988

First published 1999

2 4 6 8 10 9 7 5 3 1

Blackwell Publishers Ltd
108 Cowley Road
Oxford OX4 1JF
UK

Blackwell Publishers Inc.
350 Main Street
Malden, Massachusetts 02148
USA

British Library Cataloguing in Publication Data

A CIP catalogue record for this book is available from the British Library

Library of Congress Cataloging-in-Publication Data
Luntley, Michael, 1953–
Contemporary philosophy of thought: truth, world, content / Michael Luntley.
p.   cm. — (Contemporary philosophy)
Includes bibliographical references and index.
ISBN 0-631-19076-7 (alk. paper). — ISBN 0-631-19077-5 (pbk. : alk. paper)
1. Thought and thinking.   2. Language and languages—Philosophy.
3. Truth.   I. Title.   II. Series: Contemporary philosophy
(Cambridge, Mass.)
B105.T54L86   1999
121'.68—dc21   98-8525   CIP

Typeset in 11 on 13 pt Garamond 3
by Best-set Typesetter Ltd., Hong Kong
Printed in Great Britain by TJ International, Padstow, Cornwall

This book is printed on acid-free paper

Contents

Preface

A new paradigm is emerging in the philosophy of thought. What it is to be a thinker is to be an embodied agent acting on, and being acted upon by, the world. Descartes thought mind was out of this world. Most contemporary thinkers still agree, despite their materialism; for they mostly think that if there are such things as thoughts, they are characterizable independently of the world that they represent. The new paradigm has thought constitutively in the world. In this book I put the case for this new paradigm. I put it in the context of the standard options that get taught in most philosophy courses on thought and language.

The embodiment of thought characteristic of this new paradigm has been around in empirical work for some time, in situated robotics, artificial life research and, of course, amongst connectionist groupies. The philosophical story that brings thought into our embodied actions is now catching up. The version of this story that I tell derives from Frege, but owes its distinctiveness to Evans's seminal *The Varieties of Reference*. That book is still massively misunderstood. It is not uncommon to meet people at conferences who have no idea what a singular sense is and, when told, always respond, 'But what about empty names?' The difficulty here arises from the absence of an appreciation of the metaphysical reorientation required for understanding neo-Fregean theory of content. This book is centred on getting clear what that metaphysical reorientation amounts to. The new paradigm is a way of understanding the metaphysics of thought and of our place in the world.

The paradigm is generalizable to areas beyond the immediate concerns of the philosophy of thought. I touch on such matters occasionally, but if the sort of embodied account of thought that I defend is anywhere near right, there are morals to be drawn for the nature of ethical reasoning and the nature of the self. Our paradigm of intelligence has for too long been the ability to manipulate formal languages, play chess, do maths, etc. In contrast, I think the paradigm of intelligence is being able to cross a room at a crowded party without spilling your drink or bumping into anyone else. Now, that's smart. It involves a practical cognitive sense of embodiment, bearing and orientation that is not disengageable from being in the world. Getting an account of the concepts of embodiment, orientation, etc. straight offers the option of treating ethical reasoning in terms of a practical mastery of how we fit (or fail to fit), and how we live, in our world. There is exciting stuff that could be done on these fronts. I leave it out, for this book concentrates on the basics.

The book is intended for upper-level undergraduates and first-year graduate students of philosophy. It is, however, a basic book. Some books in the field provide a survey of advanced results in the philosophy of content. The trouble with them is that the results are only ever as advanced as the methodology employed. In addition, they rarely make transparent that the methodology might be optional, let alone how it stands with regard to competing methodologies. This book is basic, for I do not concentrate on providing advanced results in this theory or that. I concentrate on the basic metaphysical, epistemological and methodological issues that shape theorizing about content. I am as evangelical about my preferred methodology as the next guy, but the account I give is, I hope, fair, even if not balanced.

For a basic book it is pretty long, but I wanted to cover enough to give a fulsome overview of how the whole neo-Fregean story about content hangs together. That meant getting clear about a number of things that, although part of the familiar furniture of the philosophy of thought, had got a bit lost under the accumulated wisdom of several generations. So I get Russell out and dust off his theory of descriptions. I rub through the veneer of contemporary *angst* about how to do misrepresentation and reference to distal stimuli to get a picture of Quine grappling with the same problems. I plot Davidson's account of why we can't do meaning without truth, and why and how, in doing that, we gain the world and lose the conceptual relativists on the way. These things are necessary if we are to get a firm grip on how and why you cannot afford to do one bit of the philosophy of thought without having your metaphysical antennae finely tuned to what's going on everywhere else. I say I defend a neo-Fregean theory of content, but I don't really get to that until the second half of the book. But the account of reference I defend there is best understood against the backdrop of what goes before in the chapters on meaning, truth and logic and against the recurring theme of what constitutes a naturalized theory of content.

If there is one thing that I hope will be come clear in all this, it is that you can never reread the classics too often. The heart of Russell's theory of thought is, I think, right. The same applies to Frege. The trouble is, Russell buried his key insight in a Cartesian epistemology that is, frankly, rather quaint and embarrassing. Frege left us a methodology, but never applied it himself to those aspects of language use that would reveal its great power. Everyone knows Kripke disproved description theories of names, but hardly anyone seems to know who the descriptivists are! Kripke's positive account of names is full of important insights, but whether it really makes sense to call it a causal *theory* is still contestable. 'New theories of reference' have been 'new' for about thirty years now, but people still characterize them with the metaphor of 'directness'. I argue in chapter 8 that there is an important sense (*the* important sense, I think) in which these theories provide an indirect account of reference! Here, then, is the other big lesson I hope becomes clear. It has taken us the best part of a hundred years to begin to see the scope available within a Fregean account of thought. And people are still arguing about Russell's theory of descriptions! If you are to understand how contemporary philosophy of thought is going, and if you are to be in a position to contribute to it, there is no substitute for an appreciation both of the broad view and of its contestability.

A long book takes a long time. Thanks to Steve Smith for originally suggesting I write it and for bearing with me while I did. And thanks to Mary Riso, who managed to sound enthusiastic everytime I came up with a new submission date. Thanks to the many colleagues who have heard me out on various aspects of this work and related material. I have been fortunate that everytime I say, 'Let's do a reading group' on such-and-such new book in the philosophy of thought, I have found a critical mass of colleagues, not to mention a clutch of graduates eager to work together. For keeping me educated, thanks to Naomi Eilan, Christoph Hoerl, Ian Lyne, David Miller, Peter Poellner, Johannes Roessler, Tim Thornton, Martin Warner, and Chris Woodard. Numerous graduate students have taught me much, but special thanks to John Collins and Simon Prosser.

On a broader front, the influences on what follows are obvious. I should, however, mention one. For the last two years, Warwick has been host to an interdisciplinary inter-institutional research project on Consciousness and Self-Consciousness that is redefining the cutting edge of issues about content and doing it in a conversation constituted as much by pyschologists as philosophers. My ideas about how a naturalized theory of content should go derive from what I have learnt at the project's seminars and workshops. So a second special thanks to Naomi, Christoph and Johannes for getting the show on the road.

Neo-Fregean theory of content is sometimes thought to be a rather local speciality with its roots in the work that Evans and McDowell did in Oxford in the late seventies. I first learnt philosophy of thought in Oxford from Michael Dummett. His work still powerfully shapes my thinking. The source for inspiration is, however, spreading across a locale of like-mindedness from Barcelona to Paris, Geneva to Utrecht, California to Massachussetts.

Doing the philosophy of thought helps us understand how we fit in the world. The place where I fit, with Dee, Chris, Sam and Nicky, has helped make it all possible.

Michael Luntley
Warwick

1

Methodologies

1.1 Introduction

Like other animals, we get wet if left out in the rain. We get crushed if trapped under falling rocks. We become ill if we ingest toxins and various kinds of microorganisms. There is a natural pattern to the way these things impinge upon us and affect our behaviour. The patterns connecting these stimuli and our responses are continuous with the patterns that apply to other species. What makes a difference in our case is that in addition to being creatures with a capacity for getting wet, being crushed and poisoned, we have a capacity for thought and talk. Other species may have some capacity for thought and language, but with us this capacity makes a profound difference to everything we do. We have the capacity to represent in thought and talk what has happened and what could happen. We can recall the past and make plans for the future. We can think about what would happen if we went out without an umbrella.

The capacity for thought and talk gives us a history and enables us to shape the future. Other species respond to the immediate environment in regular natural patterns. We respond in patterns shaped by the content of our thought and talk. We are possessors of content. Our possession of content interrupts the otherwise regular flow of stimuli and responses and gives us the ability to shape our behaviour. It gives us intentionality. This book is about our capacity to possess content.

The central task of the philosophy of thought is to give an account of what it is to possess content. What are the relations between thought, language and the world? How does thought connect with the world? How is it that the set of ink marks 'Dog' directs our attention to dogs? Why does the sound sequence produced when someone says 'Bill Clinton' get everyone thinking about just one individual? Indeed, what is it to think of an individual? How well does the public language in which we communicate capture the content of our thoughts? And, hardest of all:

1

How can it be that creatures made of the same physical stuff as the rest of the world possess psychological states with content?

The last problem is a difficult one. The distinguishing mark of possession of content is that our capacity for thought and talk *interrupts* the otherwise straightforward causal flow of stimuli and responses. This interruption need not be thought of as an exception to our causal physical encounters with the world, for perhaps the way that content interrupts our engagement with the world could be modelled in terms of distinctive patterns of causal engagements that are available only to creatures with a sufficiently complex brain. What is problematic, however, with giving a physical account of content and the way it shapes our behaviour is that we can have false thoughts as well as true ones. Our contents can misrepresent. On the face of it, it is unclear how to give an account of false thoughts in terms of causal relations between psychological states and the world. A simple example illustrates the problem.

The pollen-sensitive cells in our nasal passages interact with the environment causally. If the right-shape particles are in the atmosphere, the cells react, and we get swollen eyes and runny noses. Short of a malfunction, these cells do not misrepresent the presence of pollen and other irritants in the environment. Short of a malfunction, the cells in our noses cannot lie. Unlike our noses, we can. So the puzzle is: How can properly functioning causal processes produce false thoughts? Of course, the most plausible view we have of ourselves is that we are physical entities located in and interacting physically with the physical world. If that is right, then finding room for the phenomenon of meaning, of misrepresentation and false belief looks to be about as hard a philosophical problem as you could wish for.[1]

The problem of misrepresentation is an instance of an even more general problem. Our everyday notion of content is a normative concept. The content of a thought, or the content expressed by a sentence, is characterized in terms of the circumstances under which it is correct and incorrect to assent to it. It is expression of content that makes our sentences subject to evaluation for truth or falsity. The terms of semantic evaluation (truth and falsity) are normative concepts. If a sentence is false, then, other things being equal, you ought not to utter it; it would be incorrect to hold to the thought it expresses. The problem about the normativity of content is then: How are we to capture these normative semantic ideas in terms of our physical interactions with the world? Our physical interactions are causal, but causal patterns are not normative patterns. Causal patterns trace the structure of what is the case, not what ought to be the case. A physicalistic theory of content is a theory that attempts to account for our possession of content in terms employed by the natural sciences – causal patterns of physical relations with the world. The normativity of content threatens to block any physicalistic theory of content.

Perhaps it will just take a lot of hard work to define the normativity of content causally, but already these simple reflections risk prompting familiar metaphysical extravagances. Suppose you thought that the normativity of semantic concepts could not be defined causally. You might be tempted to think that the normativity of content consisted not in the way in which we were causally related to the physical world, but in the way in which we were rationally related to a non-physical realm – a realm of ideas or Platonic Forms. You might be tempted to think that fundamentally we are only properly at home in this special realm of ideas, not in the physical world. In short, you might be tempted into Cartesianism, or even a Platonic model of content. Speculative metaphysics has few defenders in contemporary work, but the problem about the normativity of content reveals how our deepest metaphysical views about ourselves and the nature of mind are never far from the surface once we begin to raise the question: What is it to be a possessor of content?

In the remainder of this chapter I consider the different methodologies that shape investigations of this question, and I sketch the methodology that I adopt throughout most of this book. I also want to explain how and why the philosophy of thought is central to contemporary philosophy, for it is now almost inconceivable to think that basic issues in metaphysics and epistemology could be tackled without engagement with the philosophy of thought.

1.2 Intentional Realism, Representationalism and the Standard Model

Our central question is

(1)   What is it to be a possessor of content?

Regardless of the metaphysical oddity of the Platonist and Cartesian answers to (1), they illustrate a pair of theses that characterize most theories of content. The theses are intentional realism and representationalism. Together they characterize the standard model.

By 'intentional realism' I mean the thesis that there is such a thing as content, that there are such things as thoughts. There are thoughts, for any theory that failed to acknowledge them would be inadequate for explaining behaviour. Intentional realism commits us to no particular theory about what kind of thing content is or what kind of things thoughts are. It commits us only to the reality of the propositional attitudes: When we believe, hope, wish, etc., then the concept of our believing that . . . , hoping that . . . , wishing that . . . , etc. is ineliminable from any satisfactory explanation of behaviour. I use 'intentional realism' in a way that is weaker than most writers. I use it only to signal that there is such a thing as belief – the concept of belief content is ineliminable from any adequate account of ourselves and our actions. It does not follow from this that belief contents are to be reified and theorized as entities characterizable independently of the environment they are about. On my understanding, you could be an intentional realist and treat belief contents relationally and so not capable of individuation independently of the environment. How you treat belief contents will depend on the principles you settle on for the individuation of content. This is separate from the minimal acceptance that there are beliefs – intentional realism. Keeping our options open on what count as adequate principles of individuation for belief contents is the motivation for distinguishing between intentional realism and representationalism.[2]

Intentional realism also picks out the basic constraint on how we individuate the content of beliefs, hopes, wishes, etc. We are realists about belief, hope, etc., because they are necessary for explaining behaviour. We need a theory of content in order to get a theory of behaviour, for it is our possession of content that explains the rationality of our behaviour.[3] Prima facie, the explanation of behaviour obtained by appeal to belief is a rationalizing one. If a physicalist theory of content is possible, rationalizing explanations will be reducible to causal ones. For the moment I remain agnostic about whether this can be done, and I take the ordinary rationalizing explanations of behaviour as data to be accommodated.

Intentional realism has two components. First, there is the acknowledgement of the idea that there is such a thing as the way our possession of concepts shapes our experience of the world. We face the world with beliefs and thoughts, not just with stimuli receptors – there is something distinct about possessing content. The way our encounters with the world are thus organized constitutes our intentionality. Second, we individuate content to whatever degree of discrimination is required in order to make sense of the rational structure of behaviour. I call the first component of intentional realism the phenomenology component, for there is such a thing as the way we intentionally confront the world, and it can be described. The second component I call the individuation constraint. In summary:

> **Intentional realism:** There is such a thing as the way we experience the world where that way is shaped by our possession of content (phenomenology component) and content is individuated in response to the need to make rational sense of behaviour shaped by our possession of content (individuation constraint).

This is how I shall use 'intentional realism' throughout this book. Both components are clear in the work of a number of contemporary writers.[4] Whatever else is included in a theory of content, and for some writers it could be a good deal more, endorsing intentional realism requires that a theory of content offer a description of the way content shapes our encounters with the world where that description is constrained by the demand that it make rational sense of behaviour.

Intentional realism commits us to no particular theory of what kind of thing content is. The most common version of intentional realism is representationalism. A representationalist theory reifies content. This means that the propositional attitudes of believing that . . . , hoping that . . . , etc., are attitudes to entities of some kind. The simplest version of this is the Cartesian model: the propositional attitudes are conceived as relations to Ideas, and Ideas are non-physical entities uncovered by introspection. The Platonist version treats Ideas as abstract entities uncovered by a mysterious act of intellect. Representationalist theories of content need not involve such problematic metaphysics. Most contemporary representationalists are physicalists. The key idea is that there are states, characterizable independently of the world, and that our possession of content is defined in terms of the properties of these states.

The reification of content that produces representationalism captures the intuitive idea offered in the previous section, that what is distinctive of the way we engage the world is the way that content interrupts the otherwise regular flow of causal stimuli and responses. A representationalist theory of content treats this interruption literally as the result of the configuration of intermediary states – beliefs mostly, but also desires, hopes, wishes, etc. For the representationalist, our rationality and our cognition in general are defined over the arrangements of and operations performed upon these states. A representationalist theory of content is analogous to a representative theory of perception that theorizes perceptual experience in terms of our possession of sense-data. For the representationalist, our possession of content is a possession of a configuration of states the structure of which explains the rationality of our behaviour.

The idea that possession of representations explains our rationality entails the thesis that representations are, in principle, characterizable independently of that which they represent. The idea that in thought we deal with representational entities (Ideas, Platonic Forms, sentences in an internal language of thought, states defined by their causal role in the production of behaviour) is the idea that we deal with these states rather than with the world directly. The whole point to a representationalist theory of content is that the rationality of our dealings with the world is explained by our dealings with, or operations upon, representations. It is because, as it were, we first think (manipulate representations) that our consequent dealings with the world have a rational structure to them. The rationality of our behaviour is a consequence of our engagement with representations.

The best argument for representationalism, and this independence of representations from that for which they stand, turns on the claim that representations figure in causal explanations.[5] Suppose we hold that representations causally explain behaviour, and suppose that the semantic power of representations is explained by their causal connections with the world. If two things are causally connected, then, given that causal relations are external relations, it must be possible to characterize them independently of one another. The causal properties of a thing are local, they are properties of it; they are not relational properties.[6] The causal properties of a thing are capable of a context-free characterization – independently of the causal relations the thing happens to stand in. The representation's causal powers will explain what it happens to be related to, but a specification of the causal powers must be possible independently of the representation actually standing in such relations.[7] If we think of representations as quasi-linguistic items, things that can be characterized syntactically, then we are guaranteed that their causal properties will be characterizable in this context-free way. They will be characterizable independently of that which they represent. Accordingly, the simplest way of conceiving of representations, other than the Cartesian way, is to think of them as linguistic entities capable of syntactic individuation. It is not necessary to think of representations this way, as involving a linguistic individuation of belief states, but this is the easiest way to understand it. A physicalist theory of content that defined contentful states functionally in terms of the states' causal powers would still count as representationalist by my lights, for it would capture the idea that the state and that which gave it content (its causal powers) were capable of individuation independently of the environment. The characterizability of the state independently of the world is guaranteed by the causal individuation of the state on such a theory. The functionalist does not treat contentful states as quasi-linguistic entities connected to one another as combinable elements of a language. The connectedness of states on the functionalist account will be causal. Nevertheless, the functionalist has content-bearing states characterizable independently of the environment, and that is the key point for me. Fodor's version of representationalism treats contentful states as components within a language, the Language of Thought, and therefore subject to a linguistic combinatorial structure. I use Fodor's version as the paradigm of the standard model, because it is the simplest version of an idea that is common to many theories regardless of whether they endorse his linguistic model of psychological states with content.[8]

Representations are blueprints for the world. This provides a simple model for error. Misrepresentation occurs when you have the blueprint in your mind, but the world does not oblige with what it is standardly causally hooked up to. For the representationalist, error can, in principle, occur with representations of any category: thoughts can be false, thought components that stand for objects can be empty, and, although this point is rarely acknowledged, it should also be possible for thought components that stand for properties to be empty.

To summarize:

> **Representationalism** is the thesis that our possession of content consists in our possession of entities/states of some specified kind called 'representations', where these are characterizable independently of that which they represent.

Representationalism offers an account of what it is to be an intentional realist. In its physicalist form, representationalism is one of the most dominant options in the philosophy of thought. I take Fodor's version as the paradigm.[9] Fodor accepts intentional realism for the reason canvassed: content is required in order to make sense of behaviour. He believes that the systematicity of content (the way that the meaning of any one thought is systematically connected to the meaning of others via inferential relations) can only be explained by positing a 'Language of Thought' (LOT). This is the point that differentiates Fodor from functionalists. LOT is a system of representations the existence of which explains the rationality of our behaviour. In addition, Fodor believes that the entities posited in LOT must be given a physicalist characterization and that their semantic properties must be accounted for causally. Fodor's position is instructive, for it captures many common intuitions about content. He accepts that there is such a thing as content, which interrupts the otherwise regular flow of stimulus and response and marks us out as creatures with the power to have a history and plan our future. This interruption is not, however, the result of spooky non-physical entities. It is due to entities that causally produce behaviour. These are beliefs, characterized syntactically in LOT and identified with brain states. Fodor's position exemplifies representationalism. It is a model that endorses both intentional realism and representationalism. It is the endorsement of both theses that I call the standard model of content.

The standard model is a satisfying blend of metaphysical assumptions. It is well motivated and a plausible way of constructing a naturalized theory of content. Its attraction lies in the attempt to perform two different tasks that we might expect of a general theory of content: the *constitutive* task and the *engineering* task.[10] Like all intentional realists, Fodor accepts that there is something that we speak of when we say that someone believes that Bill Clinton is president of the USA. In saying this, we are describing the subject's intentional layout, their point of view upon the world, and we are describing it in terms of its normative role in rationalizing behaviour. We are making a minor contribution to a phenomenology of their point of view. At the same time, the entities picked out in this phenomenology are, on the standard model, identifiable with states in an engineering account of content that specifies the causal relations that beliefs, identified as brain states, must stand in with the world. These causal relations constitute the state's representational capacity.

The standard model is instructive. It enables us to identify problems that have become central to contemporary work in the philosophy of thought. A key problem concerns the relation between the constitutive and the engineering tasks. The former characterizes content in terms of its role in rationalizing explanations of behaviour (the individuation constraint of intentional realism). It employs normative concepts. In contrast, the engineering task employs causal concepts to define the relations between physical states of the brain/nervous system and the environment. On the standard model, the descriptions we deploy in rationalizing behaviour pick out real things – beliefs, desires, etc. However, because the standard model requires these things to explain behaviour causally, we must be able to identify them with entities appealed to in an engineering account of content. So the standard model is committed to reductionism. Our ordinary concept of belief is made respectable by showing how it picks out just the same sort of thing that is picked out in an engineering account of content. For this programme to work, it must be possible to show how the normative concepts of the constitutive task can be analysed in the causal concepts available within the engineering task. This looks problematic. Since Quine's seminal work, many have concluded that the analysis cannot be achieved and have given up intentional realism – e.g. Dennett, Stich, the Churchlands. Others, like Fodor and Dretske, have persevered with trying to make the programme work.[11]

The standard model has the two enterprises of the constitutive and the engineering tasks married together, usually by a theory of reduction of the former to the latter. The two tasks make up complementary levels in an overall theory of content. An important variation concerns the way that the engineering level is conceptualized – the scientific paradigms that are employed in framing the conceptual resources of the engineering level. For example, a theory that characterizes the engineering level in natural science categories borrowed from biology, rather than physics, might stand a better chance of marrying the two levels.[12]

Suppose it is impossible to analyse the categories employed by the constitutive level in terms employed by the engineering level.[13] We seem to be left with two options. Either we give up the aspiration to naturalize content, or we give up the aspirations of the constitutive level. On the former option, we endorse the constitutive level, but see it as no failure if the categories of belief, desire, etc. find no analogue in our best scientific theories of ourselves.[14] It is not clear that this is a satisfactory option, for it leaves our possession of content ultimately mysterious. The second option is to naturalize content, drop the aspirations of the constitutive level, and proceed only with the engineering level.[15] This option is only tenable if we can make sense of the idea that intentional realism is a mistake, for this option eliminates the whole apparatus of normative rationalizing concepts that we ordinarily employ in understanding ourselves and others. The second option treats this ordinary understanding as a theorizing that is fundamentally mistaken about what is going on in thought and talk. As such, this option is also profoundly unsatisfactory.[16] The variant on the second option in which the constitutive level is not fully eliminated but treated instrumentally as a way of talking that we find useful to employ, but which carries no real significance, hardly improves the plausibility of the second option.[17]

In light of the obvious difficulties that these two responses face, the standard model can seem compelling. However difficult it may be, the standard model holds out the hope of analysing normative concepts causally. Given an almost universal reluctance to treat meaning as non-natural, the standard model and the eliminativist position seem to be the chief contenders for a general theory of content. They share a common assumption: that if we are to naturalize content and the normative concepts that figure in our ordinary descriptions of content, we can do so only by reducing those concepts to the concepts employed in the scientific engineering level of theory. The standard model tries to make this reduction work; the eliminativist holds that it cannot work, and so gives up on the constitutive enterprise altogether. There is, however, another way of developing a naturalized theory of content that avoids the dichotomy that arises if we think it impossible to analyse normative concepts causally.

Suppose no analysis of the normative concepts employed in our constitutive account of content can be given in causal concepts. We could still give a naturalized theory of content if we could show how and why the two levels were complementary, without trying to reduce the constitutive to the engineering. If we could show how the accounts can lie side by side – and it might take a priori argumentation to show this – then providing the constitutive account was not incompatible with a view in which we take ourselves to be natural creatures inhabiting the natural world, this would be the abstract formula for a different kind of naturalized theory of content. This third option is non-reductionist. It endorses the claim, which otherwise seems mysterious, that no analysis can be given of constitutive content notions in causal terms. Rather than remain content with the apparently mysterious status of the concepts employed in the constitutive task, the non-reductionist naturalized theory offers an account of how it can be possible for creatures who possess content to be part of the natural world. A good example of this sort of approach is Davidson's work and his advocacy of an anomalous monism.[18] More recent developments in this vein come from the contemporary neo-Fregean tradition arising out of Evans's seminal *The Varieties of Reference*, Clark's case for the complementary status of the constitutive and engineering tasks on the basis of his defence of a connectionist theory at the engineering level, and the work of Lynne Rudder-Baker.[19]

These different approaches share a common thesis: the denial of representationalism. If you are an intentional realist but do not reify content, then the constitutive task will not be committed to states characterizable independently of what they represent. An intentional realist who does not endorse representationalism supports externalism about content – content is not characterizable independently of that (the environment) which it represents. For such theorists, the natural world that we think about and speak about will be implicated in the constitutive phenomenology of content. The fact that this constitutive task is not reducible to the causal engineering task (although the two tasks may offer illuminating constraints on one another) does not require the mysterious non-naturalism of Cartesianism. Indeed, in neo-Fregean theory the case is stronger. It is not that it shows it possible for creatures with content to inhabit the natural world; rather, it shows that the natural world is necessarily implicated in the constitutive account of content.

This third option may seem counter-intuitive. It is a sophisticated and recent addition to the extant options in the philosophy of thought. It faces many difficulties, the most striking of which is how, in the absence of a reification of content, we are to give an account of false thoughts. This problem looks insurmountable for externalist theories of thought. As noted, representationalism has a ready and simple model for error – the blueprint model. The representationalist has their own problem about misrepresentation, but that is the problem of how to account for the normative notion of falsity in terms of properly functioning causal processes. The non-representationalist's problem with error is different. It arises from the inability to detach content from the world. As I shall show, this turns out not to be a problem, even though, prima facie, it looks fatal. For the moment, it is enough to note the abstract possibility of a non-representationalist intentional realism that supports a non-reductionist naturalization of content.

Representationalism is intuitively plausible, but it is important that the possibility of a non-reductionist naturalized theory of content that denies representationalism is visible. This is the type of theory of content that I shall defend throughout this book. I believe that the denial of representationalism is set to be one of the most significant advances in our theorizing about content. It marks the final break with a variety of options that, in broad structure, have changed little since Descartes' time. The externalism of this denial of representationalism has profound effects upon our self-conception as rational beings. It will take most of this book to work out these effects, but in terms of simple slogans, the options that I have now sketched can be captured like this.

For the Cartesian, the answer to our question 'What is it to be a possessor of content?' is that possession of content amounts to possession of Ideas. For the Platonist, possession of content amounts to possession of Forms. For the standard model, possession of content amounts to possession of states characterizable independently of the world, which in turn amounts to possession of items characterizable within the typology of brain states. For the eliminativist there is no such thing as content, belief, desire, etc.; but the eliminativist at least holds that when we mistakenly believe that we are in possession of content, what we are really in possession of are states characterizable within the typology of brain states. The eliminativist denies representationalism, for beliefs, desires, etc. cannot be defined in terms of the favoured conceptual resources drawn from a scientific engineering study of the brain and central nervous system. The non-representationalist intentional realist shares with the eliminativist the denial that our constitutive categories of belief, desire, etc. are definable in engineering terms, but takes this to be due to the fact that the constitutive categories are characterizable only externalistically. Beliefs are not characterizable independently of that which they represent – the world. But this means that for such a theorist, possession of content amounts to possession of the world! That's a striking claim. By the end of this book we shall be in a position to see why it might be true.

1.3   A Central Fregean Claim

The options sketched in the previous section present a complex of metaphysical, epistemological and methodological issues. The denial of representationalism has major metaphysical and epistemological consequences, but on the basis of what kind of argument are we to judge the different options available in the philosophy of thought? The methodology that I think is the most fruitful derives from Frege, although in its contemporary form it owes almost as much to Davidson.

Frege's importance in the history of philosophy turns on a number of achievements. The aspect of his work that I focus on concerns the methodological claim that the philosophy of thought is central to all other issues in philosophy.

It is often said that Frege was one of the initiators of the 'linguistic turn' in philosophy. This label disguises an important issue, namely: Is the philosophy of thought the same as the philosophy of language? I think the answer to this is 'No'. The structure of thought is not exhaustively identifiable in language. Frege's interest in language is due to the fact that language normally marks the structure of thought. I shall frequently be concerned with questions about language, about what it is for it to have meaning, how language refers, etc., but this is only because of the role language plays in identifying the structure of thought. Language is important, but the structure of language is not constitutive of the structure of thought. We are not doing philosophy of language; we are doing philosophy of thought. We study language only in so far as we thereby study thought. It so happens that the sorts of thoughts that Frege was primarily concerned to investigate – mathematical thoughts – are thoughts the structure of which can, plausibly, be individuated with linguistic structures. This explains why Frege is thought party to the linguistic turn.

The idea of the linguistic turn is that whereas for seventeenth- and eighteenth-century thinkers the theory of Ideas had been the foundation for philosophy, from the end of the nineteenth century onwards, it is the theory of language that is foundational. For Hume, the theory of Ideas is prior to metaphysics. His account of the world depends on his theory of Ideas. After the linguistic turn, the theory of language is prior to metaphysics.

This is an odd claim. When properly understood, and when the relationship between thought and language is got right, I think it marks out not only a fruitful methodology, but a correct one. It needs, however, considerable qualification. A way of stating Frege's central methodological claim that is neutral on the thought/language issue would be that the study of semantics is prior to metaphysics, or, in a slogan:

(2)   Semantics exhausts ontology.

I want to note the sense in which (2) picks out something extractable from Frege's work.[20]

The idea that semantics exhausts ontology looks to be topsy-turvy. Consider, for example, the standard model and the eliminativist position. Both want to provide a physicalist account of our cognitive faculties that produce thought and talk. Despite their differences, both positions share a methodology that gives a priority to the scientific study of our cognitive abilities.[21] For both positions the key issue is how to show that our linguistic inputs and outputs figure in sequences of events amenable to characterization and explanation in just the same sort of way as our physical and chemical interactions with the environment. We know, roughly, how to write the laws governing what happens to us, and how our bodies respond to the influence of gravity, noxious chemicals, extremes of heat and cold, and so on. What we do not yet know is how to write comparable natural laws governing the patterns of responses that occur when people speak to us, or the sequences of neural activity when we entertain thoughts. Prioritizing the scientific/engineering account of cognition is an expression of a commitment to a metaphysical picture over our semantic enterprise. On this view, we know, roughly, what the world is like. It is a place describable with the resources of the natural sciences. All that has to be done in the theory of content, or semantics, is to show how content can be made to fit within the scientific world-view. On this way of thinking, metaphysics has priority over semantics. Semantics must be fitted into an ontology derived from science. Frege begs to differ! Before outlining the reasons why Frege adopts what appears to be a topsy-turvy methodology, let me consolidate a claim that I have already made and clarify the methodological prescription that I take from Frege.

Intentional realism includes a thesis about the proper individuation of content: namely, that we individuate content to whatever degree of precision is required in order to make rational sense of behaviour. When I say that Frege endorses the thesis that semantics exhausts ontology, what I mean by 'semantics' is a theory of content designed for the purpose of making rational sense of behaviour. Frege is important for a number of developments of major philosophical significance: the invention of quantification theory, the logicist programme for the reduction of arithmetic to logic, the idea of a semantic theory for a formal language which, eventually, through Tarski's work, has developed into the idea of model-theoretic semantics. The idea of a semantic theory for a formal language, where the theory is required in order to show that the account of validity for the formal language is sound and complete, is an important conception of semantics. Tarski showed us how to write such a semantic theory for a language of the complexity of first-order predicate calculus. It is a general problem whenever we consider languages of greater complexity – e.g. a language including modal operators, indexicals, etc. – how to write a formal semantic theory for such a language. But the task of a formal semantic theory is, chiefly, to show that validity for the language in question is properly defined, and that the account of validity is sound and complete. This is different from the business of semantics as I use that label. What I mean by 'semantics' is the study of the notion of content that is required in order to make rational sense of behaviour.[22] Given Frege's significance in both traditions of semantics, it is important to remember that it is the idea that the latter study exhausts ontology that I am taking as Frege's central claim.

I do not want to insist at this stage that the idea of a formal semantic theory can have no bearing on semantics as I understand that study. I insist only that we do not at the outset assume that the enterprises are the same or even closely connected. One way that formal semantics could be related to semantics would be the following. Suppose that representationalism is true. If so, possession of content equals possession of states characterized independently of what they stand for. If we think of these items as linguistic items (as Fodor does), we can only do so if we treat them syntactically, for then we guarantee that they are characterizable independently of what they stand for. But that means that it should, in principle, be possible to treat the philosophy of thought as the study of this privileged language. It still does not follow that a semantics for the privileged language will be exhausted by a formal semantic theory, and indeed it is quite unlikely that it would, for a formal theory works only by assigning objects to primitive expressions, and a representationalist will need a substantive account of how primitive signs get attached to things. The connection between formal semantics and representationalism is, however, this. For a formal semantic theory, a key distinction is between signs whose semantic value is assigned (the primitives) and those whose semantic value is computed from the assignments to the primitives. This issue is a purely formal or linguistic one concerning the relative status of different categories of expression. As we proceed, we will see that there are a number of instances in which a correct formal claim that, say, expressions of one category (e.g. names) are not definable in terms of expressions of another category (e.g. descriptions) is taken as endorsing a claim about the semantics of expressions with respect to rationalization of behaviour. The reason that the move from correct formal semantic claim to contentious semantic claim is made is that it is implicitly assumed that the theory of thought content is equivalent to the theory of language. It is the assumption that the structure of thought is a linguistic structure. This assumption entails representationalism, although not vice versa.[23] The assumption that the structure of thought is a linguistic structure is contentious. We need to leave room for the idea that it might be wrong. One way of guaranteeing that we make room for this is to ensure that we do not assume that semantics as I am using the label is equivalent to, or closely connected with, formal semantic theories.

For Frege, the precedence of semantics over ontology equally applied to the semantic theory for formal language – e.g. the language of arithmetic. For most of his career, Frege's interest lay in formal languages and the semantics necessary in order to pursue his logicist reduction of arithmetic. So although he lay the foundations for a general theory of content (semantics as the study constrained by the need to make rational sense of behaviour), most of his energies were not devoted to this enterprise. That is just one of the many reasons why it is important to note that the methodology that I am going to defend is better described as Fregean, rather than Frege's.

1.4   Semantics Exhausts Ontology

To endorse the 'Semantics exhausts ontology' thesis is to make a choice from among what has, historically, been a set of three options. Giving an account of what it is to be possessors of content would seem to involve giving an account of the relationship between language, mind and world. Clearly, we need to know how language is related to the world, how it represents the world. In addition, because our interest is focused on the use of language that marks our behaviour as rational, it is the use of language by creatures with minds that interests us. It is language as an expression of thought and intentionality in which we are interested. Historically, there have been three starting-points for a theory of the rationality of this language use. We could start with a theory of the mind and use that to explain the relations between thought and world. We could start with a general metaphysics about the nature of reality and construct a theory of thought and mind within its parameters. Less obviously, we could start with a theory of thought content and hope thereby to illuminate our view of the mind and reality.

The first option, typical of seventeenth- and eighteenth-century philosophers from Descartes to Hume, is now largely discredited. The second option characterizes the standard model and also the eliminativist position. The third option is Frege's. It is typical of theories that take one of the first two options that they support representationalism, for they normally assume that the three items (thought, mind and world) whose connections they seek to plot are characterizable

14

independently of one another. So, from the standpoint of the traditional theory of Ideas, you first characterize Ideas and their relationships with one another. This exercise is an introspectionist one. Then you try to define the relationships that obtain between these items and the worldly items that they represent. The second option, as exemplified in the standard model, first characterizes the world by drawing upon our best scientific theories of it. It then tries to characterize representational states with the resources made available by this prior metaphysical option.

Not all versions of the first option will be representationalist. For an idealist, there is no independent account of the world, for the world is defined over sets of Ideas. What this observation reveals is a deep-rooted intuition that acceptance of representationalism is a condition for the possibility of being a realist. The idea is that the realist belief in the existence of a world independent of thought is made possible only if you hold the representationalist thesis that thought and world can be characterized independently of one another. Being a representationalist is a safeguard against lapsing into idealism. This point is a more general version of the point noted in section 1.2 that most people think that representationalism is required in order to accommodate the possibility of misrepresentation. A false belief is one that is at odds with that which is independent of belief. If that is right, then it seems natural to suppose that belief must be characterizable independently of that which it represents – hence representationalism. This connection between realism and representationalism is, I believe, mistaken. Indeed, it had better be mistaken if Frege's prioritizing of semantics over ontology is to be compatible with realism. Although representationalism is a safeguard against idealism, having got a specification of representations independently of what they stand for, the representationalist's problem is to show how, given their constitutive separateness from the world, they nevertheless have the property of being about the world. It is not clear that this makes sense. Despite the ease with which many theorists assume that they have safeguarded realism by endorsing representationalism, they do so at the risk of leaving our thoughts (representations) wholly out of touch with the world.[24] But for the moment, it is instructive to note the bearing that our investigations into the theory of content have upon fundamental metaphysical issues such as realism.

Frege's prioritizing of semantics over metaphysics means that the constitutive theory of content, in which we account for content in terms of our rationalizing explanations of behaviour, has priority over the account of the mechanisms by which we think about the world. For Frege, there is such a thing as an investigation of our capacities for thought and talk that is not dependent on our scientific theories of the mechanisms that underpin those capacities.[25] Furthermore, the constitutive account has a general priority over metaphysics. This means that, for Frege, the starting-point to philosophy is a description of our intentionality – how things are for us in our thought and experience shaped by thought. This is a description of the patterns of thought that structure our linguistic and psychological abilities. Furthermore, the description offered is an a priori description. This enterprise needs to be undertaken before we can offer credible scientific models of these abilities. We need to start with an accurate description of the phenomena to be modelled.

The idea that the starting-point in philosophy is a description of intentionality looks like an old-fashioned Cartesian idea, but it is not. Recall the non-reductionist naturalism noted in section 1.2. The requirement that our theorizing about content be compatible with our being physical creatures in a physical world is weaker than the requirement that our theorizing about content be couched in a physicalistic vocabulary, let alone that all our explanations of content be physical ones.[26] A naturalized theory of content that is anti-representationalist and hence externalist turns out to endorse a radically anti-Cartesian conception of mind. Nevertheless, what the Fregean methodology shares with the older traditions is the idea that the study of content is both objective and conceptual.

The reason why the constitutive task is conceptual is because content is normative. This simple point has profound ramifications. The normativity of content means that understanding the meaning of an expression requires that you grasp certain patterns of use. These are patterns of use that you have to grasp if you understand the concept. For example, you have failed to understand the concept 'green' if you think that something can be both red and green all over. The pattern of use of 'green' rules out that possibility. Understanding the concept places certain obligations upon the speaker to use the concept in a patterned manner.[27]

These patterns of use are not empirical patterns. They are normative patterns that show how words ought to be used. These normative patterns can be described independently of the physical mechanisms that underlie our competence with the concept. We can describe these normative patterns a priori, for they are not patterns concerned with what we actually do, they are the patterns concerned with what we ought to do with our concepts. The former can be traced in an empirical study. It is the oddity of engaging in an empirical study of what we ought to do that provides the first sketch of a justification for an answer to the question, 'Why is a conceptual a priori study of content possible?'

The priority that Frege gives to semantics over ontology was announced in his formulation of the context principle: a word has meaning only in the context of a sentence. In section 62 of the *Grundlagen* Frege asks the Kantian question, 'How are numbers given to us?' In reply he says: 'it is only in the context of a proposition that words have any meaning'.[28] His point is that there is no such thing as a pre-linguistic encounter with numbers. More generally, there can be no non-conceptual encounter with ontology. This, of course, has become a familiar point throughout twentieth-century philosophy. It is the thesis that there is no such thing as a transparent experience of reality, one that is stripped of all theoretical and conceptual presuppositions. You cannot direct-dial into the nature of the world.[29] Frege's interest is restricted to numbers. There is no pre-linguistic, or pre-conceptual, encounter with numbers, but Frege nevertheless believes that numbers are objects. He derives that ontological claim from the context principle. In saying that words have a meaning only in the context of a proposition, he is endorsing the following argument.

His claim that numbers are objects depends on the claim that numerals – 'π', '5', '$\sqrt{3}$', etc. – are names. We cannot determine whether numerals are names by, as it were, simply looking to see if they denote objects. This is not because if numbers are objects, they are abstract objects and so cannot be observed. The reason why we cannot look to see if numerals denote objects is that the very notion of something being a name is not determined by it standing in a special sort of relation, whether epistemological or otherwise, to an object. The relation between name and object is not some queer sort of relation, to be identified by an epistemological ostensive fixation upon the name and object.[30] A sign is a name only in so far as it has the appropriate pattern of use within the context of propositions. If numerals are names, they must exhibit the right normative pattern of use in the context of whole propositions. The question of whether or not they exhibit the right pattern of use exhausts the issue of whether they are names.

So, Frege is saying that the issue of whether numerals are names, and therefore whether numbers are objects, can be resolved by asking whether numerals exhibit the appropriate pattern of use in the context of whole propositions. It is only in the context of a proposition that names have meaning. It makes no sense to ask for the meaning of a name independently of it having a well-defined pattern of use in propositions. Let me introduce the notion of grammar to replace 'pattern of use'. Frege's thesis is then this: If numerals exhibit the grammar of names, numbers are objects.[31]

More has yet to be said about the concept of grammar. But enough has been said to see the sense in which Frege's argument in section 62 of the *Grundlagen* marks the moment when philosophy shifted from the epistemological basis for metaphysics found in the traditional theory of ideas to a semantic basis. For Frege, the concept of an object is not an epistemological one. It is not a concept shaped by such questions as, 'What is it to experience an object?', 'Are objects observable?', 'What sorts of things can we be acquainted with?' For Frege, the concept of an object is a grammatical – or, we might also say, a semantic – concept. It is a concept shaped by an investigation into the grammar of naming.

The above illustrates how the a priori study of the grammar of language is the starting-point in philosophy. The a priori study of grammar is a study of the patterns of thought and, in so far as those patterns are revealed in language, a study of language. That is the Fregean methodology in the philosophy of thought. It is by

17

undertaking the study of grammar that we will delineate the basic metaphysical categories of our thought and discover, amongst other things, what sorts of objects there are. The study of grammar is the study of thought, and grammar exhausts metaphysics. In this sense, the philosophy of thought is foundational to the rest of philosophy.

The above sketch of the importance of the context principle invites a number of obvious objections:

(i)   How is the argument compatible with the idea of compositional semantics: namely, that the meaning of a sentence is a function of a meaning of its parts?

(ii)   If we are to study metaphysics via studying grammar, what sense of grammar is involved? Is this ordinary language grammar or some other notion?

(iii) Whatever notion of grammar is implicated in the context principle, why does it provide a privileged starting-point to, say, a psychologistic investigation of Ideas?

(iv)   If the study of grammar is prior to metaphysics, doesn't this commit us to a form of linguistic idealism?

The above objections raise important issues. I believe they can all be met, although a full response will take up most of the book. In the next three sections I outline a response to these questions and trace a number of key theses that have become landmarks in contemporary philosophy of thought.

1.5   Bottom-up or Top-down?

The importance of Frege's context principle is that it shows that the concept of a name is a semantic concept, not an epistemological concept. Something is a name if and only if it exhibits the right grammar in the formation of sentences that express thoughts. The context principle appears to contradict another key Fregean thesis that has become commonplace: the idea of the compositionality of meaning.

> **Compositionality thesis:** The meaning of a sentence (a thought) is a function of the meaning of its parts.

The compositionality thesis is basic to our understanding of language and of our cognitive abilities in general. The most common argument employed in support of the compositionality thesis concerns the productivity of our understanding. The number of sentences we are able to understand outstrips the number we encounter in our acquisition of language. Our understanding exploits the structure of language. We do not learn new sentences one by one, but assimilate them, via their structure of repeatable component parts, to those already mastered. In addition, the grammatical structure of language enable us to construct sentences that have never been used before. With only a few years' experience of our native language, we acquire the capacity to understand and produce sentences that we have not encountered before and that no one has encountered before.[32] The compositionality thesis suggests a building-block model of language. By this, I mean a model of language in which sub-sentential expressions – like names – acquire a meaning independently of their use in sentences. Sentences and the thoughts they express are then literally constructed out of the building blocks of meaning. This is sometimes also called a 'bottom-up' strategy in the theory of meaning.[33]

Contrast the bottom-up strategy with a top-down strategy. A top-down strategy takes the basic unit of meaning as a sentence. But if that is the case, how can its meaning be a function of the meaning of its parts? This question has a simple answer, but it makes better sense if we clarify the argument for endorsing the compositionality thesis. First the simple answer, then the clarification.

The simple answer to the problem of the compatibility of the context principle and the compositionality thesis is that neither requires us to adopt a claim about the temporal priority of the meaning of sentences over sub-sentential expressions, or vice versa. To endorse the compositionality thesis is not to endorse the idea that first we acquire a grasp of the meaning of names and other sub-sentential expressions, and then we calculate the meaning of sentences. That is the view that is captured by the idea of a bottom-up strategy. It is not forced on us by acknowledging the compositionality thesis.

Further, it is difficult to see how you could acquire a grasp of the meaning of a name without thereby grasping a good deal about its grammar, its role in whole sentences. To think that you could give an account of the meaning of a name independently of its grammar would be to think that naming was some queer sort of connection, fixed perhaps by a well-focused ostensive contact between mind and object. There has been no shortage of philosophers who have been tempted to hold such a view; it is a view of names that belongs to an older, more traditional, epistemological and even Cartesian theory of language.[34] If we accept Frege's context principle, we have to adopt a top-down strategy in which the sentence is the fundamental unit of meaning. We therefore account for the meaning of sub-sentential expressions, like names, in terms of their role in fixing the meaning of sentences. But as long as the priority given to sentences acknowledges that sentences essentially possess a combinatorial structure, nothing in the context principle is incompatible with the compositionality thesis. The whole point of the context principle is that the semantic evaluation of sentences has an explanatory priority over the semantic evaluation of sub-sentential expression. Truth is the primitive semantic concept, not reference. Our grasp of what it is for a name to refer is no more than a grasp of the role it plays in sentences that are true.

In defending the compatibility of the context principle with the compositionality thesis, I have acknowledged that the priority given to sentences in our theorizing requires that sentences and the thoughts they express essentially possess a combinatorial structure. Therefore, we need a further defence of the compositionality thesis. Why are thoughts necessarily composite? Why are the sentences that express them necessarily composite? The favourite answer to this question in the literature turns on the productivity of language use and comprehension. Only in so far as sentence comprehension is modelled in terms of an ability to manage a recursive combinatorial structure, will we be able to give an account of our capacity to understand and employ novel sentences. This answer is not, however, the fundamental one.

The fundamental reason why sentences must be structured entities turns on the fact that sentences can be used to say things with. The argument goes like this. Whatever else we do with sentences, a basic use is to make assertions with them. To make an assertion is to make a move that is to be assessed as true or false. Truth and falsity do not apply to names, for you cannot say anything with a name. The very act of saying something is the act of saying of something that it is a certain way. Whether or not the saying is true depends on whether or not the thing spoken of is the way it is claimed to be. In saying something, there are always at least two components: the thing spoken of and the way it is claimed to be.

What about one-word sentences as spoken by young children, e.g. 'Doggy'? But such sentences are elliptical for, e.g., 'Doggy here', which is composite. Indeed, unless such one-word sentences are elliptical for something complex, it is difficult to see what could be meant by an assertion of one word on its own. That, of course, is the point. If the word 'Doggy' is used on its own as a name to name something, we are still waiting to hear what is being said, we do not yet have something that can be assessed for being true or false.

The above argument can be elaborated by considering what Gareth Evans called the 'generality constraint'.[35] Start with the thought that sentences are things that can be used to make judgements.[36] Further, judgements are things to be assessed as true or false. Indeed, to make a judgement is to have some conception of the conditions that would render the judgement incorrect; it is to have a conception of the conditions that would force one to retract the judgement. We can encapsulate this point by saying:

> **Judgement principle:** To make a judgement is to be responsive to conditions that would force one to retract the judgement.

The point of this principle is to capture the normativity of meaning. It is not an empirical generalization; it is a constitutive claim. Judging something to be the case is to lay yourself hostage to a normative standard of evaluation of what you have done – have you judged truly? A vocalization that was not responsive to a notion of conditions that would force the speaker to retract would not count as a judgement.

Now, suppose someone makes a judgement of the form

Fa,

where '*a*' is a name for some object and '*F*' a predicate, such as '. . . is white'. What is it for the judgement to be sensitive to conditions that would force the retraction of the utterance? One fundamental way for such a sensitivity to manifest itself is this: In saying that *a* is white, the speaker is saying that it is the same way as other white things. It makes no sense to think that a speaker might say that *a* is white and not see any connection between the way *a* is and the way a piece of chalk is. For example, the simplest way in which you can be forced to retract the judgement is because *a* is not the same as the piece of chalk. If *a* is white, then it is the same colour as the piece of chalk. If there is not this in common between *a* and the chalk, then, in the absence of further considerations, the original judgement must be withdrawn.

This is a very elementary point, but note what flows from it. There is a generality to the notion of judging of some thing that it is a certain way. To say that *a* is white is to say that it is a way that other things can be. It is because of this generality that we get a notion of the conditions that would force us to retract the claim. So, if we understand the idea that *a* is *F*, we must in principle understand the idea that *b* is *F*, that *c* is *F*, and so on. There must be a common component to these judgements.

The connection between these judgements is a connection that accounts for their inferential relationships. If *b* is white, then anything that is the same colour as *b* is white. It is this inferential connection that provides the argument to force the retraction of the original judgement if *a* is not the same colour as *b* and *b* is white. This shows the sense in which the inferential connections between one judgement and others provides the sense of what is said by any one. We know what has been said when we know, in part, how it stands in relation to other sayings.

The generality involved in the judgement '*Fa*' does not just concern the predicate; it also involves the name. The judgement is not just about whiteness, it is about the whiteness of an object, *a*, not *b*, or *c*, or *d*. In order for the judgement to be focused on *a*, rather than any other object, it must be the case that the speaker is able to understand other things about *a*: where it is, how large it is, what kind of object it is, etc. Without an understanding of these other things that may be said about *a*, the initial judegment has nothing to distinguish it from a judgement that *b* is *F*. Therefore, in order to make the judgement '*Fa*', the speaker must understand what it would be to make other judgements about *a*: *Ga*, *Ha*, etc. Once again, this generality is involved in the way in which we evaluate the original claim. Someone says that *a* is *F*, meaning that the object over there, under the light beside the chair, . . . is white.

The judgement that *a* is *F* involves a two-way generality. It involves the capacity to understand judgements such as '*Fb*', '*Fc*', '*Fd*', etc., and it involves the capacity to understand judgements such as '*Ga*', '*Ha*', etc. Grasping the meaning of the judgement involves the combination of a pair of separable capacities: the capacity to use the name in a variety of judgements and the capacity to use the predicate in a variety of judgements. Sentences that fully express judgements are necessarily structured.[37] There can be one-word sentences that are elliptical expressions for something complex and structured – for example, the one-word sentence 'Doggy' is a sentence, rather than a name – if and only if it is elliptical for something such as 'Doggy here'.

The above argument is very abstract. It makes a small but fundamental point. We shall return to consider the importance of the argument in later chapters, but note that the argument is a conceptual one. It is an a priori conceptual argument for the compositionality thesis. The argument does not turn on the creativity of language use, but on the basic notion of what it is for a sentence as an expression of a judgement to be an item of semantic evaluation. The fact that it gives a conceptual reason for the compositionality thesis is important with regard to both the compositionality of language and the compositionality of thought. The former is a thesis associated most famously with Davidson's work. His argument about the principles employed in radical interpretation is closely related to the above argument.[38] We shall examine Davidson's account in chapter 4. The idea that the compositionality of thought is a conceptual requirement, not an empirical constraint, will occupy us in chapter 12.[39]

1.6 Logical Grammar

I have now sketched an answer to the question of how the priority given to the study of grammar by acceptance of the context principle is compatible with the acceptance of the compositionality thesis. The next question is: What concept of grammar is implicated when we say that the study of grammar is prior to metaphysics?

The simple answer is that the concept of grammar is logical grammar, not linguistic grammar. This distinction has shaped most twentieth-century philosophy of thought, from Russell's theory of descriptions to Davidson's programme for a general theory of meaning by modelling natural language within the logical grammar of first-order predicate calculus. To say that the concept of grammar implicated in the Fregean methodology is logical grammar is not, however, to say what this concept is or why it is required.

The core of the concept of logical as opposed to linguistic grammar derives from the argument of the previous section. I have argued that (i) judgements (what sentences express) are the fundamental unit of meaning, and (ii) judgements (and those sentences that fully express them) are necessarily structured. Structure is required in order that judgements be seen as subject to semantic evaluation. The grammatical structures of ordinary language do not necessarily mark the way in which sentences are subject to truth and falsity. Linguistic structures vary from one language to another with regard to the way that tense is marked, how word order is used to indicate differences between main clause and subordinate clause, etc. These are all features to do with the concept of linguistic grammar.

Logical grammar, however, is the structure that a judgement has to have in order that it be truth-evaluable. Logical grammar is the structure a judgement possesses that makes it suitable for aiming at truth. This means that the fundamental concept in our enquiry is the concept of truth, for naming is understood in terms of grammar that in turn, is understood in terms of truth. The concept of logical grammar is defined relative to truth, for it is the structure that enables judgements to be manoeuvred with respect to truth. The manoeuvres that judgements go on are called inferences.

In section 1.3 I said that a Fregean philosophy of thought holds that the study of grammar is prior to metaphysics; semantics exhausts ontology. The study of grammar involved is now seen to be the study of that structure of our thought and language that makes it truth-evaluable. That is to say, the priority of semantics over metaphysics amounts to the claim that it is by studying the structure of our thought necessary for it to be aimed at truth that we uncover the structure of the world. Semantics provides an account of the structure of thought. If provides an account of the structure of language that makes it suitable for thinking and saying things that can be true or false. In so far as we restrict metaphysics to what can be thought about or talked about, then a study of the structure of thought and talk will, *ipso facto*, be a study of the general structure of what is. On such a view, semantics gives us the outline structure of what is thinkable. The only metaphysical issues left untouched by such a study will be issues concerned with the unthinkable. It is not clear that that amounts to anything at all.[40]

Logical grammar is the structure that is necessary for our judgements (whether of thought or talk) to be aimed at truth. Suppose for the moment that some particular judgement P appears to have a structure that involves a reference to certain kinds of entities – for example, events. You might then think that in accepting P as a bona fide judgement suitable for aiming at truth, you were

23

committed to the existence of events. One job of semantics will then be to see whether this commitment is necessary in order for *P* to remain a judgement that can be aimed at truth. That is to say, if it is possible to give an analysis of the judgement that, with regard to its truth-evaluability, leaves *P* as truth-evaluable but removes the apparent reference to events, then semantics will have shown that the commitment to the existence of events is unwarranted. With regard to truth-evaluability, everything that was said with *P* can still be said without taking the judgement as endorsing the commitment to events. In broad outline, this is the justification for the twentieth-century preoccupation with the analysis of language. The analysis is justified in so far as it seeks to uncover logical grammar, the structure necessary for aiming a judgement at truth.[41]

Two points should be noted about this notion of logical grammar. First, the investigation of logical grammar involves analysis. It requires us to analyse judgements and the moves that can be undertaken with them in order to uncover the structures that enable the whole business of judgement and inference to be truth-oriented. This analysis has nothing to do with ordinary language analysis. It is not an analysis that is undertaken in order to remove conceptual confusions from ordinary language, although, if ordinary language were a conceptually confusing structure, this would be revealed by the study of logical grammar. The study of logical grammar is not, however, premissed on the idea that ordinary language is a confusing structure.[42] Second, the idea of an investigation of logical grammar does not require that logical grammar should be susceptible to an explicit definition that defines validity over a formal symbolism. That is to say, acceptance of the idea of logical grammar does not mean that it is possible to construct a language in which all instances of valid inferences are fully definable solely in terms of the formal or syntactic properties of the linguistic components.[43] The basic idea is that logical grammar is the truth-oriented structure of judgement. It does not follow from this that logical grammar can be identified with the structure of a language, for we do not yet know whether all judgements are fully codifiable linguistically. We need to keep an open mind on this. It is nothing less than the issue of representationalism versus anti-representationalism. We should not assume that the structure of language is prior to the structure of thought. We start with the more abstract idea of the structure of judgement (meaning, if you prefer), where this is the normative pattern that shapes all judgements, whether of thought or language.

The concept of logical grammar and the above justification for the idea of the analysis of judgement flow directly from the Fregean methodology. The account given is not without problems. If the justification for the analysis of judgements to reveal their logical grammar is viable, much weight rests on our theory of truth. The defence of the analysis of logical grammar that I have sketched is premissed on the idea that judgements are things to be aimed at truth. But for the above argument to provide a defence of the Fregean idea that semantics is prior to metaphysics, it will be necessary to give an account of truth that is neutral with regard to metaphysics. Our account of truth guides the analysis of logical grammar; the account of logical grammar is supposed to reveal the structure of metaphysics. But for that to work, we had better not start with an account of truth that already presupposes a substantive metaphysics.

It is not clear that this can be achieved. One of the main issues to be addressed through the first half of this book concerns the interplay between metaphysics and our grasp of the concepts of meaning and logic. It is not clear that we can start with a neutral conception of truth and then proceed to an account of meaning and logical grammar. We will need to practice a reflective equilibrium between the demands of metaphysics, meaning and logic in working out the details of the above strategy.[44]

Without prejudging the work of later chapters, we can note one response to the above problem now. One way of ensuring that the study of logical grammar is not prejudiced by a metaphysically loaded concept of truth would be for it to be a transcendental study. That is to say, the justification that I have sketched for the study of logical grammar is that it is the study of structure necessary for judgements to be aimed at truth. The starting-point to the deduction is the claim that we make judgements that are truth-evaluable. The conclusion is the claim that, for this to be possible, judgements must exhibit certain patterns of structure, a logical grammar.

This is a way of defending the analysis of logical grammar that has become more explicit in recent years. For example, in recent work, Peacocke uses the notion of the 'canonical commitments' of a judgement.[45] The canonical commitments are those commitments that you must accept in making a judgement. They are commitments to holding true various other judgements given the judgement in question. Such an approach leaves open the possibility that the necessity, if any, of the form of logical grammar is more a reflection of an unnoticed metaphysical input from our theory of truth. For the transcendental turn to work, we would need our theory of truth to be delivered by a transcendental deduction. This is a move I take in chapter 5.

We should not assume at the outset that the logical grammar of judgement and of the inferential connections of judgement can be fully and explicitly modelled syntactically. For much of the twentieth century, philosophers assumed that the way to uncover logical grammar was to provide an explicit model of the truth-evaluable structure of judgements in a formal syntactic language. If representationalism is true, it is plausible to expect such an explicit model of logical grammar. It is now a contentious point whether such a transparent presentation of logical grammar is possible.[46]

1.7 Anti-psychologism and the Threat of Linguistic Idealism

One of the most famous aspects of Frege's philosophy of thought is his anti-psychologism. For Frege, thoughts – which are the contents of judgements – are not to be conceived as psychologistic entities like ideas; rather, they are objective items. The reason that Frege gives for this turns on two key points. First, thoughts are the means of communication. We cannot share ideas; they are subjective and private. We can, however, share thoughts, but only if they have some kind of objective status. Second, for Frege it is thoughts that are the bearers of truth and falsity, not ideas. And for Frege, truth is always conceived of as objective truth.

Both of the above points explain why the study of logical grammar should be given priority over an introspectionist study of ideas. There is, however, a deeper reason why an introspectionist study of ideas cannot be taken as a starting-point for a theory of meaning and why the concept of logical grammar has to be endorsed. This further reason turns on the problems inherent in introspectionist psychology with regard to capturing the normativity of meaning. I shall defer discussion of this argument until chapter 7, where it will be considered in the context of Wittgenstein's celebrated discussion of rule-following.

Given the methodology I am pursuing, there is a threat of linguistic idealism. It will take much work to render it harmless. I have already noted the intuitive connection between endorsing representationalism and realism. Clearly, if we deny representationalism, some kind of realism is under threat, for the denial amounts to the claim that the characterization of content is not possible in isolation from our account of the world. A metaphysical realist may wonder whether we can have, on this option, a realist enough conception of the world. I believe that we can. The threat of linguistic idealism is this. If semantics exhausts ontology, how can a purely semantic study tell us anything ontological, for it will amount to no more than a study of signs and the way we use them. The problem is particularly vivid in Brandom's way of setting out options in this area.[47]

Brandom distinguishes between what he calls representationalist and inferentialist approaches to content. Representationalists provide a piecemeal (bottom-up) account of the semantic properties of signs (reference, satisfaction, truth) and then account for the signs' inferential role in terms of set-theoretic constructions upon the assignment of semantic properties. Brandom's conception of representationalism is different to mine, although most representationalists on his definition will also count as representationalist on mine. Brandom's representationalism is defined in terms of an atomistic account of semantic properties. Unless the atomist thinks that the relations of reference, satisfaction and truth that signs bear to the world are internal, they will be representationalist by my definition. The only atomist (representationalist in Brandom's sense) who is not a representationalist in my sense is Russell. Russell held that primitive signs were internally connected to simple objects. I call this semantic Cartesianism (section 1.8 below). Russell's anti-representationalism is extremely important. I return to it briefly in chapter 2 and again in chapter 11.

The difference between representationalism and inferentialism on Brandom's portrayal is that the former holds it possible to give an account of what names stand for independently of their grammar. Brandom sees inferentialism as the opposite strategy, whereby we start with an account of the name's grammar and then deliver an account of reference (satisfaction and truth for other categories of expression). That looks just as odd as the representationalist position; for how can the study of inferential role tell us anything about the *aboutness* of language? But the denial of representationalism does not have to involve Brandom's swing to the opposing option of inferentialism. The Fregean approach opposes the idea that you can give an account of the reference of a sign independently of an account of its grammar, but it does not mean that the two things, reference and grammar, are not interdependent. As I noted in section 1.4, the denial of a bottom-up approach merely denies the explanatory priority of reference; it does not mean that there is no such thing as reference. All it means is that there is no account of reference independent of grammar/inference. Nevertheless, a problem remains.

For the study of grammar to be revelatory of ontology, there must be some objectivity to the patterns of use we characterize in this study. It is not clear that this is the case if the study of grammar is a purely formal or linguistic study.[48] If the study cannot be undertaken formally, then there must be some metaphysical input to logical grammar. That sounds like a disaster for the 'Semantics exhausts ontology' thesis, but in fact it is what makes the whole method exciting. Suppose that the metaphysical input to grammar is transcendentally justified; that is, it is not a gratuitous metaphysics plugged in just to get the right results, it is there in order that we cut content at just the points necessary to get that which rationally explains behaviour. That, then, is anti-representationalism, for it is the idea that the individuation of thought and its logical grammar is world-involving. The logical grammar of thought, the structure by which it is truth-evaluable, is not, then, a linguistic structure. It is a structure of how we are in the world. The possession of content is the possession of the world. Furthermore, if in our responsiveness to reasons, we take ourselves to be responsive to contents (beliefs, etc.), this means that our responsiveness to reasons can be a direct responsiveness to the world. The world comes within the province of our thoughts, it falls within the space of reasons.[49] This is heady stuff!

The above picture illustrates the metaphysical results that flow from thinking through the Fregean methodology. It also makes vivid why semantics as I understand it cannot be identified with formal semantics. There is much to do to make it all work. The claim I shall defend is that, in order to capture the normativity of meaning, we need a concept of truth that introduces a conception of states that exist independently of the mind. This is a minimal realism. The minimal realism defended is, nevertheless, shaped by our best account of meaning, so it is a content-driven account of truth, and semantics still exhausts ontology. The details of this programme will occupy most of the rest of the book.

1.8 Summary

We are creatures who think about the world around us. We talk about the world around us. We have the ability to perceive strings of signs as carrying a meaning. At its most basic, the philosophy of thought is concerned with explaining how this is possible; but there are many forms such an explanation may take.

An older, Cartesian approach would have explained these phenomena in terms of the power of our Ideas. That, however, is no real explanation. It demands of our Ideas the power to represent, the power to imbue linguistic signs with content.[50] It does not explain what it is for us to have such power, to be possessors of content. If we want an explanation of this, there are at least a couple of stages such an explanation will need to go through.

First, we will need a reasonably accurate description of the phenomena in question. We will need to map our intentionality. We need an account of the range of abilities and capacities that go to make up our intentional stance – our ability to handle meaning and to think, talk and argue about the world around us.

Second, we will need some account of how these abilities are grounded in our physical make-up. It is, of course, possible that the map of intentionality we produce at the first stage will show that our intentionality cannot be accounted for in terms of our physical make-up. Such a result would not prove that the description offered was mistaken, but it would call it into question. It is difficult to see how we can make sense of the idea that such central capacities of our humanity should turn out to be grounded in a mysterious non-physical make-up. However, having acknowledged that, we should not at the outset presuppose any particular account of the relationship between the first and second stages of our theory of meaning. Indeed, if we give precedence to the first stage of the explanation, it is likely that the map of intentionality produced will provide some basic constraints on how we should go about the second stage.[51]

To adopt a Fregean methodology is to give precedence to the first stage of our explanation of meaning. It is to attempt to draw the map of intentionality without presupposing any particular scientific model and without making assumptions about the way the first and second stages are related. This is not incompatible with the idea that the second stage will, one day, be completable, and that doing that will be the job of a naturalized theory of content. It is also compatible with the thought that a naturalized theory of content need have no reductionist aspirations, but will rather seek only to show how the constitutive and engineering levels of theory cohabit.

There is an alternative order of precedence between these two stages, in which philosophers take the dominant scientific paradigm of the day and see what a map of our intentionality would look like if it were written according to that paradigm. This is the approach of different forms of physicalism: for example, Fodor's standard model, in which the constitutive account is reduced to the engineering account, and Millikan's theory of content, based upon biological models of explanation.[52] On extreme versions of this approach, the map of our intentionality turns out to be non-existent.[53]

I propose to follow a Fregean methodology and take the constitutive level as prior, because that way we ensure that we capture the normativity of meaning. The question of whether physicalism can capture the normativity of meaning is a recurrent theme in contemporary work. The Fregean approach is evident in many contemporary philosophers, whether or not they explicitly represent themselves as working within a Fregean methodology.[54] It is an approach that embodies the following thesis:

> The mapping of our intentionality is accomplished by an a priori objective study of meaning.

Because this study is an objective one, the items studied are not subjective ideas. Thought contents have an objective status. This, then, is opposed to what I shall call semantic Cartesianism – the thesis that ideas are mental items with a basic, unexplained power to represent. For semantic Cartesianism, the ability to grasp meaning and possess representations is treated as a basic given about the furniture of the mind; it is not something to be explained. Semantic Cartesianism is typical of most philosophers from the seventeenth and eighteenth centuries; it also seeps into the work of some twentieth-century theorists. To engage in an objective study of meaning is to begin the task of understanding the structure of the capacities by which we are possessors of content.

An important claim that is central to the theory of content is:

> Meaning is necessarily structured, the study of meaning is the study of logical grammar.

Logical grammar is the structure that meaning has in order that it be truth-evaluable. This way of understanding the idea of logical grammar means that, from the point of view of a study of logical grammar,

> Truth is the basic semantic concept, not reference.

It is this that then explains Frege's central ontological dependency on semantics, the thesis that

> The concept of an object is a semantic concept, not an epistemological or metaphysical concept.

This is why it makes sense to say that

> Semantics exhausts ontology.

In practice, most philosophers working in the area of the philosophy of thought and language indulge in some sort of mix of the two levels of theory I have described. My claim is only that a Fregean methodology that give precedence to the constitutive level would endorse the above theses. In developing arguments for this approach, we will need to watch the way that constitutive investigations either lead or follow scientific models of meaning. We need to ask what metaphysical assumptions are motivating the direction of precedence. We will need to examine to what extent it is possible to frame an a priori study of logical grammar and hold that study prior to metaphysics. In particular, we will need to trace the connections between our metaphysical intuitions, our intuitions about validity and truth, and our account of the structures of logical grammar. At times philosophers produce metaphysical results from apparently formal studies of logical grammar, and at other times they produce results in the theory of meaning from metaphysical theses. We will need to mark the direction of explanation and derivation of such claims, and to locate the point at which the direction of argument pivots, so that we can make rational choices about which direction looks correct. I start this process in the next chapter with Russell's theory of descriptions – the paradigm case of the employment of the concept of logical grammar. It is also, when properly understood, a rich resource for the general outline of an anti-representationalist theory of content.

2

Russell's Theory of Descriptions

2.1   Introduction

Russell's 'On denoting' has become a classic of twentieth-century philosophy.[1] In it Russell provides a theory of how we are to understand sentences containing definite descriptions, expressions of the form 'the so-and-so'. His theory offers an analysis of the logical grammar of sentences involving such expressions. His theory is often seen as a paradigm in the philosophy of language.[2] It is, however, properly a contribution to the philosophy of thought. Russell's interest is only in language in so far as it expresses our intentionality – the way we think of things and especially the way in which language can lead us to mistake the nature of our intentionality.

In this chapter I explain Russell's theory, offer an evaluation of whether or not it is correct, and assess its implications for a theory of content. In the first place, we need to know why Russell needed the theory. It is relatively simple to state the theory of descriptions and the standard objections to it. The important task is to understand the philosophical problems that are being addressed by it. To do this, we need to plot the epistemological and metaphysical theses that prompted the theory. This involves giving a preliminary sketch of Russell's theory of reference.[3]

The theory of reference will not occupy us properly until chapter 8. According to the methodology I have adopted, truth is the primary semantic concept, not reference. The first half of this book is concerned with the connections between truth and meaning, and also truth and logic. At this point, then, my account of Russell's theory of reference will provide only sufficient detail to motivate his need to begin the excavations into logical grammar.

2.2   Russell's Theory of Reference

Russell's theory of reference is a contribution to the theory of thought; language features only in so far as it is the expression of thought. Russell held what

31

I shall call the object theory of reference.[4] It is the simplest theory of reference available.

> **Object theory of reference:** The meaning of an expression is the entity for which it stands.

This is a general claim for all categories of expressions. For singular terms – expressions that refer to objects – the object theory of reference says that the meaning of a name '*a*' is the object *a*. Names stand for their associated objects, and employing a name in a judgement introduces the object named as the immediate object of thought or assertion. This is how Russell expresses the theory:

> Words all have meaning in the simple sense that they are symbols which stand for something other than themselves.[5]

There are two central features of the object theory of reference. First, if the meaning of an expression is the entity for which it stands, it is a condition on the meaningfulness of an expression that it have an associated entity. An expression which lacks an associated entity has no meaning. This is a general thesis that applies to all categories of expression. Let me introduce the term 'semantic value' as a general label for the entity associated with an expression. The semantic value of a name is an object. The semantic value of a predicate is a universal. The semantic value of a sentence is truth or falsity. The first point about the object theory of reference as applied to all categories of expression can now be expressed as:

> **Semantic value dependence thesis:** In order for an expression to be meaningful, it must have an entity of an appropriate kind associated with it.

The semantic value dependence thesis figures prominently in Russell's argument in 'On denoting'. It is also endorsed by a number of contemporary writers.[6] It follows from this thesis that the only kind of error available in thought is having a false thought. I shall call this molecular error, for it occurs only for whole judgements. There is, for Russell, no such thing as atomic error, for if a singular term lacks a semantic value, it is meaningless. The semantic value dependence thesis guarantees semantic success for atomic expressions, and error can only occur when atomic expressions are combined to make a judgement that is false.

The second feature of the object theory of reference concerns the nature of the association between expression and entity. With regard to names, the association is usually described as 'direct', or it is said that the relation is simple and unmediated. In his *Lectures on the Philosophy of Logical Atomism*, Russell says:

the name itself is merely a means of pointing to the thing and does not occur in what you are asserting, so that if one thing has two names, you make exactly the same assertion whichever of the names you use, provided that they are really names and not truncated descriptions.[7]

The final caveat is important. The claim that exactly the same assertion is made regardless of which name, of a set of co-referring names, is employed is a key consequence of the claim that the word/object association is direct. The point can be made in the following way.

First, in order to make the judgement that

a is *F*,

whether in thought or talk, you must understand the meaning of the expressions involved. If the meaning of the name '*a*' is the object *a*, then understanding the meaning of the judgement requires direct contact with the object. It is a condition of the understanding of the meaning of this judgement that you have a direct contact with the object.[8] Many contemporary theories of reference have tried to capture this Russellian notion that reference involves direct contact between the mind of the speaker/thinker and the object referred to. The idea of 'directness' gets employed in a variety of ways, but one thing that is meant by this, and was meant by Russell, is easily stated.

Suppose that, where 'S' is a subject of thought or assertion,

(1)   S judges that *a* is *F*.

According to the object theory of reference, grasp of the meaning of this judgement requires that S grasps the object *a*. The name simply directs S to the object. There is nothing to be said about how the name achieves this contact between S and the object. The contact exists as a condition of S understanding the name. We might note this point as follows:

> **The principle of contact:** Understanding the meaning of a name requires an unmediated contact with the object it denotes.

It follows from this that any co-referring name will, if understood by S, provide S with just the same unmediated contact.

Suppose then that '*b*' is another name for the same object,

(2)   *a* = *b*.

It must follow from (1) and (2) that

(3)   S judges that *b* is *F*.

There is no difference, with regard to the meaning of the judgement, which name is employed in making a judgement about an object. To judge that *a* is *F* is no different from judging that *b* is *F*.

This last point could be expressed by saying that on the object theory of reference, judgement is relational, and the relation is extensional. Russell characterizes judgement in this way. His example is:

(4)   Othello judges that Desdemona loves Cassio.[9]

Russell analyses (4) in terms of Othello standing in a complex relation to Desdemona, Cassio and the dyadic relation . . . loves ____. This complex relation can be represented as

(5)   Othello **R** <Desdemona, Cassio, . . . loving____>,

and the salient point about relation **R** is that it is extensional. It is because **R** is extensional that it does not matter how each item is picked out; any co-referring expression for an entity that figures within the relation will do as well as any other. The object theory of reference commits us to an extensional theory of judgement. The relation between the thinker/speaker and the entities judged is extensional. This is why, for the object theory of reference, the inference from (1) and (2) to (3) is valid. The second feature of the object theory of reference is the endorsement of an extensional theory of judgement.

Historically, it has been the extensional theory of judgement that has generated most of the debate surrounding the object theory of reference. It would not be an exaggeration to say that twentieth-century work in the theory of reference has been an extended argument about whether or not an extensional theory of judgement is viable and, therefore, whether or not the object theory of reference is viable.[10] The semantic value dependence thesis has, largely, gone unremarked. In part, no doubt, this is because it conflicts with the representationalist orthodoxy that permits atomic error. It is partly due also to its being treated guilty by association with Russell's obscure view that relations are objects. My own view is that the thesis is correct and that the extensional theory of judgement is false. We shall turn to these issues in chapter 8. For the moment it is important that the only account of the directness of association between word and object that I am currently attributing to the object theory of reference is the acceptance of an extensional theory of judgement. The idea of directness is a metaphor, and it has been variously expressed in different theories. Before proceeding further, let me note just one way in which the directness of the word/object relation is sometimes expressed.

The directness of the word/object relation is sometimes expressed by saying that names have denotation, but no connotation. As such, the theory has been associated with J. S. Mill. The association with Mill, however, is incorrect. Although he is often cited as a paradigm example of a direct reference theorist, there is little connection with Russell's notion of directness. First, what Mill says applies only to proper names, which Russell never held to be direct. Furthermore, what Mill says about names hardly supports a direct reference theory for names.[11] In *A System of Logic* Mill says:

> When we impose a proper name . . . we put a mark, not indeed upon the object itself, but, so to speak, upon the idea of the object. A proper name is but an unmeaning mark which we connect in our minds with the idea of the object, in order that whenever the mark meets our eyes or occurs to our thoughts, we may think of that individual object.[12]

Mill's theory involves a two-stage relation between word and object. In the first place, a word is associated with an idea; the idea is then associated with the object. Mill does not tell us how ideas are associated with objects, and it is therefore unclear whether Mill's views as cited support an extensional theory of judgement. I think the prima-facie view must be that Mill does not endorse an extensional theory of judgement, for it seems likely that, for Mill, co-referring names might be associated with different ideas, despite the fact that these ideas further associate with one object. Whether or not Mill's theory supports an extensional theory of judgement turns on whether or not we individuate judgements with ideas or with objects. It is not clear that Mill has a ready answer to this question, and we cannot look for one until we have a better idea of what we expect of a theory of judgement. So these matters will be left until we look at reference in detail from chapter 8 onwards.

There is, however, an important lesson we should take from this otherwise minor point about the common misreading of Mill. Mill is usually taken as standard-bearer for direct reference theorists. What the above passage shows, however, is that we have to draw a distinction between Mill's philosophy of language and his philosophy of thought. Construed as a purely linguistic claim, there is a sense in which Mill is a direct reference theorist. He is a direct reference theorist in the sense that names lack connotation and so are not semantically equivalent to any other category of expression. They are, therefore, signs whose semantic value is assigned, not computed. But that thesis of 'direct reference' (names lack connotation) is a purely linguistic thesis. It matters in the production of a formal semantic theory, for any formal theory that treated names as expressions whose value was computed from the assignment of values to expressions of another category would be mistaken. The linguistic thesis of direct reference, however, has nothing to do with an account of the semantics of names that individuates content in a way that makes rational sense of behaviour. Mill does not have a developed theory of the latter variety, but it seems clear from the passage quoted that ideas figure in his account of the naming relation just in order to capture something like the concept of content that we are interested in.[13]

2.3   The Need for a Theory of Descriptions

The fundamental need for a theory of descriptions concerns a metaphysical problem that arises for the object theory of reference. The semantic value dependence thesis says that it is a condition of the meaningfulness of an expression that it have an entity of an appropriate sort associated with it. So, a meaningful singular term must have an object associated with it. But this leads to an extravagantly bloated ontology. The following sentences are meaningful (they express judgements):

> Sherlock Holmes plays the violin.
> The round square does not exist.
> The King of France is bald.

Furthermore, they appear to contain singular terms: 'Sherlock Holmes', 'The round square', and 'The King of France'. If the object theory of reference is correct, then these terms must have associated with them the entities Sherlock Holmes, the round square, and the King of France.

The theory of descriptions is needed to remove this ontological extravagance. If it can be shown that the above expressions are not genuine singular terms, we can deflate our ontology. The idea that something is not a genuine singular term is the idea that, despite its superficial ordinary linguistic grammatical role, its logical grammar reveals that it belongs to a different category of expression. The logical grammar of a term is its role in determining the truth-value of sentences containing it. The theory of descriptions shows that the logical grammar of descriptions is not that of singular terms.

The theory of descriptions shows that most apparent occurrences of singular terms can be analysed into expressions containing only predicates and quantifiers. Informally, the analysis of

> (6)   The King of France is bald

amounts to:

(7) (i) There is a King of France, and
    (ii) There is only one King of France, and
    (iii) Anything which is a King of France is bald.

The three clauses that provide the analysis of (6) are all representable with quantifiers and predicates. Accordingly, the need for the object the King of France in order to permit the meaningfulness of (6) lapses.

The analysis will need predicates, but understanding the meaning of predicates requires the existence of universals, not of objects. So the object, the King of France, will no longer be required as a condition of the meaningfulness of (6). The universals, kinghood, being French, will be required, but these are required for understanding all sorts of expressions – e.g. 'The King of Spain', 'The President of France', etc. Therefore, ontological economy is achieved if one and the same set of entities, universals, is sufficient for giving the meaning of such expressions without the added need for an ontological commitment to objects, like the King of France, that patently do not exist. The fact that the King of France does not exist was not always acknowledged by Russell. Prior to the development of the theory of descriptions, he accepted the ontological consequences of the object theory of reference. He followed Meinong and admitted the category of subsistence in which to accommodate entities like the round square and the King of France. The theory of descriptions liberated him from this ontological silliness.[14]

Although the metaphysical problem with the object theory of reference was the main reason why Russell needed the theory of descriptions, his development of the theory flowed from an epistemological constraint that he imposed upon the object theory of reference. It is this constraint – the principle of acquaintance – that explains Russell's broad application of the theory of descriptions; it explains why, for example, Russell thought it removed not only descriptions, but also proper names, from the category of singular terms.

Acceptance of the object theory of reference entails acceptance of the principle of contact. In his earliest period Russell had not worked through this consequence of the object theory of reference. When he did, his account of the contact required between thinker and object was an epistemological one:

> Every proposition which we can understand must be composed wholly of constituents with which we are acquainted.[15]

This is Russell's principle of acquaintance,

> **Principle of acquaintance:** Understanding the meaning of an expression requires acquaintance with that entity which is its meaning.

37

The principle of acquaintance is not entailed by the object theory of reference. The object theory of reference entails only the more abstract principle of contact, and leaves undetermined how that contact is to be understood. The concept of contact employed must be an extensional relation, but that leaves open a number of possibilities for theorizing the contact. For example, contemporary theorists have attempted to preserve a Russellian view of reference by characterizing the contact between thinker and object causally.[16] For Russell, however, the contact is defined epistemologically, and his epistemology is Cartesian:

> I say that I am acquainted with an object when I have a direct cognitive relation to that object, i.e. when I am directly aware of the object itself.[17]

The point of the 'directly' is to ensure that this relation of awareness is extensional, but it also emphasizes the Cartesianism of Russell's epistemology. Russell held that ordinary physical objects, including other people, could not be direct objects of awareness.

For Russell, the range of entities with which we can be acquainted is extraordinarily small. Apart from universals, the only objects that Russell believes we can be aquainted with are sense-data.[18] Consequently, he believes that the range of genuine singular terms is extraordinarily small. It comprises just those terms that are used to refer to sense-data and the self. It follows from this that there are only three genuine singular terms: 'this', 'that' and 'I'. A genuine singular term is a term for which the object theory of reference applies.

It is because Russell understood 'acquaintance' in this Cartesian way that he held that ordinary proper names were not genuine singular terms. He treats them as truncated descriptions. The meaning of a proper name is given by a definite description. The meaning of the definite description is given by the theory of descriptions, which shows that they can be analysed into predicate terms and quantifiers. It follows from this that in order to understand descriptions and, therefore, to understand proper names, all that is required is that you be acquainted with the universals associated with the relevant predicates. This means that in ordinary language there is very little reference going on. The only time that reference occurs is when the expressions 'this', 'that' and 'I' are used to pick out sense-data and the self. All the other apparent apparatus of reference within ordinary language – names, descriptions, kind terms, pronouns – will be subject to analysis via the theory of descriptions.

Russell's theory of reference stands in contrast to the Fregean methodology sketched in chapter 1. First, Russell is a semantic Cartesian. Semantic Cartesianism is the doctrine that ideas have a basic, unexplained power to represent, to stand for things. As such, it might seem unfair to charge Russell with this, for he does not speak of ideas.[19] Nevertheless, the charge sticks. With regard to the only genuine singular terms that Russell admits, his explanation of the association between name and object goes no further than to say that the mind has a primitive unexplained power to reach out and impose the name upon the object. For Russell, the dominant partner in the exchange between mind, word and object is the mind. It is a power of the mind that attaches a 'this' to an object and that holds that attachment in place for as long as the mind continues to focus its ostensive gaze upon the object.

This point is clear in a notorious exchange in one of the discussions published with Russell's 'Lectures on the Philosophy of Logical Atomism'. A questioner asks how long communication can survive if the only objects ever genuinely referred to are sense-data.[20] The question is a good one and poses an obvious difficulty. Russell's response is simply to say:

> You can keep 'this' going for about a minute or two . . . If you argue quickly, you can get some little way before it is finished.[21]

Regardless of the adequacy of this reply to the question, what is clear is the way that Russell conceives of the mind as the dominant partner in the account of the relation between mind, word and object. It is the power of the mind that forms the association between word and object. This is semantic Cartesianism.

The charge of semantic Cartesianism is not, of itself, a criticism of Russell's position. Given the Cartesian epistemology with which Russell constrains his theory of reference, it is hardly surprising that he is a semantic Cartesian too. His principle of acquaintance restricts the range of singular terms to such a degree that the only objects left to be referred to are, as it were, so close to the mind that it is difficult to see what explanation could be given of how the mind attaches names to such things. Given the epistemological restrictions on his theory of reference, Russell's semantic Cartesianism is probably inevitable.

The second point to note is that, for Russell, the concept of an object is an epistemological concept. It is not a semantic concept. Again, this follows directly from his underlying epistemology and the way that his principle of acquaintance constrains the range of objects to which we can refer.

2.4   The Apparatus of the Theory of Descriptions

The first key aspect of the object theory of reference is the semantic value dependence thesis. For Russell this was a basic constraint upon a general theory of judgement. In 'On denoting' he sets himself the task of providing an account of the meaning of sentences of the form

The *F* is *G*.

In those cases where there is nothing which is *F*, then the apparent singular term is empty. If the description lacks a semantic value, then, given the compositionality thesis that the semantic value of a sentence is a function of the semantic values of its parts, the whole sentence will lack a semantic value. As Russell puts the point, without an account of descriptions that shows that they are not empty singular terms, the law of excluded middle will fail for sentences such as

(6)   The King of France is bald.

This point reiterates the importance of the semantic value dependence thesis, but note that the thesis affects not only what Russell says about the semantics of singular terms and definite descriptions, but also logic.

The law of excluded middle (LEM) says that, for any proposition *P*, either *P* or not-*P*. One way of responding to Russell's predicament with (6) would be to abandon the law of excluded middle. This is an expensive option. Russell thinks it is preposterous. For Russell, the threat to LEM underlined the seriousness of the demand for a theory to handle (6). Although it is rather hasty to suggest without further argument that you could abandon LEM rather than adopt the theory of descriptions, there is an important point about the availability of this option: Issues concerning meaning and reference interconnect with issues concerning the theory of logic. In addition to the metaphysical and epistemological pressures that led Russell to develop the theory of descriptions, there is also the pressure to preserve a theory of logic in which LEM holds.

An informal representation of Russell's analysis of (6) provides us with:

(7)   (i)   There is a King of France, and
      (ii)   There is only one King of France, and
      (iii)   Anything which is a King of France is bald.

In the symbolism of first-order predicate calculus the first two clauses come to:

(8)   (i) $\exists x \, Fx \, \&,$
      (ii) $\forall y \, (Fy \rightarrow y = x) \, \&.$

(i) makes an existential claim that there is a King of France. (ii) provides the uniqueness claim that in ordinary language is captured by the definite article, for it says that anything which is a King of France is identical to the item picked out by the existential clause. We then need to capture the third clause (7 iii). This appears to require another universal quantifier. However, we already have that in (ii), which introduces the idea of anything which is a King of France and requires of it that it is identical to x. Therefore we need only add further that the thing that is the King of France is also bald. Accordingly, we only need the following three clauses

(9) (i) $\exists x\ Fx\ \&,$

(ii) $\forall y\ (Fy \rightarrow y = x)\ \&,$

(iii) $Gx,$

or,

(10) $\exists x\ (Fx\ \&\ [\forall y\ (Fy \rightarrow y = x)]\ \&\ Gx).$

This analysis looks complicated. The justification for it flows from asking the following question: What am I committed to in saying 'The King of France is bald'? The notion of commitment concerns what I must hold true if I hold the sentence in question true. The commitments here are what I called in chapter 1 the 'canonical commitments' of the judgement. The analysis uncovers the structure which the sentence must have for it to be truth-evaluable; if you like, the structure of the claims implicated by taking the sentence to be true. Put that way, it is clear that if you take (6) to be true, you must be committed to taking as true that there is something which is a King of France, that there is only one such thing, and, furthermore, that it is bald. That is what Russell's analysis says in (9); (10) is merely the succinct representation of all this. It presents the logical grammar of the original sentence (6).[22]

The representation of the logical grammar of (6) provided by (10) has a number of important features. Most importantly, it represents clearly and unambiguously what is meant by (6). We say that (10) states the truth-conditions for (6); it gives an account of the conditions under which (6) is true. However, the advantage of (10) is that it gives the truth-conditions of (6) in a particularly perspicuous manner. (10) represents the conjunction of claims that Russell's analysis shows is involved in (6). But in revealing that (6) involves a conjunction of claims, (10) provides a way of representing the meaning of (6) in which the structure of the meaning is fully represented syntactically. In terms of the superficial linguistic grammar, (6) does not appear to be a conjunction; that fact is, if you like, hidden from view. It is made transparent by having it unambiguously marked in the syntactic structure employed in (10).

The transparent mapping of the structure of the meaning of a sentence – its logical grammar – helps explain away the puzzles that led Russell to develop his theory. The logical grammar of (6) reveals that it is really a complex conjunction of claims. Like any conjunction, it is false if one of the conjuncts is false. This is a key advantage of Russell's theory.

Suppose, contrary to Russell's analysis, that 'the King of France' was a genuine referring expression. In this case, the logical grammar of (6) would be '*a* is *G*'. Now, as Russell notes, by the law of excluded middle, either '*a* is *G*' is true or '*a* is not *G*' is true. Yet if one 'enumerates all the things that are bald, and then the things that are not bald, one would not find the King of France in either list'.[23] That is the worry that LEM is threatened unless we either grant the King of France subsistence or find an analysis that shows that the description is not a singular term. The analysis at (7) shows why the sentence at (6) is false. It is false because the first conjunct

   (i)   There is a King of France

is false. Russell's analysis shows that (6) entails, amongst other things, the existential claim above. That claim is false, therefore, so too is (6). LEM is preserved, and we can also acknowledge the common-sense ontology that does not have the King of France lurking in subsistence alongside round squares, golden mountains, Sherlock Holmes, etc.

This shows that if anyone judges that the King of France is bald, they have made a false judgement. If it is false that the King of France is bald, then it is true that

   (11) $\neg \exists x$ (Fx & $\forall y$ [Fy $\to$ y = x] & Gx).

However, the syntactic marking of logical grammar provided by Russell's analysis also makes plain the availability of a different judgement of the form,

   (12) $\exists x$ (Fx & $\forall y$ [Fy $\to$ y = x] & $\neg$Gx).

(12) is not the contradictory of (10), but only its contrary. As such, (12) cannot be true if (10) is true, but they can both be false together. This shows that, once properly analysed, LEM is not threatened; for the fact that the King of France fails to appear on the list of either bald things or hairy things just shows that both (10) and (12) fail to be true. But as they are only contraries and not contradictories, that is no problem. If there is a bald King of France, (10) is true. It is (12) that is true if there is a hairy King of France. If there is no King of France at all, both (10) and (12) are false. The difference between (11) and (12) is brought out elegantly in Russell's theory in terms of the different scope of the negation operator in each sentence. This difference in scope does not exist with regard to genuine singular judgements, and this fact explains why, unless Russell can show that 'the King of France' is not a referring expression, he is at risk of losing LEM.

With regard to genuine singular terms, the reason that there is no difference between

(13) $\neg a$ is F

and

(14) a is $\neg F$

turns on the point made in the previous section, that for genuine referring expressions, for which the object theory of reference applies, we get an extensional theory of judgement. (13) and (14) are both true in the same circumstances: namely, when the object a is not a member of the set of Fs.

The above points become visible through the explicit recording of the logical grammar of (6) in the notation of Russell's theory of descriptions (10). By marking the logical grammar of the sentence in terms of the syntactic structure of the preferred symbolism, a number of facts become clear. The structure uncovered in (6) reveals that it is a conjunction. It shows why (6) is false, and it uncovers the availability of different negated judgements formed from (10) depending on the position of the negation operator.

It is important to note that, for Russell, the investigation of logical grammar provides the means to produce an explicit representation of the structure of judgements. It provides this representation by marking logical grammar syntactically. The differences between e.g. (11) and (12) are differences that Russell's theory allows to be marked syntactically. This offers the prospect of an ideal language in which the discriminations of logical grammar receive syntactic marking. In possession of such a language, so the hope goes, we would then be able to resist the philosophical errors into which we are led by the superficial structures of ordinary linguistic grammar. Such is the diagnosis Russell came to accept of his own earlier mistaken advocacy of the theory of subsistence for entities like the King of France. The new symbolism lays out transparently the structure of judgement.

Historically, the idea of logical grammar has continued to be connected with the ideal of a new improved symbolism in which logical grammar would be marked by syntactic structures. Frege seems to have been party to this idea, hence his original impulse to construct a language fit for recording the judgements of arithmetic. As we will see in later chapters, it is a moot point whether we should accept that logical grammar can be marked exhaustively by syntactic structures. But note that, given the epistemological restriction on acquaintance, most of the judgements we make are, according to Russell, descriptive. Most of our judgements will then be susceptible to a syntactic individuation, for the difference between any two descriptive judgements is marked by the different arrangement of symbols. This is a context-free individuation of judgements. If this is right, then, for most of our judgements, Russell is a representationalist; for a context-free individuation is one that can be done independently of how things actually are in the world. This is a plausible view of Russell's position, although by the end of this chapter we will see that it is incomplete.

2.5 Theory of Descriptions – Summary

The theory of descriptions offers analyses of sentences containing denoting phrases of the form 'The *F*', the simplest case being a sentence of the form 'The *F* is *G*'. The analysis provides an account of the truth-conditions of the sentence. The salient features of the analysis are these:

> **DD1:** A sentence of the form 'The *F* is *G*' contains no genuine singular term.

Now, by the semantic value dependence thesis, we know that, of any given type of expression, it is a condition on the meaningfulness of sentences containing that expression that the expression's semantic value exists. In the case of singular terms, this means that for sentences containing genuine singular terms to be meaningful, the relevant object must exist. I shall say that judgements expressed with such sentences are object-dependent; this is the special case of semantic value dependence applied to singular terms.

Given the analysis that shows that DD1 is true, it follows that

> **DD2:** A sentence of the form 'The *F* is *G*' expresses a well-formed judgement regardless of whether or not anything satisfies the description 'The *F*'.

The point that the judgement is well formed is the point that Russell's analysis shows, that the judgement satisfies the law of excluded middle; either the judgement is true, or its negation is true. The intuitive idea here is that something definite has been said with such a judgement, so that there are only two possibilities with regard to assessing it; either it is true or it is false.[24]

It is because Russell endorses DD2 that he holds:

> **DD3:** Judgements of the form 'The *F* is *G*' are object-independent judgements.

Note, DD3 might be thought identical in content to DD2, but it is not, for DD3 is a thesis about judgements. DD2 is a thesis about sentences. Thus DD3 is a weaker thesis, for someone may endorse DD3 but deny that DD2 reports a semantic fact about sentences. However, it does follow immediately from DD2 that

> **DD4:** Sentences of the form 'The *F* is *G*' express judgements with a purely general content, for their content can be fully specified with general terms – predicates and relations – and quantifiers.

In the wider context of providing a general theory of reference, DD4 is an extraordinarily important thesis.[25] Because of the epistemology that underpins his principle of acquaintance, Russell believes that all of the referential apparatus of natural language, with the exception of 'this' and 'that', is subject to a descriptive analysis. If Russell is right, all the judgements we make about the world are general judgements. The only occasions on which we are able to entertain singular judgements are when we make judgements about our sense-data!

The above point concerns the application of the theory of descriptions, not the theory as such, which can be considered in isolation from Russell's Cartesian epistemology. Nevertheless, as we shall see in later chapters, the idea that our thinking about the world is fundamentally general and descriptive is an idea that captures a lot of deep-seated intuitions.[26] As a thesis about descriptive judgements regardless of the range of such judgements, DD4 looks to be simply correct. Nevertheless, DD4 has been challenged.

There are two basic kinds of criticism of Russell's theory. The first criticism, due to Strawson, takes issue with the whole basis of the theory, and objects to DD1, DD2 and DD4. The second kind of objection, most famously proposed by Donnellan, restricts the range of sentences of which DD1, DD2 and DD4 hold. Donnellan argues that, in certain contexts, Russell's analysis is inapplicable.[27] I review these two kinds of criticism of Russell's theory in the next two sections.

2.6   Strawson's Objection to the Theory of Descriptions

Strawson objects to DD1, DD2 and DD4. The fundamental source of his objection concerns not the adequacy of Russell's analysis, but the need for it. At the heart of Strawson's criticism of Russell is the idea that sentences are not the sort of things that are true or false, for truth and falsity apply to statements. A statement is what is said by an utterance of a sentence on a particular date at a particular place. The sentence (6) can be used on different occasions to make different statements. Someone who uttered the sentence during the reign of Louis XIV will have said something different (made a different statement) to that said by someone who uttered the sentence during the reign of Louis XV. Furthermore, one of these speakers may have uttered a true statement and one a false statement. To ask, as Russell asks, whether the sentence is true or false is to make a mistake about the proper objects of semantic evaluation. Statements get evaluated, not sentences.

Strawson accepts that sentence (6) has a meaning; as a sentence-type it has a type-meaning. But it does not follow from this that any given utterance of that sentence expresses a true or false statement. In particular, Strawson claims that if someone were to utter (6) now, they would 'fail to say anything true or false'.[28] Furthermore, this failure is explained by Strawson by saying that an utterance of (6) does not entail the existence of the King of France; rather, it presupposes the existence of the King of France. Now, A presupposes B just in case it is a condition of A being either true or false that B is true. If B is false, then A will fail to be either true or false. That is why an utterance of (6) now would result in a failure to say anything true or false.

The above brief statement of Strawson's criticism has a number of ambiguities in it, but they run deep in Strawson's position. Let me distinguish the following claims that Strawson appears to be making:

S1: Russell fails to distinguish between the meaning of an expression and what is expressed by a particular utterance of the expression.

S2: In the absence of a King of France, an utterance of (6) fails to say anything true or false.

S3: The existence of the King of France is presupposed by an utterance of (6); it is not entailed by it.

It is S2 and S3 that are ambiguous. Let me deal first with S1.

S1 is a general claim. With regard to descriptions, it is S1 which supports Strawson's view that, in contrast to Russell, descriptions are devices used for referring. However, his point is that it is uses of descriptions that refer, not descriptions themselves. There is a clear distinction between the meaning of a sentence construed as a particular type of arrangement of symbols and what is expressed by a given use of a sentence of that type. The existence of this distinction is obvious in the case of indexical expressions like 'I', 'here', 'this', 'to the right of'. These expressions are meaningful, and with them we can construct sentences that have a clear linguistic meaning. The linguistic meaning of e.g.

(15)   This book is to the right of me

is the meaning that is carried by the sentence construed as an arrangement of symbols. It is therefore the meaning that is common to all utterances which use tokens of that sentence-type. With regard to the meaning of the sentence, two people make use of the same linguistic meaning if they both utter (15), even if they are sitting opposite one another and are looking at different books. In such a situation, we have a common sentence meaning to our utterances, but we clearly make different statements. Or, to put the point in the terminology that I favour, we make different judgements by our utterances of (15).

The need to distinguish between the linguistic meaning of sentences and the judgements that can be expressed by particular utterances of sentences is acknowledged by Russell. One of Russell's examples in 'On denoting' involves the indexical 'my', and this is prima-facie evidence that Russell did not regard the denotation of a phrase as something that was separable from the way the phrase is used, or standardly used. Anyway, Russell's general concern is with the judgements that are expressed by sentences. He repeatedly speaks of a theory of judgements, not a theory of sentences. Accordingly, it is harmless to transpose the analysis of the sentence (6) by the sentence (10) into an analysis of the judgement expressed by (6) into the judgement expressed by (10). We need only take Russell's talk of sentences as shorthand for the judgements expressed by uses of sentences. The theory of descriptions remains intact.

There is an important issue underlying this move. Are semantic properties the properties of symbols/sentences or of uses of symbols? If the former, then this amounts to representationalism. If the latter, the idea of 'uses of symbols' is a non-context-free constraint on symbols, so this cannot support representationalism. The idea of 'uses of symbols' is more than merely shorthand for those causal properties of symbols that explain their use. If the idea were shorthand for further causal properties of symbols, then, on the assumption that causal properties are 'local', these properties would be properties of the symbols themselves that explain their use. Semantic properties would then be properties of symbols, for the idea of use would have been reduced to context-free properties, and that would be compatible with representationalism.[29] Alternatively, if the phrase 'uses of symbols' significantly qualifies the idea that semantic properties are not properties of symbols *qua* symbols, then it introduces an element into the basic issue of what the proper objects of semantic evaluation are that is incompatible with representationalism. This issue is a particular instance of a general point made in chapter 1. If 'uses of symbols' significantly qualifies the idea that semantic properties are properties of symbols, then in studying semantics, we cannot be engaging in a purely linguistic/symbolic study. The study of use is not formal. It must thus have some non-formal element in it. This, as it turns out, is precisely Russell's position. The non-formal elements come from his epistemology and metaphysics. This is often ignored, in part, no doubt, because Russell's epistemology is so embarrassingly old-fashioned and Cartesian. That may be, but it is central to the way his semantic system works. Furthermore, the Cartesian element can be factored out without changing the basic structure.

S2 and S3 are ambiguous. The ambiguities are connected. S2 is ambiguous between

> S2.1: In the absence of a King of France, an utterance of (6) fails to express a judgement

and

S2.2: In the absence of a King of France, an utterance of (6) expresses a judgement which is neither true nor false.

The ambiguity in S3 concerns whether presupposition is a logical or a pragmatic relation. If logical, it is presumably a relation between judgements; if pragmatic, it is less clear what the relation relates. However, if pragmatic, presupposition is plausibly thought of as a relation between a speech act and a judgement such that a speech act presupposes the truth of a judgement. S3 is then ambiguous between

S3.1: The judgement that the King of France exists is presupposed by the judgement expressed by an utterance of (6)

and

S3.2: The judgement that the King of France exists is presupposed by the act of uttering (6).

I start with the difference between S2.1 and S2.2. Suppose that someone utters (6) now. Have they failed to make a judgement (S2.1), or have they succeeded in expressing a judgement, but one that lacks both truth and falsity (S2.2)? Strawson's own formulation, 'fails to say anything true or false', might seem to favour the second interpretation, and it also fits most people's intuitions if they are sympathetic to Strawson's position. Surely, our speaker has said something, but perhaps what they have said fails to have a truth-value? However, in later writings, Strawson made clear that he thought that such a speaker would have failed to make a judgement, that no proposition is expressed when such a speaker utters (6).[30] There is good reason for Strawson favouring S2.1 over S2.2.

Strawson's general point against Russell was that descriptions are devices for referring, just as sentences are devices for expressing judgements. In the case of a speaker now uttering sentence (6), they fail to employ the description in referring, for there is no King of France. It thus makes sense to suppose that the speaker also fails to make a judgement. If a sub-sentential component fails to achieve what it is designed for, it seems reasonable to suppose that the whole sentence will suffer a similar failure.[31]

This reading of S2, however, seems wrong. On this account, Strawson is saying that utterances of sentences containing the description 'The King of France' will fail to express judgements because the presupposition that there is a King of France is false. (Remember, because this is a presupposition, not an entailment, the falsity of it does not make the utterance false.) However, if I say,

(16)   The King of France had supper with President Clinton last night,

48

I have clearly said something false. Note, I have said something, and it is false.[32] At the least, Strawson would have to admit that sometimes a speech act can be accomplished with an empty description.[33]

There is then pressure to interpret Strawson's position as favouring S2.2, despite his own later accounts of it. This has the virtue of making better sense of the concept of presupposition. A key difference between Strawson and Russell is that Strawson holds that if I utter (6), my statement presupposes the existence of the King of France, but it does not entail his existence. As noted, presupposition is meant to be a relation such that A presupposes B just in case B's being true is a condition for A being either true or false. Now, if presupposition is a semantic relation, it presumably relates judgements. But in that case, if in uttering (6) the existence of the King of France is presupposed, by what is it presupposed? If the relation is a semantic one, there must be a judgement expressed by my utterance of (6), albeit one which, because of the falsity of the presupposition, turns out to be neither true nor false. What this means is that if S3 is interpreted as S3.1, then we have to interpret S2 as S2.2.

Although S2.2 fits better with the intuition that something has indeed been said in such cases, it requires us to accept the possibility that judgements can be neither true nor false. At the very least, for this position to be sustainable, we need some outline of the consequences for our theory of logic in accepting this possibility. One of Russell's worries in developing his theory of descriptions was to avoid a challenge to the law of excluded middle. What Strawson now looks to be offering is something more radical: the acceptance of a third semantic value – 'neither true nor false', and this without any worked-out account of the logic of presupposition.[34]

Perhaps, then, we should stick with the earlier reading of S2, S2.1, and deny that a judgement is made by my uttering (6). However, that means that we will have to give up S3.1 and opt for S3.2, thus taking the presupposition relation as a pragmatic relation linking my speech act to the judgement that the King of France exists.[35] On this account of presupposition, however, it is no longer clear that we can make sense of the general schema: A presupposes B just in case B's being true is a condition for A's being either true or false. For if it is my speech act that presupposes the existence of the King of France, rather than the judgement that I attempted but, on the present account, failed to make, then how can it make sense to say that it has to be true that there is a King of France in order for my speech act to be either true or false? Speech acts are not true or false; rather, they are successful or not in producing items, judgements, which are either true or false.

Furthermore, if presupposition is a relation of pragmatics, relating speech acts to existential judgements, then it is no longer clear that this is a criticism of Russell. Russell was not concerned with the pragmatics of what you might commit yourself to in uttering (6). His concern was with the semantics of (6), or, better, with the semantics of what is said or judged on uttering (6). Russell's concern was with logical grammar, not with what we might call pragmatic grammar.

So, if we interpret S2 as S2.2, in which a judgement is expressed which is neither true nor false, then we will need to treat S3 as S3.1. But then the Strawsonian position will be incomplete until it offers a systematic semantics that shows how something can be neither true nor false and how this affects logic. If we retreat from that option and take presupposition as a non-logical relation, S3.2, then we will have to interpret S2 as S2.1 and hold that utterances of sentences containing descriptions fail to express a judgement at all. But that is (a) extraordinarily counter-intuitive, and (b) begins to miss the point of Russell's whole enterprise, which was an examination of the semantics of what is said with (6). It is logical grammar that Russell shows us how to investigate, not pragmatic grammar. The connections between the ambiguities in S2 and S3 leave no stable interpretation for Strawson's account of descriptions to be tenable, or for it to offer a satisfactory critique of Russell's theory.

2.7   Donnellan and Referential Uses of Descriptions

A more fruitful-looking critique of Russell's theory was instigated by Donnellan.[36] Donnellan questions whether Russell's theory applies to all sentences that employ descriptions to make judgements. Donnellan distinguishes between referential and attributive uses of definite descriptions. In the attributive role, descriptions function exactly as Russell claimed, and DD1–DD4 hold. However, Donnellan believes that there are referential uses of descriptions in which DD1–DD4 fail. To say that Russell's account fails in these cases is, in effect, to say that there are cases in which the semantic value of a description is *assigned* rather than computed as Russell's theory shows. If Donnellan is right, the description is, in such cases, a semantic primitive.

One of his original examples illustrates Donnellan's idea. Consider the sentence

(17)   Smith's murderer is insane

and the following contrasting contexts of utterance:

Context (a): (17) is uttered by a detective on discovering the severely mutilated body of Smith

and

Context (b): (17) is uttered by a journalist in court observing the erratic behaviour of the defendant charged with Smith's murder.

In context (a) Donnellan believes that Russell's analysis is correct. The detective is making a purely general judgement which we could paraphrase as, 'Smith's murderer, whoever he or she may be, is insane'. In context (a) the judgement expressed contains no referring expression or genuine singular term (DD1); the judgement is well formed, even if it turns out that no one murdered Smith (DD2); the judgement is object-independent (DD3); and the content of the judgement is purely general (DD4). Of course, if Smith was not murdered, the detective has made a false judgement, but he has still made a judgement. Russell's analysis is correct.

Now consider context (b). In this context Donnellan says the description is operating referentially. The intuitive way of capturing this idea is to say that in context (b) we could paraphrase the judgement being made as 'That man there is insane'. In such a context the description is used to pick out an individual so that a property may be predicated of it, regardless of whether or not the description actually fits the individual. If we share Donnellan's intuitions about these sorts of cases, then we have contexts in which a description is used referentially (DD1 fails); the success of the use depends on there actually being the individual who is being picked out (DD2 fails); the judgement expressed is then object-dependent (DD3 fails); and in such contexts the judgement expressed is not purely general (DD4 fails).

It is no accident that in looking for a paraphrase of the judgement made in context (b) type cases we instinctively reach for a demonstrative. Demonstratives were Russell's only legitimate singular terms. Demonstratives are purely referential terms which do no more than point to an object without describing it. Donnellan's claim is that, in certain contexts, descriptions can perform in this way too. Note also that, if Donnellan is right, he must accept a different epistemology from Russell's restrictive Cartesian epistemology. Russell believed that you could only know physical objects and other persons by description, not by acquaintance. Donnellan is suggesting that we can make referential contact with an individual regardless of whether we have the correct description. The description employed can, as it were, reach out and refer to an individual, even if that individual does not satisfy the description. I shall not address the epistemological aspect of this debate here, for it is something that we will have to investigate in greater depth in the chapters on reference. The fact that the epistemology is integral to Donnellan's account shows that Donnellan is not making a purely linguistic claim that the semantic value of descriptions is not always computed but is sometimes assigned. He sees this as showing something about the directness of our thinking in such cases. For the time being, the extension of the idea of acquaintance beyond the restrictive range of Russell's Cartesian handling of the concept is a bonus.

Does the existence of context (b) type cases show that Russell's analysis is incomplete? Donnellan's central claim is that there are different uses of descriptions. For his critique to succeed, it needs to be shown that the different uses (referential and attributive) turn on a semantic ambiguity in descriptions. If Donnellan is offering a counter-example to Russell's analysis, it had better not transpire that referential uses of descriptions can be accommodated by an account of the pragmatics of the use of descriptions, rather than as an adjustment to the semantics of descriptions.

It is tempting to think that because the difference between the referential and attributive uses is a contextual difference, the distinction must be pragmatic and not semantic. This is tempting because we are prone to think that the semantic properties of an expression are context-insensitive properties. What an expression means is a feature of it regardless of the contexts in which it is used. Indeed, if this were not the case, the expression would have no uniform meaning in the language. This temptation is misleading, although it does push us in a direction that appears to blunt Donnellan critique of Russell.

Grice noted a similar distinction to Donnellan.[37] Grice, however, took the referential use of descriptions to be a non-semantic phenomenon, and believed that 'descriptive phrases have no relevant systematic duplicity of meaning; their meaning is given by a Russellian account'.[38] The existence of the referential usage is explained by drawing a distinction between what the speaker says in context (b) type cases and what the speaker means. What is said is the judgement articulated by the expressions employed and is captured by the Russellian analysis. In contrast, what is meant is a pragmatic notion to do with the judgement the speaker had in mind and was trying to get across by employing a particular form of words. The notion of what is meant is captured in terms of the speaker's intentions, as opposed to the semantic meaning of the expressions employed.

If a distinction between speaker's intentions and the expression's semantic meaning can be sustained, Donnellan's objection to Russell lapses. With such a distinction we could hold that Russell has given the correct analysis of the semantics of descriptions. This means that the Russellian analysis captures the truth-conditions for all sentences employing descriptions where the truth-conditions specify the judgement expressed by the sentence in question. The existence of referential uses, as in context (b) type cases, will then be accommodated by an account of the pragmatics of sentence employment. There will be no semantic ambiguity in sentences employing descriptions. Such a defence of Russell is elegantly constructed by Kripke, who distinguishes between semantic reference and speaker's reference.[39]

The speaker's reference of an expression is a property of a dated, particular use of the expression. In contrast, the semantic reference is not tied to a particular use. Note, this does not mean that semantic reference is a property of an expression independently of its use by speakers. It means only that semantic reference is not a property of an expression that depends on particular uses. We need to be careful to avoid defending Russell by making semantics concerned with properties of words that they possess independently of their use by speakers. This would then prompt an inaccurate reading of Russell.

As noted in the previous section, Strawson's objection that Russell failed to distinguish between sentences and statements misses the point. Russell's concern is with semantics, where semantics is construed as a study of the linguistic meaning of expressions, where this is a property of the expression that is common to its uses on different occasions. Now, no doubt, the linguistic meaning of an expression is not a property of the word as such, considered independently of the way it is standardly used. But this means that the best way to express Kripke's distinction is by defining semantic reference as a property of an expression as standardly used to make a judgement.[40] In general, the point is that semantic properties attach to standard uses of expressions, not to expressions *per se*. Generally:

> **Standard use thesis:** The semantic properties of an expression are properties of the expression *as standardly used.*

If this is right, we can treat speaker's reference as a property of an expression as used on particular occasions where the speaker's intentions override standard use. As the point of speaker's reference is that the speaker's intentions override standard use, this is not a semantic property of the expression, but a pragmatic property.

Semantic properties may be investigated by studying the standard patterns of use of an expression – what I am calling its logical grammar. The logical grammar is something that is true of an expression independently of the particular uses by particular people at particular times. Logical grammar indicates the judgement standardly made by employing a given expression. In contrast, whether or not a speaker's intentions are overriding logical grammar is something that can only be detected pragmatically within the particular context of particular use. For example, I say, 'The man drinking martini is the Dean', and it transpires that the man I indicated is drinking lemonade. We can only count this as speaker's reference if I then count his failure to be drinking martini as irrelevant to the purposes of my communication. And that is something that can only be discovered in relation to the pragmatics of the context.

Accordingly, as long as we are careful to be clear about what we mean by semantics and the semantic properties of expressions, I conclude that neither Strawson nor Donnellan give sufficient grounds for thinking that Russell's theory fails to give the correct semantics of sentences containing descriptions. This conclusion has important consequences for how we conceive the business of semantics.

2.8   Conclusion – the Businesses of Semantics

It is tempting to think of semantics as the study of properties that expressions have *qua* expressions, as if the semantic properties of an expression were properties it had regardless of how, or indeed whether, it is used. But the semantic properties of an expression are the properties that connect an expression with items in the world. Therefore, if we think of semantics in the way suggested, we would be thinking of the connections between words and things as something that could be studied independently of the way words are used by speakers. And it is tempting to respond to this by saying that, at the end of the day, words do not have semantic properties independently of the way they are used by speakers. Signs and symbols only succeed in standing for things because they are read and used in that manner by speakers.[41] As noted at the end of the previous section, such a remark does not constitute an objection to Russell if we restrict semantics to the study of the standard uses of expressions. Nevertheless, the issue of the proper province of semantics is an important one, and from the examination of Russell's theory of descriptions, we have sufficient material at hand to make some preliminary remarks on the matter.

Let me call the idea that semantics is concerned with the properties of expressions *qua* expressions independently of their use sign-semantics, for it is the view that the semantic properties of words are properties of words *qua* signs regardless of how they are used by speakers. In contrast to sign-semantics, there is the study of the logical grammar of signs, where this is understood as the standard pattern of use of a sign by speakers.[42] Of course, no one would endorse sign-semantics with respect to ordinary language signs, but with respect to the signs that constitute the entities over which Fodor's version of representationalism defines our possession of content (items in LOT), the idea of sign-semantics picks out a common orthodoxy. For such a representationalist, the idea of the 'use of signs' can only at best be shorthand for causal properties of the signs *qua* signs that explain the way that they get employed by us. Such causal properties will, once again, be specifiable in a context-free way.

It is tempting to think that sign-semantics must be fundamental, and it is this that will give an account of how words connect with things. The reason for this is that the study of logical grammar is focused on the systematic connections between the use of one sign and another; and such a study, it will be objected, is not concerned with the connection between sign and object. Note how this objection depends on the representationalist assumption that sign and object are specifiable independently. If that is the case, then you cannot learn anything about the sign–object relation by studying the patterns connecting one sign with another. On this picture, we might think of semantics as having two levels of theorizing. On one level, there will be the business of sign-semantics that accounts for the way that signs connect with things. On the second level, the study of logical grammar will plot the systematic connections that exist between the use of one sign and another. This way of construing the relation between the two levels gives a distinctive justification for the business of analysis. Analysis takes us to, as it were, the edge of language. It identifies the point at which language reaches out and touches the world. If an expression is analysable, it is not one of the expressions on the semantic edge of language. Notice that this is a powerfully representationalist model. Language and world stand apart. We need to identify the semantic edge in order to work out the relation that holds them together. This model also allows that purely formal/linguistic results have a bearing on our semantic theory; for such results will help identify the primitives on the edge of language by showing how their semantic value cannot be computable from more primitive expressions. At that point, rather than treat their possession of semantic value as assigned, the representationalist looks for a substantive account of their possession of semantic value. This model is almost Russell's. Russell does analysis in order to reach the semantic edge of language, but then two things cloud his version of this model. First, his account of the semantic edge is thoroughly epistemological. Second, given the nature of the epistemology he applies to the primitive expressions, it turns out that they are object-dependent, so he is not, with respect to the semantic edge of language, a representationalist. Indeed, the primitive expressions are not really the semantic edge of language in the sense that we then have to reach out to contact the world. The edge, for Russell, is where language and world are inseparable.

Disregarding Russell's particular version of the two-level model, if we add to the model one further element, we get a model that has come to dominate much contemporary philosophy of thought and language. Suppose that the sign-semantics lays down the semantic properties of a class of primitive expressions, expressions for which the only account of their semantic properties is one that relates them *qua* expressions with things. Suppose then that all other signs available within the language can be treated as logical products of the primitive signs. That is to say, non-primitive signs can be defined recursively in terms of truth-functional combinations of the primitives. On this supposition, the study of logical grammar would amount to an analysis of all complex signs into their logical simples. The primitive signs would be assigned their semantic value by the sign-semantics. The semantic value of non-primitive signs is computed via the theory of logical grammar.

The idea that semantics comprises two levels of theory, sign-semantics and the study of logical grammar provides a common model for the businesses of semantics. It is a model that provides a way of locating the different interests and concerns of the two tasks, constitutive and engineering, distinguished in chapter 1. On this two-level model, the theory of sign-semantics is primitive. This is to take reference as prior to truth. On this model we would have to think of the Fregean concern with logical grammar as occupied with the second-level business of semantics, and a physicalistic theory with the first-level business of sign-semantics. On this two-levels model, Frege's concern with the study of grammar becomes equivalent to the formal semanticist's concern to identify the means by which the semantic value of complex signs is computed. This two-levels model is a useful way of thinking of physicalistic theories of meaning: for example, theories that explain the semantic value of an expression in terms of the causal connections between words and things.[43]

The two-level model does not capture the Fregean methodology, for it ignores the Fregean claim that truth is prior to reference. From a Fregean perspective, the study of logical grammar exhausts the business of semantics, so there is no real business to be conducted at the level of sign-semantics. That is the whole point of the context principle. From the representationalist's point of view, the study of logical grammar is just the banal plotting of relations between signs – in particular, the relations between primitive and complex signs. The idea that the study of grammar is banal looks compelling. It is less so, however, when we recall that from a non-representationalist perspective content is not specifiable independently of that which is represented. If such externalism flows from the Fregean methodology, then the study of logical grammar is not merely the study of a system that is detachable from the world. Instead, the study of logical grammar is a study of a sign use that is *engaged* with the world.[44] The idea of 'standard use' is a significant qualification to the idea that semantic properties are properties of signs, because what goes into standard use/logical grammar is a structure that is world-involving. The world is in our language use. It is not detached from it. If this is right, then the Fregean study of grammar has to be conceived as involving more than the merely formal semanticist's interest in the relation between primitive and complex expressions.

It is important to have the two-level model in focus, for it captures a way of thinking about semantics that is common and that leaves scope for the study of logical grammar in addition to the business of the study of word/object relations. On the two-level model, the second-level study of logical grammar provides the descriptive enterprise of mapping the structure of our judgements, while the first-level theory of sign-semantics pins that structure to the world with a theory of the connection between words and things. On such a two-level model, the study of logical grammar could still be an a priori study, and the sign-semantics an a posteriori scientific theory.

This model accommodates some features of the Fregean methodology, but mistakenly identifies semantics with formal semantics. It captures well a physicalistic methodology. In its implicit assignment of precedence to the theory of sign-semantics, such a model is hostile to the Fregean methodology properly understood, in which the study of logical grammar exhausts the business of semantics and also of metaphysics. In broad outline, some such two-level model of the businesses of semantics is evident in Russell, Carnap, Quine and many recent theories of thought: the standard model as characterized in chapter 1 and represented in the work of Fodor and Dretske. With the exception of Russell, this two-level conception of semantics comes at the price of endorsing representationalism. The task of a causal theory of sign-semantics is to connect the separate realms of world and language or, in some versions, world and thought. The Fregean hostility to the notion of sign-semantics comes from rejecting the metaphysics that prompts representationalism. It is a moot point whether the two-level model applies to Wittgenstein; it seems clearly not to apply to Wittgenstein's later work or to Davidson, and it does not apply to Frege.[45]

Russell did not have a theory of sign-semantics as I have defined it, and, indeed, he turns out not to be a representationalist. Nevertheless, he had a two-level model of semantics. For Russell, the semantic value of primitive signs was not a property of the sign *qua* expression; rather, it was a property of the sign granted to it by the power of the mind to attach signs to objects. This is his semantic Cartesianism. The signs that have their semantic values assigned in this way are the demonstratives 'this' and 'that' and predicate expressions. All other signs are then analysed as logical complexes of these via the theory of descriptions; the logical grammar of descriptions reveals that they are logical products of predicates and quantifiers. Russell endorses the standard use thesis:

> **Standard use thesis:** The semantic properties of an expression are properties of the expression *as standardly used*,

but for Russell, the 'standard use' is constrained by his semantic Cartesianism. It is this that makes Russell's position anti-representationalist in two respects. First, the endorsement of the standard use thesis, as noted in the previous section, is incompatible with representationalism if the idea of standard use is more than shorthand for further properties of signs *qua* signs. In Russell's theory, this is clearly the case. Second, for Russell, the only kind of misrepresentation that is possible is molecular misrepresentation – the falsity of a judgement. Even if a judgement component like a description fails, the failure is complex, and is really the failure of a sentence that is but a component of a larger sentential unit. An empty description like

> The present King of France

is the false sentence,

> There is something that is a present King of France and anything else that is a present King of France is identical with it,

57

the complexity of which is due to its quantificational structure. For Russell, there is no such thing as atomic misrepresentation. Hence, at the atomic level, Russell is not a representationalist.

In light of the development of this two-level model of the businesses of semantics, we can see that Russell's overall semantic theory is quite complicated, for it operates on both levels. There is a clear sense in which Russell subscribes to the thesis that the study of meaning is an objective a priori study. This is true of Russell's approach to the theory of the logical grammar of complex judgements. Nevertheless, with regard to the level of sign-semantics, Russell is a semantic Cartesian. In his account of the meaning of atomic judgements, semantic value is assigned by the power of the mind to attach a sign to an object. He partially endorses the thesis that meaning is structured, but the study of meaning is not exhausted by the study of logical grammar. He holds too that there is a theory of the semantics of primitive signs, his account of which is Cartesian. He nevertheless still endorses the standard use thesis, for even with atomic signs, their meaning is defined in terms of standard use. It is just that Russell's notion of standard use for atomic signs involves his Cartesian conception of the mind using the sign to attach to a momentary object of acquaintance. What is distinctive of Russell's account of atomic signs is his atomism – the idea that these signs can, because of the power of the mind, be given content piecemeal, one by one. That is why, for Russell, logical grammar does not exhaust his account of meaning, because fundamentally he has a piecemeal conception of content that grants signs content independent of their inferential role. But note also that the atomism that most people now reject is separable from the semantic value dependence thesis and the idea that language can reach right out to objects, so that language and world are inseparable. Russell also holds that logical grammar is the structure that meaning has in order to be truth-evaluable with regard to complex judgements, although, once again, with regard to atomic judgements they are truth-evaluable simply because the mind has the power to make them so.

Russell does not endorse the idea that truth is the basic semantic concept, for he has a two-levels model of semantics, in which the account of the assignment of semantic values to primitive expressions is explanatorily basic. Similarly, as already noted (section 2.3), for Russell the concept of an object is an epistemological concept, not a semantic concept. For the same reason, Russell does not endorse the Fregean idea that the study of logical grammar is prior to metaphysics. Indeed, for Russell, it is his metaphysics and epistemology that shape the first level of his semantics (the point at which he is a semantic Cartesian). His study of logical grammar at the second level of his semantics merely shows how to analyse all judgements into the apparatus of primitive signs.

If we strip out Russell's epistemology and metaphysics and replace the first level of his semantics with a causal theory of sign-semantics based upon a physicalistic metaphysics, we then have the general shape of the dominant approach in English-speaking philosophy of thought and language. This is the standard model: Primitive signs are connected to the world causally, and complex signs are analysed via the study of logical grammar into logical products of primitive signs. On this approach, the descriptive enterprise of studying logical grammar is an addendum to a physicalistic methodology. Frege fits in, if at all, as an appendage to a model of the businesses of semantics that, in broad outline, Russell had right. As indicated, I believe that this seriously misrepresents what the Fregean methodology has to offer. It misrepresents what Davidson's work has to offer the philosophy of thought and language. It also misrepresents Russell's main insight, that language does not stand apart from the world. Rather, in the case of context-sensitive expressions like demonstratives, language is inseparable from the world. The world is present to us in our thought and talk. All we have to do is erase the epistemology and atomism that make Russell's picture unattractive. In a model that replaced the atomistic account of reference with one in which reference was inseparable from logical grammar/standard use, there would be scope to enlarge our epistemology and acknowledge that ordinary objects, rather than mere sense-data, could be present to us in thought and talk. That is what happens in contemporary Fregean work on reference. We will not get to such matters until chapter 8 onwards. But the issue about the proper businesses of semantics is fraught with some of the deepest metaphysical conundrums regarding our conception of mind and thought and their place in the world.

Russell gives us our first clear grasp of the concept of logical grammar. He also articulates a semantic theory that is anti-representationalist and that, in the priority given to acquaintance, shows why falsity is the only possible kind of misrepresentation. This latter point is often missed. It is, however, of enormous significance, for it marks a dividing line between representationalist and anti-representationalist theories of content. Before we can proceed any further and decide whether to adopt a two-level approach to the businesses of semantics, and whether to endorse representationalism, we need to know much more about truth. That is the job of the next chapter.

3

The Semantic Theory of Truth

3.1 Introduction

Truth is the central semantic concept. There is, however, as much disagreement about the nature of truth as there is about any other semantic concept. Even with respect to Tarski's celebrated theory of truth, although most people agree that it succeeds in defining truth for a first-order language, there is disagreement about what this accomplishes. In this chapter I distinguish two broad conceptions of a theory of truth: the metaphysical and the modest, or semantic, theory. I shall briefly review why I think it is no part of the philosophy of thought and content to even so much as attempt a metaphysical theory of truth. I shall then outline the semantic conception of truth and show how it serves one central purpose, that of defining the concept of logical grammar. The issue of whether we need a metaphysical theory of truth or a semantic theory turns out to depend on whether we demand that our semantics be restricted to a theory of logical grammar, or whether we expect a two-level theory of semantics as sketched in the last chapter.

I count amongst semantic theorists of truth all those writers who not only eschew a metaphysical theory of truth, but also deny that truth is a genuine property at all. There are a number of positions available in the literature, ranging from redundancy and deflationary theories to minimalist theories of truth. I do not discuss these variants of a non-metaphysical theory of truth in detail, but I do note what seems to me to be the central insight on which they all depend.[1]

3.2 Two Conceptions of a Theory of Truth

I want to distinguish between metaphysical and semantic theories of truth. Suppose representationalism is true. If so, it is reasonable to expect that a theory of truth would contribute to an account of the connections between the separate realms of thought, language and world. The obvious way of characterizing this connection would be to say that the judgement I express with the linguistic structure

(1)   Snow is white

is true just in case it corresponds with the fact that snow is white. It is truth that relates judgement and world, and it does so via the relation of correspondence. For this to be more than a banal platitude about the relationships between our concepts of truth, fact and correspondence, much will have to be done to specify the nature of the correspondence relation and the relata that it brings together. Such is the job of correspondence theories of truth.[2]

If representationalism is true, some account must be forthcoming of the relationships that obtain between thought, language and world. It is when a correspondence theory is offered as such an account that it offers what I am calling a metaphysical theory of truth. Such a theory has to explicate the relationships between realms of entities – judgements and facts – which, by hypothesis, can be characterized independently of one another. Because these realms are distinct, some substantive account must be given of that which relates them. The classification I am using has the consequence that many of the writers who explicate truth employing the concept of correspondence are not correspondence theorists, for they do not subscribe to representationalism.[3] Nevertheless, in the final section we see that the classification draws together the aspirations of traditional correspondence theorists and contemporary physicalist critics of Tarski.

There are a number of problems with the correspondence theory of truth. The most obvious problems concern the nature of the correspondence relation and the nature of facts. The correspondence relation is classically thought to involve an isomorphism between truth-bearers and the facts, a congruence of facts and truth-bearers.[4] To even begin to get such an account working, there will need to be considerable metaphysical work to demarcate the domain of genuine facts. For example, even if you thought that

'Murder is wrong' is true,

it is unlikely that you would take this to consist in a congruence of the judgement expressed by the sentence and the wrongness of murder. For a utilitarian, the relevant facts would be facts about human happiness. There is no easy route to demarcating the realm of facts.

The correspondence theorist's metaphysics will determine what sorts of things count as facts. You might, however, question whether metaphysics should admit the concept of facts at all. You might think that the world is made not of facts, but of things, properties and events. This means that the correspondence theorist is offering a metaphysics that endorses a substantive claim that the world is made of facts, not of things. Furthermore, this claim is supposed to be about a world the characterization of which is independent of the characterization of language and judgement (representationalism).[5]

The oddity of the last claim points up the key flaw in correspondence theories; it is unclear what could constitute a non-semantic individuation of facts. Facts look to be things which, by definition, or at least by convention, are suited to be related to true judgements. Facts are not natural entities. To speak of a fact is already to have categorized the world in a way fit for making true judgements about it. If the world is the world of facts, not of things, it is a world that has already been subject to the same categorization as the categorization of judgement. Unless the concept of fact can be characterized independently of the concept of true judgement (perhaps by naturalizing the concept of fact), this is not a representationalist position. The problem of naturalizing facts is the mirror image of the key problem that affects contemporary physicalist critics of Tarksi.[6]

The problem about facts means that the correspondence theory is in danger of being either a substantive but highly contentious metaphysical theory, or a platitude about the conventional relation between talk of true judgements and talk of facts. The outlook for a metaphysical theory is not good, and what follows from platitudes is yet to be decided. Let us consider instead the idea of a semantic theory of truth and see where that takes us. I return to metaphysical issues in section 3.7.[7]

The modest, or semantic, conception of a theory of truth arises when we recall that we need a theory of truth to legitimize the concept of logical grammar. Logical grammar is the structure that a judgement has to have in order to be truth-evaluable. In chapter 1 I argued that in order for a judgement to be truth-evaluable, it had to be structured.[8] The argument concerned the way that items suited to evaluation as true or false are systematically related to one another. The claim that one judgement is true has bearings upon what other judgements we hold true. This systematicity of judgement is explained in terms of a common component structure shared between judgements. If I judge that '*a* is white', I am thereby judging that it is the same way that other things, *b*, *c*, *d*, etc. can be. But the idea of the possibility of these other things also being white arises only because my initial judgement has a combinatorial structure that includes the predicate '. . . is white', and this predicate can be applied to other things. It is a repeatable component part of judgements.

The study of logical grammar is the study of the systematic patterns of use of repeatable components of judgements and of the range of possible judgements that can be formed with such components. Given that this idea of structure is the idea of a structure necessary in order to aim a judgement at truth, we could do with a theory of truth that showed how the truth of judgements was systematically computed from an account of their structure. That is to say, we could do with a theory that shows in a systematic way how the combinatorial structure of a judgement determines the truth-condition of the judgement. Any theory of truth which does just that, we can call a semantic theory of truth. Tarski's theory of truth is a semantic theory of truth.

Tarski's theory shows how the truth-condition of any judgement expressible within first-order predicate calculus can be derived from an account of the structure of the judgement and an assignment of semantic values to the judgement's components. This means that for any judgement in natural language which is expressible in first-order predicate calculus, that expression will amount to a transparent display of the judgement's logical grammar. Once a natural language judgement has been translated into the first-order predicate calculus, we know we have a representation of the judgement's logical grammar, for, with Tarski's theory, we then know how to calculate the truth-condition of the judgement in a systematic structure-discerning way.

In short, Tarski's theory provides us with an account of the general categories of logical grammar. It shows us how we can represent the logical grammar of any judgement expressible within first-order predicate calculus. It is a theory that belongs to what I have called the second level of semantics. In the next three sections I shall give an account of Tarski's theory. Mastery of Tarski's theory of truth is often seen as a technical initiation rite that all must pass before being allowed to engage in serious work in the philosophy of language. In part, this is because the philosophy of language is often taken to be concerned with no more than the development of formal semantic theories.[9] This has the effect of disguising the philosophical issues raised by Tarski's theory as students labour on the technicalities. It also ignores the deep need for a semantic theory of truth for the philosophy of thought that focuses on an account of content that figures in rationalizing explanations of behaviour. Even on this conception of semantics, we still need an account of the systematicity of judgement, the way that thought contents are systematically related to one another. Tarski's theory provides such an account and, furthermore, lays the foundations for the anti-representationalism of Davidson's work on content. These consequences become apparent in the next two chapters. For now we need to clarify the idea of a semantic theory of truth. I begin with a very simple semantic theory in the next section, which, although not Tarski's theory, shares all the key structural features of Tarski's theory. Because the theory in the next section is simple, it makes issues about the point and pretensions of a semantic theory of truth accessible. I turn to an account of Tarski's theory proper in section 3.5.

3.3   A Simple Semantic Theory

Tarski's theory shows how the truth-condition of a sentence can be systematically computed from an account of the structure of the sentence and an assignment of semantic values to the component parts of the sentence structure. This produces a recursive definition of truth. The definition shows how we can calculate the truth-condition of any sentence within the potentially infinite number of sentences expressible in a language by repeated use of the recursive rules. These rules show that all sentences have a common structural lineage and are composed out of a finite base of components. Through an assignment of semantic value to a finite stock of sentence components and a set of combinatorial rules cataloguing the permissible combinations of the components, the theory defines the semantic outcome of every such combination. The idea is best illustrated with a very simple language.

Consider a language **L** which has only three atomic sentences, *P*, *Q* and *R*, plus the structural facilities of the propositional calculus. By laying down the above two stipulations, we have, in effect, provided a syntax for **L**, for we have implicitly defined the concept of a well-formed sentence of **L**. If something is a well-formed sentence of **L**, it is either *P*, *Q* or *R*, or some combination of these employing the connectives of the propositional calculus. We can note this explicitly as follows.

> *Syntax for **L**:*
> (i)   *P*, *Q* and *R* are basic sentences of **L**.
> (ii)   If A is a sentence of **L**, $\neg$A is a sentence of **L**.
> (iii)   If A and B are sentences of **L**, (A&B) is a sentence of **L**.
> (iv)   Nothing else is a sentence of **L**.

In the syntax for **L**, '*P*', '*Q*' and '*R*' are individual sentences, 'A' and 'B' are variables for sentences. So 'A' could be the sentence '(*P*&*Q*)', and 'B' could be the sentence '$\neg R$'. Note, by the syntax provided, that

> *P*&*Q*

is not a sentence of **L**, for clause (iii) of the syntax demands that conjunctions have a pair of brackets around them in order to be a sentence of the language. However,

> (((*P*&*P*)& $\neg P$)&*Q*)

is a sentence of **L**, for it can be recursively generated from the sentences *P* and *Q* by repeated applications of the syntax rules. So, by (i) we know that

P

is a sentence of **L**. But by (iii) we know that

(P&P)

is also a sentence of **L**. By (ii) we know, given that P is a sentence, then so too is

$\neg P$.

Therefore, by (iii) again, we know that

((P&P)&$\neg P$)

is a sentence. By (i) we know that

Q

is a sentence, and so, by (iii) once more, we know that

(((P&$\neg P$)&$\neg P$)&Q)

is a sentence.

The example is, of course, tedious, but it illustrates how the concept of being a sentence of **L** can be defined recursively. Note also that, because the connectives of the propositional calculus are interdefinable, such that negation plus any one other is sufficient to define the rest, we need only two combinatorial rules in our syntax for **L**: one rule governing the negation operator and a rule for one other connective. Note also that **L** possesses a potentially infinite number of sentences. Most of the sentences of **L** have no interest for us; nevertheless, sentences like

(((((P&P)&P)&Q)&R)&$\neg Q$)

are well-defined sentences of **L**.

The syntax for **L** recursively characterizes the set of sentences expressible in **L**. The semantics for **L** will show how the syntactic structure of **L**-sentences enables us to specify the truth-conditions for any sentence of **L**. The truth-conditions of a sentence are the conditions under which the sentence is true. By providing a systematic way of specifying the truth-conditions for any sentence of **L**, our semantics will show how the truth-conditions of any sentence are a function of the assignment of semantic values to the atomic components of the language.

So, a semantic theory for **L** will first provide an assignment of what constitutes possession of a semantic value for the atoms; then it will provide rules for calculating what it is for complex sentences formulated by the syntax of **L** to be true. Given the assignment of semantic value to the atoms, such a theory will provide an account of what it is for any sentence expressible in **L** to be true that draws upon the structure of the sentences of **L**.

Suppose '*s*' is a name for a sentence of **L**; the semantic theory will provide a systematic account of what it is to say of *s* that it is true. Because the theory provides this account systematically, drawing upon the recursive definition of the syntactic structure of **L**-sentences, the theory will be able to provide an account of the conditions under which we would say of any sentence of **L**, '*s*' is true. Therefore, the theory will provide a solution to the schema,

(2) '*s*' is true iff . . .

for every sentence of **L**. This schema applies to all sentences of **L**; therefore the semantic theory provides an account for every possible predication of '. . . is true' of **L**-sentences. A theory that entailed all true instances of this schema for all sentences of **L** would have provided an extensionally accurate definition of truth for the language **L**. The theory provides an account of what it is for every predication of truth of **L**-sentences to obtain. Note, this is not to provide a definition of truth in the abstract; it is to provide a definition of the concept 'true-in-**L**'.[10]

Two further points need noting about the idea of a semantic theory of truth. The language **L** has an infinite number of sentences within it. The semantic theory tells us what it is to say of any of these sentences that they are true. The semantic theory tells us what it is to say, e.g.,

(3) '(*P&R*)' is true.

In (3), '. . . is true' is a predicate, and '(*P&R*)' is a name. The predicate '. . . is true' is not a predicate of the language **L**, and the name '(*P&R*)' is not a name of the language **L**. **L** has no names or predicates, but only three atomic sentences whose internal structure is unspecified, plus the logical operators of the propositional calculus. This means that the sentence in (3), which says of a sentence of **L** that it is true, is not itself a sentence of **L**. (3) is not constructble according to the syntax of **L**. Therefore, (3) is a sentence from some language other than **L**. We say that (3) is a sentence of the metalanguage in which we formulate our semantic theory of truth for **L**. The semantic theory is produced in metalanguage **ML** and defines truth as it applies to sentences of **L**.

This means that the schema (2) is a schema for making claims in the metalanguage **ML** about sentences of **L**. Accordingly, the completion of the schema requires that we have a way of expressing in the metalanguage what it is for any sentence of L to be true. That means that in order to complete schema (2), we would require in the metalanguage **ML** a translation of each of the sentences of **L**. In general, we can re-form our schema (2), then, to this:

(4)   *s* is true iff *p*,

where *s* is a name for a sentence of **L**, and *p* is a translation of *s* into the metalanguage **ML**. Instances of this schema will be sentences of **ML**. Any theory that entails all and only all the correct instances of (4) for some given language **L** will then have succeeded in defining the concept true-in-L. The requirement that a theory of truth entail all true instances of (4) is Tarski's material adequacy condition. Let us now see how it works in the simple case of our language **L** with three atomic sentences.

In the case of our example **L**, a semantic theory will start with an account of what it is for each of '*P*', '*Q*' and '*R*' to be true. It will then provide rules governing the way that the truth of complex sentences is a function of the truth of their components, the atomic sentences '*P*', '*Q*' and '*R*'. These two stages correspond with the account of the syntax of **L**. To make the example more revealing, let us assume that the sentences '*P*', '*Q*' and '*R*' are German sentences, respectively: 'Der Schnee ist weiss', 'Das Grass ist grun', and 'Die Sonne tragt seine Hut'. The semantics for **L** can then be explicitly stated as follows.

Semantics for **L**:
(i)   '*P*' is true iff snow is white.
       '*Q*' is true iff grass is green.
       '*R*' is true iff the sun has got his hat on.

Where A and B are sentences of **L**,

(ii)   ¬A is true iff A is not true.
(iii)   (A&B) is true iff A is true and B is true.

The clauses in this theory are stated in the metalanguage, and they provide a translation of the object language sentences. The clauses in (i) employ translations in **ML** of the atomic sentences of **L** to provide an account of the truth-conditions of the sentences '*P*', '*Q*' and '*R*'. The clauses (ii) and (iii) employ a translation of '¬' and '&' into the metalinguistic terms 'not' and 'and' to provide recursive clauses governing the truth-conditions of complex sentences of L employing '¬' and '&'. Again, note that the words 'not' and 'and' are not part of **L**. **L** contains the expressions '¬' and '&', whose semantic role is governed by the clauses (ii) and (iii), which make use of the metalinguistic terms 'not' and 'and'. This makes clear that the provision of a semantic theory of truth for our language L presupposes mastery of a metalanguage of greater expressive power than L.

The above semantics for L allows us to derive all true instances of our schema (4). For example, let '*s*' be

'(Der Schnee ist weiss & Die Sonne tragt seine Hut).'

By application of clause (iii) and the first and third sub-clauses of clause (i) of the semantics, we now know that

(5) '(Der Schnee ist weiss & Die Sonne tragt seine Hut)' is true iff snow is white and the sun has got his hat on.

Use of the appropriate clauses will provide similar instances of the general schema for all sentences expressible within the syntax of L, including,

(6) 'Der Schnee ist weiss' is true iff snow is white.

Note, clause (i) of the semantic theory provides the basic assignment of the conditions under which the atoms possess a semantic value. In this simple example of language L, the atoms are whole sentences, and so the assignment of conditions under which the atoms possess a semantic value is an account of the truth-conditions of the atoms. This makes the whole exercise for language L look more trivial than it really is. The semantics for L is trivial, but only because L is such a simple language. The structure of what is going on in this trivial semantic theory is no different from the much more complex language for which Tarski provided a semantic theory of truth. So that we not be misled by the triviality of L, let me introduce the general notion of the *semantic conditions* of an expression, in order to make this example do some work for us.

The semantic conditions of an expression are the conditions under which the expression possesses a semantic value. The semantic value for a sentence is either true or false. So, the semantic conditions for a sentence are the conditions under which the sentence is true or false. The semantic conditions for a sentence are its truth-conditions. The semantic value for a singular term is the object for which it stands. So, the semantic conditions for a singular term are the conditions under which it refers; e.g. the name 'Bill Clinton' refers just in case the expression stands for Bill Clinton. The semantic value for predicates is the set of objects which satisfy the predicate. So, the semantic conditions for a predicate are the conditions under which it has a non-empty extension; e.g. the predicate '. . . is a president' has a non-empty extension just in case something is a president.

Now, the syntax for L lacks any reference to singular terms and predicates. This is why it provides such a simple semantic theory. Nevertheless, the point of the conceptual house cleaning of the previous paragraph allows me to state the general point of a Tarskian semantic theory on the basis of the semantics given for L. The semantic theory shows how we can define what it is for any sentence of L to be true. To say what it is for a sentence of L to be true is to state its truth-conditions. The semantic theory for L shows how the truth-conditions of any sentence in L can be systematically derived from an assignment of semantic conditions to the atoms of L. This claim is true of a semantic theory of truth for richer languages than L.

In general:

> For any language L, a semantic theory of truth shows how the truth-conditions of any sentence in L can be recursively defined, the recursion based upon an assignment of semantic conditions to the atoms.

This is a general characterization of a semantic theory of truth. It remains true no matter how complex or trivial our language L for which we write a Tarskian truth theory. We now need to see what problems are solved and what issues are raised by constructing such a semantic theory.

3.4   The Point of a Semantic Theory – I

The obvious problem with the simple semantic theory of section 3.3 is that the definition of truth is a recursion upon clauses that employ the concept of truth, because the atoms of the language are sentences. This, however, is just a particularly trivial example of the general idea of a semantic theory adumbrated at the end of section 3.3. Any semantic theory will provide a recursive definition of truth where the recursion is based upon an assignment of semantic conditions to the atoms of the language. Where the atoms are sentences, the assignment of semantic conditions will have to employ the concept of truth. Nevertheless, our simple semantic theory defines true-in-L recursively, on a set of base clauses the right-hand sides of which contain no semantic terms. The base clauses are listed under (i) above, e.g.

'*P*' is true iff snow is white.

For sure, the right-hand side exploits the expressive power of the metalanguage in specifying the truth-conditions of the sentence, but true-in-L is extensionally defined on the basis of the equivalences in clause (i).

It is important to be clear that our simple theory achieves two distinct things. First, it defines truth for complex sentences of L in terms of truth for atomic sentences – call this a structural definition. Second, it defines truth for the atomic sentences via the extensional equivalences in the base clause (i) – call this the base-extensional definition. If we had a semantic theory that applied to a language in which the atoms were sub-sentential units, then in stating the semantic conditions for sub-sentential units, we would not need the concept of truth. In such a case, the concept of truth would be defined in a recursion employing whatever semantic concept is required to state the semantic conditions of sub-sentential units. This is what Tarski achieved. Tarski showed how to write a semantic definition of truth for a language with the structure of first-order predicate calculus. The atoms of that language are sub-sentential units. Tarski showed how truth for such a language could be defined recursively over the assignment of semantic conditions for such atoms. The concept Tarski employed in assigning the semantic conditions for the atoms was the concept of satisfaction. In Tarski's theory, truth is structurally defined in terms of the satisfaction of sub-sentential strings, and satisfaction has a base-extensional definition in the base clauses of the theory.

Returning to the initial objection to the simple semantic theory of section 3.3, we can now reformulate that objection. The objection is that the theory of section 3.3 merely shows how the application of the predicate '. . . is true' to logically complex sentences can be defined in terms of its application to atomic sentences. This is correct, but as the application of '. . . is true' to the atomic sentences is defined extensionally in the base clause, we can still say that our simple theory is a theory of truth. Perhaps the objection can be reformulated as follows: Although the base-extensional definition does not employ a semantic concept, for it extensionally defines that semantic concept in the base clauses, those base clauses appeal to the expressive power of the metalanguage in providing this basic definition.

To answer this, let me state generally the two tasks that a semantic theory of truth performs. A semantic theory (1) defines the truth of complex sentences in terms of the semantic conditions for atomic expressions in the language; and (2) defines the semantic conditions for atomic expressions extensionally with the base list. The only difference between the section 3.3 theory and Tarski's is that Tarski has sub-sentential atoms the semantic conditions of which are satisfaction conditions. To keep matters simple, let us stick with our simple theory.

The base clauses in the theory exploit the expressive power of the metalanguage; but why does this matter? When we find in the base clause

    '*P*' is true iff snow is white,

then what appears on the right-hand side is the condition under which the sentence is true. That condition is not a linguistic entity. It is the condition of snow being white.[11] What more could we want of a theory of truth than that it extensionally link up true sentences with such conditions? The idea that we have been short-changed by a semantic theory arises from the assumption of representationalism. It arises from assuming that world and language can be characterized independently of one another, so that only an account of worldly states that did not draw upon the expressive power and categorization of language would do in a theory of truth. The assumption is that we should be able, as it were, to identify the 'edge of language' in the structure of our theory, and then show how this edge hooks up with the world. Russell wanted to identify the edge of language, but his account of the edge was non-representational, for it was internally connected to things by the activity of the mind; it was not specifiable independently of those things it was hooked up to. As we will see, Tarski's metaphysical critics seem to expect an account of what I am calling the 'edge of language'. The aspiration for a representationalist or metaphysical account of truth is, however, mistaken. It asks for something that cannot be given: namely, an account of worldly states that has not been passed through the filter of language and its categories! There is no such thing. If there were such a thing as the edge of language, we would probably approach it only with a rush of metaphysical vertigo, for it is impossible to see how there could be anything (certainly anything worth talking about) beyond the expressive power of language. Of course, contemporary representationalists whose representationalism is premissed on physicalism would deny the thirst for such speculative nonsense as the edge of language. But that is only because they have first assumed that the world is physical, and that the edge between language and world is merely a point in a causal chain of connections. Nevertheless, even physicalist representationalists assume that there needs to be some substantive account of how and where language hooks up with things. So, although their conception of the 'edge' will not be as speculative as, say, Descartes', they still have the basic idea that there is such a thing, for they refuse to accept that what appears on the right-hand side of the base clauses of a truth theory really amounts to the world.[12]

We could, at this point, say that a semantic theory of truth does, after all, supply a kind of correspondence theory, although not as I defined it above. It is, however, harmless to speak of what is picked out on the right-hand side of the base clauses as facts, as long as you do not mistake it for a metaphysical or representationalist account of facts. The facts appealed to are the facts as categorized by human thought and language, but so what? There is no other kind.[13] A semantic theory of truth does not, as it were, reach outside the representational power of language to say what it is for a language to express truths. The theory exploits the representational power of a language, the metalanguage, in order to state what it is for the object language to express truths. The fact that the theory exploits the expressive power of the metalanguage illustrates that the theory presupposes our pre-theoretic grasp of truth. This means that there is a pre-theoretic notion of truth that is implicit in the very idea of content or meaning. That notion of truth is drawn upon in our grasp of the meaning of the metalanguage. It is, however, that very same notion which is then codified by a semantic theory that reveals the systematic structure of meaningful truth-oriented language. The theory is modest compared to some metaphysical aspirations, but it is revelatory of the structure of logical grammar.

The point applies to all semantic theories of truth, whatever their sophistication or complexity. In all the biconditionals entailed by a semantic theory, we can plot the appearance on the right-hand side of a term that translates a term on the left-hand side. This is obvious in the case of the logical connectives. Clause (iii) of the our simple semantic theory was:

> (iii)   (A&B) is true iff A is true and B is true.

On the left-hand side we have the expression '&', and on the right-hand side we have its translation in the metalanguage, 'and'. You might wonder what benefit is gained by a theory that succeeds only in defining the conditions under which a conjunction is true by exploiting the use of the conjunction in the metalanguage! The benefit will be just this: Such a theory will show how truth can be defined in the base-extensional definition of the appropriate terms of semantic evaluation appropriate to the atoms of the language under discussion. Some have doubted whether this is, of itself, any great achievement.[14] I shall come to this objection shortly. For the moment, note the following achievement of a semantic theory of truth: A semantic theory of truth shows how the truth of a judgement expressible in the language is definable via a recursion over the judgement's structure. For any judgement J in the language L for which we have a semantic theory of truth, the truth-conditions of J are systematically definable in terms of J's structure as represented by its formation from the atomic elements of L plus whatever combinatorial rules apply to L. But now recall the discussion of the previous chapters. I defined 'logical grammar' as the structure necessary in order for a judgement to be aimed at truth; it is the structure that judgement possesses that makes judgement something apt for semantic evaluation. Tarski's semantic theory of truth achieves an explicit rendering of what that structure is. Tarski's theory applies to any language with the expressive power of first-order predicate logic. Therefore, Tarski's theory exhibits the logical grammar of such a language; it shows that the notion of logical grammar is well-defined, for it shows how the truth-oriented structure of any judgement expressible within a language of first-order predicate logic is systematically related to the truth-oriented structure of all other judgements expressible in the language. The semantic theory of truth systematically connects the concepts of truth and structure, by showing how the notion of what it is for a judgement to be true is definable in terms of that judgement's compositional structure, a structure that explains its systematic relatedness to other judgements.

To have shown that the concept of logical grammar is well-defined for languages with the expressive power of first-order predicate logic is a considerable achievement. It is, however, this achievement that can look like a mere technicality with no wider philosophical and metaphysical significance. To put the point another way, what is the philosophical significance of having a well-defined concept of logical grammar? For sure, possession of such a concept will enable the study of the logical grammar of all manner of expressions of natural language – all those that are definable in terms of the apparatus of first-order predicate logic – but how, if at all, will such a study provide any philosophical results? There must be a worry at this stage that the pursuit of this study will amount to no more than an idle parlour game for the amusement of otherwise unoccupied philosophers. This worry is well founded. It can be addressed in two quite different ways. But before addressing this worry, I give an account of how Tarski defined truth for languages with the expressive power of first-order predicate logic. I do this in the next section. In the following section I shall sum up the discussion so far, and reformulate the present concern with the pretensions and point of a semantic theory of truth. After that I shall return to look at the two ways that this concern can be addressed.

3.5 A Semantic Theory of Truth for First-order Predicate Logic

Writing the semantic theory of section 3.3 was easy. The theory is no more than what is represented in the familiar truth tables as a model for the semantics of complex sentences in propositional calculus. The truth tables start with an assignment of truth-values for atomic sentences and provide a means for calculating, for any sentence expressible by combining atomic sentences according to the compositional rules of propositional logic, the conditions under which they are true and false. Tarski showed how to produce a semantic theory of truth for a language subject to a finer level of analysis than propositional structure, a language with the resources of first-order predicate calculus. I begin with an informal sketch of Tarski's theory.

For a language with the resources of first-order predicate calculus, the atomic components of the language will be predicates and quantifiers. Depending on your theory of names, it might also contain names as atoms. For the moment, I shall assume a simplified picture, and adopt Russell's theory of names as outlined in the previous chapter. For Russell, the contribution that a name makes to the truth-conditions of a sentence in which it appears can be defined in terms of the contribution that a definite description (or some set of definite descriptions) makes to the truth-conditions of a sentence. On such a view, names are complex expressions whose semantic power is equivalent to that of an arrangement of quantifiers and predicates.

So, for the language under consideration, we will need a way of specifying the semantic conditions for the atomic elements – predicates and those constructions formed by the application of quantifiers to predicates. Predicates may be familiar one-place predicates, e.g.

Fx,

where this stands for '. . . plays the saxophone' (the 'x' merely marks the gap), or they may be many-place predicates like the relation

x loves y.

The intuitive idea about a predicate is that it is something with a hole or gap in it. A predicate is what you get if you take a whole sentence,

Bill Clinton plays the saxophone,

and extract the singular term.[15] The gap may be closed by applying a quantifier to it; e.g.

∃xFx,

something plays the saxophone. In cases where all the gaps of a predicate are governed by a quantifier, we have a *closed* sentence, otherwise we have an *open* sentence. The above sentence is closed; the following,

∃x (x loves y),

is open, for the gap marked by 'y' is not quantified over. An open sentence is thus a linguistic item of lower structure than a closed sentence. A closed sentence is a complex combination of symbols formed by the combinatorial rules of quantification given the atomic elements of open sentences. Closed sentences are the sorts of things that are true or false. A semantic theory for such a language needs to define what it is for a closed sentence to be true or false in terms of what it is for open sentences to be subject to semantic evaluation. The term of semantic evaluation for open sentences is satisfaction. Remember, the simplest open sentence is the one-place predicate

Fx,

and we speak of predicates being satisfied by objects. The predicate '. . . plays the saxophone' is satisfied by various objects; for example, it is satisfied by

Bill Clinton

and by

Courtney Pine.

It is not satisfied by

Tony Blair.

In order to be able to write the base clauses of a recursive definition of truth for closed sentences in terms of the satisfaction conditions for open sentences, we need to be able to handle cases of predicates with multiple gaps – two-, three-, four-place predicates, etc. We will say that two-place predicates are satisfied by ordered pairs of objects, for not only do we need two things to satisfy a relation like x loves y, but it matters what order the objects come in. Although the ordered pair

<Charlie Brown, the little red-haired girl>

satisfies the predicate

x loves y

to Charlie Brown's eternal misfortune, the ordered pair

<the little red-haired girl, Charlie Brown>

does not. In general, we will say that an open sentence with n gaps is satisfied by ordered n tuples – ordered pairs, ordered triples, ordered quadruples, etc. There is, in principle, no limit on the complexity of predicate structures, so we need a device in order to be able to define truth recursively in terms of the satisfaction of open sentences formed from predicates of any number of places. Let us avail ourselves of the notion of an infinite sequence of objects (an ordered pair is merely a sequence of two objects). We can then stipulate that a two-place predicate is satisfied by an infinite sequence of objects just in case it is satisfied by the first two places. So, once again,

x loves y

is satisfied by the sequence

<Charlie Brown, the little red-haired girl, Bill Clinton, . . .>

but not by the sequence

<the little red-haired girl, Charlie Brown, Bill Clinton, . . .>

nor, for all I know, by the sequence

<Bill Clinton, the little red-haired girl, Charlie Brown, . . .>

and so on. We can make similar claims about three-place predicates, four-place predicates, etc.

In general, for n-place predicates $R(x_1, \ldots, x_n)$ and infinite sequences of objects, e.g. $\langle O_1, \ldots, O_n, O_{n+1}, \ldots \rangle$, we need instances of the schema

$R(x_1, \ldots, x_n)$ is satisfied by the sequence $\langle O_1, \ldots, O_n, O_{n+1}, \ldots \rangle$ iff it is satisfied by the first n places.

Such instances will provide, for each n-place predicate, a separate base clause to define satisfaction, e.g.

(7) Fx_1 is satisfied by the sequence $\langle O_1, O_2, \ldots, O_n \rangle$ iff O_1 plays the saxophone, and
x_1 loves x_2 is satisfied by the sequence $\langle O_1, O_2, \ldots, O_n \rangle$ iff O_1 loves O_2.

The above clauses provide the starting-point for a general semantic theory for the language. They govern the simplest casees of open sentences. In order to be able to define truth for closed sentences, i.e. sentences in which all the gaps are bound by quantifiers, we need to see how to define the satisfaction conditions for the intermediary case of an open sentence that nevertheless has a quantifier governing one of the gaps, e.g.

(8) $\exists x$ (x loves y).

Once we can handle (8), the account of closed sentences can be developed. The rule we need must show the semantic contribution made by the existential quantifier. Without the quantifier, the open sentence

x loves y

is governed by (7). With a quantifier governing the first position, the sentence is still an open sentence, so the semantic contribution of the quantifier will be expressible in terms of satisfaction conditions.

A quantified sentence like (8) expresses generality. It says that there is something that loves y, where 'y' is unbound. The open sentence 'x loves y' is satisfied by particular sequences of objects, but the quantified open sentence (8) is, intuitively, not talking about particular sequences of objects. The content of (8) is general. It is making the claim that there are sequences of objects which are such that the first two members satisfy the predicate '. . . loves . . .'; or, in other words, there are sequences of objects that satisfy the open sentence 'x loves y'. Informally, the way of expressing this is to say that the open sentence with one bound variable, 'Something loves y', is satisfied by the sequence <Bill Clinton, the little red-haired girl, . . .> just in case there is another sequence – e.g. <Charlie Brown, the little red-haired girl, . . .> – that satisfies the open sentence obtained by removing the quantifier on the bound variable. And of course, we know from our basic clause governing satisfaction that the other sequence does indeed satisfy the open sentence 'x loves y'. Notice that we are not saying that the sequence

<Bill Clinton, the little red-haired girl, . . .>

satisfies (8) *simpliciter*. It cannot do that, for our notion of satisfaction *simpliciter* applies only to open sentences with no bound variable and sequences of objects as governed by (7). The informal expression of the contribution that the quantifier makes to the satisfaction conditions of (8) makes a general point about how (8) is satisfied, given that there are certain sequences of objects. The clause governing an open sentence with one bound variable, like (8), builds upon the basic notion of an open sentence being satisfied by a sequence, and lays down the general conditions of relationships between sequences of objects under which statements of generality, like the open sentence (8), are satisfied.

We can summarize the example as follows:

(9) $\exists x$ (x loves y) is satisfied by the sequence S_1, <Bill Clinton, the little red-haired girl, . . .>, iff there is another sequence S_2, <Charlie Brown, the little red-haired girl, . . .> (where S_2 differs in at most the first place), and S_2 satisfies the open sentence obtained by removing the quantifier from the closed sentence.

We now need to provide for the fact that there is no limit to the number of variables, free or bound, that may appear in a sentence. Generalizing to cover for this fact, we then have:

(10) $\exists x_i R(x_1, \ldots, x_n)$ is satisfied by the sequence S_1 iff there is another sequence S_2, that differs from S_1 in at most the ith place (where the ith place is the position bound by the quantifier), and which satisfies the open sentence obtained by dropping the quantifier.

(9) is merely an instance of (10) which, for present purposes, will do as a general rule governing the semantic contribution of the existential quantifier.[16]

Recall the simple semantic theory of section 3.3 and the trivial clauses governing the contribution of the logical constants '&' and '¬' to complex sentences. Recall that in those clauses a translation of the constant appeared on the right-hand side of the clause; e.g.

'(A&B)' is true iff 'A' is true *and* 'B' is true.

Clause (10) does for the existential quantifier what this clause does for conjunction, and, in just the same way, a translation of the constant appears on the right-hand side. Notice the appearance of the phrase '. . . *there is* another sequence . . .' on the right-hand side of (10), or in the example (9). This should not be surprising. The point is best made with a concrete example, so I will return to (9), rather than to the general (10). (9) says that the open sentence 'There is something that loves y' is satisfied by the sequence S_1 if and only if *there is* a sequence S_2, differing at the first place, and S_2 satisfies the open sentence 'x loves y'. Clauses like (9) and (10) are written in the metalanguage in which we write our semantic theory for a language L, which now contains, in addition to the apparatus of the propositional calculus, the existential quantifier, predicate letters and variables. It should be no surprise, then, that the metalanguage contains a translation of all the logical machinery of the object language that is used in writing the rules governing the compositional structure of L and the way that its structure determines the truth-conditions of sentences of L.

So far, we have considered only open sentences of L, whether those with a bound variable, like (8), or those with all free variables. Open sentences are artificial devices used for describing the compositional structure of languages with predicate calculus complexity. There are no natural language equivalents to the open sentences that we have been considering. Natural language sentences are closed. It is closed sentences to which the predicate '. . . is true' applies. But now, with the apparatus of open sentences and clauses governing their satisfaction conditions in place, it is relatively easy to see how to define truth for closed sentences.

Take the simplest case of a closed sentence with one quantifier, 'Something plays the saxophone':

(11) $\exists x F x.$

A closed sentence like (11) is the limit case of an open sentence; it is an open sentence with no free places. When considering sequences that will satisfy (11), then, there are no places in the sequence that are relevant to (11). Accordingly, for all sequences, as far as (11) is concerned, there are only two options: either they satisfy it, or they do not. And so we say that a closed sentence like (11) is satisfied either by all sequences or by none, and its being true is its being satisfied by all sequences. This can sound odd, but the point is seen when we realize that (11) is satisfied by the sequence

<Tony Blair, . . .>

because there is another sequence, differing at the first place, e.g.

<Bill Clinton, . . .>

that satisfies the open sentence obtained by dropping the quantifier in (11). But whatever sequence we think of, there is that other sequence beginning <Bill Clinton, . . .>, so (11) is satisfied by all sequences, and that is what it means to say it is true. If there were no such sequence that satisfied the open sentence

Fx,

then no sequence would satisfy the closed sentence (11); for we could not say that

<Tony Blair, . . .>

satisfies (11), because there is a sequence differing from this at the first place that satisfies the open sentence. So, (11) is true iff it is satisfied by all sequences, false if satisfied by none.

In this section I have developed an informal sketch of Tarski's theory. It has taken some time to get to the definition of truth for closed sentences – a closed sentence is true iff it is satisfied by all sequences, but patience is required in order to observe the structural similarity between the simple semantic theory of section 3.3 and the more complex one now before us. What this section has tried to make clear is merely the nature of the technical devices employed by Tarski in order to be able to produce, for a language with the compositional structure of first-order predicate calculus, the compositional semantic rules analogous to the very simple rules that apply in the propositional case. All that the current section reveals is the technical ingenuity required to do for the predicate calculus what truth tables do for propositional calculus – produce a systematic semantics in which truth is defined over the compositional structure of sentences of the language.

I conclude this section with a brief formal summary of Tarski's theory of truth. First, the syntax for **L**. **L** contains simple predicates F, G, etc.; relations, ... R____, of an unrestricted number of places; variables x, y, ... ; the negation operator ' ¬ '; conjunction '&'; and the existential quantifier '∃'. We can represent the syntax of **L** schematically, and rather than provide a list of all atomic expressions in the language, we write a general schema for what constitutes atomic elements of **L**. An atomic element for **L** is an open sentence in which all variables are free. We can call open sentences 'sentential functions', to distinguish them from sentences, for it is only the latter that are true or false. To keep matters simple, I assume that we can distinguish sentential functions from sentences and allow 'A' and 'B' to range over both sentences and sentential functions of **L**. If we then allow '$(\exists x_n)$' to represent n existential quantifiers binding n places of a sentential function, and X and Y to range over sequences of objects with 'X_i' representing the ith member of the sequence, we can produce a schematic syntax for **L** as follows.

> Syntax for **L**:
> (i)   An n-place predicate followed by n variables is a sentential function of **L**.
> (ii)   If A is a sentential function of **L**, ¬A is a sentential function of **L**.
> (iii)   If A and B are sentential functions of **L**, (A&B) is a sentential function of **L**.
> (iv)   If A is a sentential function with $n + 1$ variables of **L**, $(\exists x_n)$A is a sentential function of **L**.
> (v)   If A is a sentential function with n variables of **L**, $(\exists x_n)$A is a sentence of **L**.
> (vi)   Nothing else is a sentential function or sentence of **L**.

Note, clause (v) of the syntax defines a closed sentence, something that we would recognize as a normal sentence capable of being true or false. By the above syntax we can show that

(Fx & Ryz)

is a sentential function of **L**, as is

(∃x)(∃y)(Fx & Ryz).

Also, we know that

(∃x)Fx

is a sentence of **L**. The task of the semantics is to define what it is for any sentence expressible with this syntax to be true. As in the simple semantic theory of section 3.3, the semantics follows the structure of the syntax. The first clause of the semantics provides the base list of atomic predicates and relations stating the satisfaction conditions for each.

The semantics for **L** recursively define satisfaction:

(i)   'Fx' is satisfied by X iff X_1 is F, and so on for all one-place predicates. . . .
        'Fx$_1$, . . . , x$_n$' is satisfied by X iff $X_1 - X_n$ stand in the relation F, and so on for all relations of whatever complexity the language possesses. . . .

(ii)   '$\neg$A' is satisfied by X iff X does not satisfy 'A'.

(iii)   'A&B' is satisfied by X iff 'A' is satisfied by X and 'B' is satisfied by X.

(iv) $(\exists x_n)A_{n+1}$ is satisfied by X iff there is a Y such that $X_n \neq Y_n$ and Y satisfies A_n.

(v) $(\exists x_n)A_n$ is satisfied by X iff $(\exists x_{n-1})A_n$ is satisfied by X.

Truth is then defined such that for any sentence *s* of L, '*s*' is true iff *s* is satisfied by all sequences. The simple closed sentence with one bound variable, e.g.

$$(\exists x)Fx,$$

is true iff it is satisfied by all sequences. Where 'F' is the predicate '. . . plays the saxophone', this means that the quantified sentence 'Someone plays the saxophone' is true just in case it is satisfied by all sequences, and we know that this is the case, for whatever sequence we look at, *there is* the sequence different at the first place containing Bill Clinton, and that sequence satisfies the open sentence obtained when the number of quantifiers is one less than the number of variables – i.e. the open sentence 'x plays the saxophone'.

3.6   The Point of a Semantic Theory – II

Now that we know how to write a semantic theory of truth for any language expressible with the resources of the predicate calculus, we need to address the question, 'Just what have we achieved?' To repeat the claim made at the end of section 3.4, a claim that, having seen how Tarski's actual theory works, we are now fully entitled to make: Tarski's theory shows that the notion of logical grammar is well-defined. The semantic theory of truth reveals the systematic connectedness between the concepts of truth and structure, a connection for which I argued in chapter 1. That is a significant achievement. Furthermore, it was an achievement to have spotted how to do this for a language with predicate calculus structure. But what is the point? What do we achieve by plotting the systematic connectedness of the components of our language and the way that this connectedness underpins our notion of what it is for a judgement to be true and to bear inferential connections with other judgements?

81

These questions look to be no more than reflections of the modesty of the semantic theory of truth under the implicit assumption that a theory of truth should have higher pretensions. They concern no more than the question whether we should have a two-level semantic theory or should rest content with the single-level theory of logical grammar. The situation can be represented as follows:

Level 2	Complex expressions, e.g. sentences, compound sentences	Semantic conditions computed by theory of logical grammar
Level 1	Atomic expressions	Semantic conditions assigned

The complaint is that the semantic theory of truth defines only the semantic power of complex expressions, for the assignment of semantic power to atomic expressions presupposes an employment of equivalent semantic power in the metalanguage. What it presupposes at level 1 is the use of the semantic notion employed in making the assignment of semantic conditions in the metalanguage. The complaint is that if the theory of logical grammar that defines the semantic conditions of complex expressions as a function of the assignment of semantic conditions to atoms is to be interesting, we will need to add a theory of sign-semantics that explains the assignment of semantic conditions to the atoms, and we will need to do this without exploiting the equivalent semantic power in the metalanguage. Without the addition of a theory of sign-semantics, the theory of logical grammar merely plots the relations that obtain between one set of linguistic items and another. The second-level semantic theory is a theory of language–language relations. But semantics concerns the relations between language and world. Therefore, a semantic theory of truth begs all the interesting questions about the language–world relation. The real semantic power of language is grounded in the language–world relations that atomic expressions stand in. These relations are not explained by a semantic theory of truth; therefore the really important semantic work is left undone.

In outline, the above paragraph expresses a powerful complaint against the semantic theory of truth. It is a complaint put by Field.[17] Field claims that, in addition to the second-level theory of logical grammar, the semantic theory of truth needs to be supplemented by a causal theory that explains the assignment of semantic power to linguistic items. Field thinks that the semantic notion of satisfaction (and also reference if our language contains singular terms not definable in terms of descriptions) needs to be causally explicated. On this view, it is at the atomic level that language is hooked up to the world, and the hook-up is to be explained physicalistically in terms of a causal theory of satisfaction and a causal theory of reference. The atomic level is the edge of language, and we need a theory to take us over the edge and hook up with the world.

I shall sketch Field's argument in the next section, but for the moment consider this. If we resist the above complaint and insist that our semantic theory does not require grounding at level 1 via a causal theory of satisfaction and reference, where will that leave the methodological prescription that I have been pressing, a prescription summed up in the slogan 'Semantics exhausts ontology'? In the face of the current complaint against the modesty of the semantic theory of truth, the 'Semantics exhausts ontology' methodology appears bankrupt. If semantics does exhaust ontology, and if the only work for semantics to undertake is the second-level theory of logical grammar, then how can this even so much as reveal a glimpse of ontology, let alone exhaust it? The modest exercise of plotting the contours of the logical grammar of language appears to amount to a mapping of the conceptual connections that exist within language. Without endorsing linguistic idealism, it looks difficult to credit such an enterprise with any ontological illumination.

The challenge is to show that it can be coherent both to insist that semantics exhausts ontology and that a modest semantic theory of truth is as much as one requires in semantics. Such a challenge can be met. It requires that we legitimize the observation, made in section 3.4, that the conditions that appear on the right-hand side of the base clauses are genuinely worldly conditions. This can be done. It will, however, take us most of the way through the next two chapters to see how to do it. For the moment, in the next section, I shall review Field's criticism of Tarski. I shall also outline first moves required to resuscitate the 'Semantics exhausts ontology' methodology that I have said I will defend.

3.7 Getting Physical with Tarski

According to the complaint identified in the last section, Tarski's semantic theory of truth is ontologically impotent. The ontological import of a theory of truth can come only from a physicalist theory that explains the assignment of semantic conditions to the linguistic atoms. Such a theory is extraneous to the theory of logical grammar provided by the semantic theory of truth; it is strapped on like some prosthetic device, to put semantic power into the overall structure.

Field's criticism of Tarski centres on two theses that many philosophers take as obvious.[18] The two theses are:

(12)   The semantic power of a language is grounded in the relation between its atomic elements and extra-linguistic items,

and

(13)   The relation between the atomic elements of a language and extra-linguistic items is to be understood physically in terms of causal relations.

Note that (12) contradicts the Fregean methodology that I characterized in section 1.7, for it amounts to the view that the semantic notions of reference and satisfaction are prior to truth. According to (12), truth is to be understood in terms of the semantic notions of reference, satisfaction and the compositional rules for the language. (12), then, is aptly labelled 'semantic atomism'.[19] This is representationalism; for, according to (13), the notions of reference and satisfaction are then explained physicalistically in terms of the causal relations that obtain between e.g. names and their bearers. These relations are external; therefore what they relate can be characterized independently of each other.

It seems natural to adopt this order of explanation, and, having adopted it, it seems equally natural to expect that we might be able to ground the whole enterprise in a causal theory of reference and satisfaction. This is the model I referred to at the end of chapter 2. It is like Russell's conception of the businesses of semantics, but with the causal theory replacing Russell's Cartesian epistemology. We have to be careful to distinguish Russell's version of atomism from the representationalist variety. Russell's semantic Cartesianism makes the relation between the edge of language and world internal, not external. Curiously, the same point applies to Descartes. Descartes appears to be a representationalist only if we think of the relation between Ideas and the material world. If, however, we reflect on the relation between Ideas and what, for Descartes, is the ultimate ground of objectivity, God, then Descartes is not a representationalist. The whole point of the Ontological Argument is to show that the existence of God is a condition for the possibility of possessing the idea of God. Russell did not, of course, have an ontological argument. But his acquaintance relation for atomic expressions has a similar effect, for it establishes the semantic value dependence thesis; so, for Russell's singular terms, the existence of the object is a condition for the possibility of possessing a demonstrative idea.

The replacement of Russell's Cartesian epistemology with a causal theory is an improvement, but it reintroduces the problems of representationalism. The real issue concerns the viability of semantic atomism, for it seems plausible to think that if we accept semantic atomism, then we might as well work with a causal theory of the semantic relations of the atoms as with the ineffable Cartesianism that Russell employed. That seems a sound methodological principle.[20] Note also that there is reason to think not only that semantic atomism naturally encourages causal theories of the semantics of the atoms, but also that a predilection for causal theories pushes us in favour of semantic atomism. The reason for this is that it is commonplace in our scientific investigations of things and their properties that their gross causal powers are explicable in terms of the causal powers of their component parts. It then seems natural that if we are to explain the semantic properties of sentences (their truth and falsity) causally, this will be explicable in terms of the causal properties of their parts, hence semantic atomism. Semantic atomism and causal theories naturally go together. It is no accident that this combination is common among contemporary theorists.[21] The atomism is not essential to this combination, although it is natural. The same point applies if molecular expressions are taken as primitives. What matters is that it endorses a piecemeal account of semantic properties of expressions. Whether atomistic or molecular, a piecemeal account still faces two problems. One is the general problem of capturing the 'aboutness' of expressions without any information concerning their grammar or inferential role. The danger is that the aboutness is either left unexplained (Russell) or causal (Field), and its normativity eludes us. Second, the normativity of aboutness becomes most visible at the molecular level with the concept of truth. Truth as defined modestly is interdependent with grammar – the inferential structure of thought. That idea can be defined set-theoretically in a formal system, but that does not capture the right normative patterns, the patterns that are involved in rationalizing explanations of behaviour. A formal theory can define notions of inference and structure, but the structure we need is the structure that picks out rational behaviour, and that structure, as we saw in the previous chapter, involves not just properties of symbols, but properties of symbols as standardly used. The latter is a non-formal concept.[22]

Field's basic complaint is that Tarski's theory does not *reduce* the concept of satisfaction in the base clauses. The complaint is not that Tarski has not defined truth in non-semantic terms, for he has done. Recall that, first, Tarski defines truth in terms of satisfaction (structural definition); second, satisfaction for complex sentences and complex sentential functions is defined in terms of satisfaction for simple sentential functions (structural definition); third, satisfaction for simple sentential functions is defined extensionally in the base clauses (base-extensional definition). Given the third point, it is clear that Tarski defines truth in non-semantic terms. Satisfaction gets defined extensionally at the base clauses. Why, then, does Field think that this is not a physicalistically respectable definition of truth that reduces the concept of satisfaction?[23]

The real thrust of Field's criticism turns on the point I have repeatedly emphasized: that the base clause definition of satisfaction exploits the expressive power of the metalanguage and so does not give an account of the world–language connection in general. The translation of the base sentential functions into the metalanguage to define the satisfaction conditions on the right-hand side presupposes an ability to move, as it were, within a conceptual space, and to move in a way that presupposes a pre-theoretic grasp of semantic notions.[24] The pre-theoretic grasp of semantic notions is evident in the fact that in the base clauses the 'iff' expresses only extensional equivalence. Field thinks that reduction requires a stronger connection.[25]

Definitions of semantic terms in which the base clause is a list will be extensionally correct, but presuppose mastery of the semantic terms in order to produce the correct list in the base. The base clause for the predicate '. . . plays the saxophone' exploits mastery of that concept to produce the extensionally correct clause,

Fx is satisfied by X iff X_1 plays the saxophone.

The fact that the extensional equivalence '. . . iff____' does not reduce or explain satisfaction, but exploits our mastery with the predicate, is revealed by the observation that the above clause is only true in possible worlds in which the expression '. . . plays the saxophone' is used of people who play the saxophone. But that very same symbol string could have been used to express '. . . makes a good cup of coffee'. The meaning of the words is conventional, and it is such conventions that the semantic theory of truth exploits.[26] In contrast, Field wants a theory that uses a stronger connection than the equivalence '. . . iff____'. A stronger connection would explain or reduce the relation between the words '. . . plays the saxophone' and the people who play the instrument.[27] Call the stronger connection that Field wants 'natural equivalence'. Field's own analogy helps capture the point here.[28]

Consider the chemical concept of valence. The valence of a chemical element is an integer associated with the element that represents the sorts of chemical combinations that the element can enter into. Field holds that 'If physicalism is true it ought to be possible to find structural properties of atoms of each element that determine what the valence of that element will be'.[29] Now consider the following definitions of valence:

V_1:   Let 'E' range over elements and 'n' over integers, then
(E) (n) (E has valence n is extensionally equivalent to
    E is potassium, and n is 1,
    or E is tungsten, and n is 6,
    or [. . . for all elements in the actual world]),

and

V_2:   Let 'E' range over elements, 'n' over integers, and 'F' for some function, of unspecified complexity, of basic properties of atoms of elements, 'v' for the value of the function, and we write 'FEv' for the value of the function F for element E, then
(E) (n) (E has valence n is naturally equivalent to
    $(\exists v)(FEv$ and $v = n)$.

In V_2, the valence of an element is defined as a function of basic properties of the element's atoms. In V_1 the valence is defined via a list. V_1 is true only in those possible worlds in which the elements listed exist. There are many possible worlds, compatible with physical laws, in which V_1 does not apply. In contrast, because V_2 defines valence in terms of basic properties of atoms, V_2 is true for all possible worlds in which physical laws apply. That is why the equivalence if offers is natural equivalence.

There is a difference between V_1 and V_2. Furthermore, V_1 defines valence only by presupposing that the list in the base clause has got it right – picked out all the chemical elements. But V_1 is indexed to the elements in the actual world from which we get the list. There is no deeper explanation of valence other than listing the valence of elements that exist. There could be more elements, hence V_1 defines valence only on the presupposition that we already have an accurate employment of the concept.

Just as V_1 presupposes that we have an accurate grasp of valence, so an extensional definition of semantic terms presupposes the conventional connection between language and world. It is that conventional connection that Field wants explicated, and it is here that he wants a physical definition of satisfaction via a causal theory of satisfaction. Field wants an analogue of V_2 in which the satisfaction of '. . . plays the saxophone' will be determined not by our convention to use the expression of saxophone-players, but by a function of the causal connections between saxophone-players and the expression. Such a causal connection would then hold in all possible worlds with the same physical laws. It would not be a merely conventional connection, for the connection would depend only on the preservation of physical laws, and would not then presuppose conceptual mastery of satisfaction. Such a theory would show how semantics is reducible to physics, and how our contentful interactions with the environment could be brought into line with our scientific accounts of all other physical phenomena.

The idea of a causal theory of satisfaction presupposes representationalism, for causal relations are external, not internal. It must therefore be possible to characterize the relata of causal relations independently of one another. But how can Field endorse representationalism, for that requires that world and language be characterized independently of one another? The answer is that Field's representationalism is premissed on a prior metaphysics of physicalism. The world is what physicists tells us that it is. Language is a set of linguistic entities characterizable physicalistically. Field must then be committed to the view that the linguistic relata of his causal theory are tokens of physically described sound sequences and ink marks. These are the sorts of things that get causally related to saxophone-players. The fundamental objection to Field's methodology is the charge that from such resources he cannot reconstruct the normative intentional character of meaningful language use. The objection is a general one, but it is common. It is the objection that no physicalist reduction of intentional terms works.[30] He is asking for too much, but we at least know what he wants.

This objection is not incompatible with the view that we are physical entities in a physical universe with only physical substances. The objection requires only a non-reductionist physicalism in which all events are physical and have physical descriptions under which they are susceptible to complete explanation. But there are, in addition to the physical, other explanatory spaces, other levels of explanation.[31] If you are realist about meaning and intentional phenomena, then Field's physicalism is problematic, for the realist takes the normative rationalizing explanations in which content figures as constitutive of content. Of course, if you were willing to pay the eliminativist price with regard to intentional phenomena, there would be no problem. But that is too high a price to pay.[32]

Field's problem is the mirror image of the problem facing the correspondence theorist. Both presuppose representationalism. The correspondence theorist is faced with the charge that facts are not natural entities; they are intentional entities. The correspondence theorist's problem is to naturalize facts. Field's problem is to intentionalize natural causal sequences in order to recover the normativity of meaning. I leave this as a general challenge for the causal reductionist. We will return to it in a number of places, especially chapters 7 and 10.

If this challenge is not met, where does that leave us? It leaves us accepting *sui generis* the characterization of contentful states by their familiar role in rationalizing explanations of behaviour. It also leaves us with a threat of linguistic idealism. How do we put content into our 'Semantics exhausts ontology' methodology with a modest semantic theory of truth? In outline, the answer goes like this: There is a pre-theoretical grasp of truth that is presupposed by the very idea of content. We uncover the character of this concept of truth by asking, 'What must truth be like for content to be possible?' This is compatible with a modest semantic theory of truth. Suppose, however, that this transcendental enquiry reveals that truth has a minimally realist character that introduces some notion of states independent of the mind. If that is so, then we are licensed to hold that the conditions that appear on the right-hand side of the T-schema are indeed worldly states, even though our account of them is not that of the metaphysical realist. They are not characterized independently of the characterization of the structure of our thought and talk. They are, however, conceived as having an existence independently of judgement. This defends a modest, though not insignificant, realism.

I develop the above programme through the next four chapters (esp. chapters 5 and 7). In the next chapter I turn to Davidson's claims for a Tarskian theory as the core of a general theory of meaning.

4

Truth and Meaning

4.1 Introduction

Tarski shows us how to define truth. The definition presupposes our grasp of meaning for the metalanguage in which the definition is written and the capacity to translate object language expressions into the metalanguage. Davidson proposes to construct a general theory of meaning for a natural language.[1] Davidson's proposal is that Tarski's theory of truth should form the heart of a theory of meaning, and that to know the meaning of a language is to know a Tarskian truth theory for the language. The suggestion builds on the idea that to know the meaning of a sentence is to know its truth-conditions – the conditions under which the sentence would be true or false. The thought is that knowing a Tarskian truth theory for a natural language like English would be to know, in a systematic way, the truth-conditions of any sentence expressible in the language. Hence, understanding a natural language amounts to knowing a Tarskian truth theory for the language. Of course, not a lot of people explicitly know a Tarskian truth theory for their home tongue, so the use of the concept of 'knowledge' must be qualified. The idea is that a competent user of a natural language implicitly knows a Tarskian truth theory for the language.

There are many aspects of this proposal that need examining. One is worth immediate attention. The proposal looks circular. Tarski has shown how, if we take for granted our grasp of the meaning of the metalanguage and the meaning of the object language as it is translated into the former, then we can define truth for the object language. Davidson's proposal is that if we take our grasp of the concept of truth for granted, then we can give an account of meaning. But we cannot do that, for our grasp of the concept of truth itself presupposes our grasp of the concept of meaning. The circularity is, however, only apparent. Just as we have seen that Tarski's semantic conception of truth is, in an important sense, a modest theory of truth; so too is Davidson's theory a modest theory of meaning. The apparent

89

circularity arises only if we expect from a theory of meaning an account of a natural language that would render its meaning clear to a point of view wholly unconnected with the human enterprise of employing language to utter truths. We shall pin down the character of the modesty of Davidson's idea of a theory of meaning in due course. For now, note that his notion of a theory of meaning is not intended to be an account of meaning that would render a language transparent to a total alien, one who has no inkling of what using a language for truth-bearing communication is all about. The account of meaning that Davidson offers is not a theory of meaning from the point of view of the cosmic exile. It is a homely account of meaning.[2] Its central achievement is to display the systematicity of meaning comprehension, the systematicity of our intentionality, and the way that our intentionality confronts the world directly. The last point, Davidson's anti-representationalism, will not be covered until the next chapter, although it flows from his holism discussed below in sections 4.4 and 4.5. It is important also to note that Davidson has said that there is no such thing as a theory of thought or an account of intentionality. An account of meaning is, for Davidson, exhausted by a Tarskian truth theory that makes best overall sense of behaviour. Although that is Davidson's official line, given the richness that goes into his description of behaviour, his position comes very close to the neo-Fregean, quasi-behaviourist theory of thought that I defend in chapters 8ff. For the moment, then, I will continue to treat Davidson's contribution to the philosophy of language as a contribution to the theory of thought and intentionality.[3]

Rather than jeopardize the enterprise at first base, the threat of circularity that arises from using Tarski's theory of truth as the basis for a theory of meaning reveals the deep connections that exist between a trio of concepts central to the philosophy of thought and language: truth, meaning and inference. As we hold one of these concepts steady, so we gain a foothold in the account we give of the others. Which we should give priority to, and which we should mould to suit those priorities, are large and difficult questions. The connections between these three concepts will occupy us for this and much of the next three chapters, but we should note one facet of the way these concepts interact now.

It is tempting to think that any account of the interconnections between truth, meaning and inference will be incomplete if it is not informed by metaphysics. Surely, so the thought goes, our account of meaning, and also of valid inference, is informed by our account of truth only in tandem with an account, however implicit, of the world. The virtue of the 'Semantics exhausts ontology' methodology that I defend is that no such fourth term is needed to make complete sense of the interplay of our trio of concepts. Indeed, as we shall see in the next chapter, one of the most interesting results of Davidson's theory is the light it throws on the idea that our account of the interplay between the concepts of truth, meaning and inference exhausts our account of the world.

Our starting-point must be to examine what we can expect of a theory of meaning. I begin in the next section with an account of the kind of knowledge that understanding a language is supposed to be. I then distinguish two different concepts of theory at play in the idea of a theory of meaning, and follow them with an account of Davidson's argument for the enterprise.

4.2   Skills, Combinatoriality and Theoretical Knowledge

If we ask, 'What do competent language-users know when they understand a natural language?', Davidson says that they know a Tarskian truth theory for that language. The first point that needs noting about this is the identification of understanding and knowledge.[4] Understanding a language involves a complex array of skills and capacities: knowing how to conjugate verbs, knowing how to invert word order to change assertions into questions, knowing how to achieve the same effect by changes in intonation, knowing how to recognize valid inferences, etc. Understanding a language is a complex skill. If we think of understanding as a skill, we might think that it would resist representation as theoretical knowledge. If that were right, we could not begin to represent understanding a language as knowledge of a Tarskian truth theory.

The distinction between theoretical knowledge and practical knowledge is not sharp, but at the extremes it looks clear enough. Some knowledge is straight-forwardly propositional. This is theoretical knowledge, like knowing that heavy water is water formed from an isotope of hydrogen that contains a neutron in the nucleus of the hydrogen atom. If you know that, it is not a matter of knowing how to do something; it is a matter of having a true representation of the state of affairs at issue. In contrast, there are many types of practical knowledge – knowing how – that have no obvious connection with theoretical knowledge. If you know how to make perfect pastry, if you know how to ride a bike or to swim, there would appear to be no theoretical knowledge that you have to possess in order to know how to do these things. With the case of knowing how to speak and comprehend a language, matters appear different.

I take the following example from Michael Dummett.[5] Suppose you have never ridden a bike, and you are asked if you know how to ride one. It is an intelligible response to say, 'I don't know, I have never tried.' With the practical knowledge involved in this sort of activity, you could, as it were, plunge straight in and try to ride without any previous training or instruction. You simply have a go. Similar remarks apply to knowing how to swim. In contrast, suppose you have never spoken Spanish, listened to Spanish, or read Spanish. Suppose now that someone asks you if you can speak Spanish. It doesn't make sense to respond, 'I don't know, I've never tried.'[6] If the request was, 'Can you make Spanish-type sounds?', the response would be reasonable. Making sounds as if you were speaking Spanish is something you could 'have a go' at. Speaking Spanish is not something you could have a go at. The explanation for this difference seems plain. Knowing how to speak Spanish, in contrast to knowing how to ride a bike or knowing how to swim, depends on possession of theoretical knowledge. It depends on knowing that *No hablo mucho español* means 'I don't speak much Spanish', that *A que hora empiezan las atracciones* means 'At what time does the floor show start?', etc.

The idea that knowing how to speak a language depends on theoretical knowledge and that, therefore, the complex skill of language mastery can be represented by knowledge of a body of theoretical knowledge looks plausible. The distinction between theoretical and practical knowledge, however, is not sharp. Furthermore, in later chapters of this book I shall be considering cases of knowledge that resist codification into explicitly statable theoretical knowledge.[7] I would, then, prefer to rest the case for the theoretical representation of linguistic competence on more general ground.

In addition, there is a general problem with ascriptions of tacit theoretical knowledge to explain practical competence. The example of speaking Spanish above suggests that there is some point to the ascription, but consider this. The ascription of tacit knowledge must be testable. The obvious test is to take the ascription of tacit knowledge as correct just in case it fits the subject's behaviour. The notion of 'fitting the behaviour', however, looks too weak, for it underdetermines the choice between different truth theories.

Call two truth theories extensionally equivalent if and only if they entail all and only all the same theorems. Theorems are instances of the T-schema 's is true iff p'; they give the truth-conditions for the sentence that appears on the left-hand side. A pair of extensionally equivalent truth theories may differ in their axiomatic structure. For example, contrast a 'list' theory T_1, whose axioms are simply a list of all the instances of the T-schema, with a structure-discerning theory T_2. T_2 has an axiom set that states a semantic condition for every atom of the language and includes rules of combination that together entail all the theorems that, in T_1, occur as a basic list. Now, all that is detectable in behaviour is a subject's use of sentences; sentences are the behaviourally salient units of language. There is no such thing as the way a subject behaves with a name other than how they employ it in sentences. This means that T_1 and T_2 both fit the behaviour. In this case, there is no detectable difference between an ascription of tacit knowledge of T_1 or T_2 to the subject. What, then, does it mean to say that a competent speaker of a language tacitly knows a structure-discerning theory like Tarski's?

The obvious answer is that although T_1 and T_2 are behaviourally equivalent, they have different explanatory force with respect to novel behaviour. T_2 explains how a speaker is able to understand and produce novel sentences. Although the ascription of tacit knowledge is testable only in terms of whole sentence use, if the knowledge of the structure is construed realistically – there really are discriminable states of the subject causally responsible for sentence comprehension – then the following considerations are surely right. A subject who has encountered and understood '*Fa*' and '*Gb*' but not '*Fb*' or '*Ga*' should, if they tacitly know a structure-discerning theory, T_2, be able to understand the new sentences. They understand because tacit knowledge of T_2 equals knowledge of the axiomatic structure. This knowledge of axioms is then treated realistically as discrete internal states causally responsible in processing and producing novel sentences. So tacitly knowing T_2 really is like explicitly knowing it, for the tacit knowledge amounts to having discrete states whose causal role in comprehension mirrors the role which explicit theoretical knowledge of T_2 would play if you explicitly knew T_2.

This argument, which is due to Evans, does not turn on the speaker's potential for understanding an infinite number of sentences.[8] It turns on the capacity to understand novel sentences. The argument requires a realistic construal of knowledge of linguistic structure – there are internal states corresponding with axioms in the truth theory. It is important to note, however, that it is possible to develop an alternative way of thinking of tacit knowledge that does not require this kind of realism about internal states. Evans's model treats practical mastery of a language as really a form of theoretical knowledge represented in the realistic acceptance of discrete internal states. The alternative model applies to practical knowledge just as much as to theoretical knowledge. In other words, the capacity for novel behaviour is not restricted to theoretical knowledge; hence, nothing in Davidson's idea need commit us to the view that linguistic understanding is really a species of theoretical knowledge.[9]

Consider the range of skills: knowing how to make pastry, knowing how to swim, knowing how to play a musical instrument, knowing how to speak a language. Possession of these skills enables a subject to undertake certain activities, and these activities are all, potentially, subject to a combinatorial analysis that reveals how the skilful activity can be broken down into component actions that have come together in an appropriate manner. In the case of the first two skills, it is possible for a subject to undertake the activity without any awareness of its potential for a combinatorial analysis and, therefore, without receiving any detailed instruction in the component actions. In the case of playing a musical instrument, it is implausible to suppose that a subject could undertake the activity without some grasp of the combinatorial structure of the activity. In the case of knowing how to speak a language, there is, I suggest, no scope whatsoever for a subject to exercise the activity without that activity being representable as a function of combinatorial elements. It does not matter whether the subject is actually aware of the combinatorial analysis that applies to speaking a language. What matters is this: If the activity that the speaker engages in is not susceptible to an analysis that reveals its combinatorial structure, then the activity cannot be the activity of speaking a language. That requirement does not hold of some of the other examples of skill-based knowing how – swimming, riding a bike, etc. – regardless of whether or not we think of these things as raw behavioural skills.

The point that differentiates the intelligent deployment of language and the sort of skill the execution of which you could 'have a go at' independently of any training and learning, is that the skill of language mastery is *necessarily* a combinatorial skill; it is necessarily subject to a combinatorial analysis. Swimming is not necessarily like this. The young child who jumps in the water and swims without instruction is not handicapped in their ability to swim if they are unable to separate the component parts of the activity and, for example, make the connection between different types of swimming strokes. For such a child, their capacity to swim has no generality to it because for such a child swimming is an undifferentiated action. Matters are different for the trained competitive swimmer.

The trained competitive swimmer has a capacity for swimming that has generality, for they have learnt how to distinguish different component actions of the activity. They can adjust their breathing independently of their arm movements. They can make slight changes in their leg movements independently of the rest of the action. The trained competitive swimmer has learnt how to decompose swimming into its component sub-actions and to recombine those parts in different ways in order to find the optimum style for their physique and the prevailing conditions.

There are two points that flow from this. First, what the trained competitive swimmer knows in knowing how to swim is how to perform an action that is subject to a combinatorial analysis. It is because their knowing how to perform the action has a combinatorial structure that we say they are a trained swimmer. For such an individual, knowing how to swim is a complex knowledge subject to a combinatorial analysis.

Second, it does not follow from this that the trained swimmer's knowing how to swim consists in the theoretical knowledge that a sports scientist would employ in characterizing the component sub-actions of successful swimming. The trained swimmer's knowledge of the various component sub-actions of successful swimming may be all instances of knowing-how, for they might not have any propositionally codified representations of the sub-actions. They simply know that when they are doing the crawl, they have to move their legs in a certain way – a way that they can feel to be the correct way in terms of their proprioceptive sense. Nevertheless, although the trained swimmer's knowing how to swim need not consist in their possession of the theoretical knowledge that the sports scientist employs to analyse their skill, that theoretical representation of their skill is an empirically testable model of what they know. For every atomic component of the theoretical analysis, there will be a discrete sub-action that the swimmer is capable of distinguishing. For every principle of combination of atomic components represented in the theoretical analysis, given their possession of the capacity to perform the sub-actions, there will be a capacity on the swimmer's part to produce novel molecular actions composed of the sub-actions without explicit training in the novel molecular action.

Even with the relatively simple business of knowing how to swim, we have to be careful how we express these points. To say that the swimmer is capable of distinguishing a sub-action does not mean that the sub-action can be performed in isolation from any other component of the overall activity. Consider a finely discriminated sub-action of competitive swimming: e.g. the action of entering the leading hand into the water at one specified angle rather than another. To say that this is a sub-action that the agent can distinguish does not mean that they can perform this sub-action independently of swimming, although that may be true for some sub-actions. A first stab at what the discriminative ability to distinguish a particular sub-action means is the idea that there be two whole actions of swimming the only difference between which is that in one the leading hand enters the water at such-and-such an angle and in the other action it enters at a different angle. This, however, is not quite right. If there were two such distinct whole actions of swimming that differed only in this respect, this does not show that the respect in which they differ is a genuinely discrete sub-action, for the two different actions may have originated and been learned quite independently of one another.

To capture the idea of a distinguishable sub-action, we need to capture the thought that the sub-action can be repeated and combined with other action components in a way that rules out the possibility that the action comprising the combination was learnt as a one-off whole routine. But that is to require that the sub-action be a repeatable action component that can, in the light of the recursive combinatorial structure of the actions, give rise to novel whole actions. More generally:

> Where $a_1, \ldots, a_n$ are distinguishable sub-actions of a range of distinct actions represented as simple concatenations of sub-actions '$a_1{\wedge}a_2$' etc., then a_1 is a distinguishable sub-action iff for any pair of discrete whole actions, e.g. '$a_1{\wedge}a_2$' and '$a_2{\wedge}a_3$' that the agent can perform, they have the capacity without further training to perform the action '$a_1{\wedge}a_3$'.

In real life the situation is much more complicated, for the above treats whole actions as concatenations of component routines. In real life there will be constraints on which routines can be concatenated together, constraints that come from physical limitations of the human body and the general rules of the activity. These constraints amount to a grammar for the activity in question.

Nevertheless, the above idea shows the way that the atomic routines appealed to in the combinatorial analysis of the skill are fundamentally identified as what is common between a trio of molecular actions. It is the notion of the molecular action

95

that is prior; the notion of the atomic sub-action is defined by decomposition on a range of molecular actions. Sub-actions are fixed by a triangulation from three distinct whole actions.[10]

The idea that the theoretical knowledge of the sports scientist represents what the trained swimmer knows amounts to the following claim: The theoretical representation of the swimmer's skill will be accurate just in case the systematic structure of the theoretical knowledge successfully predicts the swimmer's behaviour: in particular, that it predicts the swimmer's capacity for novel behaviour, where novel behaviour is represented as the outcome of combinations of behavioural routines not previously concatenated together. The 'knowing that' embodied within the theory of swimming is empirically testable against the swimmer's behaviour. The reality of the ascription of a systematic structure of theoretical knowledge consists in the successful prediction of, and explanation of, the swimmer's capacity to produce new behaviour on the basis of the combinatorial structure of the behaviour acquired in training. In this respect, the theory represents the systematicity of knowing how to swim. The only difference between this case and the much more sophisticated case of using knowledge of a truth theory to represent knowing how to understand a language is that understanding a language is necessarily a skill with a combinatorial structure, whereas swimming is not necessarily combinatorial.

The reason why understanding a language is necessarily a skill with a combinatorial structure is that it is a pre-condition for language production and understanding to be semantically evaluable that it be systematically structured. In so far as our linguistic behaviour is a behaviour oriented towards truth, it must be subject to a combinatorial analysis. It is in virtue of the systematicity of the structure of that behaviour that we make sense of the behaviour being aimed at truth and it being assessable in terms of adequacy of aim.[11]

Given this essential systematicity of language mastery, then even if we thought that knowing how to understand a language was not fully representable in terms of theoretical knowledge, no harm would be done by a theoretical representation of the combinatorial structure of understanding. The reality of that structure does not require items of theoretical knowledge in the subject's head. The reality of the structure requires only the empirical testability of the postulation of systematic structure in the production of novel behaviour. There are two senses in which it is true that the reality of structure does not require positing in-the-head states. First, it does not require the representationalist model, in which the knowledge is conceived as internal representations. Second, it does not require the positing of internal states that are causally responsible for the overt behaviour. Evans's model of tacit knowledge, while not representationalist, treats that ascription of tacit knowledge as placing constraints on cognitive science, for he treats the ascription as requiring discrete internal states that are causally responsible for behaviour.

Cognitive science is then expected to produce models compatible with the individuation of internal states provided by the ascription of tacit knowledge. The reality of the ascription as I have now characterized it is weaker than in Evans's account.[12] My account is not, however, merely behaviourist, for the behavioural adequacy required for ascription of tacit knowledge includes the facility for novel behaviour. This means that the behaviour appealed to is described in intentionally rich vocabulary. It cannot be behaviour as causally trained response to stimuli, for the requirement for a capacity for novelty is, arguably, richer than behaviour described in terms of its training history.[13]

The ascription of tacit knowledge of the theory is empirically testable against the behaviour of the subject. The fact that the tacit theoretical knowledge ascribes knowledge with a systematic combinatorial structure means that it predicts that whole actions have common component parts, and on that claim turns the predictive and explanatory power of the ascription of tacit knowledge. If whole actions really have component parts, then the agent will have the capacity to recombine them in ways permissible by the theory and to produce novel whole actions for which the agent has not been specifically trained. In conclusion, the ascription of tacit theoretical knowledge in explanation of a case of knowing how does not require that we treat the ascription of structural theoretical knowledge as theoretical knowledge in the subject's head. What we need to assume is that the structure represented in the theoretical knowledge is in the subject's behaviour; that is where the real structure lies. Only if we assume that behaviour is to be explained causally in terms of in-the-head states will this have implications for what we take to be in the head. If we make that assumption, then if our behaviour has a combinatorial structure, so too we will expect the causal states that produce the behaviour to have a structure suitable for producing the combinatorial possibilities of behaviour.[14] Although this model of explanation is not required, it does suggest an important sort of case for the empirical testability of ascriptions of tacit knowledge.

The assumption of tacit knowledge is empirically testable in terms of its success in predicting novel whole behaviours. In addition, the assumption that component behavioural routines each have a common cause in the head requires a modularity to neurophysiological mechanisms. These are not perhaps directly testable, but they do suggest an important category of cases. The modularity hypothesis means that certain kinds of dysfunctionality will be possible. If a discrete behavioural routine has an isolatable causal source in the head, it should be possible for that causal source to suffer damage without impairing performance of other routines in the overall behavioural repertoire. Put simply, it should be possible for trained swimmers to lose the ability to control their hands without the losing the ability to control their legs. Case-studies of cognitive dysfunction are an important source for empirically testing ascriptions of tacit knowledge as models of knowing how. Such cases will not necessarily discriminate between the Evans account of tacit knowledge and the behaviourist account that I have defended. It will all depend on the fineness of discrimination of dysfunction whether we get something that tells in favour of a realism about in-the-head states. The behaviourist account suggested is compatible with allowing some relation between rationalizing explanations of behaviour and the account of the mechanisms that underpin its production. All it denies is that the relationship is one of identity.[15]

4.3   Two Conceptions of Theory

In the light of the previous section, the idea of employing a systematic body of theoretical knowledge as a means of representing linguistic understanding is legitimate. I have suggested that the ascription of theoretical knowledge as an explanation of linguistic mastery does not have to been taken at face value, for the reality of the ascription is tested in how we behave, not in terms of packages of theoretical knowledge in the head. But this immediately raises a further general issue about the very point of a theory of meaning as Davidson conceives of it.

Contrast two conceptions of a theory of meaning. The first conception I call the manual-theory of meaning, the second I shall call the theory-theory of meaning. The first conception is the idea of a theory of meaning as a manual of meanings that is, in principle, completable for a natural language like English. The manual-theory of meaning aims to produce a manual that catalogues what a competent speaker of English knows. The theory has to produce a full codification of all the meanings expressible in a language. It is natural, I think, to assume that what Davidson originally had in mind was the production of a manual-theory of meaning.

The theory-theory of meaning has different aspirations. By the theory-theory of meaning, I mean a project to theorize about meaning and to provide in outline a general account of the skills and knowledge a subject has to have in order to possess linguistic competence and intentionality. Such an account would need to address in general what the constraints are on ascribing linguistic competence to a subject: for example, the capacity for novel sentence production and comprehension on the basis of the combinatorial systematicity of the knowledge that underlies competence. In providing this general account, it seems reasonable to expect that the theory-theory would, in addition, plot the general connections between our concepts of meaning, inference, truth and the world.

There are a number of points to bear in mind in considering whether Davidson was proposing a manual-theory of meaning or a theory-theory of meaning. First, if the proposal was for the former, we can ask for whom the manual is to be written. And then, the more we emphasize the modesty of Davidson's proposal, the more we shall be drawn to conclude that Davidson was not proposing a manual-theory of meaning. That is, the more we emphasize that the theory of meaning describes the systematic structure of meaning in a way that is graspable only to those who already employ the language at issue, the less likely it is that we can see the pretensions of the theory as transcending those of a theory-theory of meaning. Contrariwise, if we expect a theory of meaning to represent the meaning of a natural language like English in such a way that a visiting alien to our planet could, on receipt of Davidson's theory, become a fully competent speaker of English, then we are expecting a manual-theory of meaning.

Second, in so far as Davidson uses his idea of a theory of meaning to underwrite a theory of radical interpretation, it is natural to construe him as offering a manual-theory of meaning, for the theory provides the manual for the interpretation of the radical alien. This point will be dealt with below; for now I merely note the temptation to connect the idea of a manual-theory of meaning with the enterprise of radical interpretation, although if we succumb to this temptation, we ignore the difference between Davidson's project of radical interpretation and Quine's more extreme project of radical translation.[16]

Third, if the theory is offered as a manual-theory of meaning, it is tempting to treat the ascription of tacit knowledge realistically, as literal reports of the repertoire of knowledge states in the head of the competent linguist. If the theory is to have explanatory power, and if the theory is understood as a manual-theory, then the in principle completable codification of knowledge of meanings for distinct linguistic items must serve some explanatory purpose. The natural thought is to suppose that the explanatory purpose of the ascription of this knowledge resides in the fact that for each tacitly known axiom of the theory, there is a real discrete state in the head that is causally responsible for each occurrence of understanding of, and competent production of, the linguistic item specified in that axiom. On the other hand, the more we stress the idea that the ascriptions of tacit knowledge should not be read so literally, that the reality of the ascription resides in the combinatorial character of the subject's behaviour rather than in the combinatorial structure of the insides of the head, the more we might expect that the theory is a theory-theory of meaning, not a manual-theory.

It is important also to bear in mind that, even construed as a theory-theory of meaning, the theory may have substantive consequences for issues in the philosophy of psychology. We should not assume that it is only if the theory is construed as a manual-theory, with the ascription of tacit knowledge viewed as the postulation of discrete states in the head, that the theory places any interesting constraints on work in the philosophy of psychology. To make that assumption is to assume a host of connected points about the relation between explanations in cognitive science, explanations in our ordinary folk-psychological understanding of ourselves, assumptions about the proper constraints of physicalism, and much else besides. It is tempting to suppose that only a manual-theory of meaning, with its literal construal of linguistic competence modelled on a combinatorial structure of in-the-head items, will bear upon matters in the philosophy of mind and philosophy of psychology, and that this, in some way, speaks in favour of a manual-theory of meaning. But this temptation should be resisted.

Note, the present point about the kind of theory that the theory of meaning is supposed to be connects with the methodological issues raised in chapter 1. I advocated a Fregean approach to the study of thought and language. One of the components of that approach is the idea that an a priori study of thought could be undertaken independently of empirical theories of the way that our competent use of language is implemented in our physical nature. I contrasted the Fregean and physicalistic methodologies in the philosophy of thought. The issue about whether Davidson offers a manual-theory of meaning or a theory-theory of meaning is related. To think that a manual-theory of meaning is to be preferred because it gives a ready purchase on our theorizing in the philosophy of psychology is to demand of the theory of meaning that it should directly link up with scientific models of our intelligence – models that treat intelligence as a function of the combinatorial structure of items within the head. This is the classical model in AI work. But to think this is to constrain the theory of meaning by its fitness to map on to current empirical models.[17]

In contrast, if the theory that Davidson is proposing is a theory-theory of meaning, and the ascriptions of tacit knowledge are understood as making claims about the combinatorial character of the subject's behaviour rather than their in-the-head states, this is more likely to be seen as a contribution to an a priori study of our intentionality. Again, this is not to say that such a study has no bearing on the adequacy of empirical models of the physical structures that implement our intelligence; it is only to say that the bearing is not direct, and that the structure of the theory-theory is not directly constrained by current fashions regarding the best account to be offered of these physical structures.

4.4   From Platitude to Theory

The argument of section 4.2 establishes a number of methodological claims that have become central to contemporary philosophy of thought and also to the philosophy of psychology. If that argument is right, the programme to characterize understanding a language by producing a model of understanding as tacit theoretical knowledge is legitimate. What we do not yet know is why that theoretical knowledge should be knowledge of a truth theory. In this section I show how Davidson originally argued for this, and then explain the way that the justification for characterizing understanding meaning in terms of knowledge of the truth-conditions of sentences flows from a platitudinous connection between our concept of assertoric content and truth.[18]

The model for linguistic competence is knowledge of a Tarskian truth theory for a natural language. By modelling understanding in terms of knowledge of such a theory, the theory of meaning will (i) give the meaning of every sentence expressible in the language; (ii) show how sentences are constructed from a finite stock of components with a recursively specifiable set of construction rules; and (iii) be empirically testable. The idea expressed in (i) suggests that the theory will be a manual-theory of meaning, and that is the way that it is naturally read in Davidson's original presentation.

Davidson begins by suggesting that we need a theory of meaning to be able to complete the following schema for all sentences of a natural language:

(1)   *s* means *m*,

where '*s*' is a structural description of a sentence, and '*m*' an expression that picks out its meaning. The requirement that '*s*' is a structural description of a sentence is the requirement that the theory should be a structure-discerning theory and have the ability, in terms of its account of the recursive structure of the language, to describe every sentence expressible in the language. The problem with using (1) as the basic schema for a theory of meaning is that it presupposes a notion of sentence meaning, the very idea that we want some purchase on.

Davidson's next suggestion is that, were we to require instead that a theory of meaning be able to complete the schema,

(2)   *s* means that *p*,

we would be no better off; for the notion of 'means that' is no less problematic than the concept of meaning that the theory is supposed to elucidate. Note the way in which in these manoeuvrings Davidson is requiring that a theory of meaning should be able to give an account of meaning for every sentence in the language, without presupposing semantic notions synonymous with '. . . means . . .', '. . . means that . . .', etc. We want a theory that will, for every sentence of the language, give an account of what knowing the meaning of that sentence is; but we do not want the theory to employ the concept of meaning, or something synonymous with it, in specifying the meaning. This seems to place us in an intolerable bind. Surely any theory that really captures the meaning of any given sentence will have to employ some concept synonymous with meaning, or it will fail to capture the pre-theoretic notion with which we started.

Suppose the aim of a theory of meaning is to produce an individual clause governing each sentence expressible in the language such that that clause alone specifies the meaning of the sentence. If the theory is capable of producing such a piecemeal account of meaning, it must be susceptible to the charge of being vacuous or fallacious. The supposition that the theory works piecemeal is the supposition that we could complete a schema for arbitrary sentence *s* such that the completion of that individual clause said everything that needed saying about the meaning of *s*. But suppose the schema employed a semantic concept less than synonymous with 'means that'. It does not matter what that concept is, but schematically it can be represented as

    (3)   *s* approximately means that *p*.

Clearly, this is inadequate, and not because the word 'means' appears within it. (3) is inadequate because any theory that produced instances of this would, *ex hypothesi*, produce a clause regarding the arbitrary sentence *s* such that the clause did not account in full for the meaning of *s*, but would leave something unsaid. Such a theory would then be false. But for a piecemeal theory there is no way to remedy this failing other than to admit as the central semantic concept either the concept of meaning itself or something synonymous with it or so close to the concept of meaning that the theory is vacuous. For example, we would not expect a theory that produced instances of the following schema to be an informative theory of meaning,

    (4)   *s* is translatable as *p*.

A theory of meaning that produced instances of (4) would leave the account of meaning too closely tied to a concept every much in need of explication as the concept of meaning is.

The requirement that the theory of meaning explicate the concept of meaning in a way that is not totally vacuous is the requirement that prompts Davidson's rejection of (1) and (2) as adequate schema for a theory of meaning to complete. The requirement appears licit. It also seems right to think that this requirement is impossible to meet if we assume that the theory is a piecemeal theory. Davidson's central insight was that we could, and should, dispense with the idea of a piecemeal theory of meaning. In its place, Davidson thought that a theory that produced instances of a schema

    s xxxxxx *p*,

where the x's were filled in with a semantic concept less rich than that of meaning, could still amount to a theory of meaning if we drop the idea that individual instances of the schema exhaust the account of the meaning of the sentences that appear on the left-hand side of those instances. As we have seen, no such piecemeal approach can work; but by dropping the piecemeal approach, we can gain explanatory illumination on the concept of meaning with a central semantic concept in the schema that is less than meaning itself. The illumination is provided by the way that the theory derives each instance of this schema systematically from an overall theory for the whole language. The unit of significance is not, then, the individual piecemeal instance of the schema. It is the whole language. That is Davidson's suggestion.

Davidson notes that if we replace the 'means that' in (2) with the extensional idiom

    . . . is T iff____,

we get

    (5)   *s* is T iff *p*,

where once again *s* is a structural description of a sentence of the language and *p* a sentence that translates *s*; then, any predicate that takes the place of 'T' in (5) is truth, for the condition that a theory be capable of producing instances of (5) is Tarski's material adequacy condition on a definition of truth. There is no more to having a materially adequate definition of truth than having a theory that allows us to derive for any sentence of the language an instance of (5). Davidson's claim is that a theory of truth that entailed all true instances of schema (5) would be the heart of a theory of meaning, for knowing such a truth theory would amount to knowing the meaning of all sentences expressible in the language. Knowing the meaning of a sentence is knowing its truth-conditions. A theory of truth applied to a natural language like English containing e.g. the sentence 'Snow is white' is a theory that allows us to derive for all sentences of English a statement of their truth-conditions:

    (6)   'Snow is white' is true iff Snow is white.

Therefore, knowing a theory that entails all and only all the correct statements of the truth-conditions for sentences of English is knowing the meaning of English.

Many people, on being confronted with the above suggestion, feel that they have been subjected to a sleight of hand. In order to clarify what is going on, let me summarize Davidson's key suggestion:

> **D:** To know the meaning of English is to know a truth theory that entails all true instances of *s* is true iff *p*; e.g. to know a truth theory that entails 'Snow is white' is true iff snow is white.

Here are four concerns regarding the adequacy of **D**. (i) Although the suggestion that employing the '. . . is true iff____' locution would result in a theory that appears to give the right results, no justification has been given for why we should employ truth as the central semantic concept rather than any other semantic concept, such as warranted assertibility. (ii) The '. . . is true iff____' construction is an extensional idiom; as such, it cannot help but fail to give an account of the meaning of the sentence that appears on the left-hand side. (iii) The clauses produced by the proposed theory of truth – e.g. 'Snow is white' is true iff snow is white – are trivially true, and so cannot be constitutive of the grasp of the meaning of the sentence 'Snow is white'. (iv) Any theory that produced the theorems as required would have to be stated in a metalanguage. Suppose the metalanguage is English. But that is to presuppose that all the meanings of alien tongues are expressible in English or we would not be able to produce the kind of theory which **D** says that we can. This amounts to semantic imperialism.

None of the above four charges sticks to Davidson's work, but in seeing how and why they get addressed, we are led to a much better appreciation both of what Davidson is saying and also of the philosophical and metaphysical import of his work for a general theory of thought. In the rest of this section I reply to the first charge; the remaining three sections will then deal with charges (ii) and (iii) and introduce some ideas about the modesty of Davidson's programme. I tackle (iv) in the next chapter.

The idea that we could produce a theory of meaning with something other than truth as the central semantic concept has become the rallying point for a number of writers. It lies at the heart of a protracted debate about realism and anti-realism. I leave a full discussion of that debate to a later chapter.[19] For now, I want to locate the idea that the use of truth as the central semantic concept is legitimized by a series of platitudes about the nature of assertoric content.[20]

Although it does not exhaust the notion of linguistic meaning, the idea of assertoric content is a central component to our intuitive idea of meaning. Assertoric content is the notion of what is said by a sincere utterance of a sentence. The notion of what is said is the notion of something that is subject to semantic evaluation; it is the notion of that which stands to be assessed as correct or incorrect. In so far as to make an assertion – issue an assertoric content – is to do something that can be assessed for the correctness of that content, then the notion of assertoric content presupposes some notion of standards of correctness and incorrectness. Now, there is room for a debate about quite what those standards of correctness and incorrectness amount to; but the following seems a minimal requirement: the idea of an assertoric content being incorrect amounts to the idea that an assertion of that content is mistaken, where the concept of a mistake invokes the idea of things independent of the speaker not being as the speaker claims. This, surely, is a banal platitude about the connection between the idea of assertoric content and the idea that such contents are to be disciplined or corrected by things independent of the speaker. There is no extravagant metaphysics implicated in this notion of discipline; it is the baseline required for the very idea of assertoric content to get off the ground. There is no harm in saying that the idea of truth-conditions appealed to by Davidson is no more and no less than the idea of the conditions of correct and incorrect assertion, where that provides some notion of discipline to assertoric contents, provides content to the notion of a mistake.[21]

4.5   One More Brush-stroke

The theory, knowledge of which is supposed to model knowledge of meaning, is a theory that employs an extensional idiom in its axioms and theorems. The second concern with **D** was this: Can an extensional theory capture the notion of meaning? Completion of the schema '. . . is true iff_____' requires only that the items on either side are true under the same circumstances and false under the same circumstances. This is less than the requirement that they have the same meaning. You can't get meaning out of extensional equivalence. Therefore the theory cannot work.

This concern misses the central point that Davidson is making. If the theory were offering a piecemeal account of meaning, such that the theorem for any given sentence *s* on its own gave an account of the meaning of *s*, then, as already argued in the previous section, no such theory could work. But even in his earliest writings, Davidson was clear that he was not proposing a piecemeal theory. The suggestion in **D** is that knowledge of a theory that entails all true instances of the schema counts as knowing the meaning of the language. The knowledge at issue is not piecemeal knowledge of the meaning of sentences one by one; it is holistic knowledge of the meaning of a whole language. This holistic knowledge is modelled in terms of knowledge of a theory that entails all true instances of the schema. Here is how Davidson put the point:

> The theory reveals nothing new about the conditions under which an individual sentence is true: it does not make those conditions any clearer than the sentence itself does. The work of the theory is in relating the known truth conditions of each sentence to those aspects (words) of the sentence that recur in other sentences and can be assigned identical roles in other sentences.[22]

The work of the theory consists in the way that it displays the systematicity of meaning, the way that the account of the truth-conditions for any one sentence is systematically related to the account of the truth-conditions for a whole range of other sentences. Our understanding of meaning is essentially holistic.

> What appears to the right of the biconditional plays its role in determining the meaning of *s* not by pretending synonymy but by adding one more brush-

stroke to the picture which taken as a whole tells what there is to know of the meaning of *s*.[23]

The point is central to Davidson's conception of a theory of meaning and to a proper understanding of everything that has flowed from Davidson's work – in particular, the connection between holism in the theory of meaning and the holistic character of our very concept of what it is to be rational. Davidson's claim is that to know the meaning of *s* is not simply to know a theorem of the form *s* is true iff *p*; it is to know a theory that entails such a theorem.[24]

The point is best seen in the context of interpretation when we are trying to fix the meaning of sentences of an alien language. Suppose an alien speaker produces the sentence

nows si hitew,

and suppose that we spot that

(7)   'nows si hitew' is true iff snow is white.

Even if we know that (7) is true, we do not yet know the meaning of 'nows si hitew'. It might be a lucky coincidence that 'nows si hitew' is true in just those circumstances in which snow is white and false when it is not the case that snow is white. The extensional equivalence between the alien sentence and our own is not sufficient to determine sameness of meaning.

Now consider an alternative situation. Suppose as above that we spot that (7) is true, but also that we have spotted a systematicity to alien sentence production. For example, '. . . si hitew' crops up systematically in the production of sentences whose truth-value is extensionally equivalent to the truth-value of a series of our sentences predicating whiteness of different things – chalk, the cliffs of Dover, the US presidential residency, etc. Suppose also that the other part of the alien sentence crops up systematically in the production of sentences whose truth-value is extensionally equivalent to the truth-value of a series of our sentences about snow – its coldness, its preponderance in northern latitudes in winter, its suitability as a surface for skiing on, etc. In this alternative situation we have, in effect, supposed that we could order the complexity of alien sentence production by seeing it as systematically dependent on the deployment and redeployment of a recurrent component structure. Where we can impose this much structure upon the alien sentence production, we can, in effect, suppose that the aliens' sentence production is the joint upshot of a grasp of the semantic role of distinct sentence components plus rules for combining these components in truth-determining ways.

Once we can detect such structure, we are licensed to suppose that the aliens' mastery of their language consists in their tacit knowledge that, amongst other things

    (8)   x satisfies '. . . si hitew' iff x is white

and

    (9)   'nows' denotes snow

and, amongst other rules of combination they know,

    (10)   'NN^F' is true iff the item denoted by 'NN' satisfies 'F'.

Indeed, were the aliens to see no connection between their utterance of 'nows si hitew' and other remarks either about white things or about snow, then that would be conclusive evidence that whatever 'nows si hitew' means, it could not mean that snow is white, even if it were the case that 'nows si hitew' was true just in case snow is white.[25]

The holistic character of linguistic understanding is central to Davidson's conception of a theory of meaning. As I argued in chapter 1, the requirement that our language and thought have this systematicity is a condition for the possibility that our thought and talk be subject to semantic evaluation. Again, consider the alien production of the sentence 'nows si hitew'. Suppose not only that we can detect no systematic way that the production of this string is related to noises produced in the presence of either white things or of snow, but also that we can detect no systematic way that the production of this string is related to any other noise production or behaviour that could aptly be seen as a mode of assertoric expression. Given this last supposition, it is difficult to see what it amounts to to say that the alien is saying that snow is white. If someone has the capacity to say this, then should they not have the capacity to say that things other than snow are white also? If they lack that general capacity, then they lack the capacity to assert the target assertion that snow is white.

The point here is the same as the point argued for in chapter 1 – Evans's generality constraint. It is the point that explains why the parrot that has been trained to say 'Snow is white' does not mean that snow is white even if it only ever utters the sentence in the presence of snow. It cannot mean that snow is white, because it lacks the concept of whiteness, and it lacks that because it lacks the general capacity to predicate whiteness of different things. Grasp of meaning – concept possession – does not come piecemeal; it is essentially holistic.

Now, if understanding a language is essentially holistic, we appear to face a potentially insuperable problem *vis-à-vis* Davidson's theory construed as a manual-theory of meaning. The problem concerns the principles of individuation for languages. Holism says that the unit of significance is the whole language, but what constitutes a whole language? From the developmental point of view, the problem becomes the issue of at what point we would be right to say that the infant learning the language has grasped the concept of whiteness as opposed to merely mimicking discrete productions of sentences with '. . . is white' in them. The developmental problem is less pressing, for although it is difficult to define the point at which an infant moves beyond mimicry to meaningful language production, we know that there is a difference, and furthermore that human infants cross that boundary with alacrity. What is more pressing is the question about the individuation of a language.

Suppose a speaker S understands that whiteness can be predicated of snow, but not of anything else. Our speaker has no capacity to predicate whiteness of any other kind of object. This amounts to saying that she has no capacity for making the inference from

Snow is white

to

Something is white,

for if she could do that, then she could also understand the sentence obtained by replacing the existential quantifier with any arbitrary name. Such a speaker is then like a parrot. She has no real grasp of the concept of whiteness at all. But how much else, beyond the capacity to form the sentence 'Snow is white', must our speaker be capable of before we say that she understands the concept of whiteness? What is the minimum size for a language?

In the absence of a well-motivated individuation of what constitutes a language, we can have no principled account of what constitutes the manual of meanings that a manual-theory of meaning aims to provide. It is, nevertheless, tempting to think that this problem can be avoided in the following way. What the manual-theory imputes to the speaker is the tacit knowledge of axioms and rules of combination that underpin the systematicity of sentence production and understanding. All that need appear in the manual is the list of the axioms and recursive rules of combination. What size language, in the sense of the number of sentences that our speaker actually produces, is irrelevant. Unfortunately, to say this would be to get the order of priority wrong. The positing of tacit knowledge of axioms and recursive rules is made to account for concept mastery. Concept mastery is constituted by a capacity for sentence production and understanding that satisfies the generality constraint. Of course, we think that concept mastery can be modelled by ascribing tacit knowledge of the axioms and recursive rules, but the question about the individuation of a language is a question about the basis on which it would be legitimate to posit the existence of such tacit knowledge; it cannot be ignored by merely going ahead and positing the tacit knowledge.

In section 4.3 I distinguished two different ways in which one might construe the realistic ascription of tacit knowledge of axioms. One way is to treat the ascription as true in virtue of discrete in-the-head states of the speaker. The other way is to see it as true in virtue of the common component structure of the speaker's behaviour. The latter way is incompatible with the manual-theory of meaning, especially given the holism that is essential to the enterprise. But even if the ascription of tacit knowledge is construed as making reference to discrete in-the-head states, it remains the case that the evidence for this ascription has to lie in the combinatorial complexity of the speaker's behaviour. So the problem about the identity conditions of a language becomes: How complex must a speaker's behaviour be in order to license ascription of the in-the-head states that constitutes the tacit knowledge of the axiom governing the predicate '. . . is white'? There must be an answer to this question if the theory is to be construed as a manual-theory of meaning. The absence of any well-motivated way of providing an answer to this question is reason for thinking of the idea of a theory of meaning as the idea of a theory-theory.

4.6   Not a Lot of People Know That . . .

Davidson's idea of a theory of meaning looks plausible when we state a theory of meaning for one language – say German – in a different language – e.g. English. Such a theory provides theorems of the kind

'Der Schnee ist weiss' is true iff snow is white,

and such theorems have the advantage of appearing to convey real information, in contrast to

(11)   'Snow is white' is true iff snow is white.

A theory that produces theorems like (11), in which the metalanguage in which the theory is stated is an extension of the object language, is called a homophonic theory of meaning. The temptation that needs resisting is to think that (11) is trivially true. This is a mistake, but one that many students are prone to make on first reading Davidson. It is the mistake of assuming that only a non-homophonic theory of meaning – a theory of translation – can be informative.

The fact that (11) is not trivial is borne out by the fact that a lot of people do not know that (11) is true. Monolingual French speakers do not know (11). The reason that they do not know (11) is that they do not understand the sentence embedded within it. The same point applies to the axioms employed with a Davidsonian theory of meaning, e.g.

(12)   x satisfies '. . . is white' iff x is white.

As Evans and McDowell succinctly put it, (12) states an 'eminently learnable and forgettable fact about the relationship between an English word and [the world]'.[26]

The point is general. Whether we consider the axioms or the theorems produced by the theory, the items on the right-hand side of clauses like (11) and (12) pick out worldly states of affairs. The whole clause states a relationship between linguistic items – on the left-hand side – and worldly items. The relationship picked out is, in the case of (11), the relationship that the linguistic item bears to the world when it is true. The relationship is not the correspondence relationship of truth. The relationship is merely that of extensional correlation of truth of a sentence with a worldly circumstance. All (11) says is that if the sentence is true, snow is white, and if snow is white, the sentence is true.[27]

Extensional equivalence is not a relation of correspondence. Nevertheless, two points follow. First, knowing that (11) is true is still knowing a substantial fact that correlates language and world. Second, knowing a theory that equips you with such knowledge because your derivation of (11) is systematically related to knowledge of theorems for the rest of the language is to know a general correlation between language and world which rules out the possibility that knowing (11) is, as it were, merely a one-off stroke of luck. If this explanation of why knowing (11), let alone knowing a theory that entails (11), still leaves you feeling shortchanged, consider the following explanation of why a homophonic theory of truth can be the basis for an account of the substantial knowledge that underpins understanding.

Let '*P*' be a sentence variable. We need to distinguish between knowing that *P*, and knowing that '*P*' is a truth. For example, if you accept that I am a competent speaker of Welsh and that I am a sincere speaker of Welsh sentences, then, on hearing me utter,

(13)   Y mae'r ddraig goch,

you will be entitled to say that you know that 'Y mae'r ddraig goch' is a truth. In such circumstances you will be an accurate reporter of a fact about a Welsh sentence. Of course, if you do not understand Welsh, then although you know that 'Y mae'r ddraig goch' is true, you will not know what is being said. You will not know what this sentence means, and so it could not be right for a competent Welsh speaker to say that you know that *Y mae'r ddraig goch*.[28] The distinction between the schema

knowing that '*P*' is a truth

and

knowing that *P*

is a distinction that turns on whether or not you understand the embedded sentence. A more limited example would be one in which someone failed to understand a component of the embedded sentence – e.g. a young child who hears her parents utter the sentence 'Uncle George is in Vancouver'. The child knows that this is about Uncle George, and, furthermore, that it is about him being in something called 'Vancouver'. But perhaps she knows nothing of what kind of object Vancouver is – it could be a mental state! The child knows that 'Uncle George is in Vancouver' is a truth, but we would hesitate to say that she knew that Uncle George is in Vancouver, for she does not understand the name 'Vancouver'.[29]

Given the above distinction, consider its application to complex sentence constructions. Consider again the Welsh sentence. It is, despite your lack of knowledge of Welsh, true to say that you know that

(14)   ' "Y mae'r ddraig goch" is true iff Y mae'r ddraig goch'

is a truth. You know that (14) is a truth, because you know that it is an instance of the general trick of disquotation. You know that anything of the form

'*P*' is true iff *P*

will be a truth simply in virtue of your grasp of the meaning of the predicate '. . . is true', the logical connective '. . . iff____', the notion of a dummy letter standing for any one sentence, plus the facility of forming a name by placing quotation marks around a sentence. Now, knowing that (14) is a truth is, if you know the above general points, trivial. Knowing that (14) is a truth is something that a monolingual speaker of English can know. Suppose we had a homophonic theory of meaning for Welsh, and, just to make matters simpler, suppose that the Welsh for '. . . is true', and '. . . iff____' is the same as the English. Now, Davidson's central claim is that competent speakers of Welsh know a homophonic theory that entails the theorem

(15)   'Y mae'r ddraig goch' is true iff Y mae'r ddraig goch,

111

and that, of course, is precisely what you do not know.

You know that (14) is a truth; that is trivial. You do not know (15), for that reports on the substantive relation between a Welsh sentence and worldly affairs. The difference between (14) and (15) is an instance of the difference between the two schema noted above. The reason you do not know (15) is because you do not understand Welsh. The difference between knowing that (14) is true and knowing (15) is the difference between competent Welsh speakers and the rest. But that is as it should be on Davidson's proposal, for that says that knowing a theory that entails (15) is what it is to understand Welsh. If you understood Welsh, you would know (15), and would then know what we would represent in a non-homophonic translation theory as

    (16)   'Y mae'r ddraig goch' is true iff the dragon is red.

A homophonic truth theory is a non-negligible theory of truth for a language. Furthermore, knowledge of such a truth theory for a natural language is non-trivial knowledge. Competent Welsh speakers are competent in virtue of their knowledge of a theory that entails (15), for that is something that non-Welsh speakers do not know. An immediate question is prompted by this recognition that knowledge of a theory that entails (15) is non-trivial: namely, is it possible for there to be a homophonic truth theory for a language that adequately represents what it is to understand that language, yet for it not to be possible to translate that language into English? This question forces us to address issues about the modesty of Davidson's conception of a theory of meaning.

Given the non-triviality of a homophonic truth theory as a basis for a theory of meaning, we can, as it were, give a theory of meaning for Welsh in Welsh. This, however, would appear to be a very modest achievement. Suppose such a theory were written down in a manual. Would possession of such a manual provide a non-Welsh speaker with the resources to understand Welsh? The point is not just that if you think that such a manual would not suffice for understanding Welsh, then Davidson's theory cannot be a manual-theory of meaning. The point goes deeper. The question whether possession of the homophonic manual-theory of meaning for Welsh is adequate for understanding Welsh turns on whether or not Welsh contains concepts that are untranslatable into English. If Welsh concepts are fully translatable into English, you might think that a homophonic Welsh theory of meaning would suffice for understanding; for the systematic structure described by the theory would provide sufficient theoretical constraint to pin down the meaning of any given sentence and, as it were, grant us entry to the Welsh view of the world. But now, suppose the Welsh view of the world is different. Suppose, that is, that there are Welsh concepts that do not translate into English, and that all one can do is to provide the homophonic axiom,[30]

(17)   x satisfies 'Y mae'r . . . prydferth' iff Y mae'r x prydferth.

If that were the case, the idea of a theory of meaning would be a very modest idea, for it would amount to no more than a description of the systematic structure of the meaning of any given language from within the conceptual scheme embedded in that language. It would display the structure of our conceptual scheme, but the display would be of only local interest.

In a sense, Davidson does think that a theory of meaning is a homely local exercise, except that he also believes that the relevant locale includes all rational creatures, for he believes that there are no homophonic axioms that could not be translated. The consequence of this can be roughly stated by saying that on Davidson's account there is only one conceptual scheme, one that all rational creatures share. As we shall see, this is not an accurate way of reporting Davidson's position, for he believes that there is no such thing as a conceptual scheme. Whatever that means, it certainly means that Davidson is committed to the idea that there is no homophonic axiom that cannot be translated. These are powerful conclusions, especially given the apparent modesty of Davidson's enterprise. In the next section I distinguish different senses in which Davidson's idea of a theory of meaning is modest, a theory that describes the structure of the meanings through which we view the world. In the next chapter I examine the claim that there is no such thing as a conceptual scheme.

4.7   Modesty

I want to distinguish four senses in which Davidson's conception of a theory of meaning is a modest conception. These four senses involve the claims that

(i)   the theory involves no conceptual analysis;
(ii)   the theory merely describes the systematicity of meaning in a language by revealing its logical grammar;
(iii) the theory presupposes an uncontentious although realist concept of truth;
(iv)   in describing the systematicity of meaning in a language, the theory describes the structure of our conceptual scheme.

I shall discuss the third kind of modesty in chapter 6. Discussion of the fourth variety will occupy most of the next chapter.

The point that the theory of meaning provides no conceptual analysis was clear in Davidson's earliest writings. With regard to the sentence 'Bardot is good', he says that it is no part of the job of a theory of meaning as he conceives it that it should explain the meaning of the concept 'good' other than by showing how the concept is systematically related to others in the production of sentences that are true.[31] The point that the theory provides no conceptual analysis is then simply that the combinatorial structure employed by the theory will be a structure the axioms of which are axioms governing the use of concept words, like

x satisfies '. . . is good' iff x is good.

Any systematic theory of meaning will have to have some basic level represented in the theory's axioms. This basic level will consist of axioms governing the assignment of semantic value to the atoms of the language. An atom is no more than a linguistic item whose semantic value is assigned, rather than computed. To say that there is no conceptual analysis in Davidson's theory is then to say no more than that the semantic value for a concept expression is not computed from an assignment of any more basic category of linguistic item. Given that there has to be some such basic level, it is not clear that it is an objection to Davidson's theory to say that it is modest with respect to conceptual analysis.

Note also that although concepts are not treated as complex semantic items, there is one sense in which the meaning of a concept expression is not simple. This turns on the holism of Davidson's project. The axiom governing any single concept expression does not of itself specify the meaning of the expression; it does so only in the context of an overall theory that employs that axiom in a systematic manner to compute the meaning of whole sentences in which the concept expression figures. This point is expressed by saying that, for Davidson, the ideas of satisfaction as applied to predicates and reference as applied to singular terms are ideas that are secondary to the concept of truth as applied to whole sentences. Davidson does not advocate a piecemeal, let alone an atomistic, account of meaning. This means that there is no more to an account of concept possession or to an account of reference than what is achieved by producing a truth theory that makes best overall sense of a speaker's behaviour. This is a kind of behaviourism. Giving an account of meaning for a speaker is no more and no less than providing a truth theory that fits their behaviour. In his later writings Davidson has explicitly disavowed the neo-Fregean approach which has developed extended discussions of concept possession and the nature of singular thought (thought that refers to particular objects). The differences, however, are superficial. Recall that the Fregean account of content is anchored to the project of making rational sense of behaviour. It is possible, I believe, to reformulate contemporary neo-Fregean work on concept possession and singular reference as accounts of the kinds of behaviour that are distinctive of possession of specific concepts or of the ability to engage singular thoughts. For example, the idea of a singular mode of presentation may be thought of as just that network of systematically related theorems of a Davidsonian theory that is required in order to make sense of the behaviour involved in tracking a perceptually demonstrable object. Davidson's insistence that there is no more to an account of singular thought or of concept possession in general is made, in part, to guard against a reification of thought and intentionality that comes from treating these things in a piecemeal fashion. Davidson finds this problematic. There are no thoughts; there is only behaviour rationally understandable in the light of the ascription of knowledge of a Tarskian truth theory for the language in question. As we shall see in later chapters, this kind of behaviourism about content is, far from being in opposition to contemporary neo-Fregean work, the best way to understand it.[32] The holism of Davidson's theory – the priority of the concept of truth over the concepts of reference and satisfaction – will occupy us further in the next chapter, so I shall defer extended discussion of it till then.

Given that the theory is modest in the first sense described above, it seems fair to assume that it must be modest in the second sense of describing the structure of meaning in the language by displaying the logical grammar of that meaning. The work of the theory consists in its display of the systematic structure of meaning, and that is to display its logical grammar. This notion of modesty is, however, more problematic.

The second sense of modesty appears to parallel a feature of Tarski's theory of truth and, indeed, to be an inheritance from that theory. Just as Tarski provides a definition of truth from within a language (given an assignment of semantic values to the primitives in a language), so Davidson defines meaning internal to a conceptual scheme. But it is unclear that the idea of a conceptual scheme is as modest as this parallel suggests. Disregarding, for the moment, the point that Davidson claims that there is no such thing as a conceptual scheme, the present worry is this: If Davidson is merely describing the structure of our conceptual scheme, then there should not be anything contentious in the description. Yet there are many features of Davidson's programme that are contentious. The most obvious example concerns his treatment of adverbial modification and his derivation of an event ontology.

Adverbial modification concerns inferences that involve adverbial qualification of an action. For example, if it is true that

(18)   Harry sang lugubriously,

it must also be true that

(19)   Harry sang.

The inference from (18) to (19) is valid, as is any inference in which one removes the adverb from the action description. For this to be a valid inference, it must exhibit a repeatable combinatorial structure. Given the resources of first-order predicate calculus, the only way to represent the structure that the move from (18) to (19) exploits is to treat the adverb as a predicate of doings, a predicate of events. So the inference from (18) to (19) is an instance of the more general form: from

(20)   There is an event that was a Harry's singing and it was a lugubrious one,

infer

(21)   There is an event that was a Harry's singing.

More generally still, the inference is of the form, from

(22) $\exists x \, (Fx \ \& \ Gx)$

to

(23) $\exists x \, (Fx)$.

We know that the move from (22) to (23) is a valid inference, but if that is the form of the inference from (18) to (19), it is an inference that involves a quantification over events. If we take the ontological import of a discourse by looking to see what it quantifies over, then, if the above is a correct account of the logical form of action sentences, we are committed to an ontology that includes events.

This is a surprise. What started out as a modest attempt to describe the logical grammar of meaning – the logical structure of our conceptual scheme – reveals to us something that appears to be a moderately startling metaphysical result: Our acknowledgement that the inference from (18) to (19) is valid commits us to an event ontology. There is considerable debate about Davidson's derivation of an event ontology.[33] From the point of view of the 'Semantics exhausts ontology' methodology, the point of this ontological derivation must be viewed correctly. The claim is not that events should be included within a metaphysics that purports to catalogue the world independently of the way in which we talk and think about it. From the point of view of Davidson's methodology, there is no way to catalogue the world other than in terms of the way that we talk and think about it. Furthermore, the category of events is not offered as an addendum to a physicalistic classification of the world, as if scientists had forgotten to include this category, and it took a philosopher to remind them of what there is. If semantics exhausts ontology, then the concepts of object, event and other basic categories that catalogue the world are semantic concepts. They are not epistemological concepts, and they are certainly not scientific concepts. Ontological categories are not categories of things we should expect to find in our travels about the world – do not expect to bump into an event. Ontological categories are categories that figure in the basic truth-oriented structure of thought and talk. Davidson's claim is that the concept of an event picks out just such a basic category.

5

Interpretation, Minimal Truth and the World

5.1   Introduction

We cannot have a clear sight of Davidson's conception of a theory of meaning unless we can give an account of his central metaphysical claim: the scheme/content distinction is a dogma.[1] In the next section I introduce the key ideas behind this claim. In section 5.3 I outline what many commentators take to be the central argument for this claim. In section 5.4 I examine a central argument of Davidson's and distinguish between a number of related issues concerning conceptual relativism and pluralism. Section 5.5 introduces further ideas about the concept of truth taken from Wiggins's work on the marks of truth, and in section 5.6 I outline the central conceptual argument that delivers the denial of the scheme/content distinction.

5.2   Whose Language is it Anyway?

The central metaphysical result that Davidson draws from his theory of meaning is the claim that the distinction between scheme and content collapses. This is the distinction between what is given in experience (content) and the conceptual scheme that organizes that given. The choice of the word 'content' for the notion of the given is unfortunate. The point is better expressed in Kant's terminology of the distinction between intuitions and concepts.[2]

The idea that such a distinction can be made is the idea that our account of the world is a function of two separate things: the raw given or intuitions of experience, plus the structure imposed by concepts. It also means that concepts do not operate upon the world, but upon the given. Our concepts do not, as it were, reach out to the world. Davidson denies this. If the scheme/content distinction can be maintained, it seems reasonable to suppose that there could be creatures who imposed a

118

different conceptual scheme upon the raw intuitions and who would, therefore, have a different account of the world. If such creatures possessed a different conceptual scheme, we would not be able to understand their view of the world, nor they understand ours. This is the basis for conceptual relativism. Davidson denies that this is possible, for no distinction between intuitions and concepts is possible. This means that there is no such thing as a conceptual scheme which is separable from intuitions and which organizes the raw given. This means that our contact with the world is immediate. It is not mediated by concepts, for concepts reach right out to the world – the world is within our use of concepts.

On the face of it, this sounds as if it is a return to the myth of the given – an unmediated non-conceptual contact with the world. The point, however, is this: There is immediate contact, but the world thereby contacted does not then need organizing conceptually.[3] What we have immediate contact with is a world that is, if you like, already conceptually organized. It is important that we do not confuse the immediacy of contact that Davidson acknowledges with the idea of the given. To help keep the different notions of immediacy separate, I distinguish between the thesis that what we immediately contact in experience is *structured* and the thesis that what we contact is organized.

I reserve the notion of 'organization' for the activity of the mind/categories that operates upon the raw given of intuitions. It is the notion of organization that figures in the Kantian idea of a distinction between scheme and content. On this model, we have immediate non-conceptual contact with the world in the form of intuitions, and these are then organized by the conceptual scheme. Davidson's view is that there is an unmediated contact with the world, but the force of 'unmediated' is to signal that there is no activity of the mind (application of the categories) that is separable from the receipt of intuitions. This is not to deny a different sense in which concepts are involved in our contact with the world, for the world with which we have a direct contact is structured.

The difficulty here is that we seem prone to assume that the conceptual structure of our contact with the world is an achievement, an organization of a level of something non-conceptual. On this picture, it is possible, in principle, to factor out the contribution that raw intuitions play in our conception of the world. When Davidson claims that the scheme/content distinction is untenable, he is claiming that it is impossible to factor out the level of intuitions. This leaves our contact with the world as immediate, but what we contact cannot now be thought of as something that requires organization in order to figure in our thoughts and rational enquiry about the world. What we contact must already be structured.[4]

To sum up: the traditional view is that we have immediate contact with non-conceptual intuitions. These are subject to conceptual organization by the application of a conceptual scheme upon the intuitions. On this traditional view, it is possible to countenance the idea of alternative conceptual schemes. Davidson's view

119

is that the very idea of a conceptual scheme is incoherent – there is no scheme/content distinction. This means that there is still such a thing as direct contact with the world, but it must be conceived differently. Rather than speak of 'immediate contact', which I shall reserve for the contact enjoyed in the traditional view, I shall call Davidson's idea the idea of a 'direct presence' of the world. What is distinctive about the notion of direct presence is the idea that the structure of our experience of the world, which enables our experience to play the role it needs to play in disciplining our thought and reasoning, is a structure that is not imposed by the mind; it is a structure intrinsic to the very idea of being confronted by the world.

The denial of the scheme/content distinction has profound consequences. Whether it is true, and what the argument is supposed to be for this claim, are some of the most contentious issues in contemporary discussions of Davidson's work. In the view of many commentators, Davidson's argument is a verificationist argument.[5] I want to distinguish between two different arguments that are at play in Davidson's work. I call them the empirical argument from interpretation and the conceptual argument against the scheme/content distinction. The former is an argument about the procedures that have to be undertaken in the context of radical interpretation. It is an argument that shows, broadly, that it is a condition for the possibility of interpreting another that we see the other as sharing our beliefs. The key question about this argument is: How can such an argument show the impossibility of conceptual relativism, for it claims only a congruence of belief as a condition for the possibility of interpretation? Perhaps the whole point of the idea of different conceptual schemes is that we would not be able to interpret languages that expressed them. This suggests that the empirical argument from interpretation can deliver the denial of conceptual relativism only if it is a verificationist argument, for it assumes that the possibility of an alternative conceptual scheme can be assessed only from the point of view of what we can verify. By definition, what we can verify must be verifiable from within our conceptual scheme, so therefore we cannot make sense of the idea of an alternative conceptual scheme.

If the argument against the possibility of conceptual relativism is the empirical argument about interpretation, then it does not seem to be an argument against the scheme/content distinction. It looks, instead, to be an argument which says that there is only one conceptual scheme, ours![6] Nevertheless, Davidson's conclusion is supposed to be not that there is only one conceptual scheme but that there is no such thing – the scheme/content distinction collapses.[7] This suggests that this result comes from other sources. That, I think, is correct, despite the fact that most commentators locate only one argument in Davidson – the argument from interpretation, which I am calling the empirical argument. I discuss the empirical argument first, before moving on to consider the central argument whose consequences are much broader than issues in the philosophy of language and theory of interpretation. They touch our deepest conception of what it is to be a thinker and to be related to the world in thought. Davidson's position supports a radical externalism about thought, about how what it is to be possessed of intentionality is to be in the direct presence of the world.

5.3   The Empirical Argument from Interpretation

The argument from interpretation is an argument about the empirical testability of a manual-theory of meaning. Davidson has always claimed that his idea of a theory of meaning was that of an empirically testable theory.[8] In the circumstances of radical interpretation, the idea seems plain; but we need to ascertain precisely what elements of the theory are supposed to be empirically testable.

We know from section 4.5 that Davidson's conception of meaning is holistic. The argument for that claim is an a priori conceptual argument. The argument shows that in order for the theory of meaning to do real explanatory work, it cannot be a piecemeal theory. A piecemeal theory is one in which any given axiom or any given theorem could, on its own, specify the meaning of an atom or a complex clause, respectively. The thought behind the argument for holism was that the explanatory work of the theory lay in the way that it successfully captured the right account of the truth-conditions of sentences by the imposition of a structure-discerning theory. The central concept of a structure-discerning theory – truth – figured only in clauses that on their own do not specify meaning. A theory that discerned sufficient systematic truth-oriented structure in language production and comprehension would, given the extensional resources of a Tarskian truth theory, pick out meaning.

The holism of Davidson's enterprise is not an empirically testable feature of the theory. That much is clear. Holism about meaning is a constitutive claim.[9] The thought that the theory is testable, then, must amount to this: The choice of elements selected to figure in the theory's axioms is empirically testable. So, if a speaker sincerely assents to

(1)   'nows si hitew'

in the presence of white snow, and we hypothesize that 'nows' is a noun term for snow, this hypothesis can be tested empirically by seeing if the speaker employs it in other contexts involving snow. Similar thoughts apply to the phrase we hypothesize as meaning the predicate '. . . is white'.[10]

There is another respect in which Davidson's theory of meaning is holistic. We can only determine the meaning of the term 'nows' against a backdrop of assumptions about the speaker's beliefs. To hypothesize a meaning for the term is to

121

assume that when the speaker offered (1), they were expressing a belief about a kind of stuff and not merely expressing a belief about patches of visual experience. Our purchase on what beliefs the speaker is expressing is gained only via a grasp of the meaning of their expressions. Our purchase on the meaning of their expressions is constrained by our conception of what beliefs they are trying to express. There is no independent entry point into the speaker's beliefs and meanings. We have to bootstrap our way into the meaning of their language at the same time as we grasp the beliefs they are expressing about the world. The mutual independence of belief and meaning is the first aspect of the holism of Davidson's conception of meaning.

The second aspect concerns the fact that simultaneously solving the identification of the meaning of the speaker's expressions and their beliefs presupposes a third variable, which cannot be isolated independently of meaning and belief. The third variable is the speaker's desires. In trying to simultaneously fix the speaker's meaning and beliefs, we have to assume that the speaker is motivated by a desire to speak the truth in offering an utterance. We have to juggle meaning, belief and desire in one simultaneous triangulation, to provide an understanding of the speaker's behaviour. The fact that these three items are holistically related means that, in interpreting the alien speaker, we need to see them as rational; for it is the interconnectedness of desire, belief and meaning that constitutes our core notion of rationality.

Rational behaviour is that which, against a backdrop of belief and desire, makes best overall sense of satisfying desires in the light of beliefs held by the agent. A speaker who asserts the sentence

Snow is freezing cold

would prima facie exhibit irrational behaviour were they to immediately thrust several handfuls of the stuff down their vest. We do not ordinarily expect people to have the desire to have freezing cold material next to their body. If the speaker were to act in this manner, then we would, in order to preserve their rationality, have to do one of three things. We could suppose: (a) that they do not mean by 'freezing cold' what we mean by it; (b) that although they mean what we mean by the sentence, they did not believe the stuff before them was snow; (c) that, contrary to ordinary folk, they had a desire to have freezing cold material next to their skin, perhaps because they had a sudden need to cool down rapidly. Which option we take will be determined by how we hold the variables at issue in the other two options. We cannot first determine one of these variables without making assumptions about the other two.

The problem of radical interpretation is now set. Consider the case of an alien speaker who is producing sentences in the light of their confrontation with the world. We want to determine what their sentences mean; but to do this, we need to know in general the character of their beliefs and also their desires. We proceed by making hypotheses about the meaning of individual expressions that the alien employs. These hypotheses are testable, but only against further hypotheses about the belief system the alien employs and the desires they have. As there is no neutral starting-point for solving the triangulation of meaning, belief and desire, we have no choice but to start by assuming that the confrontation with the world enjoyed by the alien is, in broad outline, the same as ours.

To see this, suppose that the idea of alternative conceptual schemes made sense. Suppose, that is, that the alien's belief system encompasses novel ideas that are not expressible in our beliefs. Now, we can only tell when an alien is expressing novel beliefs once we have become good at translating them. In order to translate the alien tongue, we have to produce T-sentences the right-hand side of which we complete with an English sentence, on the left-hand side of which we mention an alien sentence. But the whole point of the holism of a theory of meaning is that to arrive at any one T-sentence that successfully provides an interpretation of an alien sentence is to arrive at a whole web of T-sentences for a significant fragment of the alien language. It follows from this that the idea that the alien has the capacity to entertain novel beliefs that are not expressible in our language presupposes that, by and large, they possess a pattern of beliefs much like ours.

The central argument is then this:

Argument from interpretation:
(i)   We can only make sense of the idea of the alien's capacity for novel beliefs if we can interpret them.
(ii) Interpreting aliens requires the production of a theory that produces T-sentences linking alien sentences and English sentences.
(iii) A theory of the kind required at (ii) is essentially holistic.
(iv) The holism of the theory of interpretation shows that there must be a significant fragment of the alien language that is translatable into English, and this means that the aliens broadly agree with us about the world – their pattern of beliefs is much like ours.

Note, this argument emphasizes a point that Davidson has repeatedly stressed and that many commentators draw attention to: that the possibility of disagreement presupposes a large shared background of belief.[11] If this is the argument that Davidson is employing to show that there is no scheme/content distinction, there are a number of flaws in it.

First, you might object to the opening claim that it is a requirement on the alien's capacity for novel belief that we be able to interpret them. For sure, if we are to make sense of the alien's having a capacity for novel beliefs, we would first have to be able to interpret them, but what if we cannot make sense of them? The proponent of the idea of different conceptual schemes might insist that we would not be able to make sense of the alien's capacity for novel beliefs; that, after all, is just what it is for them to have a different conceptual scheme. Second, the conclusion of the above argument is that the alien has a pattern of belief much like ours, and this is not a denial of the scheme/content distinction. One way of understanding the idea that the alien has a pattern of belief much like ours is to say not that there is no such thing as a conceptual scheme, but that there is only one conceptual scheme.

Both the above objections reveal the verificationist nature of the argument. The argument claims that the only way we can verify that the alien has a capacity for novel beliefs is first to verify that they have a capacity for belief. The only way we can verify that they have a capacity for belief is to verify that we can interpret their utterances. Finally, to interpret their utterances is to find them in broad agreement with our view of the world. There is, therefore, no way that we could verify that the alien has a capacity for novel beliefs. If that is what the argument is proposing, the proponent of different conceptual schemes might respond by saying that the argument begs the question; for the very idea of a different conceptual scheme is of something that could not be interpreted by us. Another way of expressing this would be to say that the kind of disagreement involved in the idea of novel belief expression is not a disagreement that presupposes a background of agreed beliefs. Rather, the idea of different conceptual schemes is not that we and the alien disagree, but that we have beliefs that are incongruent. The conceptual relativist thinks that the alien has a completely different mind-set to us.

A proponent of the empirical argument from interpretation may respond to these charges in the following manner.[12] The charge of verificationism arises because it is claimed that there is an asymmetrical relation between our capacity to interpret an alien and the notion that the alien is like-minded. It is verificationist to insist that we solve the question of whether the alien is like-minded by testing for interpretability, where we think of these as two different notions. However, what if we insist that the relation between interpretability and mindedness is a symmetrical relation? That is to say, we have no grip on the notion of mindedness independently of our grip on the notion of interpretability, and no grip on the latter notion independently of the former. Whether or not this version of the argument is legitimately labelled verificationist is a delicate point. I suspect that it is. Nevertheless, even if you think this is not now a verificationist argument, it is clear, I think, that we are presented not so much with an argument against the possibility of alternative conceptual schemes as with a refusal to countenance the possibility, for the very notion of mindedness is now definitionally dependent on the notion of interpretability.

Furthermore, this way of reading the argument still does not deliver the result that there is no scheme/content distinction. What it delivers is the claim that there is no way of conceiving of the world other than the way we do. Now, you might think that in the absence of the possibility of alternative conceptual schemes, the very idea of a scheme as something that organizes intuitions is redundant; but if so, the point has not been argued for. It would be consistent with the argument so far adumbrated to conclude that all rational creatures applied the same conceptual scheme in organizing their intuitions. It would take a further verificationist step to move from that to the claim that Davidson repeatedly makes that there is no scheme/content distinction at all.

Davidson's work on this topic is notoriously dense and tightly argued, so it is difficult to see what assumption is doing the work at any one point. Nevertheless, it is worth trying to reshuffle the arrangement of claims, in order to identify the point at which the conclusion that no scheme/content distinction makes sense is forced. So, let me restate the situation in a way that tries to be hospitable to the possibility of there being different conceptual schemes. The important aspect of the restatement is the division of point (i) in the above argument into two distinct claims, in order to avoid the charge of verificationism.

The first claim that we need to distinguish is this: Regardless of whether or not an alien's belief system is interpretable by us, to suppose that they have a way of forming beliefs about the world is to suppose that they enjoy a holistic, rationally structured view of the world. Call this the alien point of view. What is important about it is that it is a rationally structured whole. Second, the only evidence we could have that a creature enjoyed such a point of view would be that we could assimilate that point of view into the way we see the world.

The argument now becomes:

(ia) Suppose the alien has a rationally structured point of view.

(ib) We can only make sense of the idea of the alien point of view if we can interpret it.

(ii) Interpreting aliens requires the production of a theory that produces T-sentences linking alien sentences and English sentences.

(iii) A theory of the kind required at (ii) is essentially holistic.

(iv) The holism of the theory of interpretation shows that there must be a significant fragment of the alien language that is translatable into English, and this means that the aliens broadly agree with us about the world – their pattern of beliefs is much like ours.

The assumption at (i a) is meant to capture the idea that there could be such a thing as an alien conceptual scheme and to do so separate from the claim, in (i b), that the only way we can make sense of such an idea is via our verification of such a scheme in the alien's behaviour. Now, it is the argument from (i b) to (iv) that I want to call the empirical argument from interpretation. It is an argument that starts from what I take to be a correct point, that the only evidence we could have that a creature has

125

a rationally structured point of view is that it is interpretable (i b). I want to suggest, however, that it is not this argument that delivers the collapse of the scheme/content distinction. The scheme/content distinction is collapsed by the claim that the alien has a rationally structured point of view (i a). That is to say, when the very idea of what it is to have a rationally structured point of view is properly understood, we will see that the scheme/content distinction collapses.

What I am calling the empirical argument from interpretation, (i b)–(iv), is the argument that provides a home for a number of methodological principles that have sprung up in discussion of Davidson's views. One response to the empirical argument from interpretation is to say that it merely makes a methodological point, a point that could be summed up in the slogan 'Interpretation breeds concurrence'. Construed as an argument about the correct methodology for interpreting alien languages, the argument looks persuasive; for all it is saying is that if we are to understand the alien, we will have to do so in our own terms. Accordingly, commentators have suggested methodological principles that capture this claim: the principle of charity, 'Assume the natives are generally correct in their beliefs'; the principle of humanity, 'Assume the natives are interested in similar things to us'. Such principles have their place within the empirical project of making sense of alien speakers on the assumption that an interpretation is possible. It is the assumption that interpretation is possible, however, that the proponent of different conceptual schemes is likely to challenge.

Note, to accept the plausibility of such methodological principles and the empirical argument from interpretation is not to deny that the process of interpretation can reveal novel ways of thinking about the world. The methodological principles are compatible with the idea that, when engaged in the interpretation of alien tongues, we can discover ways of thinking about the world that are not fully translatable into our home tongue as it stands. There may be points at which the alien belief system conceptualizes experiences that have no direct analogue in our beliefs. All that the methodological principles require is that when this occurs, it does so against a backdrop of massive agreement. So, for example, we might learn that Eskimos have words for many different kinds of snow, where we have only the word for the white, cold, undifferentiated stuff. More commonly, we might decide that there is no good English word for translating another language's term – e.g. the German *Gemuchlichkeit* or the French *sang froid* – and so we use the foreign term instead of looking for an equivalent. Such cases are irrelevant to the truth of the methodological principles under consideration, for no one is seriously suggesting that Eskimos, Germans or the French do not share a massive background view of the world with English speakers. However finely snow or moods are differentiated in other tongues, we are all fundamentally talking about a world of persisting material objects populated by people of varying degrees of emotional and psychological complexity.

Davidson, however, has always insisted that he was offering a metaphysical argument, and not a set of methodological homilies, about the practice of interpretation.[13] Before I take the detours required to show how Davidson's basic argument impinges upon (i a), let me briefly review a key text in which Davidson attempts to construct a conceptual argument against the possibility of different conceptual schemes from the resources of the empirical argument from interpretation.

5.4   Interpretation, Omniscience, Pluralism

In 'The method of truth in metaphysics' Davidson says: 'The basic claim is that much community of belief is needed to provide a basis for communication or understanding.'[14] As such, this might be construed as no more than the methodological 'Interpretation breeds concurrence'. Davidson, however, continues,

> objective error can occur only in a setting of largely true beliefs.[15]

It is the fact that it is *objective* error that is supposed to reveal that his thesis is more than a methodological one. The thought, I take it, is this: To ascribe novel beliefs to the alien is, from our point of view, to see the alien as in error. If his argument is merely the methodological argument, the concept of error will be no more than the idea that we find the alien's beliefs incongruent with ours. Davidson, however, is interested in the conditions for finding the alien speakers objectively in error and not merely out of line with our view of the world. The device he employs to make this shift is the idea of the omniscient interpreter.

The argument that Davidson provides in 'The method of truth in metaphysics' can be summarized like this.[16]

1   Interpretation breeds concurrence; that is, if we are to interpret the alien's utterances, we will attribute meaning to them only on the basis of the interpreter's beliefs.

This is the methodological principle. Next:

2   Suppose there existed an omniscient interpreter. Any interpretation made by such an interpreter under the above methodological principle would be true.

3   Given (2), the possibility of massive error is unintelligible, for that would be to suppose that the omniscient interpreter could correctly interpret another as being massively mistaken, and this contravenes the merely methodological constraint on interpretation in (1).

This is one of the clearest passages in which Davidson explicitly rejects the idea that his argument against the possibility of conceptual relativism is a methodological argument. The device of the omniscient interpreter is supposed to move the argument beyond the methodological. It is not clear, however, that the above argument does any such thing.

The key move in this argument is the supposition of the existence of an omniscient interpreter. Is this a fair move if we are to give serious consideration to the possibility of different conceptual schemes? Davidson insists that the supposition of the omniscient interpreter is a harmless, legitimate device. We need to see in what sense this is correct. The proponent of conceptual relativism will insist that the whole point of this idea is that there is no such thing as a point of view that can encompass all conceptual schemes, for different conceptual schemes render beliefs incommensurable. This could be expressed by saying that the account of the activity of the omniscient interpreter in the above argument begs the question. In step 3 of the argument, the possibility that the existence of the omniscient interpreter rules out is the possibility of the alien speaker being in massive error. But is this the right way to describe the situation that the conceptual relativist wants us to imagine?

The conceptual relativist does not conceive of the alien as being in massive error; they conceive of them as possessing beliefs that are not expressible in our concepts. Of course, if the alien possessed beliefs not expressible in our terms, we might think of that as possessing beliefs that are not correct by our lights; but that is not the same as 'not correct, full stop'. Indeed, it is the very idea that we can have an absolute notion of beliefs being correct or incorrect that is challenged by the conceptual relativist. They think that beliefs are, at best, only ever correct or incorrect relative to a conceptual scheme. Thus, the very idea of an omniscient interpreter begs the question against the conceptual relativist.

To leave matters there is to leave the argument between Davidson on the current interpretation and the conceptual relativist at a clash of intuitions about the coherence of the idea of the omniscient interpreter. So let us describe the situation in more detail. I want to distinguish between two versions of the idea of an omniscient interpreter. I shall then argue that the sense in which the idea is plausible does not deliver the argument that Davidson wants.

The conceptual relativist must be committed to the idea that there can be conceptual schemes CS_1 and CS_2 such that beliefs expressed in one are not expressible in the other. This, however, is not yet sufficient to capture what is normally meant by conceptual relativism, for to posit the possibility of different belief systems that are understandable only *sui generis* is merely to endorse a position that I shall call pluralism. What is distinctive of pluralism is the idea of a plurality of ways of describing the world wherein the different ways are complementary, rather than in conflict. In addition, the conceptual relativist posits conceptual schemes that are not only not mutually expressible, but that introduce alternative incom-

128

mensurable notions of the world. The conceptual relativist, then, is characterized as follows:

> **CR:** There can be conceptual schemes CS_1 and CS_2 such that beliefs expressed in one are not expressible in the other, and the respective sets of beliefs cannot be seen as about a common world.

Davidson wants to say that the idea of an omniscient interpreter is both coherent and renders CR false. But the issue turns on how we conceive the understanding that the omniscient interpreter achieves. At a minimum, the idea of an omniscient interpreter must accommodate the following:

> **OI:** An omniscient interpreter is able to understand all beliefs.

Thesis OI is central to the idea of the omniscient interpreter. It renders the idea coherent and a plausible supposition. The point of view of the omniscient interpreter is simply the point of view from which nothing is hidden. As such, that is a conception of the omniscient interpreter that is prima-facie reasonable. It captures a bare possibility that there is no good reason to deny. But it is not a conception of the omniscient interpreter that shows the falsity of CR.

Thesis OI means that no belief content is hidden from the omniscient interpreter, but the significance of this claim turns on how we understand the phrase 'the point of view of the omniscient interpreter'. We think of the omniscient interpreter as someone able to access all beliefs. That is thesis OI. This thesis is compatible with the idea that the point of view of the omniscient interpreter is to be understood conjunctively; it is an additive point of view. This means that the beliefs of the alien which the omniscient interpreter accesses get added to the beliefs of ours that the omniscient interpreter also understands, in such a way that the alien beliefs do not contradict our beliefs. But it is compatible with this that the alien beliefs do not translate into our beliefs, nor ours into theirs, and that they are about different worlds, despite the fact that both sets of beliefs are accessible to the omniscient interpreter. But that is precisely the scenario that the advocate of conceptual relativism wants us to consider. Therefore, the supposition of the omniscient interpreter in OI is compatible with CR. Another way of putting this is to say that the point of view of the omniscient interpreter as defined by OI is simply the point of view characterized as

> Point of view of OI: $CS_1 + CS_2 + \ldots + CS_n$.

The notion of the omniscient interpreter as defined by OI does not entail the idea of the omniscient interpreter as a being with a unified point of view in which the beliefs of CS₁, CS₂, etc. are intertranslatable. That notion of the omniscient interpreter is:

> OI': An omniscient interpreter is able to understand all beliefs and understand them from a single unified point of view.

The difference between OI and OI' is the difference between the additive point of view of the omniscient interpreter and the unifying point of view. The former captures an idea that does justice to many intuitions we hold about belief content.

Consider beliefs about music. It is a common idea that in coming to acquire an appreciation of music or of some particular form of music, you acquire a point of view and a set of beliefs that can only be acquired by, as it were, 'going native' with the musicians. The capacity for belief formation that you acquire as you absorb yourself in the practice of music making and music criticism is not translatable – let alone reducible – to the capacity for belief formation you had before undertaking the musical apprenticeship. As long as the new beliefs about music do not contradict your previous beliefs, your new point of view is an additive one, not a unifying one; for you do not have a single unifying conceptual framework in terms of which you can translate your music beliefs and other beliefs into a common vocabulary. Undergoing the musical apprenticeship has, in a sense that is not merely metaphorical, introduced you to a new world.[17]

The notion of an additive point of view is an important idea. It is central to the idea that there is no one unifying explanatory framework in terms of which all our beliefs can be expressed. The possibility of a pluralism of explanatory frameworks is not negligible, and has an important role to play in contemporary philosophy.[18] It might be thought, however, that such pluralism hardly amounts to conceptual relativism. As it stands, the example I have used supports pluralism. Pluralism is weaker than conceptual relativism. Nevertheless, it does suggest the resources for developing the conceptual relativist case.

Suppose that musical beliefs are not translatable into a non-musical vocabulary. All the same, accepting that musical beliefs are only understandable *sui generis* is compatible with the following picture: The correctness of musical beliefs means that, in addition to our basic understanding of the world as possessing properties picked out by our scientific material object discourse, we also understand the world to possess features expressible in musical discourse. This is an additive point of view; but it is a point of view with only one world, the world that has both material properties and musical properties. What I am assuming about this point of view is that our conception of the world as material objects and processes occupying space and time plays a fundamental role in organizing our thinking. The supposition of musical discourse as being non-translatable into this basic discourse introduces a pluralism about explanatory schemes; for example, our explanations of musical responses are given *sui generis* from within musical discourse. But the pluralism thus defined does not challenge the basic role that our material object conception of the world plays, and it is the fundamental role of that discourse which substantiates the idea that, despite the pluralism, there is only one world. Pluralism merely introduces the idea that the one world has, in addition to material properties, musical properties. It is a pluralism of properties, not a pluralism of worlds.

Pluralism does not introduce conceptual relativism. It is a distinct and weaker thesis. It is also an important philosophical position.[19] Pluralism has the following characteristics:

(a) The conception of the world in material object terms provides a basic conception of the world independent of our judgements about it.

(b) Not all the properties of the world are expressible in material object discourse; there are discourses that are understandable only *sui generis*.

(c) Properties picked out by the extra discourses under (b) are nevertheless properties of items – things, events, persons – picked out in the basic conception under (a).

Pluralism does not endorse OI', for, despite the fundamental role which pluralism gives to material object discourse, this is not a unifying role. By a 'unifying role' I mean the idea that a discourse or set of concepts provides a common currency for understanding all other beliefs. It is because pluralism does not support OI' that it gives us the idea of an additive point of view. The reason that pluralism is not the same as conceptual relativism is because the additive character is additive only with respect to properties, not with respect to the basic stuff of the world. Pluralism does not introduce new kinds of things in the world; it introduces new kinds of properties which familiar material things possess. So although it is not wholly metaphorical to say that in learning the language of music one comes to occupy a new world, it is not wholly literal either. In undergoing a musical education, you come to occupy a familiar world with new properties.

Despite the fact that pluralism is a weaker thesis than conceptual relativism, it provides the resources to show that the idea of the omniscient interpreter, thesis OI, does not, of itself show the falsity of CR. Once we have the notion of an additive point of view, the difference between pluralism and conceptual relativism is the difference between points of view that are additive with respect to properties and additive with respect to substance. Although the music example is additive only with respect to properties, the general idea of an additive point of view suggests that there is, as yet, no good reason to suppose that the point of view of the omniscient interpreter could not be an additive point of view with respect to substance. If so, that would allow that the omniscient interpreter as defined by the OI thesis was compatible with CR. It would take the omniscient interpreter as defined by OI', in which the unifying point of view is unifying with respect to substance, to show the falsity of CR. That, however, is a stronger version of the omniscient interpreter. It is the OI thesis that is prima-facie plausible; but it does not do the work required for Davidson's argument in 'The method of truth in metaphysics' to go through.

5.5 The Marks of Truth

I now want to turn to what I think is the core argument that delivers the denial of the scheme/content distinction. I have suggested that the distinction is rendered untenable once we make the initial assumption that the alien has a rationally structured point of view. This was the starting-point to the empirical argument from interpretation as outlined in section 5.3. I now want to show why we do not need the empirical argument to get to the denial of the scheme/content distinction.

What is it to ascribe a rationally structured point of view to the alien or, for that matter, to ourselves? Whatever else is involved in ascribing a rationally structured point of view to a subject, it must involve the idea that the subject adjusts their beliefs with respect to truth, with respect to how things are. That, however, only pushes our question back a further step, for what is it to adjust your beliefs with respect to truth? The simple answer to this that I want to recommend is that to adjust your beliefs with respect to truth is have a direct presence of the world. This means that to be in possession of concepts and to be making judgements is already to be in confrontation with the world and to be making adjustments in light of that confrontation. Possession of concepts implies possession of the world. These are, as it stands, mere slogans. If substantiated, they entail the denial of the scheme/content distinction, for possession of concepts cannot be separated from our engagement with the world. The slogan 'Possession of concepts implies possession of the world' also elucidates the basic holism of Davidson's project. This is a holism that flows from the primacy of truth over reference and the idea that we confront the world via truth, not reference. These are the ideas that we now need to elucidate. I start with truth.

In chapter 3 we saw how, given an understanding of meaning and translation, Tarski shows us how to define truth. In the previous chapter I said that we could think of Davidson's project as showing how, taking our concept of truth for granted, we could give a theory of meaning. The concepts of truth and meaning are intimately connected. In this section I want to explore a way of getting some purchase on both concepts simultaneously.

The approach derives from David Wiggins's work on the marks of truth. The basic idea is to take the bare notion of assertoric content as primitive and see what truth must be like in order for assertion to be possible. This is not to presuppose a substantive account of meaning. It is, rather, to start from a minimal starting-point that no one could reasonably deny. The starting-point is just this: We open our mouths and say things. Given that this is so, what must truth be like? The enquiry is a transcendental enquiry, for it is an enquiry into the properties (marks) that truth must possess if the notion of assertoric content is viable. No one can deny the starting-point that assertoric content is possible, for to do so would be to employ an assertoric content.

Wiggins identifies five marks of truth.[20] The five marks are:

Mark 1:   Truth is the primary dimension of assessment for beliefs and for sentences that express them.

Mark 2:   If x is true, then under favourable circumstances x will command convergence.

Mark 3:   For all x where 'x' is a sentence expressing a belief, if x is true, then x has content, and its truth does not consist in x's being believed, being hoped for, being wished for, etc.

Mark 4:   Every true belief is true in virtue of something.

Mark 5:   If x_1 is true and x_2 is true, then $x_1 \& x_2$ is true; all truths are compatible.

The argument for these five marks is a transcendental argument on the conditions for the possibility of assertoric content. It could also be expressed as an argument about the conditions for the possibility of thought, or of judgement. At the moment, nothing turns on whether we think of the argument as an argument about the conditions for thought or for linguistic assertion. The argument for the first three marks is the important argument. Wiggins says that mark 4 is a summary of (1)–(3), and that (5), although important for the notion of an additive point of view, flows immediately from the argument for the first three. I shall present the argument for the first three marks of truth in a different order from Wiggins. I think it is more natural to order the marks (1), (3), (2). It is (3) that is central.

So, given that we take ourselves and others to be making assertions, what does this tell us about truth? What must truth be like for this activity to be possible? Note, the enquiry into the marks of truth is not an exercise in speculative metaphysics. The investigation of truth that Wiggins undertakes is not designed to resolve the debates between correspondence, coherence and pragmatist theories of truth. The account of truth that Wiggins is defending is an account of plain truth, or minimal truth: 'truth is whatever concept we appeal to in the interpretative business of trying to make sense of others where, in so doing, we see the others as party to some however tenuous norm of rationality'.[21] The datum for this enquiry is simply that people say things.

Suppose that assertion takes place. Why must truth have the first mark? The first mark says that truth is the primary dimension of assessment for beliefs. Another way of putting this is to say that falsity is the primary defect of a belief. Suppose that this was not the case. Suppose that it was not a primary defect for an assertion to be incorrect. If that were the case, then there would be no sense to the idea that in saying something you are subject to discipline. The very idea of making an assertion is the idea of ruling something out. To make an assertion is to make a claim that things are thus-and-so. If they are not thus-and-so, the assertion is incorrect. The idea that, whatever else an assertion does, it rules something out, is fundamental to the very idea of content. The point is a semantic point about the idea of content. It is not a pragmatic point about the practice of assertion or of making judgements. It is the idea that an assertoric content represents things as being a certain way, and that if they are not that way, then the assertoric content is incorrect. It has not told it how it is.

The point may seem obvious, and indeed it is. But it is important that we be clear about the point being made before we proceed to marks 3 and 2. The force of the argument that falsity is the primary defect of an assertoric content can be seen in the light of interpretation. Consider a subject who utters a string of sounds,

Blib blob blab,

and we take those sounds to express an assertoric content. If we are to interpret those sounds as bearing a content, we must know what is being ruled out by someone offering that sound sequence. Suppose, for example, that we hypothesize that 'Blib blob' is a name and 'blab' a predicate. Suppose further that we hypothesize that the predicate is 'fat' because of the way the speaker has used the word in the presence of other fat things. But suppose further still that the item for which we presume 'Blib blob' is the name is canonically not fat. Under such circumstances we would have to expect that the speaker would retract their utterance as incorrect. If they did not acknowledge their mistake, that would be canonical evidence that, in the absence of a convincing story about how they were subject to lapses of rationality or were oblivious to Blib blob's thinness, etc., the predicate did not after all mean 'fat'.

If, for such reasons, we were to discount the hypothesis that 'blab' meant fat, and were to proceed to find no regular pattern of use of 'blab', that would give us purchase on what it would be for an utterance of 'x is blab' to be incorrect, we would eventually be forced to conclude that we had no evidence that the speaker was using language at all. Note that I am not currently running the empirical argument from interpretation. I am not arguing that unless we can make sense of 'Blib blob blab', it has no content. I am simply arguing that if it has content, its component parts must possess a grammar – a pattern of use – that reveals what it would be to use them incorrectly. For the moment it does not matter whether we think of the content of these sounds as interpretable in English. But where there is content, there must be systematic patterns of use. It is these systematic patterns of use that capture the idea of a content being used incorrectly, the idea that an assertion involving such a content is semantically incorrect.[22]

What this shows is that the very idea of assertoric content involves the idea of the content being incorrect or mistaken. In terms of speech acts, the point is that the making of an assertion presupposes a notion of what it would be for the assertion to be mistaken, a conception of what it would be to have to retract the assertion. The central idea here is the idea of a mistake: the idea of a content being mistaken and a speech act being mistaken because the content is. The semantic notion of the content being mistaken is primary; the mistake of a speech act is derivative.

If the above is right, we have the resources to provide the argument for the third mark of truth. This mark says that where x is a sentence with content, its being true does not consist in its being believed, hoped for, etc. In short, this mark says that truth is independent of will. It is important to observe that as Wiggins expresses this mark, the point is that the truth of x is independent of belief. He does not say that x's truth is independent of *my* belief, the point is expressed more abstractly than that. If truth is independent of will, this introduces a minimal realism into our concept of truth. The fact that it is independence of will and not 'independence of my will' means that the notion of independence imports a genuine concept of objectivity, not merely intersubjectivity, into the concept of truth.[23]

Given the first mark of truth, we know that where x is a sentence with content, there must be some notion of what it is for that content to be semantically mistaken. This means that were a speaker to make an assertion with this content, they would be in error. The concept of a mistake here is a normative concept. It is the notion that someone making an assertion with that content ought to retract. It is this normativity that lies at the heart of our concept of rationality. It is a norm of rationality that, other things being equal, you ought not to assert a content that is semantically in error. In terms of the practice of assertion, if you have made such an assertion, you ought to retract.

But the force of this normative notion can arise only from the idea that what forces the retraction is independent of will, and it cannot just be independent of the speaker's will, because, for example, it is dependent on the will of others. The idea of being required to retract because semantically mistaken is not merely the idea of needing to conform; it is the idea of being required to retract in order to get things right. In being semantically mistaken, you are confronted with something. Semantic correctness and incorrectness are not things you can control at will.

This, then, is the third mark of truth: if x is true, it is true independent of will; for it is constitutive of the idea of semantic content that such a content be the sort of thing that can be correct or incorrect independent of our judging it to be so.[24] Of course, in saying this, we have said nothing substantive about the nature of that which is independent of will and which forces our retraction when we make a false assertion. The point of the third mark of truth is just to require that for any given discourse that obeys the marks of truth, it must be possible for the content of the discourse to provide a conception of the world in which the behaviour of that world is something that obtains independent of will. This provides a test of whether or not a discourse is genuinely a truth-apt discourse. It is a test passed by our ordinary everyday discourse about material objects, for that is a discourse the content of which is plausibly seen as actually requiring a conception of the world independent of will – the conception of the world as made up of spatio-temporal particulars occupying time and location independent of our perception of their spatio-temporal occupancy.[25]

The second mark of truth follows from the argument for the third mark. If x is true, then it is true independent of its being willed to be true, hoped to be true, etc. It is true independent of will. But that means that were I to assert x in error, the requirement that I ought to retract flows from a conception of my being out of line with something that is independent of will. The norm that I should retract is the norm that I should get in line and accord my beliefs with what is the case. But if that which forces the retraction of my false assertion is independent of will, not only is it independent of *my* will, it is also independent of *your* will. Therefore, if my assertion is false, then, in principle, it should be possible to give an account of how my belief is out of line with what is the case. But by the same token, if what is the case is independent of your will as well as independent of my will, then were you to make the same assertion, so too should it be possible, in principle, to give an account of how your belief is out of line with what is the case. If what forces me to retract is independent of will, then, were you similarly positioned and making the same assertion, the very same state of affairs should force you to retract. Of course, you may not be similarly positioned, and that in itself may have a bearing on whether you ought to retract. But, other things being equal, if that which forces me to retract does not also force you to retract, then it is not genuinely independent of will. Other things being equal, we will then converge in our responses to mistakes. We will be subject to just the same discipline to our beliefs and assertions. If x is true, then under favourable circumstances it will command convergence.

Wiggins says that mark 4 is intended only as a summary of the preceding three marks, so no more need be said on that. Mark 5 may look surprising, for you may wonder how such a minimalist enquiry into the character of truth necessary for assertoric content to be possible could yield the conclusion that all truths are compatible. The point, however, flows immediately from the arguments for marks 1 and 3, and, once seen, is very obvious.

Recall, the point of mark 1 is that, in making an assertion, the assertoric content of the assertion rules out something. What is ruled out is that which would render the content semantically mistaken. In the simple case, then, for propositions *P* and

Q, if P is true, then whatever would render it mistaken cannot obtain. In the simplest case, that which would render it mistaken is, of course, not-P. But now suppose also that Q is true. Similarly, not-Q cannot obtain. Suppose now that Q is incompatible with P. The simplest way of representing this is to suppose that Q entails not-P. But, in supposing that both P and Q are true, we have already seen that not-P cannot obtain, and yet the supposition that Q is true and incompatible with P requires not-P to obtain. We must conclude that either Q is not true, or it is not incompatible with P. What we cannot conclude is that both P and Q are true and incompatible. The point is general, so any pair of truths must be compatible. All truths are compatible.

For the purposes of understanding Davidson's denial of the scheme/content distinction, it is the third mark of truth that is significant. This mark requires that, where there is content, there must be some conception of that which is independent of will and which grounds the notion of semantic error. This is, however minimal, a notion of the world. The above argument is a transcendental argument for a minimal form of realism.[26] A subject who has the capacity for thought, a capacity for forming assertoric contents, has a capacity for being disciplined by the world. To think that thus-and-so is the case is already to have a conception of that which would render the thought erroneous.

5.6 Confrontation with the World

Davidson's basic argument for the denial of the scheme/content distinction is contained within the starting-point for consideration of the interpretation of others. That starting-point is the assumption

(i a) Suppose the alien has a rationally structured point of view.

In the light of the argument about the marks of truth, we now know that if a subject has the capacity for thought, they must be subject to discipline. To be subject to discipline is to be subject to semantic error, where this involves the idea of having your thoughts and assertions correctable by something independent of will. The notion of semantic discipline is the idea of having your thoughts tested by a confrontation with the world. The denial of the scheme/content distinction amounts to the claim that this confrontation is a direct presence; it is not mediated. Why should this be so? The answer lies in the holism of Davidson's account of meaning.

For Davidson, truth is the fundamental semantic concept, not reference or satisfaction. As he argues, reference and satisfaction are 'posits we need to implement a theory of truth'.[27] They are concepts that have an explanatory role 'within' the theory of meaning. It is the concept of truth that is used to explain the application of the theory of meaning. What does this primacy of the concept of truth amount to?

The point turns on the fundamental normativity of meaning ascription. To ascribe a content to a subject is to ascribe to the subject a content that is disciplined by the circumstances under which they ought not to hold that content. This is the fundamental normativity of content that underlies the argument for the marks of truth. Davidson's prioritizing of the concept of truth over reference and satisfaction turns on the idea that the normativity of content can be captured only holistically. The idea is this: Suppose a subject holds '*P*' true; they possess a content that stands to be disciplined by something independent of will. The holism of this notion of discipline turns on the idea that the only purchase we have on what it is for a content to be disciplined is to see it systematically related to a whole field of contents. Contents are things that by their very nature enjoy a systematicity in virtue of which they are disciplined. Content is systematic, because truth is independent of will. The systematicity of content flows from the requirement that content be answerable to something that is genuinely independent of will. For example, if a subject thinks that an object *a* is white, then, if that is to be disciplined by the whiteness of the object independent of what the subject wills, hopes, believes, etc., the issue of whether or not their thought is correct must be systematically connected to the issue of whether other things are white. Put another way, if they are mistaken in claiming that *a* is white, then, in just the same respect that they are mistaken about *a*, they would also be mistaken about *b*. Falsity, like truth, is systematic. To discover that one content is false, or true, has bearing upon the semantic status of other contents. That is the basis for inference. That is the claim of the systematicity of content.

Because of the systematicity of content, our encounter with the world is via truth, not via reference. If we start our semantic explanations with the terms of semantic evaluation for atomic expressions – reference and satisfaction – we will not be able to recover the normativity of the systematicity of content. This is, at this point, a claim, not an argument. The claim is, however, plausible. In general, the point in its favour is that if we base our semantic theory on, say, a theory of reference, the regularities governing the employment of terms will only be causal regularities. This is the idea that the base point for semantics is a causal theory of reference. A lot of people think that this is the appropriate place to begin a semantic theory.[28] Davidson disagrees. The fundamental reason for disagreeing with a building-block approach to semantics is that if we start with a description of causal regularities governing the use of terms, we will not be able to recover the normative regularities that are constitutive of the systematicity of content. The systematicity of content says that the use of linguistic terms is connected by normative rules, rules like, if you hold '*P*' to be true and you hold 'If *P*, *Q*' to be true, you ought not

to hold 'not-Q' to be true. These normative rules are nothing less than the normative patterns of use that are constitutive of the meaning of terms; the normative
rules provide the logical grammar of the expression.[29]

Davidson's advocacy of the primacy of truth is thus an advocacy of the primacy
of the study of logical grammar. That is what the theory of meaning studies. His
holism is the thesis that this grammar can be studied only *sui generis*; it cannot be
grounded in a theory of weaker regularities such as causal regularities. This means
that truth is prior to reference. Our notion of what a term refers to is dependent of
our notion of what it is for sentences containing that term to be true. This sounds
as if it has matters wholly the wrong way around.[30] I do not believe that this is so,
but it marks the profound and radical version of the 'Semantics exhausts ontology'
thesis that Davidson advocates.

Suppose for the moment that Davidson is right, and truth is primary. In so far
as a subject possesses content, the subject must be responsive to semantic discipline;
they must enjoy some kind of confrontation with the world. That is the point of the
argument about the marks of truth. If truth is prior to reference because of the
systematicity of content, the confrontation with the world must be holistic. Confrontations with the world are not obtained by causal impacts; they are obtained by
being presented with the content of a 'that' clause. The appropriate notion of
confrontation that disciplines content is a confrontation *that thus-and-so* is the case.
The holism and systematicity of content mean that, in terms of the sort of semantic
disciplinary confrontation required for meaning to be possible, coming to experience that thus-and-so is the case is not further analysable into a series of causal
confrontations tracing the causal ancestry and impact that regulates the use of
singular terms, predicates letters, etc. Our basic semantic encounter with the world
is an encounter in which, as it were, the world says, 'Take that'! For the normativity
of content to be possible, our confrontations must be molecular in character. When
we experience that thus-and-so is the case, what is represented in the 'that' clause
is the world. It has to be the world at this point, for it has to be that which is
independent of will for it to perform the disciplinary role required for content to be
possible. And that which is independent of will is the world. Our confrontations
with the world – that thus-and-so is the case – cannot be decomposed into, say,
causal confrontations as tracked by a causal theory of reference and the subsequent
application of a conceptual scheme. Our confrontations are direct encounters with
the world. This is the denial of the scheme/content distinction.[31]

Recall, the directness of encounter implicated by the denial of the scheme/
content distinction does not deny that the world we encounter is structured –
indeed, the structure is constitutive of the encounter. It has to be structured for our
encounters with the world to play the role they need to play in rationally ordering
our beliefs. Encounters with piecemeal items via causal contacts do not provide the
rational impact that we require of the world. Only a molecular encounter provides

rational impact in virtue of its structure. What is denied by the thesis of direct presence is the idea that the structure encountered is an organization that arises from the application of a conceptual scheme upon a level of confrontation that is non-conceptual. The non-conceptual confrontation would, on such a model, presumably be supplied by a causal theory of reference and satisfaction. Pictorially, the situation can be represented thus:

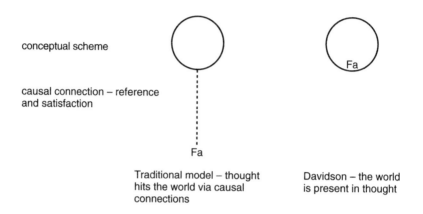

conceptual scheme

causal connection – reference and satisfaction

Fa

Traditional model – thought hits the world via causal connections

Davidson – the world is present in thought

Davidson's position is thus a radical reading of the 'Semantics exhausts ontology' thesis. If this is right, the denial of the scheme/content distinction arises not out of the empirical argument from interpretation, but from a transcendental argument about the character of our confrontation with the world, a confrontation that is necessary for content to be possible.[32]

Davidson's position captures a number of theses first noted in chapter 1. The study of meaning is a priori, for the normativity of content is not reducible to causal regularities – something that could be studied a posteriori. The study of meaning is a priori, for it is a study of the normative patterns that have to exist for meaning to be the sort of thing that is semantically disciplined. The patterns of use studied by this a priori enquiry constitute logical grammar. It is an objective study and, furthermore, a study which shows that a certain minimal, although objective, notion of realist truth is a necessary condition for the possibility of content.

Most philosophers who oppose Davidson's approach do so because they refuse to accept his approach to metaphysics. If your metaphysical starting-point is physicalism, you will be committed to providing a theory of meaning that will reduce the normative patterns of use of expressions to causal regularities. You will expect the normative patterns of use to track the causal regularities studied by empirical disciplines like psychology. Writers like Fodor acknowledge the character of the Davidsonian approach to content, but think that it is an exhausted line of enquiry. But the approach only looks exhausted because of the presumption that we make haste to ground investigations into meaning in physical theory. But that haste obscures the variety of options that are available for naturalizing content, and pushes us into the reductionist version of naturalization.[33]

It should be noted, however, that despite the very radical version of the 'Semantics exhausts ontology' that we have now uncovered in Davidson and the claim that our confrontations with the world are molecular, this is not to deny the obvious point that we are physical creatures that inhabit a physical environment that is in regular and continuous causal interaction with us. To say that our confrontations with the world are molecular is not to deny that we have causal confrontations with the world. The point is only that the confrontations that discipline thought and talk are not definable in terms of causal impacts. They are, of course, causal impacts. No doubt, in some sense, the confrontations that discipline thought and talk supervene upon causal impacts. When I say that the chalk is white and I am confronted with the redness of the chalk, I am subject to all sorts of causal impacts, including those that issue from the redness of the chalk. The point behind Davidson's claim is simply that it is an a priori constitutive claim about the nature of our semantic confrontations with the world that they enjoy a normative structure. There is no scope for an analysis of that normative structure in terms of causal regularities: the normative patterns do not track causal patterns. It does not follow from this that normative patterns are not in fact causal patterns. All that follows is that the salience of the normative patterns is anomalous with respect to the causal ones.

To look at the consequences of Davidson's position from the other point of view, consider this. If semantics exhausts ontology, then we do not start our metaphysics with a favoured world-view – say, the scientific. We start our metaphysics by looking to see which classes of thought and talk are genuinely truth-apt. Of which forms of discourse can we say that they observe a truth-predicate which obeys the marks of truth? Suppose we find that moral discourse is such a discourse. If that were so, we would then have exhausted the issue of moral realism – whether or not the world is a world of value, for our notion of the world is constituted by our notion of those thoughts that are true.[34]

For many people, this approach to metaphysics is the very opposite of that which they find most reasonable, obvious and commonsensical. The 'Semantics exhausts ontology' thesis is seen as an absurd extravagance. They think the world is whatever the sciences tell us that it is – nothing more, nothing less. From Davidson's point of view, such a privileging of one form of discourse over the rest is a prejudice; furthermore, it stands to deny the existence of the most striking feature of our lives – our capacity for thought and talk. Our thought and talk involve a direct presence of the world. The world is before us in thought. Of course, Davidson has denied that there is such a thing as thought, for meaning is what is captured by a truth theory that makes best overall sense of behaviour.[35] This is not, however, really a denial of our intentionality and our ability to think. Rather, it is the claim that what it is to think is to be a creature with a rationally systematic structure to your behaviour. Our thought and intentionality consist in our being creatures with a rational systematicity to our behaviour. This is a form of qualified behaviourism. It is 'qualified', for the description of behaviour employed is rich in normative rationalizing concepts. It is not a reductionist behaviourism. As we will see in later chapters, far from being at odds with contemporary neo-Fregean theory of thought, Davidson's position is compatible with, if not identical with, the neo-Fregean. In both cases, the behaviourism is endorsed as part of a critique of the representationalism of the standard model of thought and content. When Davidson denies that there is such a thing as thought, what he is really denying is the representationalist reification of thought. It is thoughts that Davidson denies, not thought. This leaves Davidson, like any externalist, with a problem about how to treat false thoughts in the absence of a reified representation to stand in lieu of the world when our thinking is false. But everyone has a problem with the concept of misrepresentation. I save that topic for later chapters. (See especially chapters 11 and 12.)

Davidson's fundamental metaphysical orientation is one with a long philosophical ancestry. It is not a metaphysical orientation in which you start with a metaphysics of the world and then try to accommodate thinking subjects within it. It is an orientation that starts with the thinking self and, on the basis of our capacity for thought and talk, works out what the world must be like. It is an orientation that investigates the self and its world, not the world and the selves it contains. It is an orientation that, for many writers, smacks of dualism, verificationism and idealism. The charge of dualism is thoroughly misguided, for the 'Semantics exhausts ontology' thesis commits us, at most, to substance monism with a pluralism of properties, not a pluralism of substances. The charge of verificationism is deflected by recognizing that the denial of the scheme/content distinction does not depend on the empirical argument from interpretation. The threat of idealism is removed just in case the transcendental enquiry into the conditions for the possibility of content reveal that we have to possess a concept of truth that is independent of will. That, of course, is exactly what the enquiry reveals in the investigation into the marks of truth. Whether or not the resulting position would be recognized as realist by all who have used that label is doubtful. But, in a minimal sense, the resulting position is realist, for it legitimizes a concept of truth independent of will. This is a concept of objective truth. The legitimacy of an objective concept of truth and a direct presence of the world are the major significant and, I suspect, lasting achievements of Davidson's philosophy. The metaphysical significance of these compares with the advances made by any of the greatest thinkers in our tradition.

6

Meaning, Metaphysics and Logic

6.1 Introduction

Davidson's work promotes of a pair of significant metaphysical claims: the denial of the scheme/content distinction and the defence of minimal realism. The fact that such metaphysical results flow from investigations in the theory of meaning is a reflection of the 'Semantics exhausts ontology' thesis. For anyone endorsing the broadly Fregean methodology that I am defending, the contemporary tool-bag for metaphysics is the philosophy of thought.

In Michael Dummett's hands, this fundamental dependence on the theory of meaning has given rise to a specific claim that a basic metaphysical debate between realism and anti-realism should be fought out in meaning-theoretic terms. Dummett thinks that there is an issue about whether truth is the central semantic concept for a theory of meaning.[1] Furthermore, the issue about what concept should be the central concept for a theory of meaning provides a novel way of handling the metaphysical debate about realism.

In this chapter I plot the connections between the work already done and metaphysics, especially as this bears upon our concept of valid inference. We have seen that our account of truth cannot help but implicate an account of meaning, and vice versa. In the last chapter we drew the sting of this interdependence by recasting the basic semantic investigation as a transcendental enquiry into the character of truth, given that a notion of assertoric content is possible. That investigation makes use of the concept of the systematicity of meaning, the way that contents are systematically related to one another in ways that define their inferential relationships. So whatever we say about meaning must bear upon our concept of valid inference. The concept of valid inference is as much implicated in our theorizing about meaning as the concept of truth. This trio of concepts together determine our metaphysics, or at least a core part of our metaphysics: our view of the world that is exhausted by semantics.

The way that these three concepts are connected is not obvious. The account of the connection varies from author to author. Indeed, the realism/anti-realism debate in the theory of meaning has acquired a reputation for being a highly recondite and specialized debate, if not almost a local family quarrel, the entry rules to which have become opaque to many researchers.[2] There is not space within one chapter to do justice to the variety of arguments that occupy the territory of this debate. Instead, in the next two sections I introduce the central ideas of the realism/ anti-realism debate and outline the range of options for plotting the connections between meaning, truth and validity. Having distinguished different lines of connections, in the remainder of the chapter I provide an overview and preliminary assessment of the different arguments. This chapter stands apart from most of the rest of the book. Its aim is to provide a broad survey of options, rather than to pursue the argument in detail for any one.

6.2   Intuitionistic Mathematics

Dummett's critique of realism from within the theory of meaning owes much to the development of intuitionistic mathematics. In this section I give an informal sketch of the central features of intuitionistic mathematics and of the account of validity that intuitionistic logic offers in place of classical logic. This provides a simple model of an anti-realist programme stripped of the clutter of epistemological baggage carried in more familiar domains. It provides a basis for drawing the distinctions required for a firm grip on all the issues that are involved within contemporary debates about realism and anti-realism.

Brouwer called his philosophy of mathematics 'Intuitionism', for, like Kant, he believed that mathematical objects – numbers, sets, functions, etc. – were mind-dependent.[3] He believed that mathematical objects existed only in so far as they were intuited by the human mind. He was an idealist about mathematical objects. He did not believe that mathematical objects and their properties existed independently of the human activity of intuiting them, more specifically the activity of constructing examples of numbers with specific properties through the activity of proofs. Brouwer's metaphysics is opposed to Platonism about mathematics, which holds that mathematical numbers and their properties exist independently of our activities of proof. So far, this has all the characteristics of a familiar idealist/realist controversy. The novelty arises when we consider the attitude to logically complex expressions, given the central role that the concept of proof plays in Brouwer's thought.

Because Brouwer thought that numbers were mind-dependent, a statement about numbers was to be understood not in terms of the conditions under which it was true; for no such conditions obtain independently of the conditions under which it is provable by us. So the meaning of a mathematical statement is to be

144

given in terms of its proof-conditions: the conditions under which it would be provable. Now, consider an undecidable mathematical statement *S*, one for which we have no account of what it would be to prove it, or to prove its negation. The idea that the meaning of *S* should be given in its proof-conditions, and not truth-conditions, means that, in the absence of proof one way or the other, we have no warrant for thinking that mathematical reality is either as *S* states it to be or as not-*S* states it to be. This result follows, for, according to Brouwer's point of view, the only warrant for thinking that mathematical reality is as some statement claims it to be is to be able to prove that statement. By definition, this is not possible in the case of *S*, and, crucially, neither is it the case with not-*S*. But this means that the intuitionist has no warrant (proof) for asserting

Either *S* or not-*S*.

Note how the idealist account of the meaning of atomic sentences in terms of their proof-conditions has the consequence that a logically complex sentence turns out not to be provable. This means that the intuitionist is committed to a different account of the meaning of logically complex sentences, for the above is an instance of the law of excluded middle,

(1)   A v ¬A,

which, in classical logic, is equivalent to the following three laws:

(2)   ¬¬(A v ¬A)

(3)   ¬(A & ¬A)

(4)   ¬¬A → A.

Intuitionistic logic endorses only (2) and (3).[4]

Negation is the key constant for understanding the difference between intuitionistic and classical logic. The intuitionist is committed to what seems, intuitively, to be a stronger, yet also simpler, concept of negation than the classical logician, for the intuitionist does not treat not-A as true just in case A fails to be true. In this sense the intuitionistic account of negation is more demanding than classical negation, which is an operator that, as it were, sweeps up all the sentences that fail to be true. In contrast, the intuitionist demands that for '¬A' to be true (provable), it is not enough to show that 'A' fails to be provable, but that it be provable that it is not provable. This is understood as the claim that it is provable that a proof of 'A' would lead to a contradiction. In this sense, intuitionistic negation is more demanding than classical negation.[5]

145

The above is only the briefest sketch of how the concepts of meaning, truth (understood in terms of proof) and logic are connected in intuitionistic mathematics and logic. The significance of the connection is profound. The intuitionist case connects a metaphysical thesis about mathematical reality to a logical thesis via considerations about the meaning of mathematical statements and, especially, the meaning of logically complex statements. Intuitively, Brouwer's central claim can be formulated like this: To insist that classical rules of inference are valid and to insist that all instances of (1) are true is, in effect, to give voice to the metaphysical thesis that mathematical reality exists independently of mind. To insist that all instances of (1) obtain, even for undecidable mathematical sentences, is to insist that mathematical reality already has the answer to the question 'Whether *S*?', that the answer exists independently of our ability to prove it or its negation. But this connection between the metaphysical issue 'Do numbers exist independently of us?' and the logical issue 'Are classical rules of inference or intuitionistic rules of inference valid?' suggests that we can explore our metaphysical problems by examining our logic. More specifically, Brouwer's central complaint against classical logic was that its rules of inference (double negation elimination in the case of the propositional calculus) were not genuinely rules of logic, for they encoded a metaphysical model (realism) our right to which stands in need of legitimization. This is a stunning charge. It is a philosophical insight that is truly a product of the twentieth century. It is the thought that the issue between intuitionistic and classical logic provides a non-metaphorical way of formulating the otherwise opaque and long-standing metaphysical dispute between Platonists and their opponents.

Many things in philosophy are shadows of earlier formulations, but Brouwer's idea is genuinely novel. His charge against classical logic is that its rules are, if you like, not purely logical, but import metaphysics into our very notion of what constitutes a valid argument. The patterns of argumentation employed by classical mathematicians are patterns that are valid only if the metaphysics of Platonism is tenable. The intuitive pull of Brouwer's charge is that we should employ only those patterns of inference that are, as it were, metaphysically free of suspicion. Quite what a positive account of such rules would amount to is not clear from Brouwer's writings, but I suggest that a first formulation would be to say that it amounts to the injunction to employ only those rules of inference that can be shown to be transcendentally necessary – necessary for the existence of thought and talk.[6]

Let me summarize a number of features of Brouwer's anti-realist account of the connection between metaphysics, meaning and logic. First, Brouwer employs a non-truth-conditional account of the meaning of atomic sentences: the meanings of atomic mathematical sentences are specified in terms of their proof-conditions. Second, Brouwer offers a non-truth-conditional account of the meaning of the logical constants, specifically negation. Third, the second point has the consequence that Brouwer favours a logic that challenges the classical account of valid inference. Fourth, the challenge to classical logic is seen as a non-metaphorical way of formulating the otherwise intractable metaphysical disagreement between Platonists and mathematical idealists.

Dummett's key insight on the above was that the connection Brouwer had plotted between metaphysics and logic is not domain-specific. It is generalizable across all discourses, and requires only that we replace the concept of proof with some more general epistemically constrained concept of truth. If then, as Dummett believes, there are general considerations about meaning that push us towards an epistemic conception of truth, this will *ipso facto* push us towards a non-classical account of inference in these other domains, and this will be to endorse an anti-realist attitude to those domains. That, then, is the general prescription for connecting metaphysics with logic via meaning. In the application of the general recipe, many different issues have accumulated around the core, as ideas specific to empirical discourse have clouded the central connection. In the next section I plot the four main types of anti-realist argument before going on briefly to evaluate each in turn.

6.3   Four Types of Anti-realist Argument

To instil some order into the arguments, intuitions and theories that make up the realism/anti-realism debate, I distinguish four different ways of connecting the metaphysics of realism with issues about meaning and validity. The idea that the metaphysics of realism is in some way affected by considerations of meaning is not novel. Classical verificationisms from the idealism of Berkeley to the logical positivism of the Vienna circle have based their metaphysics upon claims about the impossibility of accounting for the meaning of certain statements given a verificationist account of meaning. So, for Berkeley, the very idea of unperceived existence is unintelligible because of our supposed inability to verify it, and such a claim clearly presupposes a verificationist account of meaning. Similarly, the phenomenalism that was popular during the logical positivist period was sustained by an epistemology which held that the only things that were verifiable were statements about sense-data. What is novel in Dummett's treatment is the idea that the debate about the semantic concept at the heart of a theory of meaning (should it be truth or an epistemic concept like verification?) connects with issues in the theory of inference. This connection has not always been closely observed by Dummett, or by some of his followers and many of his critics. Nevertheless, it is a connection that characterizes three of the four argument types about realism that I want to distinguish.

147

What is central to all four types of anti-realism that I want to distinguish is the idea that our concept of truth should be constrained, and for the moment we should think of this constraint as an epistemic one. The precise nature of such a constraint is open to debate, but we can start with the idea that truth should be restricted to 'knowable truth'.[7] The natural way of thinking about this constraint is to suppose that it amounts to endorsing a verificationist theory of meaning; but to do this already blurs an important distinction that I want to draw. So, let's start by merely noting that the anti-realist thinks that truth is restricted to knowable truth. We can distinguish the four different anti-realist arguments by making a series of distinctions. First, we distinguish between those arguments in which the knowability constraint flows from an account of meaning and those that do not. The idea that the knowability constraint could be detached from an account of meaning provides us with the first type of anti-realist argument. The first argument takes the validity of classical rules of inference as the key issue, but offers a critique of classical logic not based on the theory of meaning. Such an argument sees the validity of deduction as grounded in a proof-theoretic justification, rather than a justification that is semantically constrained. This argument is apparent in Prawitz's work, and also figures in the work of Tennant and Dummett.[8]

The other three arguments all connect the knowability constraint with semantic issues. The first of these three arguments is one in which the semantic basis for knowability is a general verificationist theory of meaning that applies to all sentences, including atomic ones. This characterizes the second type of anti-realist argument. This is a powerful form of argument, for the knowability condition affects meaning in general, and this must place some constraints on the limits of intelligibility. In particular, it seems reasonable to suppose that a general verificationism that resulted in a critique of classical logic would do so via the claim that the classical account of the meaning of the logical constants was unintelligible.[9] The remaining two varieties are arguments in which the semantic basis for knowability applies only to logically complex sentences. The third type of argument questions the intelligibility of the classical account of the constants. The fourth type of argument critiques classical logic without questioning the intelligibility of the classical account of the constants. The third argument type is a verificationist argument, but is non-verificationist with respect to atomic sentences. The semantic basis for knowability in the fourth argument is less easy to state in ways that are familiar from verificationist positions elsewhere in philosophy.

We can represent the relationship between these four argument types (AR1–AR4) diagrammatically as responses to a series of questions as follows:

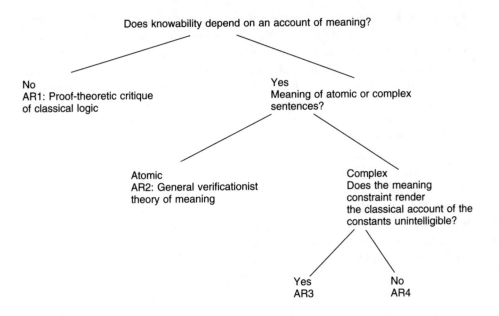

The argument types that I have labelled AR3 and AR4 do not have obvious names, although note that AR3 will share with AR2 the effect of making the classical account of the constants unintelligible. These two differ only in that AR2 has this effect as a consequence of a general theory of meaning that imposes intelligibility limits on all expressions; AR3 has this effect only on the logical constants. The difference between AR2 and AR3 requires us to make sense of the idea of a very specific theory of meaning that applies only to the logical constants. Even in the abstract, this appears an odd idea, and, indeed, I shall argue that there is no coherent way of occupying the position that I have abstractly identified as AR3. The reason that I have identified this as a potential version of an anti-realist critique is that, in the light of further distinctions that I shall offer below, AR3 characterizes a position that Tennant sometimes seems to endorse.

I call the AR2 argument reductionist anti-realism. It employs a verificationist account of meaning for atomic sentences. On the face of it, such an account is at odds with our ordinary unreflective notion of what it is to understand sentences that, prima facie, appear not to be verifiable: e.g. sentences about other minds. Reductionist anti-realism has the consequence that sentences about other minds have a weaker content than we unreflectively suppose (e.g. the content of sentences about other minds is specified in terms of behavioural dispositions). Given the emphasis on the meaning of atomic sentences, then even if the reductionist anti-realist critiques the meaning of the classical constants, it may turn out that the classical rules of inference can survive under a different account of the constants. If so, this means that the reductionist anti-realist stands to lose the connection between meaning, truth and inference and locates the debate about realism solely in questions about meaning and truth, not inference. As we will see, such reductionist anti-realism has become almost an orthodoxy in the Dummettian-inspired debate, and many defences of realism have turned out to be attacks on the reductionist concentration on the meaning of atomic sentences.

AR4 attempts to critique realism by offering a critique of classical rules of inference without subjecting the classical account of the constants to the charge of unintelligibility. This is the argument strategy that I have offered, and it is also found in some of Tennant's work.[10] I call the AR4 strategy non-reductionist anti-realism. AR3 would appear to be a possible strategy that critiques classical rules of inference but operates with a criterion of intelligibility that affects only the logical constants, not atomic sentences. As noted, it is not clear what such a criterion of intelligibility would look like, so I do not bother to give it a name.

In the next section I shall briefly sketch the ideas central to a proof-theoretic critique of classical logic, and explain why such a programme requires the support of some semantic constraints. AR1 turns out not to be a sustainable independent line of argument. I then examine the scope for reductionist anti-realism and, following that, non-reductionist anti-realism.

6.4   The Proof-theoretic Critique of Classical Logic

If a purely proof-theoretic critique of classical logic worked, the connection between metaphysics, logic and semantics would be lost. Metaphysics and logic would be connected, but semantics would drop out of the picture. I do not think that a purely proof-theoretic critique of classical logic works, for some semantic component is required in order to gain argumentative leverage over classical logic. The approach is of considerable interest, however, and worth noting, if only to help focus attention on what is central to the way our concepts of truth, meaning and inference are connected.[11]

Consider the question of how we justify logical laws. A proof-theoretic justification of deduction works by taking a basic set of rules of inference as self-evident, and then attempting to justify all other rules by appeal to the basic set. Call any deduction involving only the basic set of rules a 'canonical deduction'. The claim is then that if there is valid deduction from premises $A_1, \ldots, A_n$ to conclusion C, every step in the deduction can be reduced to steps involving only canonical deductions, so that the whole transition can be represented as a canonical deduction. Following a suggestion of Gentzen's, a popular way of effecting this reduction procedure is to take the introduction rules for the constants as the basic set and to try to justify everything else in terms of them. In the first instance, this means that we should be able to justify the elimination rules by this procedure, and this, of course, is just the requirement that the introduction and elimination rules be in harmony. Having done this, we would then need to show how all derived rules can be reduced to application of the introduction rules.[12] A couple of examples will make the idea plain.

Take the introduction and elimination rules for the conditional:

$$
\begin{array}{c}
\begin{array}{c} A \\ \gamma \\ B \end{array} \\ \hline A \to B \end{array} \to +
\qquad
\begin{array}{cc} \alpha & \beta \\ A & A \to B \\ \hline & B \end{array} \to -
$$

Suppose we have a deduction that involves an application of conditional elimination to reach B. This deduction will include the subsidiary deduction α that has A as conclusion. The deduction will also have subsidiary deduction β, to get $A \to B$ as conclusion. The deduction β will have to include within it an application of the introduction rule for the conditional. This means that β must contain, from a deduction to A as conclusion, the deduction γ that takes us from A to B, followed by an application of the introduction rule for the conditional. But if β contains γ, then instead of employing conditional elimination to obtain B, all we need do is append γ to our deduction for A, α. α followed immediately by γ will give us B directly, and the use of the introduction rule in β, followed by the elimination rule, will now appear to be a superfluous detour.

The distributive law provides a good example of the same technique applied to a derived rule. We have

$$
\frac{A \,\&\, (B \vee C)}{(A \,\&\, B) \vee (B \,\&\, C)}
$$

as the derived law. Now, in obtaining the premiss of this law, there must have been a deduction α to reach A as conclusion and a deduction to reach (B v C) as conclusion, followed by an application of conjunction introduction. The deduction to reach (B v C) must have involved the introduction rule for 'v', e.g. the rule

$$
\frac{B}{B \vee C}
$$

Call the deduction to reach B, β. We can represent the whole situation, then, as follows:

$$
\begin{array}{cc}
 & \beta \\
 & \mathrm{B} \\
\alpha & \overline{} \; \mathrm{v+} \\
\mathrm{A} & \mathrm{B\,v\,C} \; \&+ \\
\hline
\multicolumn{2}{c}{\mathrm{A\,\&\,(B\,v\,C)}} \\
\hline
\multicolumn{2}{c}{(\mathrm{A\,\&\,B})\;\mathrm{v}\;(\mathrm{A\,\&\,C})}
\end{array}
$$

But if we have deductions α and β to get A and B respectively, then it is clear that a deduction comprising α and β, followed by conjunction introduction and then the disjunction introduction rule, would get us the above conclusion; e.g.

$$
\begin{array}{cc}
\alpha & \beta \\
\mathrm{A} & \mathrm{B} \; \&+ \\
\hline
\multicolumn{2}{c}{(\mathrm{A\,\&\,B})} \; \mathrm{v+} \\
\hline
\multicolumn{2}{c}{(\mathrm{A\,\&\,B})\;\mathrm{v}\;(\mathrm{A\,\&\,C})}
\end{array}
$$

The idea that all valid deductions are reducible to applications of the introduction rules captures the familiar idea that deductive inference is non-ampliative: a valid deductive argument provides no new information. The reduction procedure outlined above may seem to render deductive arguments superfluous; for if all valid deductive arguments can be reduced to applications of the introduction rules, what point is there in introducing logical complexity? Put informally, the whole point about a valid deductive argument is that, with respect to your stock of atomic information, it provides no new information; it does not take you any further than the stock of information with which you began. Of course, unpacking the consequences of complex sentences can be informative, but it can never add to your stock of atomic information. This point is just the informal representation of the claim that

$$
\frac{\mathrm{A}}{\mathrm{B}}
$$

is not a valid argument. Indeed, the limit case of a valid argument is:

$$
\frac{\mathrm{A}}{\mathrm{A}}
$$

That is the most that you can get out of a valid deductive argument. Indeed, with respect to atomic sentences, all deductive arguments will be reducible to either the above or the weaker form

$$\frac{A}{A \vee B}$$

If the idea of a proof-theoretic justification of deduction provides any leverage on the metaphysics of realism, everything turns on how we demarcate the set of basic rules. In the case of disjunction and conjunction it is difficult to see how there could be any dispute about the introduction rules for these constants. The conditional is, perhaps, more problematic, but for present purposes I shall assume that there is no real dispute about that either.[13] When we consider negation, however, it is not clear what the self-evident rules should be governing this constant. The introduction rule is not contentious:

$$\frac{\begin{array}{c} A \\ B \& \neg B \end{array}}{\neg A} \neg +,$$

but if we take as our elimination rule the apparently self-evident

$$\frac{A \& \neg A}{B} \neg -,$$

these two together do not suffice to generate classical logic. They only provide intuitionistic logic. Indeed, the above pair of rules could be replaced by the single rule governing negation of *ex falso quodlibet* (EFQ)

$$\frac{\perp}{B} \text{EFQ}$$

otherwise known as absurdity elimination. In order to obtain classical logic, we would require the classical elimination rule for negation – double negation elimination (DNE):

$$\frac{\neg \neg A}{A} \text{DNE},$$

for that then ensures that we get excluded middle as a law, and classical *reductio*

$$\frac{\begin{array}{c} \neg A \\ \perp \end{array}}{A} \text{classical reductio}$$

as a derived rule. But now, how are we to decide whether or not DNE should appear in our basic set of self-evident rules from which the rest of logic is to be justified? The intuitionist will want no more than EFQ. Indeed, it is instructive to think of the intuitionistic restriction here as amounting to the complaint that DNE is not a generally valid rule, for it is a rule that breaks the constraint that deductive logic is non-ampliative: it should not enrich our stock of atomic information. For the intuitionist, DNE is a rule that, rather than leaving us standing still with respect to our atomic information

$$\frac{A}{A},$$

expands it just as

$$\frac{A}{B}$$

does. Putting the matter this way makes apparent that the intuitionist thinks the sentence A has a different content to $\neg\neg A$. From the classical point of view, of course, there is no difference in content between a sentence and its double negation; that is why the classical logician finds DNE self-evident and therefore a bona-fide member of the basic set of rules.[14] But this means that there is no way to settle the debate about whether EFQ and DNE should appear in the basic set of self-evident rules without some account of the meaning of the negation constant. Because the intuitionist thinks that A is a stronger claim than $\neg\neg A$ and the classical logician thinks that they are identical, they must disagree over the meaning of 'not'. A proof-theoretic justification of deduction may play a valuable role in formalizing our ordinary concept of valid inference, but it cannot provide leverage on the issue between intuitionistic and classical logic without some further semantic constraint to demarcate the basic set of self-evident rules. I conclude then that AR1 is not a viable basis for an anti-realist critique. This means that the connection noted between metaphysics and questions in the theory of valid inference must be related to issues about meaning. In the next section I turn to outline AR2, the defence and critique of which has occupied a central place in the Dummett-inspired literature debate on realism.[15]

6.5   Reductionist Anti-realism

One difficulty with plotting the connections between issues in the theory of meaning and realism is the variety of positions that are called 'realist'. It is not obvious that realism about theoretical entities in science, realism about other minds, realism about moral values, realism about colours, etc. have much in common, let alone a connection with the theory of meaning. It seems reasonable to suppose that there are domain-specific issues in each of these cases that cannot be handled by a general appeal to broad semantic enquiries.

One thing that might be thought to be domain-specific is the account of reference to the entities characteristic of different domains. For example, realism about theoretical entities in science is normally an issue about whether we treat reference to such items at face value or whether we give a reductionist account in terms of our reference to instrument readings, etc. Similarly, realism about other minds can be construed as an issue about whether reference to such things should be taken literally or reconstrued as reference to behavioural dispositions. The cases of moral values and colours bear comparison. In both these cases the anti-realist is normally thought to be committed to an account of judgements about values or colours that reveals that our ordinary talk about such things leads us into error if we take it at face value as talk about real properties of value or colour.[16]

All the above cases are types of anti-realism that are committed to some form of reductionism; for in each case the anti-realist enjoins us to take our ordinary talk about the entities or properties at issue at less than face value. I suggest we classify the above four cases into one of two different categories. The first two cases, theoretical entities in science and other minds, I shall call anti-realisms based on epistemological reductionism. Such anti-realisms typically endorse an epistemological thesis that says that the disputed entities are beyond our epistemological reach. The anti-realist advises us to construe talk about the supposed entities in terms of talk about a favoured range of entities that are within our epistemological reach.

In contrast, the cases of moral values and colours I call anti-realisms based on metaphysical reductionism. Such anti-realisms typically appeal to metaphysical principles or assumptions that render the supposed properties problematic. For example, many writers are suspicious of the reality of colours, because colours do not enjoy a 'wide explanatory role'; that is to say, colours feature in only a narrow range of explanations and are therefore not integrated into the general explanatory framework employed in the natural sciences.[17]

Of these different kinds of anti-realism, it is more likely that the first kind, based on epistemological reductionism, could be illuminated by debates about meaning. Anti-realisms based on metaphysical reductionism do not necessarily involve reductionism about the meaning of the target-class judgements. Indeed, such anti-realists will claim it a virtue of their position that they are committed to no revisionist or reductionist thesis about the meaning of talk about values or colours. They will insist that the issue with which they are concerned is wholly a metaphysical issue about the sorts of states of affairs that make judgements about value and colour true.[18] I shall not discuss metaphysical reductionist anti-realisms further. The development of such positions requires a prior acceptance of the controlling meta-physical model that motivates an anti-realist account of, for example, values. This approach is too removed from the 'Semantics exhausts ontology' methodology that I am deploying to make assessment of it viable in the present context. Epistemologi-cal reductionist anti-realisms, however, have a prima-facie compatibility with the approach to semantics on offer in this book. We need to assess their worth.

Anti-realisms that offer an epistemological reduction have the following general character. We distinguish between judgements the content of which represents states of the world that are within epistemological reach and those that represent states of the world that are beyond epistemological reach. Call the former, judge-ments that belong to the e-class. Judgments that belong to the e-class are judge-ments the evidence for which can amount to that which they represent; that is to say, the evidence can be the truth-conditions. Judgements that do not belong to the e-class must then be judgements the evidence for which falls short of their truth-conditions. Now, merely to observe that the truth-conditions of judgements that do not belong to the e-class are out of our epistemological reach does not, of itself, enjoin an anti-realist attitude to these judgements. You can be a realist about a given target class of judgements – e.g. judgements about other minds – and accept that the target class is not a subset of the e-class. Such a form of realism with respect to other minds is common.

The apparently harmless assumption that we have made is to draw a distinc-tion between judgements of the e-class and those that are not of the e-class. The semantic point to this epistemological distinction is to say that it is a distinction between judgements the truth-conditions of which fall within a conception of that which we can experience, and those whose truth-conditions are not experienceable. The assumption that such a distinction can be made is central to reductionist forms of anti-realism. I shall call it the assumption about the limit of experience (the LE assumption). The LE assumption applies to atomic judgements. It divides atomic judgements into the e-class and the rest. It is contentious where we should locate the point at which the LE assumption cuts this divide, but it is a common thought that some such division upon the range of atomic judgements is viable. For the moment we should note one respect in which the positioning of the divide effected by the LE assumption is contentious.

The division of judgements into those that are members of the e-class and those that are not is a division between judgements whose truth-conditions are verifiable and those whose truth-conditions are not verifiable, or are 'recognition-transcendent'. Now, to say that judgements not in the e-class have truth-conditions that are not verifiable is to say that it is not possible to verify or experience their truth-conditions. The impossibility evoked here, however, is only relative to what-ever epistemological assumptions motivate the deployment of the LE assumption. The LE assumption could constrain what is available within experience in a number of different ways. Some might think that it has the result that only judgements about sense-data have verifiable truth-conditions; others that judgements about material objects have verifiable truth-conditions, but not judgements about other minds, and so on. Wherever the LE assumption cuts a line between those atomic states of affairs that are verifiable and those that are not, then, on the basis of that division, the latter judgements will have truth-conditions that are non-verifiable. Because I shall have need to characterize a different concept of non-verifiability later on, I shall refer to the current idea as relative non-verifiability, to mark the point that the concept of non-verifiability is understood relative to the epistemology regarding atomic states of affairs.[19]

As noted, to employ the LE assumption is not yet to advocate an anti-realist attitude with respect to judgements that are not members of the e-class. To get an anti-realist argument on the basis of the epistemological framework just sketched, we need to add a pair of plausible constraints on what it is to know the meaning of a sentence. These constraints amount to what I will call meaning empiricism (ME).

Suppose we assume that understanding a sentence is to know its truth-conditions, to know under what conditions the sentence would be true or false. Meaning empiricism comprises a pair of plausible constraints on knowledge of truth-conditions that concern the acquisition of knowledge of meaning and the manifestation of knowledge of meaning. The constraints are:

> **ME(a):** Knowledge of the truth-conditions of sentences must be such that an account is available of how a speaker empirically acquires such knowledge.

> **ME(b):** Knowledge of the truth-conditions of sentences must be such that an account is available of how a speaker empirically manifests such knowledge.

The operation of these constraints in the pursuit of an anti-realist argument has become known as the acquisition challenge and the manifestation challenge respectively.[20]

It has become customary to think that it is ME(b) that poses the more serious challenge. Suppose that we could meet the manifestation challenge and show what it is to possess knowledge of truth-conditions of sentences. Even if we were unsure how to meet the acquisition challenge, it would hardly matter, for in meeting ME(b), we would have shown that we possessed the relevant knowledge even if we were not sure how we got it. ME(b) is therefore the more serious challenge.

6.6   Wright's Reductionist Anti-realism

I start with the simplest application of ME(b) to derive an anti-realist position. Suppose the LE assumption cuts the division between the e-class and the rest in such a way that statements about others' mental states fall in the latter category. Wright makes this assumption in his treatment of anti-realism. Let '*P*' be a statement about another's mental state, e.g.

> *P*: So-and-so is in pain.

Statements about others' behaviour we shall assume fall within the e-class. Let '*S*' be such a statement, e.g.

> *S*: So-and-so is behaving in such-and-such a way.

Now, ME(b) demands that knowledge of truth-conditions be manifestable. What does this requirement amount to?

The simplest version of ME(b) would be to insist that to manifest knowledge of truth-conditions is to show what it is to be empirically sensitive to the truth-conditions. With regard to *S*, *ex hypothesi* its truth-conditions are the sorts of states to which one can be empirically sensitive, for we have supposed that they fall within the limit of experience. There is, therefore, no problem about knowledge of the truth-conditions of *S* satisfying ME(b). With respect to *P*, however, *ex hypothesi* the truth-conditions of non-e-class statements are such that it is not possible to be empirically sensitive to them. There is no such thing as being sensitive to such states of affairs, for the LE assumption has rendered such states of affairs non-experienceable. So there is nothing that we could do that would count as a sensitivity to such truth-conditions. It is only possible to show a sensitivity to truth-conditions for statements of the e-class, like *S*. This means that knowledge of the truth-conditions of *P* fails ME(b).

Nevertheless, *P* is a meaningful statement. As knowledge of the proposed truth-conditions for *P* fails ME(b), its meaning must be accounted for in terms of knowledge of conditions that satisfy ME(b). The truth-conditions of *S* satisfy ME(b), and these conditions are the *evidence*-conditions for *P*, or, as we might also call them, the assertibility-conditions for *P*. Therefore, the only conditions available, knowledge of which could constitute knowledge of the meaning of *P*, are its assertibility-conditions. For statements that are not members of the e-class, such as *P*, we must then endorse an assertibility-conditions account of meaning. Indeed, it does no harm to say in general that the conditions, knowledge of which constitutes knowledge of meaning, are the assertibility-conditions for statements, and then note that for those statements that belong to the e-class the assertibility-conditions equal truth-conditions.

The argument of the last two paragraphs can be summarized as follows:

(i)   Knowledge of meaning is manifestable iff an account can be given of what it is to be empirically sensitive to the semantic conditions proposed.

(ii)   By hypothesis, it is not possible to be empirically sensitive to the truth-conditions of statements of the non-e-class.

(iii)   For non-e-class statements, the only conditions to which empirical sensitivity is possible are assertibility-conditions (the truth-conditions of various sets of e-class statements).

(iv)   In general, knowledge of meaning = knowledge of assertibility-conditions; in the case of e-class statements, however, assertibility-conditions = truth-conditions.

There are a number of difficulties with this argument.

First, (iii) means that the proponent of this sort of anti-realism is committed to a reductionist account of the meaning of non-e-class statements; for example, the meaning of statements like P will be defined in terms of our knowledge of the truth-conditions of statements from the e-class, like S. On its own, this renders such forms of anti-realism extraordinarily problematic, for it denies what appears to be an elementary datum about language use: namely, that P and S say different things! The anti-realist turns out to be a common-or-garden behaviourist about other minds. But matters are worse, for it is not clear that the description of the anti-realist position is coherent. The initial classification of P as not a member of the e-class would seem to acknowledge that its meaning transcends that of e-class statements. It is then rather odd to be presented with an argument that, having acknowledged a distinction between e-class and non-e-class statements (the LE assumption), then proceeds to reduce the meaning of the latter in terms of the meaning of the former, or of sets of the former! This problem is, I think, endemic to reductionist anti-realism. It is a problem that Wright, in particular, has grappled with by trying to invoke what some have taken to be Wittgenstein's concept of criterion.[21]

The concept of criterion and the idea of a relation of criterial support has been taken to offer the prospect of providing an account of the relationship between the e-class and non-e-class statements such that the former are criterial for the latter, where this relation is less than definitional. The idea of 'criterial support' is supposed to capture a relationship between statements, or classes of statements, such that the e-class statement provides defeasible support for the non-e-class; knowledge that the former is true confers knowledge that the latter is, and the former specifies the meaning of the latter. It has never been made clear, however, that any one relation could satisfy these three requirements. Indeed, it is surely incoherent to suppose that a relation could be both knowledge-conferring and defeasible, or meaning-specifying and defeasible. Yet, unless the relationship between the e-class and the non-e-class is defeasible, the anti-realist falls foul of a simple and indefensible behaviourism for which the relationship is definitional rather than defeasible.

Second, an obvious objection to reductionist anti-realism is to challenge the application of the LE assumption that generates (ii). Why should we assume that it is impossible to exhibit a sensitivity to the truth-conditions of a statement like *P*? Of course, we know that it is impossible for us to *feel* another's pain, perhaps also to *have* another's pain. But why should it follow from this that it is impossible to know directly or be sensitive to another's pain? Is there not a Cartesianism motivating the LE assumption here, to the effect that another's pain is always hidden, tucked away in a private, inaccessible realm? Without further argument for the inaccessibility of the truth-conditions of the supposedly non-e-class statements, the realist can respond that the apparatus of the LE assumption is simply mistaken. The realist will say that there is no principled division between different categories of statement. On occasion you can have a direct sensitivity to how things are with others. This realist response has been championed by John McDowell, who has also done much to emphasize the idea of direct presence in Davidson's work.[22] This response to the use of the LE assumption provides an extraordinarily liberating option that challenges deep-seated assumptions and intuitions that have fuelled a lot of traditional epistemology. I think this realist response is plausible; but if nothing else, the sheer fact that it is available reveals the weight of epistemological baggage being carried by the reductionist anti-realist.

A third objection to the reductionist anti-realist concerns the relationship between this sort of anti-realism and intuitionism. On the face of it, the reductionist anti-realist seems to support logical revisionism. Consider the following example. Let the non-e-class statement *P* be a statement about a psychological trait, e.g.

P: So-and-so is easily frightened.

If we allow the use of the LE assumption to claim that the truth-conditions of *P* are not experienceable, the meaning of *P* will have to be specified in terms of statements that belong to the e-class – behavioural reports. Now, with regard to behavioural traits, it seems likely that the appropriate behavioural reports will be conditionals. If *P* is true, then something of the form

If so-and-so is presented with circumstance C, they will produce behaviour B,

will be true. If *P* is not true, something of the following form will hold:

If so-and-so is presented with circumstance C, they will not produce behaviour B.

But what if the person in question is not, and never has been, presented with antecedent circumstance C? In that case we would have no evidence for asserting either *P* or not-*P*, and so bivalence fails. Thus construed, reductionist anti-realism supports logical revisionism. Of course, one might respond to this by claiming that not-*P* is true just in case *P* is not true, and so if the first conditional fails to hold, then *P* fails to be true, which means that not-*P* is true. Bivalence is then preserved. This response, however, seems to conflate two claims that are separable. The point of appealing to behavioural reports in giving the meaning of *P* is to give an account of the meaning of *P* in terms of its assertibility-conditions. Now, although we do not normally see a distinction between

>   not-*P* is true

and

>   *P* is not true,

there is clearly a difference between

>   not-*P* is assertible

and

>   *P* is not assertible.

The latter claim is weaker than the former, and holds in the situation in which the antecedent circumstance C fails: namely, that our subject is not presented with the circumstance that primes fright. This means that we are not in a position to assert *P*. But this is weaker than the claim that not-*P* is assertible, which obtains when the subject is confronted with the antecedent circumstance C and they show no fear.

In general, for epistemic semantic concepts, like assertibility and provability, the pairs not-provable/provable not, not-assertible/assertible not, etc. are pairs of different concepts. The second member of each pair is a stronger concept. It is the concept captured in the above case by saying that not-*P* is true if the second conditional obtains, rather than merely that the former conditional fails to obtain. Furthermore, as noted in section 6.2, intuitionistic logic is marked by its employment of a concept of negation that is, intuitively, stronger than classical negation. It is a concept of negation that does not merely sweep up all those statements that fail to be true, but requires for not-*P* to be true that it be shown that *P* is assertibly not-assertible, or provably not-provable. Wright has argued that anti-realists need not endorse logical revisionism, but his argument turns on his failure to distinguish between '*P* is not assertible' and 'not-*P* is assertible'. I will not pursue the issue here.[23] Suffice it to note that for the reductionist anti-realist there is a problem about how to understand negation, and whether or not to endorse logical revisionism.

The above three objections are, I believe, sufficient to cast doubt on the viability of reductionist anti-realism. Let me briefly mention a fourth very general objection to which reductionist anti-realism is vulnerable. The reductionist anti-realist thinks that the idea of evidence-transcendent truth-conditions does not pass the manifestability test, ME(b). The reductionist anti-realist denies that the idea of evidence-transcendent states of affairs makes sense. The classic cases of evidence-transcendent conditions are cases of statements about times and places that are not experienceable – e.g. the past or universally quantified statements where the quantifier ranges over unsurveyable spaces. If the reductionist anti-realist is right, then we can make no sense of talk about unverifiable times and places. This, however, is a strikingly strong claim; for although we might not be able to visit the past or distant places and verify how things were and are at those times and places, surely we know what it *would* be to verify a statement about such times and places. For example, suppose that it is not possible to verify statements about a distant place because it is physically impossible ever to reach it. Imagine that we know that it is physically impossible to journey to Alpha Centauri. Now consider the following statement,

(5)   There is a copy of *Contemporary Philosophy of Thought* in orbit around Alpha Centauri.

(5) is, by hypothesis, unverifiable. It is, however, understandable. Furthermore, you understand it to say, roughly, that

(6)   Were you to set off from this planet in the direction of Alpha Centauri and travel for approximately 6 light-years, you would observe a copy of this book in deep space.

Now (6) gives an account of what it means to say that (5) is true by appeal to counterfactual conditions of verification, for we have supposed that the journey required is impossible. But such conditions are the truth-conditions, for the conditions expressed in (6) give voice to a conception of things being a certain way even if we are never able to make the observations required to confirm that they are this way. The conception of what it is for (5) to be true that is expressed in (6) makes play with our ordinary conception of objects occupying positions in an unbounded spatio-temporal framework. But there is nothing surprising about this conception of the spatio-temporal framework, for it is the very same conception that is involved in our understanding of material objects as things that do not drop out of existence when we leave their presence. We understand the idea of the table in the dining-room remaining behind when we leave to do the washing-up. Note, I am not claiming that we *know* that the table still exists when we leave the room (although I think we do know that). All I am presently observing is that we *understand* the idea of it existing. If that is right, then the idea of the book in orbit around Alpha Centauri is no different in principle; it is just further away. We understand the idea of the book in circulation around Alpha Centauri by application of incremental movements away from here within the same spatio-temporal framework that makes sense of our ordinary thought about material objects. We understand the idea of moving around the spatial framework. This framework underpins the realist conception of things being thus-and-so independent of our verification of them and independent of our ability to verify them. We understand what it means to make statements about inaccessible regions of space and time by exploiting the holism of our thought about material objects, a holism that locates them all within a unified unbounded spatio-temporal framework. In short, our ordinary conception of the existence of material objects as things that do not suddenly drop out of existence when we turn our backs on them requires the conception of a unified unbounded spatio-temporal framework. But this same conception is then available to make sense of statements about inaccessible times and places. This means that the realist conception of truth-conditions is only under threat at the cost of denying our most basic conception of what it is for something to be a material object. If this is right, no wonder that the reductionist anti-realist strategy looks such an implausible one.

The fourth objection that I have just sketched derives from work following Evans's seminal *The Varieties of Reference*. Evans's book heralded a large research project on what we might call the metaphysics of thought. I explore the ramifications of this in later chapters on reference (chapters 8ff). If this objection to anti-realism is well founded, the reductionist anti-realist critique of the meaningfulness of a truth-conditional account of content cannot succeed; meaning is truth-conditional. I think this result is right, but as I now show, it leaves other versions of anti-realism in play.[24]

6.7 Dummett's Anti-realism

Dummett's arguments against realism are not easy to classify in terms of the distinctions between varieties AR1–AR4. There is a simple explanation for this. Some writers – including Wright, Tennant, and I – have tried to develop and defend an anti-realist position.[25] Dummett has never done this. He has been content to explore the idea that the tenability of realism stands or falls with various issues in the theory of meaning, without turning his explorations into an evangelism with regard to any specific anti-realist position.

Given the exploratory character of Dummett's work in this area, it is not, I think, possible to give a definitive statement of the kind of anti-realism which Dummett thinks flows from his critiques of realism. Some of his arguments look straightforwardly behaviourist. He also often expresses himself in reductionist tones, when, for example, he claims that the very sense of the classical account of the logical constants is under threat.[26] On the other hand, he has noted the possibility of a non-reductionist anti-realism.[27] What I propose to do is to look at Dummett's treatment of the manifestability requirement, ME(b), in one key example, and distinguish the different strands of argument that can be detected within it.

Dummett has always insisted that it should be possible to give an account of knowledge of meaning that does not employ an explicit statement of meaning.[28] That is to say, we are not allowed to explain the meaning of language by employing language. This means that if knowledge of meaning is knowledge of truth-conditions, the knowledge of truth-conditions must be implicit knowledge, not an explicit statement. This looks similar to Wright's version of the manifestation requirement, for the demand that knowledge of meaning be implicit knowledge means that the knowledge must be cashable in terms of behavioural dispositions. The idea seems to be that it should be possible to manifest knowledge of meaning to someone who does not know the language, e.g. an alien. An explicit statement of knowledge of truth-conditions would be circular, for it would not grant entry to the language for the alien.

Consider how this requirement operates. Consider a sentence S the truth-conditions of which are such that one can have a behavioural sensitivity to their obtaining. One such instance of this would be the case of a sentence that belongs to the e-class, although Dummett does not put the matter in this epistemological way. In the case of S, there is no harm in saying that knowledge of meaning equals knowledge of truth-conditions, for it is possible to manifest such knowledge behaviourally; for, by hypothesis, S's membership of the e-class means that its truth-conditions are the sorts of circumstances with regard to which it is possible to possess a behavioural sensitivity. As such, the alien could plot such behavioural sensitivity, and thereby grasp the meaning involved. This looks to be making the same point as Wright's argument. The difference is that Dummett's distinction between sentences for which one can manifest a behavioural sensitivity to truth-conditions and those for which this is not the case is not drawn in terms of the LE assumption.

Dummett does not employ the epistemological device of drawing a line between different categories of atomic sentences demarcated by their distance, as it were, from our epistemic contact. Dummett's examples of sentences for which a behavioural account of knowledge of meaning does not work are examples from one of three categories of unverifiability: sentences about distant times, sentences about distant places, and sentences the meaning of which is specified employing subjunctive conditionals. The latter type of case is best illustrated by sentences expressing statements about character traits, although Dummett's favourite example also involves distant times.

Consider the case of sentence

J: Jones was brave

said of someone who is now dead and who was never placed in circumstances calling for a brave response. If knowledge of the meaning of J equals knowledge of truth-conditions, these will be conditions for which it is not possible to possess a behavioural sensitivity. The point is the same as the example in the previous section about character traits. If J is true, then it will be true that

If Jones were placed in circumstance C, Jones would display behaviour B,

and if J is false, it will be because

If Jones were placed in circumstance C, Jones would not display behaviour B.

But because Jones was never placed in circumstance C and is now dead, there never was, and never can be, anything to which one could display a behavioural sensitivity that would count as manifesting knowledge of the truth-conditions of J. Therefore, with respect to J, a truth-conditional account of knowledge of meaning can only be an explicit statement of knowledge, and that affronts Dummett's understanding of the manifestation requirement.

One response to the above argument is to question the assumption that an explicit statement of knowledge of meaning would be circular. Indeed, what exactly is the circularity that Dummett thinks is problematic? I think there are two different issues about the circularity of an explicit characterization of knowledge of meaning, both of which can be located in Dummett's thinking, but only one of which is defensible. The first issue is this: If knowledge of meaning is characterized explicitly, the theory of meaning will not provide access to our language to a creature previously uninitiated into the language. The demand for non-circularity is then the demand that the theory of meaning make meaning graspable for the alien, or, as McDowell has put it, it presupposes that the task of a theory of meaning is to make meaning explicable to the point of view of the cosmic exile.[29]

The demand against circularity is then opposed to the modesty of Davidson's idea of a theory of meaning that we encountered in chapter 4. It is this modesty that McDowell defends.[30] Dummett's requirement of immodesty seems excessive. He requires that knowledge of meaning be explicable behaviourally, so that anyone observing the behaviour should be able to reconstruct the meaning of the subject's language without having any prior grasp of what the language means. But this amounts to the demand that the intentional concepts of meaning, synonymy, etc. be explicable in non-intentional concepts, and this is surely too high a price to pay. Instead, you might insist that the manifestability requirement is met by showing how you can be behaviourally responsive to the truth-conditions of *J*, by showing how your linguistic behaviour is systematically responsive to a holistic web of beliefs. That is to say that although, of course, it is not possible to exhibit a behavioural sensitivity directly to the truth-conditions of *J*, you can, in the systematicity of your linguistic behaviour, exhibit that sensitivity indirectly – for example, in the way that you take the truth of *J* to be systematically linked to the truth of other claims. You manifest knowledge of meaning from within the systematicity of your linguistic behaviour, where that behaviour is described in the only way in which it can be if we are to capture our intentionality: namely, modestly. This means that meaning is truth-conditional.

The above response is due to McDowell. I think it is right. There is, however, another kind of circularity that Dummett seems keen for us to avoid. Despite the fact that Dummett's use of the Jones example suggests that he is advocating behaviourism about meaning, this is not a reductionist behaviourism. Unlike Wright, he is not trying to reduce the meaning of *J* to behaviour. Indeed, the problem with *J* is precisely that it has a meaning that is adequately captured by the pair of subjunctive conditionals as above. This pair of conditionals specifies what it *would* be to verify *J* where the circumstances involved are incapable of verification. The sense, then, in which *J* is non-verifiable is not relative to the employment of the LE assumption. Indeed, in the light of the fourth objection to reductionist anti-realism at the end of the last section, one might think that Dummett's claim that the meaning of *J* was given by the pair of subjunctive conditionals amounted to an endorsement of a truth-conditional theory of meaning. This is because the problem cases for Dummett are not cases beyond the reach of the LE assumption. They are cases for which we have a notion of what it would be to verify them, but cannot do so. This means that we have a conception of the circumstances under which they would be true, where those circumstances are not verifiable. So we do have a conception of their meaning in terms of conditions that transcend what we are able to verify. This, then, is a truth-conditional theory of meaning! So what is Dummett going on about?

For Wright, if a sentence is unverifiable, it is, unless explicable in terms of sentences from the e-class, unintelligible. Although Dummett sometimes seems to endorse this strong challenge to the intelligibility of unverifiable sentences, more often than not his position is different. The central claim he makes about the subjunctive conditionals that give the meaning of *J* is not that we cannot understand them, but that subjunctive conditionals cannot be barely true. They must be true in virtue of something. In the case of *J*, where the subjunctive conditionals concern behaviour patterns that never happened and never will, there is nothing in virtue of which the conditional can be true, or false. This is not an epistemological constraint as such, but a metaphysical demand that where a sentence is true, there must be an account of that in virtue of which it is true, where such an account produces what I shall call an individuating circumstance of truth. I leave discussion of this notion to the next and final sections. For the moment, it is enough to contrast a verifiability constraint that makes unverifiable sentences unintelligible and the more general constraint that raises a problem about what, if anything, an unverifiable sentence is true in virtue of. The latter type of constraint does not make *J* unintelligible; it merely denies that there is an individuating circumstance in virtue of which it is true or false. We have, therefore, no right to insist that *J* is determinately either true or false. Bivalence fails for *J*.

It is the issue about bivalence that is characteristic of intuitionistic logic, and Dummett has often taken bivalence as the mark of realism. If the thought that to specify the meaning of *J* in terms of the pair of subjunctive conditionals is to endorse a truth-conditional theory of meaning, yet the failure of bivalence is a significant anti-realist claim, then the issue about realism pulls apart from the issue of whether meaning is couched in truth-conditions or verification-conditions. This is a bonus, for, as we saw in the previous section, there is a case for thinking that a truth-conditional account of meaning is unavoidable. We need, then, to distinguish between whether or not *J* has truth-conditions that transcend verifiable conditions and whether or not *J* is determinately either true or false. I suggest that the circularity with regard to specifying *J*'s truth-conditions is unproblematic, and that we endorse a modest account of truth-conditional meaning. This leaves us with a separate issue concerning whether or not there is any non-circular account of why bivalence should hold for *J*.

6.8   Non-reductionist Anti-realism

We need to distinguish between two theses both of which have, with some plausibility, been identified with realism.[31] I call the first the Objectivity of content:

> **Objectivity of content:** The meaning of sentences is specified in terms of conditions that may obtain independently of our ability to verify them. Call these truth-conditions.

The objectivity of content is a necessary condition for realism about a given class of sentences. It is, for example, something that a Berkleyan idealist would deny. If the objectivity of content holds for a given class of sentences, we may say that they have recognition-transcendent truth-conditions. Contrast this with what I call the Objectivity of truth:

> **Objectivity of truth:** Sentences with objective content have determinate truth-values independent of our ability to verify them.

To say that the objectivity of content applies to sentences is to say that we know what it would be for them to be true independently of our ability to verify them. To say that the objectivity of truth applies to such sentences is to *add* the further claim that the sentences have a truth-value independently of our ability to verify them. The move is from knowing what would have to be the case for the sentence to be true or false to the claim that determinately either one or other condition obtains. The objectivity of truth is then the principle of bivalence. But if it is this that is characteristic of realism, then the debate between realism and anti-realism is not between truth-conditional and assertibility-conditional accounts of meaning. The debate is between those who, having accepted that meaning is truth-conditional, dispute whether classical logic or intuitionistic logic is correct.

The idea that anti-realism is only a thesis about logic and not a critique of truth-conditional theories of meaning is the key to a non-reductionist form of anti-realism. For the non-reductionist anti-realist, the constraint on the theory of valid inference cannot be an epistemological constraint, for such an anti-realist allows the intelligibility of a truth-conditional account of meaning. That is the objectivity of content, and the non-reductionist anti-realist does not take issue with that. The difference between the objectivity of content and the objectivity of truth is familiar from debates in the philosophy of religion. The distinction is analogous to the distinction between the issue of whether the concept of an omnipotent, omniscient deity makes sense and the issue of whether there is any good reason to believe in the existence of such a thing. Analogously, the anti-realist might acknowledge that the idea of unverifiable truth-conditions makes sense, but question whether we have any right to believe that such things determinately obtain or not, giving our sentences determinate truth-values and thereby legitimizing the use of classical rules of inference. If the anti-realist gives away so much to the realist, what critique remains of the classical theory of inference?

The topic is a large one, but in summary the argument goes like this.[32] The key point turns on the treatment of negation. Why should we restrict the meaning of '¬A' to 'A → ⊥'? The non-reductionist anti-realist replies as follows. We are asked to consider what rules governing '¬' are necessary for thought or talk to be possible. The claim will then be that laws (2) and (3) are necessary conditions for the possibility of judgement, laws (1) and (4) being surplus to transcendental requirements.

If that is the basic challenge, the fundamental semantic constraint is not a verificationist constraint at all. It is not a constraint concerned with the issue of which states of affairs are verifiable and which are not. The fundamental semantic constraint is that we delimit the structure of thought in terms of those patterns necessary for objective thought and talk to be possible. Just as with Wiggins's enquiry into the marks of truth, which asked what marks truth must have for assertion to be possible, the non-reductionist anti-realist challenge is to ask what our patterns of inference must be for judgement to be possible. It seems to me that we can deliver a realist enough concept of truth by the lights of Davidson's arguments (reviewed in chapter 5) as long as we allow a sufficient notion of systematicity to thought. That systematicity makes use of our notion of valid inference. The issue then is: What rules go into our notion of valid inference?

An analogy will help us to answer this question. Suppose someone wants to include within our basic patterns of inference an inductive inference rule. A simple way of making plain what is wrong with that suggestion is to say that inductive rules of inference do not count as genuine logical rules, for the correctness of an inductive rule is not a formal matter. For an inductive argument to be valid, in addition to the argument satisfying whatever formal criteria you think appropriate to impose upon the argument, there is also the not inconsiderable matter of the world being a certain sort of place: namely, a regular, well-ordered environment. To put the point in a slightly different way, suppose our inductivist complains, and offers us an inductive justification of the inductive rule. We protest that the justification is circular. The inductivist then replies that our justifications of deductive rules of inference are also circular, so where's the problem? Our response can be summed up like this: The circularity of a deductive justification of a deductive rule is not vicious, for the rule is valid analytically. Given the meaning of the constants, the rule cannot take us from truth to falsehood. In contrast, an inductive justification of an inductive rule is viciously circular; for the rule, if valid, is valid not only because the terms employed carry a certain meaning, but because the world is the way that it is. The inductive rule is only valid synthetically. We could say that deductive rules of inference are metaphysically innocent. You need not know anything about how the world is in order to know that deductive rules are valid. In contrast, inductive rules of inference are metaphysically loaded; for, in order to know that they are valid, you need to know how things are in the world. That is why the circularity of the inductive justification of induction is vicious.

And here's the rub! Brouwer's central insight was that certain rules of deductive inference are not as innocent as folks would have us believe. In particular, the classical rules governing negation embody a metaphysical point of view. They are not genuine logical rules. The drive to demarcate those rules of inference that are transcendentally necessary, necessary as conditions for the possibility of judgement, is then the drive to arrive at genuinely logical rules of inference. The genuinely logical rules are those whose justification commits us to no more than is necessary in order to make thought and talk possible. We have already seen, in previous chapters, that this entails a minimal, although significant, realism. It is, however, a notion of realism captured by what I have called the Objectivity of content. It is not the notion of realism that delivers the Objectivity of truth, or bivalence. If this is right, there is a non-reductionist critique of classical logic that is semantics-based, but not verificationist. For such an anti-realist, the core purchase on semantic concepts is not epistemological, but transcendental. This is in keeping with the approach developed in earlier chapters.

The fundamental semantic constraint on truth is not, then, epistemological; it is transcendental. As I noted in section 6.7, Dummett's critique of realism often fails to fit the more straightforward epistemic critique found in Wright. Dummett does not employ the LE assumption to demarcate a privileged class of atomic sentences. His concern is with the metaphysical issue of what it is for a sentence to be barely true, and the thought that, of certain classes of sentences, the idea of bare truth does not apply. In section 6.7 I called his constraint a metaphysical one, a demand that where a sentence is true, there must be an *individuating circumstance of truth*. My preferred way of understanding this idea is in line with the transcendental approach that I have now illustrated. To demand that if a sentence is true, there be an individuating circumstance of truth, is not to demand that the sentence be know-able, provable, or any other such '-able'. It is to demand that the sentence's truth impact upon the systematicity of truth, that it bear inferentially upon the truth of other sentences. It is not that we have to know how it so bears, only that it must so bear. The issue, then, is what is the structure of the way that the truth of a sentence bears upon others? What is the general structure of the way our sentences interconnect? What is a valid inference? The transcendental non-reductionist anti-realist merely points out that a transcendental justification of logic leaves classical logic unsupported.

The point is illustrated by considering the difference between the reductionist and non-reductionist anti-realisms about the past. The reductionist anti-realist reduces our talk about the past to talk about the epistemic warrants for past-tensed sentences. Epistemically we cannot reach into the past, so its reality is deemed suspect. I do not think that there is an issue about how far we can reach epistemically. Indeed, I would be inclined to defend a direct realism about the range of our grasp of other times. The past is real. Furthermore, the logical structure of thought reaches into the past. The only issue for me is the nature of this logical structure that reaches into the past. If you like, what is the structure of the logical tendrils by which we reach in thought and connect ourselves with the past? That is the only question the non-reductionist anti-realist will press. If you now think that this hardly warrants the name *anti*-realist, nothing hangs on that either.

But there is a position here that is less than full-blooded realism. It denies what I call the Objectivity of truth.[33]

6.9 Truth, Knowability and a Knock-down Argument

There is a knock-down argument that poses problems for anti-realists who base their position on verificationist ideas. Here is a simple form of the argument.[34] Suppose the anti-realist principle is that if a proposition is true, it is knowably true:

Prin $P \to \Diamond KP$.

Now, there are things that are unknown,

(i) $P \,\&\, \neg KP$.

Prin applies to all propositions, so applied to (i) gives us

(ii) $\Diamond K (P \,\&\, \neg KP)$.

Knowledge distributes over conjunction, therefore

(iii) $\Diamond (KP \,\&\, K \neg KP)$.

You can only know something if it is true, therefore the second conjunct becomes

(iv) $\Diamond (KP \,\&\, \neg KP)$.

(iv) is a contradiction, so our only assumption (i) must be false,

(v) $\neg (P \,\&\, \neg KP)$.

(v) is equivalent to

(vi) $P \to KP$.

Hence, we have shown that given **Prin**, all truths are known!

If anti-realism is viable on an epistemic basis, it will have to respond to this argument. Unfortunately, all formulations of the anti-realist principle that constrain truth to the possibility of knowing/proving/experiencing truth are susceptible to the above argument. This neat refutation of anti-realism, however, is only as good as the anti-realist advocacy of a simple epistemic constraint on truth. The non-reductionist anti-realist that I sketched in the previous section is immune to this argument. As I noted, the non-reductionist does not reduce truth epistemically. The leading constraint is not that if something is true, it must be possible to φ it, where 'φ' substitutes for an epistemic verb. The constraint is that if something is true, its truth bears upon the truth of other sentences. Note, the constraint is not that it is *possible* for its truth to bear upon other truths – that would introduce an idea that would fall foul of the above knock-down argument. It would reintroduce the idea that truth depends on what we can do. But the non-reductionist anti-realist is, in contrast to this, minimally realist. Truth is independent of will. If a sentence is true, it bears upon other truths, regardless of whether we know it. Its inferential bearing is, if you like, out there. The structure of this connection is real. The transcendentally inspired non-reductionist anti-realist asks only that this structure be one that is necessary in order for thought and talk to be possible. It transpires that a logic that is proof-theoretically intuitionistic will do nicely.

7

The Possibility of a Naturalized Theory of Meaning

7.1 Introduction

I have defended an account of content that is modest and descriptive. There is much to be done and much to be learned by describing the logical grammar of our intentionality. The enterprise shows how our possession of content makes a difference to our interactions with the world. It delivers substantive metaphysical results: a defence of minimal realism, the idea of direct presence, a critique of the realist idea of the determinacy of truth-values. In the chapters to follow, these results will be added to, for the neo-Fregean approach to sense and reference supports a radical externalism about the mind that is opposed to the dominant representationalist theories. The approach that I have been employing is, however, at odds with the approach that many philosophers see as inevitable if we are to provide a naturalized theory of thought and language, a theory that sees our cognitive abilities as part of the natural order of things. It is time to look sideways at some of the most influential arguments concerning the possibility of a naturalized theory of meaning.

There is more than one way of developing a naturalized account of thought and content.[1] One of the things that I want to make clear by the end of this chapter is the outline of a non-reductionist naturalized theory of content. For most people, however, the idea of a naturalized theory of content is that of a reductionist theory in which the vocabulary of ordinary content ascription is captured with the conceptual resources supplied by the natural sciences. How such an approach develops will depend on which of the natural sciences is employed as the resource. In this chapter I look at two influential examples of a naturalized account of content: those of Quine and Millikan.

No account of twentieth-century philosophy of thought and language would be complete without some discussion of Quine. Quine based his naturalism on the resources available from the psychological behaviourism influential during the highpoint of his work. Quine's choice of a base physical theory would no longer be widely endorsed, but the general structure of naturalized accounts of meaning owes much to his pioneering work. The second case I discuss, Millikan's work, is significant for the way that her choice of biology as the base physical theory is determined in order to try and circumvent the problem that all naturalized theories of meaning have to face. I start with a very brief account of this problem.

7.2 A General Problem with Naturalizing Meaning

Unless I indicate otherwise, by a 'naturalized theory of meaning' I shall mean a theory that attempts to naturalize meaning by reducing our ordinary concept of belief content to concepts available from within physical theory. I call the physical theory employed the base theory. In the final section of this chapter, I return to outline the options for a non-reductionist naturalized theory of content.

Whatever base theory is selected for naturalizing meaning, it will be a theory that articulates physical laws governing the regular behaviour of entities, processes and events. The laws state regularities, and a physical event is explained when we see how it instantiates a regularity. On a standard Humean account of causation and explanation, there is no necessity that these regularities obtain in the world, and there is no more to explanation than seeing how an event fits into a regularity that simply is. Causal laws as articulated in the physical sciences have no normative standing. In the understanding of things and events provided by the natural sciences, things do not happen because they should, or because they ought to happen. They just happen, and, so the methodological assumption behind our scientific endeavours has it, when they happen, they instantiate a pattern. Natural laws are regularities.

In contrast, our ordinary ascriptions of content in terms of belief and desire fit into normative patterns. Our ascriptions of content are bounded by the rationality principle, that ascription of beliefs must make best overall rational sense of the subject's behaviour. Our ascriptions of belief hang together. If a subject believes that P & Q, they should believe that P. Or if they believe that it is dinner time and they have a desire to have dinner, then they should make a move to the dining-room. The 'should' in these cases is a normative 'should' that marks our rational expectations of possessors of content. There is a normative order to our ascriptions of content. If an ascription breaks with that order, that is prima facie evidence that the ascription is mistaken. When we explain a subject's behaviour in the light of their beliefs and desires, we show how their behaviour is something that had to happen. We see how their action, given their beliefs and desires, was something that should/ought to be done.

We have, then, a contrast between explanations that show how things, events and processes instantiate causal patterns and explanations that show how things, events and processes ought/should be in order to make rational sense of an indi-vidual.[2] The contrasting explanations deal respectively in causal patterns and normative patterns. The task for the naturalization of content is often taken to consist in showing how the items that instantiate the latter patterns (beliefs and desires) can be reduced to items that instantiate the former patterns. The intuitive idea is that our concept of belief is answerable to mature physical theory. The fitness of our ordinary concepts of belief, desire, etc. turns on whether a place can be found for them in mature physical theory.[3]

The general problem with naturalizing meaning is now obvious. The difference between causal and normative patterns is a qualitative difference. No amount of tinkering with descriptions of causal properties of things can provide the normativity required to make sense of the normative properties of belief.[4] If this is right, the dilemma for the naturalist is either to embrace a rejection of the normative descriptions of ourselves that we pre-theoretically take for granted, or to acknowledge that the failure to capture this normativity amounts to failure of the naturalization project. The first horn of the dilemma is eliminativism; the second appears to be a lazy indulgence in our pre-theoretic self-descriptions. We should not, I suggest, turn too quickly to the latter horn of the dilemma. Nevertheless, its existence signals an obvious response to the naturalist who embraces the first horn. The response accepts the eliminativist argument, which shows that meaning cannot be recovered from within the resources of the base theory, but then treats this argument not as an ontological clean-up operation, but as a *reductio ad absurdum* of naturalism. The eliminativist shows that, given such-and-such conceptual resources from physical theory, there is no such thing as meaning, to which the response is then, 'So much the worse for the assumption that we are given such limited resources'![5]

I do not think that either horn of this dilemma is tenable, and I shall show how, in outline, we can avoid the dilemma by articulating a different model of what it is to naturalize meaning. I do this in the final section of this chapter. One way in which naturalistic accounts of content try to ameliorate the threat of this dilemma is by softening the pretensions of a naturalized theory of meaning and allowing within the base theory elements designed to make the causal account of normativity more plausible. Within naturalist accounts of meaning it is possible then to distinguish two broad strategies. I shall call them tough-minded naturalism and soft-minded naturalism.

The tough-minded naturalist privileges a base physical theory and then, from the resources made available in that base, tries to capture the phenomena of intentionality. The phenomena in question are normally restricted to the data of our linguistic behaviour. Anything from our pre-theoretic understanding of the phe-nomena that cannot be accommodated within the resources of the base theory is simply not kosher. This strategy is found in Quine's work, and it underpins most contemporary eliminativism about belief. The tough-minded naturalist embraces the first horn of our dilemma. The soft-minded naturalist does not give such an overriding privileging to the base theory, and tries to find a more reflective equilibrium between our best scientific theories and our pre-theoretic under-standing of intentionality. This will most likely require a priori argumentation in order to provide a description of our pre-theoretic account of intentionality that shapes it fit so that it can be assimilated within the scientific world-view. A good example of this approach is Fodor.[6] But the case I shall discuss in this chapter is Millikan's work on a teleological account of content, for it is more accessible than Fodor's, and does not require a prior discussion of causal theories of reference, something we will not tackle until chapter 10. Once we turn to consider soft-minded naturalism, the general problem of trying to capture the normativity of content causally gives rise to a number of subsidiary problems. Two, in particular, stand out. First, on a physicalist rendering of content, it becomes difficult to account for the content of psychological states in terms of their relation to distal stimuli (the environment) rather than merely proximal stimuli (e.g. retinal stimu-lation). The second problem flows from this. In order to capture the idea of psychological states misrepresenting things, we need to see them as responsive to distal stimuli, not the proximal stimuli that, normally, are invariant between veridical and erroneous experiences. The physicalist account of content then has a problem making sense of misrepresentation. One of the great strengths of Millikan's work is the way that, at one stroke, she solves these two problems from within a naturalistic position. This is another reason for including her in the present discussion. I start, however, with Quine.

7.3   Quine and the Indeterminacy of Translation

Quine is resolutely tough-minded in his naturalism, and the basic structure of his position is thereby relatively simple to state. His version of naturalism has influ-enced two generations of philosophy. This is due to the systematic way in which he worked out in detail the consequences of assuming that all our knowledge comes from the senses; the only real knowledge is scientific knowledge, and the universe is, fundamentally, a physical system. It was Quine who inaugurated contemporary interest in naturalized theories of knowledge and of meaning. It is the latter case that interests us. The central claim in his naturalized theory of meaning is the indeterminacy of translation. He says:

> Manuals for translating one language into another can be set up on divergent ways, all compatible with the totality of speech dispositions, yet incompatible with each other.[7]

The indeterminacy of translation is the claim that there is no fact of the matter which of these manuals is correct. He allows that we can and will make pragmatic choices over which translation manual to employ, but says:

> Two translators might develop independent manuals of translation, both of them compatible with all speech behaviour, and yet one manual would offer translations that the other translator would reject. My position was that either manual could be useful, but as to which was right and which wrong there was no fact of the matter.[8]

If there is no fact of the matter which translation is correct, then there is no such thing as meaning, for there is no correct answer to the question 'What is the meaning of such-and-such utterance?'

One of the many confusions regarding Quine's thesis arises from a failure to acknowledge that the indeterminacy of translation is a metaphysical thesis, not merely an epistemological thesis about the underdetermination of choice of translation manuals. Quine accepts that all physical theories are underdetermined by the evidence, and translation manuals are, as theories of translation, similarly underdetermined. However, with regard to physical theories, Quine is a realist; for he believes that there are physical facts of the matter that determine which theories are true and which are false. The underdetermination of theory by data merely says that there is no routine for determining, on the basis of the evidence available, which theories are true and which false. With regard to theories of translation, Quine is not a realist; for in this case the underdetermination of translation manuals shows that there is no such thing as the correct manual. The explanation for this differential treatment of physical theory and translation theory is Quine's underlying physicalism. It is because Quine believes that the universe is fundamentally a physical system that the thesis of the underdetermination of theory by data is an epistemological thesis about the lack of effective decision procedures for spotting which physical theories are true and which false. There is, nevertheless, such a thing as physical theories being true or false. But it is also because of his underlying physicalism that in the case of translation manuals there is no such thing as correct/incorrect translation; for Quine believes that the manuals record all the facts there are: namely, all the facts respectable by his physicalist light. Once all the physical facts are in, there is still scope for translation manuals to offer divergent incompatible solutions to the question 'What is the meaning of such-and-such utterance?' But if all the physical facts are in, there are no further facts left to determine meaning. So there is no such thing as meaning.[9]

You might wonder how, if all the physical facts are in, there can be room for translation manuals to offer divergent solutions to the question 'What is the meaning of such-and-such utterance?' unless Quine appeals to a notion of meaning that transcends his strict physicalist view of the universe. Does not Quine have to appeal to a non-physicalistically respectable concept of meaning in order to frame the very thesis of the indeterminacy of translation? There is some tension here in Quine's thinking, but it can be eliminated. If Quine is really pursuing the tough-minded strategy, then the premiss that there are translation manuals such that the choice between them is indeterminate and they are nevertheless distinct manuals can be treated as an assumption that is required only in order to prove the point that there is no such thing as meaning. The argument is used to undermine our belief that there is such a thing as a meaningful contest between translation manuals. Quine rarely pushes the argument this far, but it is the logical result, given the indeterminacy thesis.

In places, however, Quine takes a softer line. In particular, in conference discussion responses published in 1974, Quine said that what he was really against was the 'museum myth of meaning'.[10] Quine's response here is interesting, for it shows him hovering between a tough-minded naturalism – 'there is no such thing as meaning' – and a more moderate position. The more moderate position is one in which it is acknowledged that we cannot, perhaps, stop employing intentional idioms, but we should not theorize our usage of these idioms as an engagement with entities called meanings, which have a shadowy Platonic status. The target of the moderate position is an unhelpful and metaphysically problematic reification of meanings into abstract entities our engagement with which is supposed to explain intentional behaviour. It is such Platonism that he refers to as 'the museum myth of meanings'. But of course, hostility to such metaphysically extravagant accounts of intentionality is compatible with a variety of other forms of realism about the intentional. Officially, Quine's position has to be the tough-minded one, for it is the only one that is compatible with the underlying physicalism that motivates the indeterminacy of translation thesis.

Quine's argument for the indeterminacy thesis is elaborated in the context of translation and what he calls 'radical translation'. This is the situation of the field linguist trying to understand an alien tribe with whom they can assume no shared language, beliefs, culture, etc. It is important to note the point that underpins this methodology. The methodology forces an account of meaning in which we disallow ourselves our ordinary familiar practices of interpretation and understanding of others. Our ordinary practices of understanding are thick with richly meaning-theoretic notions of belief, desire, intentionality, etc. By making us consider meaning in the context of radical translation, Quine restricts the resources available for an account of meaning to those things that are, by his physicalist lights, respectable. In confronting the alien speaker, the only evidence available concerns the native speaker's disposition to produce sounds under specific stimuli. We have, in short, a purely behaviourist characterization of the speaker. Behaviourism is Quine's chosen base physical theory.

Here is a simple way to think of Quine's argument. We are considering the activity of radical translation. The selection of radical translation guarantees that the only evidence available in understanding an alien speaker is information about the sound sequences they produce under given stimuli. On the basis of observable stimuli and the consequent sound production by the native speaker, we attempt to construct a translation manual that pairs sentences of the alien language with, say, English. The translation manual aims to provide pairings of semantically equivalent vocalizations. For the sake of argument, let us assume that we have identified alien vocalizations as sentences.[11] Semantically equivalent sentences will be sentences that are 'prompted by the same stimulatory situations'.[12] The idea of stimulatory situations is defined as 'stimulation . . . at any moment is the set of receptors triggered at that moment'.[13] This is a rigorously physicalistic concept of stimulation, and it defines Quine's basic semantic concept, the idea of stimulus meaning. The stimulus meaning of a sentence is the stimulatory situation that prompts its vocalization. The semantic equivalence that a translation manual aims at is then sameness of stimulus meaning.

The concept of stimulus meaning is physicalistically respectable. The only physical facts that are relevant to the production of a translation manual are facts about stimulus meaning. This restriction is achieved by the methodological device of radical translation; for that ensures that we do not allow clutter from inherited intentional idioms to obscure the strict physical basis for the construction of a translation manual. As we will see, the concept of stimulus meaning is so narrow that it is, perhaps, no surprise that on such a basis translation is indeterminate. We should beware, however, of too hasty a rejection of Quine's methodology for that reason alone. It is important to bear in mind that if the naturalization of meaning requires that intentional concepts be fully captured in concepts from the physical sciences, then we must be clear that the choice of physical science concepts is not infected with intentional idioms. This guarantee is ensured by Quine's concentration on radical translation. So guaranteed, it does not seem to me to be unreasonable to find that the only concepts left with which to start the reconstruction of semantics should be as restricted in content as Quine's notion of stimulus meaning.

Quine's argument for the indeterminacy of translation turns on the realization that the semantic concept of stimulus meaning does not capture the systematicity of meaning that comes from acknowledging that content is, in part, individuated by inferential role. Quine argues that differences in inferential role cannot be captured by stimulus meaning. But such differences are central to our ordinary concept of meaning. Therefore our ordinary concept of meaning is empty, for there are no physicalistically respectable answers to instances of the question schema: What is the meaning of . . . ?

The argument can best be represented as a series of reflections on the different degrees of holism that our ordinary concept of meaning enjoys. First, stimulus meaning applies to sentences, not words. Now, there are pairs of English sentences that are stimulus-synonymous but are not thereby synonymous. For example, all the following sentences are stimulus-synonymous, yet we think that they differ in meaning:

(1)   There is a rabbit.

(2)   There is an undetached rabbit part.

(3)   A time-slice of the history of a rabbit is over there.

Now consider the native who, in the presence of rabbits, habitually says,

(4)   gavagai.

(4) is stimulus-synonymous with all of (1)–(3); that much is physicalistically respectable by the lights of the demands placed upon radical translation. But now, given that (1)–(3) are stimulus-synonymous, there can be no answer to the question which of these the native means in uttering (4). By the lights of the only physically respectable notion of meaning, stimulus meaning, there is no answer to this question. Therefore, the fact of what the native means is indeterminate. There is no such thing as the fact of whether they mean (1), (2) or (3), or any other sentence that is stimulus-synonymous with these. Reference is inscrutable; for the phenomena of sentential stimulus synonymy does not, and cannot, fix the reference of sub-sentential components.

It might be thought that this argument merely begs the question, for as I have presented it, and as Quine presents it himself, the argument makes use of the assumption that (1)–(3) having different meanings. That assumption is required in order to set up the problem about what the native means – does she mean (1) or (2), etc.? I remarked earlier that in places Quine seems to vacillate between a tough-minded naturalism (there is no meaning) and a more moderate position that merely encourages caution in the way we theorize meaning. His official position has to be the tough-minded one.

Let me call the assumption regarding the different meanings of (1)–(3) the homely assumption:

> **Homely assumption:** There is such a thing as meaning in the home tongue – we are familiar (at home) with our own language.

Is Quine practising an unfair partiality in his treatment of English compared with the native's tongue? The answer to this has to be 'No'. Quine is not making the homely assumption except as part of a methodological device to get us thinking about meaning in a physicalistically respectable way. The argument looks as if it is making the homely assumption, but the argument is rapidly generalized in order to prove the very opposite.

As things stand, our problem is that we do not know, and cannot know, which of (1)–(3) the native means by (4). There is no fact of the matter to determine what (4) means beyond its stimulus synonymy with all these sentences. If we ask what the native is ontologically committed to in uttering (4), our answer will depend on which translation manual we select. On one manual, uttering (4) commits the native to rabbits, on another to time-slices of rabbits. Given that stimulus meaning is all we have to go on, there is in general no such thing as ontological commitments of a language as such, but only relative to a translation manual. This point applies just as much within our home tongue and to ourselves. As Quine says:

> The resort to a remote language was not really essential. On deeper reflection, radical translation begins at home.[14]

Of course, in understanding one another in our home tongue, we instinctively employ the homophonic translation manual, in which 'rabbit' means rabbit, and 'There is a rabbit' means that there is a rabbit. The employment of the homophonic form of manual, rather than the more exotic variants in (2) and (3), is not, however, grounded in physicalistically respectable facts about meaning – stimulus synonymy. Quine admits that all sorts of pragmatic pressures, social pressures and just sheer mimicry push us to endorse the homophonic manual. But there is no physical fact of the matter that requires me to translate your rabbit talk in the homophonic way. I could translate your 'rabbit' talk according to manuals that would support (2) as my understanding of your utterance of (1). There is no account available of why this would be incorrect. In short:

> we can reproduce the inscrutability of reference at home. . . . The problem at home differs none from radical translation ordinarily so called except in the wilfulness of this suspension of homophonic translation.[15]

We do not need, then, to consider the situation of radical translation other than for the methodological reason that I emphasized: namely, that it guarantees that we do not allow the physicalistically respectable concepts to be impugned by infection from our over familiar use of intentional idioms. As Quine clearly states in the last passage quoted, the device of radical translation is just a trick to get us to willingly suspend our familiar ways of talking about ourselves in order to get down to the only way of theorizing our linguistic output that is physicalistically respectable. If this is right, the conclusion that the indeterminacy of translation thesis offers us is not merely that there are no facts of the matter regarding what speakers of alien tongues mean but rather, that there is no objective fact of the matter about what any of us are talking about. Our ordinary intuitive concept of meaning which sees (1)–(3) as distinct in content does not survive physicalist scrutiny: there is no such thing.

This result emphasizes the fact that Quine is not making the banal epistemological point that meaning is underdetermined by physical evidence. His concern is the ontological thesis that, given his restricted physicalist account of the facts, there are no facts about meaning as we ordinarily take them to be. This is especially clear in the following passage:

> when I say there is no fact of the matter as regards, say, two rival manuals of translation, what I mean is that both manuals are compatible with all the same distributions of states and relations over elementary particles. In a word, they are physically equivalent.[16]

Of course, Quine does not deny that we prefer homophonic translation manuals; we find them simpler, and they accord with various regulative principles that have been offered for fine-tuning the selection of manuals: e.g. the principle of charity – assuming that natives are broadly speaking correct more often than not. He also admits that he would favour a manual that equated a short native phrase with 'rabbit' and a longer one with 'rabbit part', rather than vice versa. But the principles that inform such choices are not part of the physical evidence, and are not among the physical facts of the matter. They are pragmatic principles and, as such, do not reduce the indeterminacy of meaning other than in a pragmatic way. As such principles are not based in physical facts, they cannot reduce the lack of fact about what we mean.

The above account of Quine's argument concentrates on only the first aspect of the holism of meaning and the idea that the physicalistic semantic concept (stimulus meaning) does not determine inferential role, for the difference we ordinarily perceive among (1)–(3) is a difference in inferential role. Meaning, however, is subject to a further degree of holism. For although stimulus meaning is a property of sentences, not of sub-sentential components, hence the inscrutability of reference, in most cases stimulus meaning cannot be measured sentence by sentence, but only in whole clusters. We may differ in our assent to (1) not because we disagree in our ontology of rabbits over time-slices of rabbits, but for other reasons. For example, I may refuse to assent to (1) because I believe that a rabbit-hunter is within earshot, and I have a desire to protect rabbits from untimely deaths. Only in the context of a whole web of beliefs and desires does it begin to make sense to test for stimulus meaning. This second aspect of the holism of meaning therefore renders the hope for determinate meaning by the lights of stimulus meaning even less promising. I shall not pursue this further point here, for enough has been said to get the picture of Quine's project. I turn now to evaluate the above argument.

7.4 Responses to Quine

It is tempting to respond to Quine in the following way. The indeterminacy of translation arises only because Quine ignores the way that a speaker's disposition to assert any given sentence is systematically connected to their disposition to assert other sentences. For example, a speaker who asserts (1) is, unlike a speaker who asserts (2) or (3), likely also to assert

(5)   You could feed two people with that,

plus a whole load of other judgements that we would ordinarily take someone who believed (1) to be committed to. For example, judging that there is a rabbit there is to judge that there is a space-occupying physical object there, something that would resist pressure from other objects, be they other rabbits, human feet or hunters' spears. Judgements about rabbit parts, detached or not, involve similar commitments, although not, of course, to such large-scale space-occupancy. These contrast with judgements about time-slices of the history of a rabbit, which might not involve any notion of space-occupancy, although that will also depend on how thinly we slice the history of the rabbit and what we take the relationship between different slices to be.

In general, the ordinary notion of meaning whereby we say that (1)–(3) are not synonymous is a notion marked by the different inferential commitments that a speaker who asserts these sentences endorses. Their ordinary meaning is determined by their position within a web of assertions. Such holism is not, however, problematic. The holistic web in which sentence meaning is determined is connected by the common components of the sentences in the web. If we can discern sufficient structure in the native's utterances, then this structure will, in effect, close off the indeterminacy that Quine advocates. A simple example illustrates the point.

Suppose the rabbit before us is brown with white fur on its feet. If the native utterance means (1), then the native must be committed to

(6)   There is something that is brown,

or

(7)   There is something that is the same colour as this,

183

when we point to something else that is brown. If, however, the native utterance means (2), we cannot hold the native to these commitments, for the reference of (2) might be to one of the white parts of the rabbit, so nothing to do with brown things. Suppose we had independently identified 'brun' as the word that the native was disposed to utter when confronted with brown things. If (4) means (1), their assent to (4) should prompt assent to 'brun'. We can express this by saying that if we include amongst the data of our observations of the native's disposition to utter sentences not only their raw dispositions to utter a given sentence under given stimuli, but also their conditional dispositions to utter one sentence given another, then we will be able to fix their meaning. Dispositions to utter sentences conditional upon other sentences make sense on the supposition that the sentences have common component parts. If we record sufficient information on these conditional dispositions, then we will be able to fix the meaning of the native's utterances, for we will get an accurate fix on the parts of the sentences that they have in common.

The above argument is due to Evans.[17] Does it show that Quine's position is flawed? I do not think that this response shows that Quine's position is mistaken, but it does show how little is available within a strictly physicalistic world-view. It also enables us to draw some very general morals about meaning out of the discussion of Quine. First, let me dismiss a response to this argument that does not take us very far.

The charge is that Quine only allows evidence of piecemeal dispositions to make assertions, but that if he were to allow evidence of conditional dispositions to assert one sentence given the assertion of another, then we would be able to focus on the meaning of any one by locating it within the overall scheme of assertions that the native endorses. There is a counter-response to this charge that looks obvious: namely, how can we be so confident that we have accurately logged on to the meaning of 'brun' and all the other sentence components? The reply to that is that with discriminations of sufficient detail, we will in fact fix the meaning of the whole lot. Of course, we might have got 'brun' wrong, but we can check that too, by comparing the use of that component with other language parts used in the presence of colours. It is true that there will be no privileged entry point to the understanding of the native language. That, of itself, does not show that we could not fix the meaning of the language if we discerned sufficient structure in the native's utterances. We have, of course, met something like these sorts of considerations before, in chapter 5 on Davidson's argument for the denial of the scheme/content distinction. You might think that Evans, in employing Davidson's framework, is simply begging the question against Quine in two respects.

First, Davidson's project of radical interpretation is not the same as Quine's project of radical translation. The difference is that Davidson does not restrict the description of behaviour to the thin physicalistic description that Quine advocates. For Davidson starts with a description of behaviour that is replete with intentional idioms. So Evans has begged the question by adopting Davidson's approach.[18] Second, Evans's argument begs the question because of the optimistic assumption that, with enough structure, we can pin down meaning. How does he know this to be true? For sure, with enough structure imposed upon a description of behaviour that is already intentional, we could probably pin down meaning, but this is hardly to take Quine seriously.

I think the issues in the previous paragraph, although important, detract from the real import of Evans's argument. So I propose to ignore the issue of whether, with sufficient structure, we could pin down meaning. The key point behind Evans's argument does not require us to settle that matter. The central point behind Evans's argument is the thought that if the native says 'gavagai', we are entitled to ask:

What follows?

That question is legitimate, for it points to the systematicity of meaning. If the native meant something by 'gavagai', they must be committed to some other things being true. Such commitments flow from the fact that meaning is a systematic structure of contents. Systematicity is not an empirical claim. It is a constitutive claim. Meaning is systematic, for that is how it gets to be semantically evaluable. Of course, Quine himself famously endorses the holism of meaning, but he sees this holism as the source of the problem, not the solution. That Quine sees the systematicity of meaning as the source of the problem is because he does not think we can fix the meaning of the parts. In contrast, Evans thinks that by discerning a combinatorial structure we will fix meaning.

I take it that it is only by discerning a combinatorial structure in the speaker's utterances that we can treat them as subject to semantic evaluation.[19] Let us grant Evans that. Evans's main insight is that if Quine is to capture the idea that there really is meaning in the native's utterance, it is not enough to define the piecemeal stimulus meaning of 'gavagai'; he must also capture the notion of what follows. To do this, he will need to observe the conditional dispositions to utter sentences given stimulation and the previous utterance of other sentences. If we have these conditional dispositions, then will we not fix the meaning?

There are two issues here. First, can Quine admit conditional dispositions? Second, would conditional dispositions fix the meaning of 'gavagai'? Both Quine and Evans think that meaning is systematic/holistic. Quine thinks that meaning is irrecoverably lost in the whole. Evans thinks it is recoverable only because of the way it is embedded in the inferential patterns of the whole. If Quine is right, there will be no answer to the question 'What follows when someone says "gavagai"?' In other words, Evans's question is illegitimate. On the face of it, this is an extraordinarily radical claim. But I suspect it is what Quine is committed to.

The basic challenge is that if there is meaning to the native utterance, we should have some notion of 'what follows'. There are two responses that Quine can make which show that Evans's argument still begs the question against Quine. But once we see the point of these responses, we also see how impoverished any physicalist account of meaning must be.

The first response goes like this. Suppose Quine admits the idea of conditional dispositions to utter sentences, given the utterance of others. Suppose that Quine captures the point of the question, 'What follows?' To suppose this is to suppose that Quine can discriminate a structure in the native's dispositions to behave. To do this, it will be necessary to discriminate component parts in the stimulation patterns, so that we can track the linguistic components that are prompted by those stimulation components. We will also need to formulate rules for combining these linguistic components, and, once again, discriminate component parts in the stimulation patterns that prompt the use of the rule. I see no reason why Quine should not allow a discrimination of combinatorial structure in language and in the stimulation patterns that produce it. This means that Quine would be able to formulate the sort of conditional dispositions which Evans is looking for.

The second response concerns the significance of allowing conditional dispositions. Even if Quine employs a structure-discerning theory that picks out repeatable linguistic structure and related structure in the stimulations, reference will still be inscrutable. The reason for this is seen by considering a suggestion of Hookway's.[20]

Consider the inferential connections with regard to counting that follow from the utterance of 'gavagai'. Suppose we have identified the native's word for 'three', for they have been observed to assent to 'gree' whenever three things have been seen. It should then follow that if they assent to 'gavagai' three times in succession, they will then assent to 'gree gavagai'. This suggests that 'gavagai' means rabbit, not rabbit part. For suppose you had been wondering whether it was whole rabbits or rabbit parts that 'gavagai' stood for. If, for example, you suspected that they meant the latter, say rabbit feet, then evidence that they were, given three dispositions to say 'gavagai', further disposed to say 'gree gavagai' would show that it was not rabbit parts they were talking about. This argument, however, begs the question, and involves the conceptual imperialism that the idea of radical translation is meant to avoid. The argument looks compelling only by assuming that 'gree' means what we mean by 'three'. But, given that we are supposed to have left the intentional idioms at home when we go on radical translation, we are not entitled to assume that. For all we know, the axiom governing 'gree' could be:

a set of objects satisfies '. . . gree things' iff the set comprises three non-rabbits, otherwise twelve things.

We can always find an axiom to replace the one we instinctively use that will be stimulus-synonymous with the axiom for 'three', yet carries a different meaning. This means that we could produce rival theories of meaning as Evans conceives of a theory of meaning. Evans conceives of a structure-discerning theory having an axiomatic structure which has real cognitive import. The structure of the axioms tells us something about the structure of their cognitive machinery. Given the possibility of the 'bent' disjunctive axiom for 'gree', we could produce the sorts of theories Evans favours. They would be empirically equivalent in terms of the structure of cognitive machinery they impute, yet not equivalent in meaning specification. Both the theory with the 'ordinary' 'gree' axiom and the 'bent' axiom have the same explanatory potential in so far as they impute the same degree of basic structure in terms of which behaviour gets explained. But the ordinary and bent axioms are stimulus-synonymous. Therefore Evans's argument begs the question.

This response involves attributing to the natives a theory of meaning the axioms of which look ridiculously complex. It is only because the axioms are complex that the overall theory will end up with the same-size axiom base as the intuitive theory. The complex meaning in the above rule for 'gree' is buried in the internal complexity of the axioms that need to be written for the theory. But the notion of complexity here is, of course, only relative to our understanding of our counting words. It remains the case that 'gree' and 'three' are stimulus-synonymous. If they are stimulus-synonymous and that is the only physicalistically respectable notion of meaning, it must follow that there is no fact of the matter whether someone means gree or three when they say 'gree'. The same point applies to us. There is no fact of the matter whether, when you say 'three', you mean gree or three!

At this point it is tempting to give up on Quine and embrace the other horn of the dilemma that he acknowledges and take his argument as a *reductio ad absurdum* of the naturalization of meaning. That would, I think, be too hasty. There is, however, a moral worth taking from Quine.

The fact that Quine can be defended in the above manner reveals how little is captured, in Quine's framework, when we ask Evans's question, 'What follows?' When we note that the native says 'gavagai', and then ask 'What follows?', the notion of conditionality we want is the notion of what they are *committed* to in saying 'gavagai'. The most that Quine can get out of the idea of conditional dispositions is only a notion of what they are causally disposed to say next, and that has nothing to do with the normative notion of what they are committed to. The point here goes right back to the basics of Quine's position.

Quine is clear that a stimulatory situation is the 'set of receptors triggered at that moment'. So we can treat stimulations as permutations of switches. The stimulation for a given basic disposition, like the disposition to say 'gavagai', will be some setting of switches on or off. Consider a stimulus array of switches. Any given stimulation puts each switch into either on or off mode. We can represent any given stimulation as a sequence of 1s and 0s. The supposition that Quine could permit structure in the stimulations, and correspondingly in language use, is then the thought that, for example, we notice that whenever they say 'gavagai', switches 6–8 are in the setting $<0,1,1>$. We spot similar stable patterns of switches for other linguistic units. This sets up dispositions of the form

(8)   If $<\ldots, x, x, 0, 1, 1, x, x, \ldots> \rightarrow$ 'gavagai',

where the x's and dots mark the state of the switches whose setting plays no role in the production of the word. So we build up an account of the subject's behaviour with these dispositions. What about the conditional dispositions? We know that if a certain pattern of switches at a given location prompts 'gavagai', what of the notion of 'What follows?' The idea that something follows is the idea of the subject being disposed, given the stimulation that prompted 'gavagai', to say further things. So switches 6–8 must also prompt further outputs by being parts of overall stimulations that can re-figure in more complex stimulations. For example, suppose switches 9–11 in the setting $<1,0,1>$ prompt 'grite', which the natives say in the presence of white things. We can grant Quine a structure-discerning theory if we allow the segments of switch settings to play a systematic role in prompting verbal behaviour. So, for example, we allow

(9)   If $<\ldots, x, x, 0, 1, 1, 1, 0, 1, x, x, \ldots> \rightarrow$ grite gavagai.

This seems reasonable. Now, given the disposition in (9) and the native's disposition to say 'grite gavagai' in the presence of white rabbits, we now ask, 'What follows?' The obvious answer is that what follows is that they should be disposed to say 'gavagai'; for the inference

(10)   White rabbits
——————————
       Rabbits

is valid. Having allowed Quine stimulatory structure, surely he can capture this; for embedded within the complex stimulation conditions of (9) is the switch setting that prompts 'gavagai' as demanded in (8). But now we can see what has gone wrong with Quine's model, and why all this structure still leaves reference inscrutable. In the account of 'What follows', Quine's dispositions are dispositions for verbal output given a stimulatory situation. This means that the '$\rightarrow$' in the representation of these dispositions signifies causal dispositions. Quine has to say that the native is disposed to say 'grite gavagai' under a set of stimulations that also disposes him to say 'gavagai'. But the relation between saying 'White rabbit' and 'rabbit' is not one of causal disposition. When Evans wants to raise the issue of what follows from the utterance of 'gavagai', the issue is what the native *should* say. It is the issue of what they are committed to. What they are disposed to say is neither here nor there for the issue of what they are committed to.

The same applies at the level of basic dispositions. It is simply not true that a person who understands 'rabbit' is *disposed* to say 'rabbit' when they see one. They might refrain from saying anything because they do not want other hunters to muscle in on their dinner. The systematicity of meaning that needs capturing is a normative systematicity, not a causal dispositional systematicity. That is why, even if we grant Quine systematic dispositions, we still do not fix meaning. We are never going to fix meaning with causal dispositions.

The problem here is one of *reduced content*. The ordinary intentional notion of content enjoys normative systematicity. Quine proposes to naturalize meaning by constructing a theory that, at best, offers a systematicity of what we are caused to do, including vocalize, under various conditions. From that basis, an account of causal patterns and causal systematicity will not, and cannot, track the patterns of standard use that make up the normative systematicity of content. Standard use is not standard by causal lights; it is standard by the lights of the correctness/incorrectness of judgement – truth and falsity.

7.5   Millikan and the Teleology of Content

The way in which I have presented Quine's position leaves him invulnerable to Evans's argument, but at the price of being unable to capture the full truth-conditional notion of content at play in ordinary intentional idioms. Quine is not, and cannot be, an intentional realist. That is what his argument for the indeterminacy of translation shows. The last way of representing Quine's position, in terms of the problem of reduced content, connects Quine's programme with a recent attempt to 'Quine' meaning into the vocabulary of a different base physical theory.

Millikan wants to capture the phenomenon of intentionality. She also wants to naturalize it, but without eliminating it. She chooses biology as the base theory. The choice of base theory is particularly apt. Biology employs teleological explanations. These are explanations in which features of organisms are explained in terms their proper function. Now, the point that stands in the way of Quine's programme is the fact that when we ask, of a given utterance, 'What follows?', we are asking not what follows causally, but what follows in standard use. The concept of standard use is a normative concept. Millikan's central motivating insight is that we can capture the normative idea of standard use with the biologically respectable idea of proper function, for this too is a normative concept.

Millikan's work is sophisticated, and much of it is concerned with developing the terminology for theorizing biological explanation.[21] I cannot do justice to the richness of her theory here. I merely sketch some of the key ideas in order to pick out the point at which she seems to be vulnerable to a charge of reduced content. Despite the sophistication of her choice of base theory, her biological model of content generates its own indeterminacy thesis; it fails to capture the intentionalist notion of truth-conditional content.[22]

First, let me illustrate the power that her biological theory has, for, unlike most contemporary attempts at naturalizing meaning, Millikan's theory has a number of distinct points in its favour. The problem with naturalizing meaning is one of capturing normativity in causal terms. Two instances of this problem have come to dominate much of the literature: the problem of misrepresentation and what I shall call content solipsism. These problems concern the difficulty, given a causal account of a state's representational content, to capture the idea of false representations and the idea that the state represents things in the external environment, rather than merely proximal stimulations. The problems are connected. A simple example illustrates them both.[23]

The visual system of the frog detects small flying insects. The visual states represent the presence of edible bugs. When a frog's visual system is in such a state, it causes the frog to shoot out its tongue and eat the bug. Is it possible for the state S of the frog's visual system to misrepresent the presence of edible bugs? To answer this question, we need to know what S represents. If we characterize S's representational content in terms of its causal powers, we are presented with the problem of content solipsism. Causally, S is fired by anything that produces the same pattern of retinal stimulation as the pattern produced by flying bugs. If you throw lead pellets across the frog's field of view, S will be fired. In terms of the causal capacities of S, S is insensitive to the difference between edible bugs and lead pellets. This means that it is indeterminate whether S represents edible bug or lead pellet. Therefore, all that S can represent in terms of its causal capacities is that a certain pattern of retinal stimulation is occurring. This is content solipsism. It is a direct consequence of Quinean considerations about making meaning physicalistically respectable. Content gets defined with respect to proximal stimuli, not distal stimuli – the presence of a bug.

Now, if content is defined with respect to proximal, not distal, stimuli, no account of misrepresentation is available. We would like to say that S misrepresents the situation when the frog lashes out and swallows a lead pellet. But unless we can get an account of how S's representational content is definable with respect to distal stimuli, we can give no account of misrepresentation. If what S represents is proximal stimuli, then, short of a malfunction, S always gets things right. It is only if we can fix S's representational content with respect to distal stimuli that we can then treat the stimulation by a lead pellet, which is identical in terms of proximal stimuli, as a case of misrepresentation. But because the two cases of bug and lead pellet stimulation are identical in proximal stimuli, they are identical in terms of the causal character of the situations. Causal powers and capacities are concerned with local characteristics of a state; they are characteristics that are invariant between different distal sources of local causal properties.[24] Therefore, the causal theorist suffers from content solipsism and the consequent problem of misrepresentation.[25]

It is a key characteristic of Millikan's theory that she is able to solve both the above problems at a single stroke. For Millikan, the content of S is defined in terms of its proper function, not its causal powers or capacities. The proper function of S is the function for which it has been selected in a selectionist history of its causal encounters with the world. The proper function of S is to represent what, under normal conditions, provides a normal explanation of the occurrence of S. It is central to Millikan's case that the concepts of 'proper' and 'normal' here are not statistical norms, but introduce genuinely normative ideas.[26] The central insight is that a state's responsiveness to some feature of the environment F will be selected just in case under normal conditions it will increase the survival chances of the creature that S responds to F. For example, creatures with a flight response when a shadow falls across them are responding to the presence of predators. From an evolutionary point of view, it increases survival value to respond immediately to the shadow without checking to see what caused it. Creatures who prevaricated did not survive in sufficient numbers to influence the gene pool for their species. Indeed, those creatures whose response was 'twitchy' to just the right extent, given the distribution of predators in the environment, are the ones whose genes have survived. And note that 'just the right extent' is not a statistical idea; it expresses the frequency of the flight response as a norm relative to the operative conditions of the environment.

With regard to the frog, the proper function of S is to detect edible bugs. This means that S's content, defined in terms of proper function, represents the presence of edible bugs – distal stimuli rather than proximal stimuli. Frog visual systems with a capacity for state S got selected because of the survival value to the frog. Note, this survival is dependent on the state of the environment. With a different environmental history, say one in which every frog pond came equipped with a group of small boys throwing lead pellets in front of frogs, frogs that evolved a capacity for S would not have survived. They would have sunk to the bottom of the pond with a belly full of lead! But, given the normal environmental conditions, it increases survival value for frogs to have a visual system that produces S, for normally that is a response to edible bugs. So S represents the distal stimuli, the

191

environmental condition of the presence of edible bugs. The problem of content solipsism is solved. The problem of misrepresentation is also solved, for if S represents edible bug, then when S is fired by a passing lead pellet, it misrepresents, even if it ends up doing this most of the time.

Millikan's theory has powerful advantages over simpler versions of naturalized accounts of content. The externalist individuation of content in terms of distal stimuli is a significant achievement. The problems of content solipsism and misrepresentation are no more than contemporary variants of Quine's indeterminacy of translation problem. Millikan solves these problems. Nevertheless, indeterminacy returns to haunt even *her* version of a naturalized theory of content.

The simple Quine version of the problem of reduced content goes like this. If we characterize a state's content in terms of its causal powers or capacities, those causal features will not capture the normative notions of the correctness or incorrectness of content. The causal features characterize only the causal patterns a state engages in, not the normative patterns that our ordinary rationalizing notion of content demands. Now, Millikan defines the content of a state in terms of its proper function, and that is a normative idea. It might be thought, therefore, that as the patterns in which representational states engage on her account are normative patterns, there can be no problem of reduced content for her. This is wrong, for although the patterns that characterize a state's content for Millikan are normative patterns defined by proper function, the notion of proper function is itself defined as the function for which the state has been selected in a selectionist history of its causal encounters with the world. The normative patterns of response implicated in the idea of a state's proper function are patterns defined over the *actual causal encounters that figured in the creature's evolutionary history*. Our ordinary rationalizing notion of content involves the idea of normative patterns of response. For example, having a belief with a given content is characterized in terms of various canonical commitments that define the normative patterns into which the belief content enters. These patterns concern the systematic connectedness between belief and belief, and belief and action. The simple question that needs answering is: Does this ordinary pre-theoretic notion of normative pattern outstrip patterns defined over *actual causal* encounters with the environment? Peacocke, for one, thinks that it does. If so, Millikan's notion of proper function will still fail to get content right.[27]

Peacocke's example concerns the canonical commitments of a universally quantified belief. Suppose I believe that all Londoners are friendly on the basis of causal encounters with a sample of Londoners all of whom have been friendly. Is the content of this belief restricted to all Londoners who have a causal impact upon me, or to all Londoners? On Millikan's account, only the former can figure in a selectionist history of the state that codes my belief. But that reduces the content of my belief, which, realistically understood, involves a canonical commitment to hold all Londoners, regardless of their causal contact with me, as friendly. In general, Peacocke puts the point thus:

> how is the teleological theorist to block an incorrect assignment of content to beliefs, namely one that requires for its truth merely the truth of all the logical consequences of *p* that have a causal impact on the thinker, rather than the stronger condition of the truth of *p* itself?[28]

Millikan complains that Peacocke's objection is too narrowly focused, for her concern is with mechanisms that systematically underlie the production of beliefs. She does not expect an account of the causal impact between environment and thinker belief by belief, for such impacts operate upon belief-producing mechanisms.[29] The point is fair, but still begs the question; for it merely ascribes to a belief-producing mechanism the ability to pattern belief with respect to the full ordinary notion of normative patterns of commitment, rather than those patterns involved in the causal history of belief production. In short, the response requires that the belief-producing mechanism has the power to produce the right normative patterns, but does not say how it gets this power. The difficulty here is that the ordinary notion of normative patterns of commitment that define a belief content is a notion of a pattern that ranges over hypothetical situations, not merely those situations that have been causally responsible for the selection of the state that has that belief content. Clearly, hypothetical situations have no role to play in the causal selection of a state for its survival value. Therefore, the situations picked out by the notion of proper function must be less than the full range of situations intuitively implicated in possession of belief.

Furthermore, there is a potential instability in Millikan's position. Does her notion of proper function already presuppose the normative notion of content individuation that Peacocke takes for granted as part of his descriptive enterprise of characterizing intentionality? If not, it must be an issue whether a selectionist history of a belief-producing mechanism will leave indeterminate the ordinary notion of content. If proper function does not presuppose the ordinary normative concepts, there is a risk that it will be reducible to an account of the causal structure that underpins its operation. If so, proper function adds nothing to the basic causal powers taxonomy of intentional states.[30] Millikan denies this; but that leaves the taxonomy of intentional states by proper function autonomous with respect to causal powers. Having accepted this degree of autonomy, the worry for the teleologist will be that the 'proper' in 'proper function' gets content right only when it appeals to the very pre-theoretical rationalizing taxonomy that someone like Peacocke starts with. Despite the enormous advantages which Millikan's theory enjoys over more standard causal theories of content, we are left with a Quinean choice between indeterminacy and intentional realism. The latter takes the descriptive enterprise of characterizing intentionality as the starting-point for a theory of content.

7.6 Wittgenstein and the Impossibility of Naturalizing Meaning

The problem running through the discussion of this chapter turns on the claim that it is impossible to fix content in terms of causal dispositions. The patterns that constitute the systematicity of content are normative patterns. They are the patterns required to capture the normative idea of the correctness/incorrectness of belief. The argument so far has examined attempts by Quine and Millikan to naturalize content by reducing the intentional to a favoured set of concepts taken from physical theory. Both attempts fail. On one reading, Wittgenstein's celebrated rule-following argument shows in general why this standard form of naturalization must fail. In this section I show how the key discussion of rules in *Philosophical Investigations*, sections 143–242, relates to the work so far discussed.[31]

In section 185 Wittgenstein raises the following sceptical challenge. Suppose you have been taught the meaning of the rule 'Add 2' by being trained to produce the sequence, '2, 4, 6, 8, . . .'. If you understand the meaning of the rule, you know that when the sequence gets to '998, 1000, . . .' the correct continuation is '1002, 1004, 1006, . . .'. Understanding the meaning of the instruction 'Add 2' commits you to going that way in the development of the sequence rather than any other way. To develop the sequence after '1000' as '1004, 1008, 1012, . . .' would be a mistake. We would say that you were incorrectly applying the rule 'Add 2', or perhaps that you had misunderstood and were applying a different more complex rule, 'Add 2 if the sum is less than 1002, otherwise add 4'. Understanding the meaning of the rule 'Add 2' involves commitments to what constitutes the correct continuation of the sequence. These are commitments to applications of the rule that outstrip the cases covered in your learning of the rule.

The idea that the commitments concerning correct continuation outstrip the applications of the rule employed in learning is central to the very idea of content possession. It is the idea that the canonical commitments of concept possession cover hypothetical situations as well as actual ones. This is the point that is central to Peacocke's argument against Millikan. In learning any concept, we are presented with various applications that train our understanding, but that understanding is not complete until we know how to go on and extend the concept beyond the instances employed in training. If this were not the case, thought would not be answerable to the generality constraint.[32] The generality constraint demands that understanding a concept requires a capacity to use it of things other than those encountered in learning. The example of the concept of an arithmetical rule is a simple example of the phenomenon that grasp of a concept involves a grasp of its correct application to novel cases.

Wittgenstein's central sceptical challenge can now be expressed: What constitutes the commitment to how a concept is employed in novel cases? In particular, suppose you have never extended the 'Add 2' rule beyond 1000; what is it about your training with the rule 'Add 2' that makes it the case that you have to continue '1002, 1004, . . .', rather than '1004, 1008, . . .'? The question can seem absurd, for it strikes at such a basic feature of thought. Don't you simply know, as well as you know anything, that 'Add 2' means that the former extension of the sequence is right and the latter wrong? How could anyone doubt that? Wittgenstein's scepticism is not, however, a request to take seriously the possibility that you have not understood the meaning of 'Add 2'. His point is rather a request for an account of what constitutes the idea that learning the concept entails knowing that the former extension of the sequence is correct and that latter incorrect. We want to say something like, 'Given what we mean by "Add 2", we *have to* continue the sequence one way rather than the other'. But what constitutes the necessity here? What kind of necessity is it? That is the focus of Wittgenstein's investigations.

It can seem perverse to ask for the nature of the necessity that the rule continue one way rather than another, for the necessity is simply the necessity that flows from understanding meaning. But think of the initial training. You are told to develop the sequence '2, 4, 6, 8, . . .', and you perhaps also develop other segments like '162, 164, 166, 168, . . .'. You see the pattern, you spot how things develop, and so you know that it has to continue one way rather than another after 1000. But the question is, 'What is the pattern you see, and what is it to see it?' The cases you see and hear in training are compatible with an infinite number of different patterns. Suppose I am being trained and that, after seeing the above developments and others like them, I say, 'Ah, now I have it, I see the pattern.' I then proceed to develop the series into new cases, and all goes well until I reach 1000. At that point I proceed, '1004, 1008, 1012, . . .' Does this mean that I did not see the pattern, and if so, at what point in the training did I fail to see the pattern? Perhaps you say that I saw a different pattern, the one represented in the rule 'Add 2 if the sum is less than 1002, otherwise add 4'. But if so, there is nothing in the training to distinguish between seeing the 'straight' pattern and the 'bent' one. If that is right, there is nothing in the training to force the continuation of the series one way rather than the other. In other words, the training in the rule makes it indeterminate whether the rule learnt is the straight one or the bent one. The meaning of 'Add 2' is indeterminate between the two rules. But matters are worse than that. Given the fact that in any finite training in the use of an arithmetical rule, the cases employed will be compatible with an infinite number of different patterns, then it is not that the training fails to determine which of two different rules is learnt, but that it fails to determine which of an infinite number of rules is learnt. But this means that the training places no constraint on future development of the series. If learning a concept places no constraint on future use, then no content has been learnt. A concept the application of which is compatible with absolutely anything simply is not a concept. So the full force of the sceptical argument here is that there is no such thing as meaning anything with the rule 'Add 2'.

We have, then, a challenge to give an account of what constitutes grasp of the normative pattern of use that constitutes concept possession. An obvious response to this challenge is to say that training in the use of 'Add 2' establishes a disposition to continue the rule one way rather than another, and that this constitutes our notion of correct continuation of the series. This cannot be the right response for a reason that we have met on a number of occasions in this chapter. Understanding a concept is not a matter of being disposed to act in certain ways, make utterances under such-and-such conditions, etc. It is a matter of knowing that you *ought* to act in those ways. What you are disposed to do is quite different from what you ought to do. Although Kripke's reading of Wittgenstein has been much criticized, especially for his account of Wittgenstein's response to the basic challenge, his account of the challenge, and especially his insight that a dispositional response is inadequate, is well put.[33]

Here is another way of responding to Wittgenstein's challenge. You might think that the scepticism which says that our training in concepts leaves us so free that content is indeterminate amounts to no more than the banal platitude that symbols *qua* signs have no normative force. That is to say, you might respond by saying that our training with the symbols 'Add 2' only looks to be normatively inert because the symbols themselves are normatively inert. If so, this misplaces the source of normativity that constitutes understanding the concept of adding 2. The normativity arises from our *interpretation* of the symbols. It is only symbols as interpreted that carry normative force, and training is a matter of coming to place the right interpretation upon the symbols. This response goes nowhere, however, for it merely assumes the very thing that needs accounting for. If it is true that symbols gain meaning and normative force only by being interpreted, then training with symbols still leaves indeterminate what the correct interpretation is. Indeed, the idea that signs get a meaning only by having an interpretation placed upon them looks to be one of the central assumptions that generates Wittgenstein's problem. If all understanding of symbols is a matter of placing an interpretation upon them, then there is nothing to constrain the idea of correct interpretation. Each mistake I make could be accounted for by supposing that I am applying a novel, 'bent' interpretation upon the symbols. Nothing is settled, for example, by trying to make my meaning determinate when I continue '1004, 1008, 1012, . . .'

by saying that I am using the interpretation, 'Add 2 if the sum is less than 1002, otherwise add 4', for that fixes nothing. The interpretation itself is expressed with yet a further string of symbols, and, if symbols and our use of them get content only by the application of an interpretation, this 'bent' rule is just as much open to further bent interpretations as the original 'Add 2'. If symbols wait upon interpretation in order to get content, nothing is added by throwing a few more symbols into the account.[34]

The issues in the last paragraph help bring out the central assumption that Wittgenstein is targeting. I think that Wittgenstein's argument is a *reductio ad absurdum* of what I shall call the inertness of experience.[35] Suppose that experience has no intrinsic normative content; it cannot be part of the content of an experience that something has to be the case. This is the thesis of the inertness of experience. It is familiar from Hume. It is also something that a standard naturalist will have to accept, for if experience were characterizable fully in terms taken from the physical sciences, then any given experience would be characterizable in terms of causal structures. Causal structures do not, and cannot, have normative properties. They have dispositional properties, but not normative properties. Therefore, our experience of hearing 'Add 2' cannot, of itself, carry any intrinsic normative force. If no single such experience carries normative force, nothing is gained by having a number of such experiences. Given the inertness of experience, the normativity that constitutes meaning must be an imposition upon experience. We will have to see the normative force that the 'Add 2' series must continue one way rather than another as something that is applied to our experience of adding numbers, not something that is intrinsic to our experience with these concepts. The obvious model here is to hold that experiences are inert, but that the normativity that binds them together over time is a sort of contractual connection between experiences. There is an implicit contract that binds us to future use when we experience the training sessions with 'Add 2'. This, however, is to think of the normativity of meaning as an interpretation placed upon the otherwise inert experiences. But if so, then there is no contract that will tie our experiences together over time to determine the right continuation of the series. We say that having learnt '2, 4, 6, 8, . . .', we are contracted to continue one way rather than the other. But if no experience on its own carries normative force, then neither can the experience of the supposed contract that binds us to one set of results rather than another. At best, the contract can amount to no more than something expressed in a further sequence of symbols, that once more stand in need of a further contract, to enable them to carry a normative force for us. We are threatened with an infinite regress as signs empty of normative force are shored up by a never-ending scaffolding of equally empty signs, each trying to fix the meaning of the previous sign. Meaning will still be indeterminate.[36]

The response that works is to deny the inertness of experience. To put the point in different terms, if experience could have an intrinsic normative content, then there could be a grasp of meaning that did not depend on interpretation, but in which you saw immediately what had to follow.[37] As Wittgenstein puts it:

> there is a way of grasping a rule which is *not* an *interpretation*, but which is exhibited in what we call 'obeying the rule' and 'going against it' in actual cases.[38]

If this response is right, then Wittgenstein's rule-following argument is a transcendental argument to the effect that it is a condition for the possibility of meaning that we accept an account of experience, and of what is available within experience, that refuses to bend to the demands of standard forms of naturalization. This means that any adequate phenomenology of experience, and especially of experiential states with content, will have to enjoy some degree of autonomy from the natural sciences. Such a result is, of course, compatible with physicalism, but only with a non-reductionist physicalism. The attempt to naturalize intentionality will have to proceed in an indirect, non-reductionist manner.

The literature on Wittgenstein is enormous. The above brief sketch of one way of reading his rule-following considerations shows, however, that Wittgenstein's concerns are central to the philosophy of thought and language. They impinge on matters at the heart of the subject, the very possibility of naturalizing meaning as that project is standardly understood.[39]

7.7 It's not Unnatural to Think . . .

The problem that besets the attempts by Quine and others to naturalize meaning is a function of an implicit representationalism. If you assume a representationalist account of belief, and make the physicalist assumption that the only objects and states that exist are physical ones, it appears to be impossible to account for the normativity of content in natural terms. The reason is that physical objects and physical states do not possess normative properties. There are no intrinsic normative properties of such things. Quine treats meaning as something definable over physical states, and finds that such states have no properties to define the normative notion of 'what follows'. If we persist with the physicalist view that there are only physical objects and physical states in the universe, then we can find no objects or states that possess the appropriate properties for those objects or states to be identifiable with beliefs. But this means that if we also persist with representationalism, we will have to look outside the natural order to find entities that could bear these peculiar properties. This is the heart of Dennett's argument against the myth of original intentionality. As Dennett notes, many people are prepared to say that simple machines do not have real representational states – the 'aboutness' of the states of a vending machine that detects quarter-dollars is derived. Its 'aboutness' is indexed to *our* use. It means something for us, not for itself. This suggests that our states enjoy original intentionality, for otherwise intentionality would not exist anywhere. Dennett's argument that there is no such thing as original intentionality requires the Quinean insight that no physical thing has normative properties. Hence, if no physical description of a thing captures the normative properties needed for original aboutness, there is no such thing.[40] There is, however, an alternative approach to naturalizing content. It becomes available when we drop the representationalist assumption.

So, let us agree that in answer to the question, 'How can physical objects or physical states have normative properties?', the correct reply is, 'They cannot'. If we do not subscribe to the representationalist reification of content, we need not conclude either that there is no such thing as normativity, or that it resides in an intrinsically normative non-physical realm. Rather, we can treat the normative properties required for content ascription as properties of the *way we behave*. That is to say, we acknowledge that we behave and act upon the world causally, but that our behaviour falls into patterns that are not, themselves, causal patterns.[41] There are irreducibly normative patterns to our causal encounters with the physical universe. So, we are physical creatures engaged in physical causal encounters with a physical universe. The patterns of our engagement are, however, diverse. Some of the patterns are straightforwardly causal – the patterns of responses that we have in common with other species, of animals and plants, rocks and trees, spiral nebulae and bacteria. Some of the patterns of our engagement are not, however, reducible to causal patterns. They are patterns that are salient only from the point of view of intentional explanation. Being a thinker is being a creature with an irreducibly normative pattern to one's behaviour.

This, of course, is a form of behaviourism. I call it quasi-behaviourism. It is not Quine's behaviourism, for the behaviour involved is not describable in the restrictive raw physical terms that Quine advocates. The behaviour is irreducibly intentional. But it is behaviourist, for there are no entities that possess the normative properties of content; there are only patterns of behaviour.[42] To adapt Dennett's advice, we banish beliefs, but we do not banish believers.[43] Indeed, wherever there is a creature with an irreducibly normative pattern to its behaviour, there is intentionality. Intentionality is found not in the structure of inner items, but in the structure of our encounters with the world, encounters that work the only way it has ever seemed plausible for them to work – causally.

This is the abstract recipe for a non-reductionist naturalization of content that becomes visible once we drop representationalism. It is a recipe that we will see how to fill out in the remaining chapters of this book. The broad structure of the position just sketched is the structure found in the neo-Fregean account of content.

It is also Davidson's position. It is a radically externalist account of content, for content is understood relationally in terms of our encounters with the world. It is also an account that sits happily with some of the emerging paradigms in contemporary empirical work on artificial intelligence and robotics.[44]

8

What is a Theory of Reference?

8.1 Introduction

In this and the following four chapters I outline the most fruitful way of giving a theory of reference. A theory of reference is concerned with the question 'How do words refer?', but that question admits of different interpretations. I defend a Fregean response to this question, a response that invokes a distinction between sense and reference. I will also refer to the neo-Fregean theory of reference and the neo-Fregean theory of content. I use 'Fregean' to describe the general methodology initiated by Frege and, until recently, invariably misunderstood. It is the methodology that I endorsed in chapter 1. I use 'neo-Fregean' to describe contemporary work that has applied the Fregean methodology to areas of thought and to categories of expression that Frege himself rarely discussed. Here is a first stab at what Frege's concept of sense involves.

Names that refer to the same individual do not necessarily have the same inferential role within language use. The difference in inferential role is not merely a linguistic phenomenon. It is a difference explained by the different cognitive significance of co-referring names, where this, in turn, turns on the different rational force of referring to an individual with one name rather than another. Consider the names 'Superman' and 'Clark Kent'. To say the sentences

    Superman is in the next room

and

    Clark Kent is in the next room

have different cognitive significance is to say that they have different rational impacts on someone who understands them. On hearing the former sentence, Lois

Lane would doubtless rush to the next room. That response would not be so compelling on hearing the latter sentence. Despite the fact that there is a sense in which the sentences say exactly the same thing – namely, that a certain individual is in the next room – there is also an important sense in which they carry different information. They impact upon Lois in different ways, and organize her behaviour differently. On the assumption that the key to the concept of content is that it is that which rationally explains the structure of behaviour, there is a difference in content in the above sentences. We say two sentences have different cognitive significance if they prompt different responses in the rational action of those who understand them – we cut cognitive significance to just the degree of fineness of discrimination that is required in order to make rational sense of a subject's response to hearing sentences they understand. So we say that two sentences have different cognitive significance if and only if it makes sense to suppose that someone who understands them could have different rational responses to them. This notion of cognitive significance is Frege's concept of sense. Frege thinks that cognitive significance is a semantic property of the name.

In saying that sense is a semantic property of names, Frege does not mean that it is a property of names *qua* symbols. If Frege held that names were a derived category of expression and that each name was equivalent to an expression from some other category, then sense could plausibly be thought of as a property of the name as symbol. That would be the notion of semantics appropriate to a formal semantic theory, where the issue is simply whether the semantic value of a name is assigned or computed. The notion of cognitive significance, however, is a semantic property of a name in the sense that it is a property of the *standard use* of the name. Most people who object to Frege's theory of sense do so because they think of semantics as concerned with a purely formal/linguistic study of the properties of expressions. As we saw in chapters 1–3, that is not how the Fregean methodology treats semantics. Like most disputes in philosophy, the dispute between Fregeans and others is not, for the most part, due to one side being mistaken or peddling lousy arguments; it arises because they are mostly talking at cross-purposes.

Despite the fact that the phenomena that Frege appealed to in introducing his sense/reference distinction (from now on, the Frege-phenomena) are acknowledged by most writers, his notion of a theory of sense is often thought to be redundant. In the last thirty years, it has become common to speak of the 'new theory of reference' which is held to have superseded Frege's account of sense and reference. The new theory of reference is connected with the work of Kripke, Donnellan, Putnam and Kaplan.[1] It is this work that, predominantly, takes Frege as wrong, because sense is not a semantic property in the purely formal/linguistic sense.[2] I shall address some of this work in this chapter, although much will be left to later chapters. For the moment I want to clarify the central role and need for the concept of sense.

I want to suggest that Frege's idea of a theory of sense is the idea of a general theory of intentionality. The theory of sense is a description – a kind of phenomenology – of the intentional point of view, the point of view of creatures with the capacity to think about the environment. On this proposal, the theory of sense is constitutive of the very idea of content, and, mirroring the priority of explanation that occupied us in earlier chapters, the theory of sense is fundamentally a theory of thought. It is thought (the sense of a whole sentence) that has primary role in the theory of sense, not the sense of individual words.

To call the theory of sense a phenomenology of intentionality is provocative, but accurate. What is important about the kind of phenomenology that goes on in Fregean work is that it is a description of the intentional point of view (of what it is to be a thinker) that is constrained not by introspection (as in traditional phenomenology), but by the requirement that the structure of intentionality is a structure oriented towards truth. It is the phenomenology of thought, and thoughts are, primarily, things to be assessed as true or false.[3]

In this chapter I review why we need phenomenology, and why it bears upon the theory of reference. If all we wanted from a theory of reference was a formal semantic theory that determined whether the semantic value of a name was assigned or computed, then phenomenology would be irrelevant. If all we wanted from a theory of reference was a representationalist theory that, having identified the edge of language, provided an account of the hook-up between language and world, phenomenology would be irrelevant. At best, for the representationalist, the phenomenology would be a contribution to the identification of the edge of language, the category of expressions that then stood in need of a substantive hook-up to the world. In the remainder of this chapter I show why we should, and can, expect more of a theory of reference: in particular, why it must be answerable to the notion of cognitive significance.

8.2   Asking the Right Question

It seems natural to suppose that a very basic question is: 'How do names refer?' This, however, is too vague. Clarifying what the right question is about reference takes us back to the methodological issues reviewed in chapter 1. The question 'How do names refer?' appears to be the fundamental question because it draws our attention to the single most important point about language use – the fact that we use language to represent. The question invites us to say something about the power of language to represent in what seems to be the most primitive case, the case in which we use a symbol to stand for a thing. A name, like 'Bill Clinton', stands in for the object we wish to talk about or think about. Such a symbol string, whether thought of as marks on the paper or as a series of sounds, stands for an object, and allows us to think about the object, talk about it, ask questions about it, and so on. Although we are right to be impressed by all this, and although it is right that we should expect some account of how this is possible, to ask 'How do names refer?' is to put the emphasis in the wrong place.

The question invites the idea that there must be a mechanism of reference, an account of how a set of ink marks achieves the apparently magical feat of standing for 200-odd pounds of human flesh and blood. This is a significant fact about human beings – we employ something intrinsically insignificant and arbitrary to stand in for something as salient as the president of the United States of America. To our knowledge, no other species on our planet has the capacity to use a sign to stand for Bill Clinton. It is, however, unclear that if the question is understood as requesting an account of the mechanism by which 'Bill Clinton' stands for Bill Clinton, any non-trivial account could be forthcoming. One way to reply to this question is to say that 'Bill Clinton' stands for Bill Clinton by being associated with him, or by being the name that was given to him at his baptism, etc. But this is unilluminating, for it presupposes the activity of naming and using symbols to stand for objects. The reply tells the banal story about how that particular name – 'Bill Clinton' – came to be applied to that particular object. It does not address the question of what it is in general for a symbol string/set of marks to stand for an object.

If, then, we ask 'How do names refer?', our request is for a general account of what it is for a symbol to stand for an object. Although it is not obvious that such a request has to be construed as a request for a mechanism that connects name to object, many philosophers have assumed that Frege's theory of sense and reference is an account that offers a mechanism by which names stand for objects. It has become a standard view in many textbooks to suppose that Frege held that names represent objects descriptively.[4] This is the descriptive theory of names. Russell held that proper names were truncated descriptions, although he did not hold that as part of a theory of sense (cognitive significance). The descriptive theory of names says that a name is equivalent to a description or set of descriptions. As a theory of sense, it holds that it is by description that a name achieves the feat of standing for its object.

The descriptive theory of sense has fatal objections to it. It has been the target of repeated criticism throughout contemporary work. It is not, however, Frege's theory. This is just as well, for, as we shall see, the descriptive theory of sense has the result that there is no such thing as reference. We want a theory of what it is, in general, for a name to stand for an object; but we do not want an account of the mechanism of reference. Let me explain this reluctance about seeking a mechanism of reference.

The following seems to be an innocuous metaphysical picture. On the one hand there is the world, and on the other there is language. These two things, world and language, can be conceived independently of one another. As already remarked, there is nothing intrinsic about any particular piece of language that makes it especially suited to represent whatever it represents. Linguistic signs are arbitrary. 'Bill Clinton' could just as well have been the symbol string for the future tense of the verb 'to clinton', where this means 'to complete a dodgy property deal'. On this apparently innocuous picture, we have a conception of objects and of the signs that are used to represent them. If we think in these terms, then we surely need some account of how these two domains of items – objects and names – are connected. It is notoriously unclear, however, what could constitute an illuminating account of the relation of these two domains.

One option, already canvassed, would be to trot out the banal platitudes that 'Bill Clinton' stands for Bill Clinton by being the name that was given at Bill Clinton's baptism by his parents. Such an account tells us nothing about the general issue of how language and world are connected; it presupposes and makes use of the fact that language and world are connected. The problem is that once we make the apparently innocuous assumption that language and world are two thoroughly distinct domains, it appears to be impossible to see how we could find a substantive account of the relationship between them. This problem mirrors a problem we encountered in chapter 3. In section 3.2 we saw that a central difficulty with the correspondence theory of truth was that it appeared to amount to no more than banal platitudes, for talk of facts introduced entities whose individuation was fundamentally semantic, not metaphysical. To speak of the world as the world of facts is already to speak of the world as individuated in a way that is semantically significant. It is not to speak of the world as a domain that is characterizable independently of the domain of language. There is no scope for an illuminating account of the relationship between true propositions and facts where this is supposed to offer insight into the relationship between two domains (language and world) that are conceivable independently of one another. Just the same problem confronts the attempt to provide a theory of reference that tells us how it is that a name manages to stand for an object. This problem is central to twentieth-century work in the philosophy of thought, and to twentieth-century philosophy in general.

The apparently innocuous metaphysical image at work here is a version of representationalism. The key to representationalism is the idea that thought and world, or language and world, can be conceived independently of one another as two separable domains, one of which has the property of representing the other. But it is an extreme version of representationalism that prompts the difficulties addressed in the previous paragraph. It is a version that takes thought and world to be two metaphysically distinct realms because, for example, they can only be described in radically distinct vocabularies, the intentional and the physical. Call this metaphysical representationalism. I take it that metaphysical representationalism is false.[5] If so, there are two alternatives available to us. The first is to specify a non-semantic relation between word and object, and then see if the semantic fact that 'Bill Clinton' stands for Bill Clinton can be explained in terms of the non-semantic relation selected.[6]

One notable and much explored version of this option attempts to provide a causal theory of the relation between language use and world. Such a theory needs to be able to show how the semantic relation between 'Bill Clinton' and Bill Clinton can be accounted for in terms of a causal relation between the object and an utterance of the sound sequence produced by someone saying 'Bill Clinton', and also the causal relation between the object and the linguistic inscription 'Bill Clinton'. It is not clear that this can be achieved; for, amongst other things, there is an awful clutter of items that stand in causal relations to Bill Clinton that have no semantic relation with him. The task of a causal theory of names is to filter out those causal relations in which an object stands to linguistic production that characterize the semantic relation of 'standing for' or, more generally, of representation. It is not clear that this can be done. A preacher who suffered a fit of coughing brought on by the irritant of Bill Clinton's baby powder at the baptism and who, in the middle of this fit of coughing, expostulated 'Bill Clinton' would not thereby have set up the semantic relation of naming between the linguistic device 'Bill Clinton' and the young baby. That would be the wrong sort of causal connection. Intuitively, semantic relations are not contingent, as in this case. They are normative relations concerned with the correct use of words. Sneezing does not set up a norm of correctness for word use. But perhaps the right causal connections could be filtered out of the welter of causal hook-ups between young Bill and the linguistic output for which he is, in various ways, causally responsible. I leave a more detailed examination of the prospects of a causal theory of reference to the next chapter.

The causal theory is a response to metaphysical representationalism, because it starts from the assumption that both thought and world, or language use and world, can be accounted for in the same vocabulary – the vocabulary employed by the physical sciences. A causal theory is best viewed as endorsing physicalism. Note, however, that this is still to endorse representationalism as I have characterized it all along. For even if the extreme of metaphysical representationalism is denied, because thought and world are describable in the single vocabulary of the physical sciences, then, as with any two things that are causally related, any given thought must be characterizable independently of that which it represents.[7] On such an approach, language and thought are of the world. Utterances, inscriptions and thoughts are regular worldly happenings characterizable with the same set of conceptual tools necessary for describing the natural world.

Note that this idea is more than a banal worldliness of thought that comes from denying a Cartesian other-worldliness to thought. Descartes held that language was the mark of thought, and that thought resided only in beings with souls. The worldliness of physicalism is a much stronger thesis than the denial of Cartesian other-worldliness. The worldliness of physicalism is the specific thesis that the semantic properties of thought can be accounted for in the causal vocabulary that is apt for characterizing the goings-on described in the natural sciences. The worldliness of physicalism is the metaphysical claim that we know what the world is like: it is that which is describable by the causal laws of the natural sciences. For the physicalist, the central task of the philosophy of thought is to show how to fit our cognitive and linguistic capacities within the broad purview of the descriptive resources of natural science.[8]

A second alternative, if we deny metaphysical representationalism, is to deny in addition the more plausible physicalist version of representationalism. Where physicalism gives a worldly account of thought and language, the second option gives a semantic account of the world. This looks a silly response. It looks like linguistic idealism. If we give a semantic account of the world, are we not saying that the world is constituted by the language we that characterizes thought? that the only objects are those we name? that the only facts are those we take to be true? and so on? There is, however, no need to endorse such metaphysical extravagances if we deny representationalism. We need only recall the lessons to be learnt from Davidson's account of truth and interpretation, for a better way of expressing this second response would be to say this:

> There is no account of thought and language that is not, at the same time, an account of the world.

The point is that in so far as thought and language have to be seen as disciplined by truth, for that is the basic semantic concept, then for truth to provide the disciplinary function necessary in order to capture the idea of semantic correctness/incorrectness, it must introduce a conception of things independent of will. A conception of things independent of will is a conception of the world. To attempt to conceive of thought without conceiving of it as subject to discipline by some minimally realist conception of the world is to fail to conceive of thought as something that has the capacity to be semantically correct/incorrect. That, of course, is simply a restatement of the point made in section 5.6. To put the point in terms of the over-simplistic language in which it is too frequently expressed:

> It is impossible for us to step outside thought and language and inspect the world as it is in itself. We cannot escape thought and the language that clothes it. We cannot essape concepts. So, we must rest content with what is delivered to us within concepts.[9]

The point that Davidson forces upon us is the realization that what is available to us may be no less than the world, for what is revealed to us from within concepts is something that, because of the role it plays in disciplining our thoughts and utterances, is conceivable independently of will. That is the world. The trick here is to see that what is available to us from within concepts is not a restricted view (as if we could have a clearer view of the world if only we could take off the concepts); rather, what is available to us within concepts is the world, for anything less would not make thought and language the sort of thing it is: namely, a system of representation susceptible of semantic discipline.

Much twentieth-century philosophy has worked in the shadow of the denial of metaphysical representationalism. Metaphysical representationalism is a conceptual minefield. There is no way of characterizing the relationship between thought and world once you make the move that defines the metaphysical representationalist image.[10] Once we ignore the option of linguistic idealism, the two responses to this extreme metaphysical separation of world and content conform to the two methodologies that I introduced in chapter 1: the representationalism of the standard position and the Fregean methodology in which semantics exhausts ontology. In light of the defence offered of Davidson's version of the latter methodology, it is a methodology ripe for further exploration. As noted, I am deferring consideration of the physicalist version of a theory of reference – the causal theory of reference – to the next chapter. This provides an easier route into the topic.

8.3   The Right Question about Reference

We need to proceed with our question 'How do names refer?', bearing in mind that we are not seeking an account of a mechanism of reference that links distinct realms of thought and world. If we do not conceive of these realms independently of one another, it might seem that there is nothing left to ask with our question. That is wrong. Even without the extravagance of metaphysical representationalism, there must be some issue about how names refer, for it is apparent that for any given speaker/thinker names divide into two classes: those with which the subject can understand things said and things thought and those with which they cannot. What is the difference between these two categories of names? Intuitively, the difference is that the former category is a class of names that mean something to our subject, for they understand what is said by the use of a name from that category. There will be thousands of sentences to which the vast majority of readers of this book would be totally indifferent, not because they would not be interested in them, but because they would not know what was being expressed. So, if, for example, I remarked that

(1)   RM is a historian,

there would be a group of people who, on reading (1), would know precisely what was being expressed and be prompted to all sorts of different rational responses. For most people, though, there would be no rational response to reading (1). Of course, they would know that (1) says of someone who bears the name 'RM' that he is a historian, but knowing that is knowing

(2)   'RM is a historian' is a truth,

rather than

(3)   RM is a historian.

Recall the argument in section 4.6 about the distinction between knowing that '*P*' is a truth and knowing that *P*. What you know on reading (1) is that

(4)   A person named 'RM' is a historian.

But from (4) all that follows is, given you know that 'RM' is a name and you know the general rule governing disquotation for names:

> Where an object named '*a*' is *F*, the sentence formed by concatenating the name with the predicate is a truth,

you know that (2). What, then, is the difference between knowing (2) and knowing (3)? If we had the answer to that, we would then have some sort of answer to our question, 'How do names refer?'

I am going to take having an account of the difference between knowing (2) and knowing (3) as a basic constraint on an adequate answer to the question 'How do names refer?' If we had an account of the difference between knowing (2) and knowing (3), we would then have an account that would explain the rational significance of a sentence with a name in it. We would have an account of the role of names in sentences, where that account was answerable to the rational impact of sentences upon action. It is the rational impact of sentences upon action that I have been taking as constitutive of content. The fundamental constraint all along has been that we should individuate content to whatever degree of fineness is required in order to make rational sense of a subject's behaviour. To make rational sense of a subject's behaviour is not just to be able to explain behaviour as an item that instantiates a regular pattern; it is to explain behaviour by attributing intentionality to the subject. To make

209

rational sense of a subject is to make the subject out to be an intentional agent, someone responsive to reasons. And if what is at issue here is the intentionality of the subject, then to make rational sense of the subject's behaviour is to see them as a thinker about the environment. The intentional stance is the stance of a subject who thinks about the environment in addition to merely responding to it.

We have moved from the idea that we want to have an account of reference that explains the cognitive significance of sentences with names in them, to the idea that the account of cognitive significance is connected with the notion of the thought expressed by a sentence with a name in it. I think that connection is right. It captures the intuitive appeal of the Fregean programme that identifies an account of content with an account of thought. A Fregean account of reference is an account of what it is to refer to an object from the point of view of a thinker. The key issue is: How do we think about objects? Put that way, it might sound as if we were being invited to examine introspectively the character of our inner lives. That would be a mistake. The notion of thought is, for the moment, no more than whatever is invoked in rational explanations of behaviour, explanations that attribute to subjects an intentional stance to the world. This means that our question 'How do names refer?' could just as well be rephrased as 'How do we adopt an intentional stance to objects?' The trouble with the latter formulation is that it invites an unconstrained introspective phenomenology; it is unclear what constraints should properly be imposed upon an answer. The former question makes plain that one constraint upon an adequate answer will be that the character of the intentional stance we adopt with respect to objects will be plotted by logging the role of names within rational explanations of behaviour. In that case, there is no temptation for unconstrained introspective phenomenology. Instead, we stick to the familiar territory occupied whenever we provide rational explanations of one another's behaviour in the light of the sentence production of ourselves and others. So, if I say

RM is a historian

and this prompts a certain kind of response from you, this shows something about the character of your intentional stance with respect to RM; it shows something about the way in which you think about RM.

We now have the basic Fregean constraint on a theory of reference. An answer to the question 'How do names refer?' must illuminate what it is to think about objects. We want an answer that accounts for our ability to think about objects and to refer to objects. In order that we do not get misled by the impulse to theorize thinking introspectively, let me offer the following schematic definition of what it is to think of an object with a name:

Thoughts thesis: To think of an object with a name is for the name to occur in sentences that have a rational impact upon the subject's behaviour.

I will speak of a name's or a sentence's rational impotence and rational power as shorthand to pick out the inability or ability to think of an object with a name. Our task, then, is to give an account of the rational power of sentences that employ names and other singular terms. That is what our question 'How do names refer?' amounts to.

8.4   Reprise of the Object Theory of Reference

If I use a name with which you are unfamiliar, as in (1), the name does not get you thinking about the individual. My utterance of (1) unaccompanied by any further information is rationally impotent for you. The only rational response likely from you would be: 'Who are you talking about?' The intuitive explanation of the rational impotence of (1) for you is that I know something that you do not. It is possession of information that enables me to refer to RM and think about RM.

In light of the above refinement of our question about reference, it is relatively easy to state what is wrong with the object theory of reference and why we need a sense/reference distinction. The object theory of reference holds that a name stands for an object; the meaning of a name is the object for which it stands.[11] There are two ways of taking the object theory of reference. Either it is part of an exercise in formal semantics, or it is party to a general theory of judgement. I shall call these the formal object theory of reference and Russell's object theory of reference.

The formal object theory of reference has nothing to say to our question about the rational power of sentences containing singular terms. A formal semantic theory is concerned only with providing a combinatorial semantics that will compute the correct account of the semantic value for complex expressions, given an assignment of semantic values to the atoms plus a set of rules for combining the atoms into well-formed sentences. This is the only constraint on a formal semantic theory. All that a formal theory needs to do with singular terms is to provide axioms in which each singular term is assigned an object as its semantic value, or, if the term is complex, show how its semantic value is computed from an assignment of semantic values to terms of a different category. Formal theories are important and necessary if we want to develop semantic theories for formal languages in mathematics and computing. But such theories are indifferent to the rational power of sentences — the way that sentences impact upon intentional action. There are issues about reference within formal semantics, but they are issues concerned with how you vary the ontological commitments of, say, a scientific theory under different model-theoretic semantics. On one model a scientific theory may come out with reference to one kind of entity, and on a different model it may come out with different referents. This can be a way of measuring the ontological import of a given theory, constrained by issues such as which model provides the most accurate account of the inferential structure of the theory under investigation. But none of this is relevant to our task of investigating the rational power of language. It is the latter task that I am taking as constitutive of philosophical semantics. The formal object theory cannot ignore the phenomena that Frege appeals to, but it generally mislocates them. It is not possible to ignore the Frege-phenomena, for a formal semantics for a language that contains a belief operator will need to treat the semantics of belief ascription. However, there is a danger that the Frege-phenomena are then seen merely as puzzles that need ironing out in a formal semantics adequate to handle such a language.[12] Such an approach does not recognize the Frege-phenomena as constitutive of a theory of thought and judgement content, where the concept of content is fundamentally located by its role in rationalizing explanations of action.

Russell's version of the object theory of reference is different. Russell held that a name stands for the object which is its bearer. On the face of it, this looks to be wrong, for in the example above 'RM' does not succeed for you in standing for RM, because the sentence has no rational impact upon you. Put another way, if we ask, 'What is the information associated with a name that grants it semantic power for a subject?', the only answer Russell could give would be that the information is the object. On the supposition that what constitutes a name's possession of rational power is the subject's possession of information, we are then left with the claim that a name gets rational power in virtue of the subject's possession of the object for which the name stands! This sounds odd; yet not only is it Russell's thesis, in the light of his background assumptions, it makes sense.

Russell's object theory of reference is compatible with the idea that there is such a thing as the rational power of a name. It is also compatible with the idea that the rational power of a name for a subject consists in the subject's possession information. However, because the name simply stands for its object, the only candidate for the information possession of which grants the name rational power for a subject is the object itself. Given that our whole exercise is to understand the rational power of singular terms, in order to explicate what it is to think about objects, this means that the object for which a name stands is implicated in the very individuation of the subject's thought. In general, for some sentence

Fa

that has a rational power for subject S, then S's thought that a is F will be individuated by the object a and the property F-ness. S's thought will be individuated by the ordered pair

$<a, F>$.

Call this a Russellian proposition. According to Russell's object theory of reference, a Russellian proposition is offered as an account of thought and judgement about objects; it is offered as something intended to capture the rational power of sentences containing singular terms. Note also that on this analysis there are no empty singular terms, for the account of thought expressed by a sentence containing a singular term is object-dependent. Note too that two sentences differing only in containing different names with the same reference will express the same thought. So, where

$a = b,$

then the rational power of

a is F

will be the same as the rational power of

b is F.

The thought expressed is the same in both cases.

On the face of it, this all seems hopelessly wrong, for the Frege-phenomena show that sentences differing only by the substitution of co-referring names do not have the same rational power. Furthermore, it seems obscure to offer a Russellian proposition as an account of thought. A Russellian proposition contains the object, but what sense could there be to the idea that your thought contains an object? It is a common objection made by Frege that it makes no sense to speak of an object as a thought constituent.[13] Of course, in making this objection, we must be careful to express the point right. The objection does not have to be made on the basis of an introspective survey that reports an absence of the supposed object in one's mind, although if our account of thought is to capture the phenomenology of the intentional stance, there is a point to a straightforward phenomenological puzzlement in the idea that an object could be a constituent of thought. The real force of the objection is that if thoughts are individuated by Russellian propositions, we lose any account of the rational power of sentences. The account of thought is tied to the notion of the rational power of sentences; it is not tied to introspection.

These objections look fatal to the object theory of reference, though not to Russell's version. Russell's version of the theory must be set against the background of his epistemology. Russell believed that the object theory was correct, but he also believed that it only applied to genuine singular terms. For Russell, a genuine singular term was one that satisfied the principle of acquaintance. Given that Russell thought that you could only be acquainted with sense-data, it follows that the only genuine singular terms were the demonstratives 'this' and 'that' as used to pick out patches of the sensory field.[14]

Given Russell's epistemological constraint on the idea of a genuine singular term, the above objections to the object theory of reference lapse. If we restrict out attention to sentences containing demonstratives used to pick out patches in the sensory field, then it seems reasonable to conclude that co-referring singular terms will have the same rational power, although, given the transitory character of genuine Russellian reference, there will be few examples of this phenomenon. Furthermore, the objection that objects cannot be constituents of thought lapses. Construed as a phenomenological objection, it lapses, for if anything is a constituent of a thought, presumably an object of direct mental awareness is. Furthermore, construed in its proper form, the objection that objects cannot be constituents of thought amounts to the claim that Russellian propositions offer no account of the rational power of sentences. Once again, if we observe the epistemological restriction that Russell imposes, then the only Russellian propositions at issue are those comprised of a sense-datum and a property, e.g. a colour. With this restriction, it is not implausible to suppose that the rational power of the sentence

> This is yellow

is explicated in virtue of the mind's capacity to hold its ostensive gaze upon a yellow sense-datum. In defending Russell on this point, however, we only reinforce the extent of Russell's semantic Cartesianism. At the end of the day, the rational power of the above sentence is a function of the unexplained and unexplainable capacity of the mind to determine to mean by 'this' the sense-datum upon which it is fixed.

Russell's object theory of reference is immune to the standard objections provided by the Frege-phenomena, but the price of immunity is acceptance of two consequences both of which rule out Russell's theory as a viable account of reference. First, Russell's theory is committed to semantic Cartesianism. Second, it is committed to the view that, with the exception of demonstrative reference to sense-data, there is no reference within ordinary language use or ordinary thought. The second consequence is, of course, the point of Russell's theory of descriptions. It is the idea that all the apparent referential apparatus of natural language, with the exception of demonstratives, can be analysed with the apparatus of predication and quantification. According to Russell, for the most part, language represents the world descriptively. As we shall see in the next chapter when we consider the descriptive theory of sense, the idea that the semantic relation of 'standing for' is fundamentally descriptive connects with some deep-seated and powerful intuitions about the nature of the mind – intuitions that are also fundamentally Cartesian.

If we take a neutral stance on epistemology, and refuse to endorse Russell's epistemological foundations for his theory of reference, the object theory of reference construed as more than an offering in formal semantics remains open to powerful objections. The objections are basically two. First, the theory fails to capture the rational power of sentences containing singular terms, for it can give no account of the differential rational power of

a is F

and,

b is F

when

$a = b$.

Second, the object theory of reference has the result that thoughts are characterized by Russellian propositions, and this means that objects are constituents of thoughts. This objection comes in two versions. The first version consists in the perplexity of accepting that the shape of your phenomenology can include an object! The second version consists in an objection close to the objection about failure to distinguish the differential rational power of co-referring terms. The second version says this: on the object theory of reference there is no account available of the rational power of sentences, for Russellian propositions give at best the identity-conditions for what is the case, and whatever thoughts are, their identity-conditions must be independent of what is the case, otherwise we would not be able to have false thoughts. The ability to have false thoughts is central to the capacity for representation. Therefore, any theory that fails to accommodate the possibility of false thoughts is inadequate as a theory of reference that explicates the reference characteristic of thought. The whole point of the notion of the rational power of sentences is that the rational power of a sentence concerns the normative effects it has upon your actions, and this effect is independent of whether or not the sentence is true or false. If a sentence exerts a rational power upon you, then it has a content that affects what you do, irrespective of whether that content is actually true or false. Lois's belief that Superman is in the next room bears upon her actions independently of whether or not he really is in the next room. Therefore, any account of thought must be able to capture the notion of content involved here. It is a concept of content characterizable independently of whether or not the fact, represented by the ordered pair of Superman and the property of being in the next room, obtains. Therefore, the object theory of reference is fundamentally flawed.[15]

Despite the above outline argument for why we need the idea of cognitive significance, the defence of direct reference theories that deny Frege's sense/reference distinction is extraordinarily common. Many writers seem to think that it is only by having a theory of direct reference that we have a theory of genuine reference at all. They think Frege's theory is an indirect theory. Real reference is only ever direct![16] Before looking at any of these theories in detail, it will be helpful to set out in general terms the broad differences and general claims that structure contemporary work on reference. I proceed in this way because what matters in understanding contemporary work on reference is not so much the detail as the underlying motivation for the theory. It is one thing to be presented with, say, the detail of a neo-Fregean account, or of Kaplan's work. It is another thing altogether to understand the underlying questions that these different approaches are trying to address. The situation in contemporary work on reference is very complex. The complexity is due, in part, to a systematic unclarity about what the different approaches are trying to achieve. A central unclarity concerns the idea that the phrase 'direct reference theory' picks out an unambiguous set of theories.

I want to distinguish between three different senses of the idea of 'direct reference'. The phrase 'direct reference theorist' is widely used as a label that is supposed to apply to Kripke, Donnellan, Kaplan, Perry, Salmon and Recanati among others.[17] There are substantial differences between these writers. If they are united in one thing, it is in a reaction to what was once taken to be Frege's theory. It is less clear that they share much by way of positive characterization of their positions.

The first sense of 'direct reference theory' that I distinguish is the formal direct reference theory (FDRT). FDRT amounts to no more than the claim that names are not definable via descriptions. This means that in setting up a formal semantic theory for a language, the semantic value of names cannot be treated as computable from the semantic value of descriptive phrases. FDRT holds that names have to be assigned a semantic value when constructing a formal semantics. FDRT is a very weak claim, for it provides no independent leverage on what constitutes a name. Russell held that ordinary proper names were equivalent to descriptions, but that does not put him in opposition to FDRT unless we have independent reason for denying his claim that ordinary proper names are not genuine names.

Nevertheless, in the days when most people thought that Frege held a descriptive theory of sense (the cognitive significance of a name is a description), FDRT looked like a substantial result. It shows that a descriptive theory of those things that we take to be names (and Frege took ordinary proper names to be names) cannot be right.[18] In addition, if we assume that cognitive significance as a semantic property is a property of names *qua* symbols, then we would expect cognitive significance to show up in a purely formal/linguistic theory of names. But FDRT says that names are simply assigned a semantic value and no more. That, of course, does not show that FDRT is incompatible with the idea that sense, as cognitive significance, is a significant semantic property; it shows only that FDRT is incompatible with the idea that sense, thus construed, is a formal or linguistic property of symbols. As we saw in earlier chapters, it is almost incredible to think that a content notion like sense could be a formal property of symbols. Sense is content that figures in rationalizing explanations of behaviour, and such content has to be construed as a semantic property of *standard use* of symbols. The remaining chapters are no more than a working-out of the consequences of this for the theory of reference.

FDRT, then, has little to do with any theory of reference that has a major role for the concept of sense in explaining the rational power of sentences with singular terms in them. Despite this, the only thing that unites the work of direct reference theorists is their common front on the point that reference is not descriptive. For example, Recanati provides his opening definition of direct reference thus:

> A (directly) referential term is a term that serves simply to refer. It is devoid of descriptive content, in the sense . . . that what it contributes to the proposition expressed by the sentence where it occurs is not a concept, but an object.[19]

Or compare Kaplan's definition of direct reference:

> Directly referential expressions are said to refer directly without the mediation of a Fregean *Sinn* . . . the referent is not mediated by the corresponding propositional content[20]

and his definition of a singular proposition:

> if the component of the proposition . . . which corresponds to the singular term is determined by the individual and the individual is directly determined by the singular term – rather than the individual being determined by the component of the proposition, which is directly determined by the singular term – then we have what I call a singular proposition.[21]

In both these authors we see not only the negative thesis supported by FDRT – namely, that names are not equivalent to descriptions – but also a positive thesis about the proposition expressed by a sentence containing a name. It is clear in Kaplan's view that direct reference is in play in order to avoid a mediated account of propositions. It is the blueprint conception of sense, as a mediating veil between speaker/thinker and object that Kaplan is centrally reacting against. Needless to say, Fregean theory is not committed to this blueprint model. Recanati makes two claims about singular propositions. First, he makes the negative claim that the contribution of a name to the proposition expressed by a sentence containing it is not a concept. What this means depends on what he means by 'concept', but the most plausible hypothesis is that the use of 'concept' here is the use in which concept is identified with predicative content – that is, the sort of content that descriptive phrases possess.

This is not the most useful way of treating the idea of concept and conceptual content, but if this is what Recanati means, it is no more than a restatement of the negative point entailed by FDRT – that names are not equivalent to descriptions.[22] The second claim that Recanati makes is that the contribution made by the name to the proposition expressed by the sentence is an object. So Recanati is endorsing the idea of Russellian propositions that contain objects. The same point is expressed by Kaplan.

Now all direct reference theorists use the notion of Russellian propositions to capture the proposition expressed by a sentence containing a directly referring expression, or to capture 'what is said' by such a sentence. This might suggest a second notion of directness, distinct from the directness of FDRT; for if the proposition expressed by a sentence is Russellian and contains the object concerned, then this must involve some sort of direct contact between the speaker of the sentence and the object. Call this propositional directness. It is not, however, clear what propositional directness amounts to. Although the work of these writers is replete with talk of 'direct cognitive contact' between speaker and object, with the exception of Salmon, none of them takes the idea of propositional directness to deny the Frege-phenomena. That is to say, it is not generally held that propositional directness (objects as constituents of propositions) is a claim about the way we *think* about objects.[23] Propositional directness is then compatible with the Frege-phenomena. All that propositional directness involves is the idea that there is such a thing as a notion of propositional content that is individuated according to Russellian propositions. With the exception of Salmon, no direct reference theorist thinks that Russellian propositions give a complete account of belief and the other so-called propositional attitudes. In other words, the notion of propositional content identified with Russellian propositions is acknowledged by nearly everyone concerned not to capture what I have called the rational power of names and the sentences in which they occur.

The point that 'direct reference theorists' do not use the idea of proposition where a Fregean uses the idea of thought is explicit in the following example from

Kaplan.[24] Consider a subject who sees his own reflection in a window, but does not realize that he is looking at a reflection. He sees that his pants are on fire, but does not realize that it is him. Kaplan says that the sentence

(5) His pants are on fire

expresses the same proposition as

(6) My pants are on fire

just in case the same person is being referred to in each case, even if the person concerned does not realize that it is the same person. He also acknowledges that to believe that my pants are on fire is not the same thing as to believe that that person's pants are on fire. In other words, Kaplan acknowledges that there has to be a notion of content over and above that which is captured by the notion of Russellian proposition. So far, so good, for this is just to acknowledge that the idea of Russellian proposition does not capture the idea of the rational power of these sentences. That is what is captured by the ordinary concept of belief. So we need to distinguish between the propositions expressed by (5) and (6) and the way in which people 'apprehend' these propositions. The proposition is the Russellian proposition

$$<a, F>,$$

where 'a' is the person concerned, and 'F' the property of wearing burning pants. The way in which the proposition is apprehended is called by Kaplan the character. It is intended to be analogous to the Fregean idea of a mode of presentation, and to capture the idea of cognitive significance. Kaplan says:

> A given content may be presented under various characters and . . . we may hold a propositional attitude toward a given content under one character but not under another.[25]

The character is the linguistic meaning, and Kaplan says we should think of it as a function from context to propositional content. That is to say, the character or mode of presentation involved in the belief naturally expressed in (5) is the linguistic meaning of the sentence: roughly, 'The man perceptually present has pants that are on fire'. That linguistic meaning on its own does not determine propositional content. In addition, we need to know the context, in order to know what the relevant perceptual presence is, so that the 'His' fixes an individual.[26]

219

As it stands, to say that theories that invoke propositional content endorse a notion of propositional directness, tells us nothing until we know what the point is of the idea of propositional content. As it stands, the idea of propositional content is simply the idea of the truth-conditions, the 'what is said' notion of content, and everyone agrees that that is different from the Fregean notion of content that occurs in rationalizing explanations of behaviour. So propositional directness can mean no more than that the object is part of the truth-conditions of the sentence, thought, statement, etc. Given that everyone acknowledges that the idea of propositional content does not suffice for explaining behaviour, we still need to know what, if anything, this idea of content is required for. Recanati, for one, makes a great deal of the fact that direct reference theorists need not deny the Frege-phenomena, and that the Fregean idea of cognitive significance is compatible with accepting the idea of content as defined by propositional content.[27]

The ideas that underpin the notion of propositional content employed by direct reference theorists do, however, pick out a real point of difference between the Fregean approach and the direct reference theory. First, let us agree that propositional content does not capture cognitive significance. It does not capture the idea of content that figures in rationalizing explanations of behaviour. Furthermore, just about everyone agrees that we need to invoke some notion of cognitive significance, so let's call this 'sense' as Frege did. Now, for the direct reference theorist, sense equals linguistic meaning (character), and it is character plus context that determines reference and truth-conditions. So the sense whereby we think of the object when we think of it as 'Him' is different from the sense when we think of the same object as 'Me'; but, in appropriate contexts, these different senses will pick out just the same object – that is, determine just the same truth-conditions,

$$<a, F>.$$

What is clear about this notion of character is that it is a context-invariant feature of an expression. This is obvious, for character is linguistic meaning. So direct reference theorists assume that the Frege-phenomena can be captured by a notion of content that is less than propositional content, but which is explicable as linguistic meaning. This means that the idea of content that is required for explaining behaviour is, according to the direct reference theorist, a context-invariant notion of content. This in turn means that they hold that that notion of content is susceptible to a representationalist model, or blueprint conception. So, although their semantic concept of propositional content is object-involving (the Russellian proposition), their notion of content that explains behaviour is object-independent. The latter notion of content is linguistic meaning, and linguistic meaning is the meaning a sign has that it carries from context to context. So, with respect to sense, the direct reference theorist has an *indirect* notion of content. And remember, it is sense that equals cognitive significance, the idea of content that explains behaviour and that characterizes thought. Propositional content does not characterize thought; sense does that. So a direct reference theorist endorses an indirect model of thought. It is a standard representationalist model. Such a model endorses what is called a dual-component theory of content, meaning that truth-conditions are determined by two separate notions: namely, sense (character, linguistic meaning) plus context.[28]

This means that there is a third notion of directness at play in contemporary theories of reference, but one that direct reference theories do not permit. The third notion of directness is the idea of a sense or thought that directly picks out a reference without supplementation by context. Direct reference theorists have a direct model of propositional content, but an indirect model of thought content. The former, as I have indicated, really amounts to little more than the claim in FDRT that names are not semantically equivalent to some other category of expression, such as descriptions. The latter amounts to representationalism about thought. The difference between Fregean and direct reference theorists turns on whether or not sense (cognitive significance) determines reference and truth-conditions, or whether it is sense plus context that does so. The Fregean thinks the former, the direct reference theorists the latter. But this means that it is the Fregean who has a direct theory of reference at the level of thought, not the direct reference theorist!

Let me summarize the above in the following way. We acknowledge the idea of propositional content as a Russellian proposition, an ordered pair of object and property:

Proposition: $<a, F>$.

Everyone accepts that this is a notion of content. In addition, nearly everyone accepts that this notion of propositional content, although valuable in the construction of formal semantic theories, does not explain behaviour. There is then another notion of content – call it sense – that is required in order to explain behaviour. We could represent this as

Thought: $\hat{}mpa, mpF\hat{}$,

where 'mp$a$' stands for the mode of presentation of a, and 'mp$F$' stands for the mode of presentation of F-ness. Now, of course, if sense determines reference, which is what Fregeans claim, then whatever mode of presentation is involved in thinking of the object a, the thought will determine the same truth-conditions represented as the propositional content

$<a, F>$.

That is just the simple point that however we may be thinking about an object, there is such a thing as what we are thinking about that stays the same. All that changes is the way in which we think of it. For the Fregean, the thought is the notion of content that picks out cognitive significance. The direct reference theorist agrees. So, everyone endorses,

> Thought = cognitive significance.

So far, the differences might seem like mere terminological disputes, and Recanati, for one, is prone to represent the matter this way. But there is one central difference. For the direct reference theorist, the proposition (truth-condition) is determined by thought plus context. They think this because they think that thought is linguistic meaning. In other words, the direct reference theorist holds that the idea of cognitive significance, thought, is a context-invariant idea of content. That is what the neo-Fregean denies, and it is what, I think, Frege would have denied too, had he considered a wider range of categories of singular terms. Frege's basic test for individuating sense, that sense be cut to rationalize behaviour, cuts cognitive significance in a way that leaves it a contextualized notion of content. It is not context-invariant. This means that for the Fregean, thought alone determines proposition (truth-conditions). The central claim that differentiates the Fregean from the direct reference theorist is the claim that cognitive significance (the level of thought) is not context-free. Sense is not, *contra* the linguistic representational-ism model assumed by Kaplan et al., a notion of content that can be factored out of our contextual encounters with the world. In contrast, for Kaplan, sense falls short of determining reference, for context is required in order to determine the object picked out. This means that, for Kaplan, thought falls short of objects. For the Fregean, the level of sense determines reference, and so thought provides a direct contact with objects.[29]

We now have a difference between the Fregean methodology with respect to reference and the approach of direct reference theorists. We also have reason to question the appropriateness of the latter label, given the indirectness of reference at the level of thought in the work of all the major 'direct reference theorists'. Two questions immediately arise. First, with which notion of content, the propositional or the thought-theoretic, should we start? If we set out from a formal semanticist's point of view, we are likely to start with the idea of propositional content, and then add on the idea of thought content in order to get the right results in our formal semantic theory once we begin to consider languages with thought-sensitive opera-tors. For example, once we consider languages with a belief operator, we will need to invoke more than merely propositional content in order to explain which inferences employing that operator are right and which are not. From this perspective, sense is always a 'bolt-on', an ingredient added to get the formal theory to deliver the right answers.[30] Note also that if sense is construed as linguistic meaning, something that is context-invariant, then the 'bolt-on' required should be amenable to further formal specification. Context-invariant meanings will be meanings that symbols have *qua* symbols, so on this first perspective the whole of philosophical semantics will fall within the province of the formal semanticist.

The alternative strategy is the one that I have advocated from chapter 1. It is the strategy that sees the basic motivation in philosophical semantics as to get a theory of content that makes sense of behaviour. But that means we start with thought and investigate the concept of cognitive significance. This is Frege's approach. The idea that these might be alternative strategies is a late comer to many contemporary thinkers, for as long as it was assumed that sense was descriptive, then the exploration of cognitive significance simply was the investigation of a formal semantic theory. If sense is descriptive, then the semantic value of names is computed, not assigned, and this will show up in the structure of a formal semantic theory. Similarly, even if sense is not descriptive, if it is identified with linguistic meaning, it should be possible to bring the theory of sense within the province of formal semantics.[31] If, however, sense is neither descriptive nor recoverable from linguistic meaning, but is a contextually sensitive notion of content, a theory of sense cannot be modelled on a formal semantic theory.

The second question is this: Is sense, the idea of cognitive significance, something that is contextually invariant, or is it a context-dependent notion of content? Whichever perspective you adopt in response to the first question, you will still have to answer the second question. If the latter answer is correct, then the Fregean methodology that starts with sense, not propositional content, must be the correct methodology, for the formal semanticist's approach will be unable to acknowledge the context-dependent idea of thought content. If the latter answer is correct, then there are such things as direct thoughts, and representationalism is false. Direct reference theorists endorse representationalism. In the remaining chapters of this book I shall show why representationalism is false, and thereby justify the Fregean methodology that I have been employing all along.

8.5 Frege's Puzzles

We now have sufficient stage setting to introduce Frege's distinction between sense and reference in just the way that he introduced the distinction himself. We will then see why so many people have assumed that Frege was committed to a representationalist model of sense. Frege famously observed that identities of the form[32]

$a = b$

are more informative than identities of the form

$a = a.$

Now, if the object theory of reference is correct, and all a name does is stand for its object, there ought not to be this difference. Furthermore, as already noted, sentences that differ only by substitution of co-referring singular terms may have different rational power. This means that the following inference is invalid:

(7) *S* believes that *a* is *F*

$a = b$
_____
S believes that *b* is *F*.

If all that names do is simply stand for objects, then the inference at (7) should be valid, but it is not. The basic reason for saying that the inference at (7) is invalid turns on the role we envisage for the concept of belief. There are many things that we might expect of a theory of belief, but the central one, however, is surely this: We ascribe beliefs to subjects in order to make rational sense of their behaviour. Accordingly, the concept of belief finds its natural home in the arena of rationalizing explanations of intentional action. This is why I prefer to express the basic constraint on a theory of reference in terms of the need to explicate the rational power of sentences. The inference at (7) is invalid because the fact that $a = b$ gives no reason for attributing a common rational power to the sentences '*a* is *F*' and '*b* is *F*'.[33]

On the face of it, we have two related puzzles: one is a puzzle about the possibility of informative identity statements; the other is a puzzle about how to account for the failure of validity of the inference schema at (7). The second puzzle flows from the first. If identity statements of the form

$a = b$

are informative in a way that those of the form

$a = a$

are not, then the former must say more than the latter. If so, that would explain why the inference at (7) is invalid, for it relies upon an informative identity at the second premiss, and we have no right to assume that the subject is aware of it. Frege's solution to these puzzles is to say that names have sense in addition to reference. By the sense of a name Frege means its 'cognitive significance'. He also uses the phrase the 'mode of presentation'. These phrase are intended to pick out information associated with each name that characterizes the way in which the name refers to its object. A better way of putting this is to say that the sense of a name is the way in which a subject thinks of the object.[34]

Frege's distinction between sense and reference applies to all categories of expression.[35] The reference of the name is the object for which it stands, and the sense is the mode of presentation or the way in which someone who understands the name thinks of the object. Accordingly, for Frege, a thought is individuated by sense, not reference. Indeed, the fundamental purchase on the notion of sense is the idea of an ingredient of thought. Sense is invoked in order to characterize the way we think of objects. The sense of a whole sentence is a thought, and the sense of a name is an ingredient of a thought. So, just as we can treat the semantic value (true/false) of a sentence as a function of the semantic value (object) of a name and the semantic value (extension) of a predicate, so too we can treat the sense of a sentence (thought) as a function of the sense of a name (mode of presentation) and the sense of a predicate (concept).

Stalling objections to the above for the moment (and there are plenty of them), the applicability of the sense/reference distinction to all categories of expression explains a fundamental feature of Frege's mature theory of sense. The reason why the inference at (7) fails is because we characterized beliefs in terms of their role in the rational explanation of intentional action. A belief is a thought. So, when we ascribe a belief to someone, we are ascribing a thought to them. For Frege, a thought is the sense of a sentence, and is comprised of the sense of the sentence's component parts. This means that to say

S believes that a is F

is to ascribe to S a thought containing the sense of 'a'. This in turn means that what we attribute to S is made up out of the senses of the various linguistic components that follow the 'believes that . . .'. It must follow from this, then, that a name in the context of the 'S believes that . . .' construction does not stand for its referent (object), but its sense. What the dots represent in this context is a thought; so a name in belief contexts stands for its sense, not its reference. This is what Frege says:

> In reported speech one talks about the sense . . . It is quite clear that in this way of speaking words do not have their customary reference but designate what is usually their sense.[36]

Frege's theory of *oratio obliqua* has an intuitive plausibility to it; but note that the theory has acquired a somewhat baroque complexity. We have a theory in which names now have two entities associated with them, a sense and a reference.[37] Furthermore, in certain contexts the sense becomes the reference, although in extensional contexts this is not so. On the face of it, this is an ontologically extravagant theory. That, however, is the least of its problems.

The central problem with Frege's theory is this: If we think of sense as an extra entity associated with a name, there is no account available that comes anywhere near to giving a compelling statement of the identity-conditions of this entity. The favourite candidate for the sense of a name has been a description, or bundle of descriptions. Apart from the fact that this suggestion is susceptible to fatal objections, it offers an ontologically messy model of our thought about objects.[38] The model appears to be this: We think about objects with names by having before our minds entities called senses. These entities are the modes of presentation, the way in which the object is presented to us in thought. But if we think of the way the object is presented to us in thought as an entity associated with the name, then the sense turns out to be a blueprint for the object. We never directly think about objects. Rather, we think by having blueprints for objects in our minds (senses), and these are entities that are associated with the names that denote objects. The denotation of an object by a name is explained by the role of this intermediary, the blueprint in the mind.

This model of thoughts has the benefit of not allowing that objects themselves can be constituents of thoughts, but it achieves this by making the realm of thought wholly disengaged from the world. The model is reminiscent of Locke's Cartesian theory of ideas. This is embarrassing for the Fregean, for we seem to be retreating to the kind of semantic Cartesianism for which I criticized Russell. It is beginning to look as if Frege's theory has the rational power of sentences explained in terms of the power of mental items, senses, to guide the mind on to objects.

The objection that Frege's theory is committed to a representationalist model of thought in which we think about objects by possessing mental blueprints that stand in for them is a natural one. It is a potentially fatal objection. Frege would have objected that he never intended sense to be construed psychologistically, and so the talk of mental blueprints is misleading. That is a fair complaint, but it makes little difference. Certainly, Frege attacked psychologism in logic and the theory of language. He held that the realm of sense was objective, not subjective.[39] Some have compared Frege's notion of the objectivity of sense with Popper's idea of 'world 3' entities as the objects of scientific knowledge. Despite Frege's insistence on the objectivity of sense, however, this does not remove senses from the psychological realm for two reasons.

First, Frege's attack on psychologism is an attack on introspective psychology and the idea that meaning be understood in terms of possession of ideas the identity-conditions of which are definable introspectively. This means that the objectivity of the sense of a singular term is really an issue about the identity-conditions of sense being specified in terms of its role in the determination of the semantic value of sentences, the role of sense in determining truth. It is truth that is fundamentally objective for Frege, and sense is objective in so far as it is individuated with respect to its role in determining the truth/falsity of sentences. For Frege, the notion of objectivity is connected with truth, just as his concept of an object is a logical concept, not a metaphysical concept. The notion of the objective is, therefore, broader than the notion of the real. The distinction is marked in German between *Objectivität* and *Wirklichkeit*. *Wirklichkeit* is reality, that which exists within the causal nexus. Numbers are objective objects if and only if names for numbers figure in sentences that are true. This has nothing to do with whether or not numbers are real. Similarly, to say that sense is objective is to characterize sense with respect to its role in determining truth. It is to say nothing about its status within one realm of reality – the mental – or another.

Second, sense must have some psychological reality, for it is psychologically real in so far as the fundamental individuation of sense lies in its role in the explanation of intentional action. Sense constitutes thought, and the role of thought is to figure, alongside desire, in the familiar rationalizing explanations of action.[40] The objection that sense is a blueprint, and that our thought about objects is only ever indirectly about objects, in a way familiar from indirect realism in the theory of perception, shows why the idea of direct reference theory appeared to be an important alternative to Frege.

In order to resolve the issues raised at the end of the previous section, we need to know whether it is possible to define the identity-conditions of the sense of a term in such a way that it would produce an account of blueprints for objects in thought that then account for reference, or whether sense is to be defined in a way that leaves it contextualized. In addition, in sorting out whether thought is direct, if 'direct' means that the relation between thinker and object is one of acquaintance, it does not follow that we have to understand acquaintance in the atomistic way that Russell did. In particular, we should leave room for the possibility that the relation of acquaintance could be sense-sensitive.[41] Historically, the see-saw on which much contemporary philosophy of thought has played has supposedly involved the oscillation between a blueprint model of thought and a Russellian model. In light of the previous section, the labelling is thoroughly misleading.

Direct reference theorists, it turns out, have an indirect model at the level of thought. They hold that reference is direct only at the level of propositional content. In addition, that point is poorly expressed by calling the propositional content a 'Russellian proposition'. As we saw at the beginning of section 8.4, Russell's own view of these propositions was that they not only picked out the notion of 'what is said', but picked out the level of thought too. With regard to singular terms, Russell conflated the level of propositional content and thought content. That can sound outrageous, but it is acceptable and, given Russell's epistemology, is probably right. The conflation works because the class of singular terms is so small.

So far, I have merely stated that sense does not have to be identified with a representationalist idea, and that it is the Fregean who will have a notion of direct reference at the level of thought. This option remains to be explored. If it turns out to be viable, the dichotomy between blueprint and direct theory of reference is as badly labelled as any pairing of opposing positions in the history of philosophy.

The option that needs to be explored is the possibility of a direct theory of reference that also accommodates the concept of sense – a sense-sensitive concept of acquaintance. I have insisted on the individuation of sense being tied to our rationalizing explanations of action. This means that the option is one in which we have a direct thought about an object, where its directness consists in the absence of an intermediary, and yet the relation is characterized in terms of its rationalizing role in action explanation. This means that for acquaintance to be sense-sensitive, it cannot be understood atomistically; the relation of acquaintance must be a relation that has a place within the grammar of (the space of) reasons. Such is the position occupied by the theory of singular sense that has come to dominate neo-Fregean theory.[42]

If we expect our semantic theory to provide a theory of content that locates content in its role in rationalizing action, then it is unclear that we can do without a theory of sense. Wettstein's classic paper brought this issue to a head.[43] Wettstein argued that the only credible notion of meaning must be one definable in terms of linguistic meaning. Hence it must be formulable in terms of properties of symbols, so plausibly something that could be studied by investigating the patterns of behaviour of different kinds of symbol's syntax. Wettstein then argued that no notion of cognitive significance could be saved from such resources, and that therefore semantics should give up the attempt to address questions of cognitive significance. In contrast, Perry has argued that without the idea of cognitive significance, there is no point in studying meaning.[44] Perry's basic thought is the one that I have repeatedly stressed in this chapter. It is the idea that our fundamental purchase on the notion of content is provided by the role which thoughts play in the explanation of action. We want a theory of thought and content, because it is content that makes us the rational intentional creatures that we are. For Perry, this means that we must persevere with the attempt to construct a notion of cognitive significance from the notion of linguistic meaning.[45] That, I suspect, is a mistake; but Perry's insistence on the centrality we should give to rationalizing explanations of action is correct.

With these warnings and issues in mind, in the next chapter I examine the basic argument for drawing the sense/reference distinction – it does not rest on a simple puzzle about how to frame a correct formal semantic theory.

9

Sense and Reference

9.1   Introduction

In this chapter I examine the basic argument for the sense/reference distinction. The distinction is not a response to the puzzles about informative identity statements and the consequent failure of validity for inferences involving substitution of co-referring singular terms within the context of beliefs. The distinction is needed to capture the rational power of sentences. The rational power of a sentence is its capacity to impact upon behaviour in a way that makes behaviour rational. The intuitive explanation of this is to say that the sentence expresses a thought, and it is the thought that explains the behaviour. There is nothing wrong with this intuitive explanation just so long as we do not assume a reification of thoughts as entities that play an intermediary role in our cognitive attitude to the environment. I want to resist the idea that sense is a surrogate for objects and the environment to which we are related in thought. The idea that sense is a surrogate for objects is the blueprint conception of thought. I shall defend the thesis that thoughts are modes of orientation to the environment rather than surrogates for the environment.

We need to keep the following points in mind:

(1)   We should not assume a blueprint conception of thought.
(2)   We should hold fast to the idea that the fundamental need for the notion of sense is the role that content plays in rationalizing explanations of behaviour.

There is one further point that is central to an understanding of the Fregean approach to content. Frege held both of the following theses about names, and about singular terms in general:

Thesis I: Names have sense

230

and

Thesis II: Each name has a unique sense.

Thesis I introduces the very idea of a sense/reference distinction. It commits us to the idea that in order to understand the rational power of sentences and the names they contain, we need to invoke the concept of sense. Thesis II is the stronger claim that the sense of a name is an objective body of information that is unique to a given name. It is this unique body of information that is a component of the objective thought expressed by any sentence employing the name. It is because sense is objective in this sense – a unique package of information associated with a name – that Frege thinks that communication is possible. If sense were not objective, Frege believes that communication would be impossible.[1]

It is thesis II that has caused most difficulty for Fregean theories of sense and reference, for if you are asked to state the sense of a name, you normally have to use a definite description. If there is one thing, however, on which most philosophers now agree, it is that names and definite descriptions have different semantic roles. In particular, names and definite descriptions make different contributions to the semantic value of sentences within the context of modal operators.[2] Given the different semantic roles of names and definite descriptions, any attempt to state the sense of a name with a description is open to counter-example.

For the moment I ignore thesis II in order to focus attention on the more fundamental thesis I. If there is a sound argument for thesis I, the role for the notion of sense will be unavoidable. Only when we are clear about this, shall I return to thesis II. I believe we can make sense of thesis II, but that we make better progress if, for the moment, we neglect it. This order of exposition serves another purpose.

In chapter 4 I argued that we should distinguish between two different ways of understanding Davidson's proposal for a theory of meaning. I called these the theory-theory of meaning and the manual-theory of meaning. The latter aims to state the meaning of every sentence formulable within the language under consideration. The former aims only to theorize the relationships between our concepts of meaning, truth, reference and knowledge in such a way as to make plain what sort of thing meaning is and what sorts of abilities – cognitive abilities, abilities to track the truth and follow inference, etc. – a creature with a grasp of meaning possesses. A theory-theory aims to illuminate the conceptual role that the concept of meaning plays within our broader philosophical self-conception. A similar distinction can be drawn between two conceptions of a theory of sense.

We can distinguish between the theory of sense and a theory of senses. The latter is a theory capable of specifying, for any given linguistic unit, the sense of that unit. A theory of senses would be expected to deliver for any given singular term a theorem of the form

231

(3) The sense of *s* is_____.

In contrast, the theory of sense has no such aspirations. The theory of sense specifies the kind of thing sense is: its fundamental role within our self-conception as creatures with intentionality, what kind of information sense is, and how this will differ systematically for different categories of expressions. In short, the theory of sense explicates the rational power of sentences within our broader philosophical self-conception. It does not complete instances of schema (3). This does not mean that the theory of sense should not address the issue of thesis II. The theory of sense must give some account of how we could understand the claim that each singular term has an objective package of information associated with it that constituted its sense. It does not follow from this that it should be always possible to state what that package is, let alone that it could be done systematically as part of a theory with the capacity to produce theorems that instantiate schema (3).

9.2 The Basic Claim for the Sense/Reference Distinction

The fundamental claim that underpins the idea of sense is that there is no such thing as simple thing-knowledge, or bare acquaintance with particulars.[3] The central claim is a rejection of a piecemeal approach to content. It is a rejection of Russell's atomism.[4] A better, albeit more obscure, way of expressing the central claim is to say that thing-knowledge always depends on truth-knowledge. This formulation is close to Dummett's.[5] The simplest way of seeing what these claims amount to, and of uncovering the argument that supports them, is to return to Russell's object theory of reference.

For Russell there are two different kinds of thoughts that we can have about particulars. There are acquaintance-based thoughts and descriptive thoughts.[6] Consider a sentence of the form

(4) *a* is *F*.

If '*a*' is a genuine singular term (this means that '*a*' is either a demonstrative or the first-person pronoun 'I'), the thought expressed by (4) is individuated by a Russellian proposition

(5) $<a, F>$.

If '*a*' is any other category of singular term, including proper names, then '*a*' will be equivalent to a description or set of descriptions. In such cases the thought expressed by (4) is individuated by a descriptive proposition

(6)   F [the φ].

Note, the issue here is an issue about thought, not about propositions. Although Russell speaks of propositions, and we call the ordered pair of object and property a 'Russellian proposition', for Russell, this was part of an overall theory of thought and judgement. The issue before us is what is a singular *thought*? That is to say, are there thoughts, things that figure in rationalizing explanations of behaviour, that are singular? What is the rational power of a singular expression? It is important to bear in mind that Russell has quite different motivations from those of contemporary 'Russellians' who employ the idea of propositional content, which is explicitly not a notion of thought content.

For Russell, only those thoughts capable of individuation by a Russellian proposition are genuinely thoughts about particulars. The intuition behind this claim seems right, for thoughts capable of individuation by a descriptive proposition like (6) have a general content. The content of such thoughts is specifiable with the apparatus of predicates and quantifiers. In contrast, thoughts specifiable with Russellian propositions have a genuinely singular content. The idea of a singular content is of great importance. Only of thoughts with a singular content can we say that they are thoughts about a particular. Russell struggles with the epistemological consequences of his restriction on the range of genuine singular terms and, hence, the range of singular thoughts in which reference to particulars takes place. He acknowledges the need to save the appearance of more singular thought going on in our lives than is officially allowed under the constraints of his theory. He says that when we speak of Bismarck, there is a singular thought about Bismarck individuated by the Russellian proposition

(7)   <Bismarck, great statesmanship>,

and that this is the thought we would like to have when we use the sentence

(8)   Bismarck was a great statesman.

However, only Bismarck himself can have the thought individuated by (7); the rest of us, because we cannot be acquainted with Bismarck, have to make do with the descriptive thought[7]

(9)   a great statesman [the first chancellor of the German Empire].

What is clear in this model of thought is that the category of singular thoughts (those with a singular rather than a general content) is a category of thoughts that require a bare acquaintance with the object by the thinker. The relationship of acquaintance is immediate, unmediated and unanalysable. Once again, given the epistemological restrictions at play in Russell's theorizing, there is no real scope to call these features of the acquaintance relation into doubt. Call this acquaintance thing-knowledge. It is a form of knowledge that is not susceptible of further analysis and that involves a direct contact between thinker and object.[8] It is an atomistic concept of acquaintance. Suppose we were to consider the possibility of singular thoughts about particulars like ordinary material objects, other people, etc. Once again, because the object theory of reference entails an extensional theory of judgement, with thoughts individuated by Russellian propositions, the relationship between thinker and particular must be one of bare acquaintance: thing-knowledge.

The notion of bare acquaintance is simply the notion that singular thoughts are individuated by the objects that are their referent. We know from chapter 8 that this means that there will be a problem accounting for the differential rational power of sentences containing co-referring singular terms. We know also that Frege took this to lead to the apparent absurdity that the object thought about is a constituent of thought. We know also that Frege's response to all this was to propose that singular terms have sense as well as reference, and that a favourite metaphor for the sense of a singular term is the mode of presentation by which it represents the object thought about. What we do not yet know is what independent argument there is for all this. My suggestion is that the argument centres on the claim that there is no such thing as thing-knowledge that does not depend on knowledge of truths, or truth-knowledge. The basic claim is then that thing-knowledge always depends on truth-knowledge, or

> BC: Knowledge of truths is more primitive than knowledge of things.

BC looks to have things topsy-turvy, for it says that we account for our knowledge and thought about things in terms of our knowledge and thought about truths. In contrast, the familiar idea of compositional semantics is that knowledge of truths is compositionally analysable as the product of knowledge of the semantic role of sub-sentential units. BC appears to be incompatible with the very idea of compositional semantics. The appearance is illusory, but the point needs some explaining.

9.3 The Basic Argument for the Sense/Reference Distinction

The argument goes like this. First, here is the criterion that Frege uses time and again in individuating thoughts:

> **Intuitive criterion of difference (ICD):** Sentences S_1 and S_2 express different thoughts iff it is possible for a subject to understand both and to assent to one and dissent to the other.[9]

ICD takes for granted the idea of sentences having rational power, for it employs the differential rational power of sentences in defining the criterion for individuating thoughts. The fact that, for some given pair of sentences, one elicits assent and the other dissent is the simplest example of their differential rational power. To note the role of ICD is not yet to provide an argument for the sense/reference distinction. It is simply to record that the idea of a sentence's rational power is taken for granted by the Fregean. This is not necessarily a problem, for as we concluded at the end of the previous chapter, the bottom line for the theory of content is that content is needed because of its role in rationalizing explanations of behaviour. Accordingly, a theory that defines the principles of thought individuation in terms of the rational power of sentences is bound to meet our bottom-line constraint on content. So far, we are merely in agreement with all those writers who endorse intentional realism as defined in chapter 1 and who accept the legitimacy of ordinary rationalizing explanations of behaviour.[10]

What we need an argument for is the thesis that knowledge of truths is more basic than knowledge of things. As a thesis about thoughts and what it is to think about objects, BC says that the idea of a molecular thought is more primitive than the idea of a mode of presentation of an object. There is no such thing as thinking about an object that is not a thinking of a whole thought. If this is the basic claim that underpins the theory of sense, it is the analogue for thought and sense of Davidson's claim that truth is a more primitive semantic concept than reference. The basic argument for Frege's sense/reference distinction is an argument for the claim that the sense of a sentence (a thought) is a more primitive concept than the sense of a singular term (the mode of presentation of an object).

I call the claim that the idea of the sense of a sentence is more primitive than the idea of the sense of a singular term the molecular theory of sense, for the sense of molecular units is prior to that of the sense of the atoms that compose molecular senses. The central claim for the molecular theory of sense is that it is not possible to think of an object without thinking some whole thoughts about it. If you are thinking of a, you must be thinking some thoughts – e.g. Fa, Ga, etc. – and the thinking of these thoughts constitutes the way in which you think of a; it constitutes the sense of the singular term. Note that an argument for the claim that it is not possible to think of a without thinking some thoughts (Fa, Ga, etc.) is only an argument for Frege's thesis I. An argument for thesis II would require some means of identifying the set of thoughts that constituted the sense of the singular term and an account of how that set constituted an objective body of information that was the sense of a. I start with an argument for the claim that it is impossible to think of an object without thinking some set of thoughts.

One argument for the molecular theory of sense consists of an appeal to the apparent difficulty of articulating what it would be to think of an object without thinking whole thoughts about it. For example, suppose that in the middle of a crowded, rowdy meeting I say

(10)   That heckler should be ejected.

Suppose now that my purported reference and thought about the individual is not responsive to an enquiry from you as to whom I mean. Suppose you ask if I mean the man with the red hair, or the man behind the tall security guard, or the man who . . . , etc., and in response to all these questions I simply shrug and insist that I simply mean that that heckler should be ejected. So you then ask if I mean that one there, and you point; or you ask if I mean the one next to that one there, and you point to a different place. Suppose I still refuse to see any of this as relevant to the thought I expressed with (10). You have offered a series of thoughts to which you took the truth of my original claim to be sensitive, and I refuse point-blank to acknowledge any such sensitivity. In the face of my attempt to hold my original claim insensitive to such further thoughts, it is tempting to wonder whether I could really have meant anything at all by my original claim. To take the matter further, consider this.

Suppose that as I uttered (10), you fixed the angle of my gaze and proceeded into the crowd along a trajectory defined by that angle. Suppose that at each person located on that trajectory you then asked, 'Do you mean this person?', and I replied, 'Oh no, not them'! In the absence of further complicated explanations about the variance between the physical orientation of my head and eyeballs and the real direction of my sight, these further suppositions surely confirm that my original utterance of (10) could not have amounted to a thinking about an object.

The suppositions that I have considered are all ways of revealing the way in which thought about an object must be sensitive to a cluster of thoughts that, as it were, provide the triangulation that fixes thought on a particular. You cannot, for example, demonstratively think about an object without having some idea of how it stands above, behind and to the side of other things, for if you did not have some idea about that, you would have no idea of its space-occupancy at all.

What is the force of the above considerations? On the face of it, they appear to support an epistemological claim that we might express as follows:

Epistemological molecularity: The only way that we can tell that someone is thinking about *a* is by their preparedness to think a bundle of thoughts about *a*.

If epistemological molecularity is all that is at stake, this does not support the molecular theory of sense. Epistemological molecularity is compatible with the idea that there is such a thing as thinking about an object that could be characterized independently of thinking a bundle of thoughts; it is only that thinking some such bundle is a guide or test for the occurrence of the thinking about the object. In contrast, the molecular theory of sense holds that thinking about an object is constituted by thinking a bundle of thoughts.

A second response to the above considerations that would add further support to the idea that they support, at best, the notion of epistemological molecularity is the following. Someone might say that if thinking about an object is constituted by thinking a bundle of thoughts, how is this bundle individuated? What makes it a bundle of thoughts relevant to thinking about *a*? To this the inescapable answer would seem to be that what makes the bundle of thoughts relevant to thinking about *a* is that they are all thoughts that involve thinking about *a*. But in that case, the very individuation of the bundle presupposes the idea of thinking about *a*; it cannot be constitutive of thinking about *a*. This is a natural response to the above considerations, but it trades on the initial epistemological way in which I have represented the central claim.

The picture so far suggests that sense is required in order to focus thought on objects. There is something right about this suggestion, but it needs to be stripped of the epistemological idea of sense as a 'search and refer' criterion for applying a name. For example, consider thinking about the number 2. The danger with the epistemological considerations is that they suggest a model in which thinking of the number 2 amounts to thinking a privileged set of thoughts that constitute the way we think of the number. The privileged set would include, for example, the thought that 2 is greater than 1 and less than 3. This model falls foul of two central objections. First, it treats sense as a 'test', a method for targeting objects, which suggests that the method might fail. If so, the model endorses a blueprint conception of thought. Second, even in the arithmetical case, it is contentious which whole thoughts should go into the privileged set.

The epistemological considerations do not, then, capture the best way of articulating the need for the concept of sense. They do, however, capture the sorts of ideas that many people have of Frege – that sense is fundamentally an epistemological concept concerned with a 'search-and-refer' model of thinking of objects. But sense is not an epistemological concept. It is not concerned with the epistemology of thought about objects; it is a constitutive thesis about thought about objects.

Consider again the number 2. The question to ask is not, 'How do you think of 2 without thinking a privileged set of whole thoughts?' The question is, 'Is it possible to factor out the ability to think of 2 from the ability to think things like, "2 is greater than 1 and less than 3"?' The epistemological question suggests that in thinking of 2 you have a privileged set of thoughts before the mind – hence the threat of the blueprint model. To ask the constitutive question is to make no assumptions about sense as mental entity before the mind.

Consider a different example. Consider a subject looking at a surface covered by grains of rice and thinking of a perceptually demonstrated grain the thought 'That grain is discoloured'. Again, the question that needs considering is, 'Is it possible to factor out the ability to think about that grain from the ability to think things like "It is to the left of that one", "It is behind this one", etc.?' The central claim that grounds the need for the sense/reference distinction is that it is not possible to factor out the ability to think of an object from the ability to think whole thoughts. But now you might think that reference never gets explained, but at best elucidated within a holistic web of reference and thought about objects.[11]

This last point is correct, but it is not an objection! Recall that our task is not to explain reference as a relation that connects disparate realms – thought and world – that can be characterized independently of one another. The task is to explain what the rational power of sentences with singular terms consists in. The answer to which we have been moving is simply this: The rational power of a sentence with a singular term in it consists in the way that the sentence is systematically connected to a web of sentences. For sure, this web will employ singular terms; it might also employ the same singular term as the original target sentence. This, however, is no objection. Indeed, it points to the fundamental insight that drives the whole conception of sense and reference.

The fundamental insight is that if you could factor out grasp of the sense of a singular term from grasp of the sense of whole sentences, you would have no account of the rational power of the sense of the singular term. Thinking of an object is normative. To think of an object is to have your cognitive attitude to it subject to normative rational evaluation. The normativity of thought consists in the way a thought is systematically connected to others. The idea that we could factor out a sense of a singular term is that we could specify its content independently of its role in explaining the inferential connections between whole thoughts. This would make it possible to have a sense as a stand-alone item – a blueprint conception of sense. Sense would be atomic and permit the possibility of atomic error. But the notion of atomic error plays no role in accounting for the systematic connectedness of thought. Atomic error does not, and cannot, bear on the error of other thought elements; for, by being atomic, there is nothing about it that other thoughts can share.[12]

It still might seem that the argument for the molecular theory of sense is incomplete, for it might be thought that the above considerations really take us no further than a point reached in chapter 1 when we reviewed the argument for what Evans calls the generality constraint.[13] The generality constraint says that in thinking that *a* is *F*, you are exercising a pair of capacities; the ability to think the molecular thought presupposes the ability to understand other molecular thoughts employing the constituents found in the first thought. Similarly, it might be objected that the argument for the molecular theory of sense shows only that grasp of the sense of a singular term has to be grasp of something that is capable of figuring in a whole thought, not that the idea of grasping whole thoughts is more basic.

But the argument for the molecular theory of sense does go further than the argument for the generality constraint. If the requirement was only that in grasping the sense of a singular term, you grasped something that was capable of figuring in a whole thought, then in principle there could be a singular sense that never in fact figured in a whole thought. It would be an atomic representation. It would then be possible to think of an object without ever thinking anything about it. It is that possibility that is ruled out by the fundamental argument for the sense/reference distinction. That possibility is ruled out because it is a scenario in which your thinking would not be subject to normative rational evaluation. Piecemeal and atomic representations have no rational impact. The rational impact of a content consists in its connectivity with other contents. Contents get connectivity by sharing components. 'Ah,' you might now say, 'so there are such things as components?' Well of course there are, but the idea of a component is explained via the idea of whole thoughts, not the other way round. A component is what whole thoughts have in common; it is defined in terms of its grammar in connecting whole thoughts. It is not something whose characterization can be factored out of its role in connecting whole thoughts. If you never thought anything about the object, you would not be able to evaluate your thought. The sort of thinking about an object that is envisaged by the possibility of a sense of a singular term as something that could be factored out of a whole thought would be a thinking that involved no evaluation. Semantic evaluation is essentially true/false evaluation; there is no such thing as referential evaluation. This is the reason why there cannot be empty names. This can sound surprising. As noted in chapter 1, in principle, representationalism permits the possibility of atomic error. The present argument points out that a notion of atomic error can play no role in accounting for the normative connectivity of thought.[14]

Thinking about objects is essentially a thinking of whole thoughts. The idea of the sense of a singular term, a thought component, is not the idea of something that can be factored out of a thought and that, on its own, could constitute a rational attitude to an object. The idea of the sense of a singular term is the idea of that which is common between a web of whole thoughts. The sense of a singular term is defined as that which a number of whole thoughts have in common. In other words, the very idea of the sense of a singular term is a theoretical construct or posit, something that is posited to account for ways that webs of whole thoughts are taken to be rationally connected to one another. It is entertaining such whole thoughts that constitutes the idea of the *way in which you think of an object*. The phrase 'the way of thinking of an object' does not pick out a repeatable thought component that could be characterized independently of its grammar as a common component of thoughts. The sense of a sentence – a thought – is the notion that has real application; the sense of a singular term is a theoretical posit.[15] To say that the sense of a sentence has real application is just to repeat that it is that notion that is applied in the fundamental role that thoughts play in rationalizing explanations of action.

9.4   The Reified Model of Sense and Quasi-behaviourism

If the sense of a singular term turns out to be a theoretical posit, where does this leave the central theses that Frege applied to sense. Frege held (i) that in belief contexts a name stands for its sense, not its reference; (ii) that sense is objective; (iii) that each name has a unique sense, thus making communication possible. I return to (iii) in the next chapter. The thesis that looks most under threat from my reading of the argument for the sense/reference distinction is (i). To say that the sense of a singular term is a theoretical posit is to deny the reification of sense; but this means that sense is not available as an object to be referred to in belief contexts. The loss of the reification of sense is a bonus. Can Frege's account of *oratio obliqua* survive this bonus?

Frege says that in the simple sentence

> (11)   Bill Clinton plays the saxophone,

the name 'Bill Clinton' refers to Bill Clinton, but also possesses a sense. In the more complex case,

> (12)   Hillary believes that Bill Clinton plays the saxophone,

the name 'Bill Clinton' stands for its sense, not its reference. How much of this do we have to accept if we retain a sense/reference distinction along the lines argued for above? The thrust of Frege's thesis about (12) is to account for the familiar failures of inference, for even if

> (13)   Bill Clinton is the tallest man in the Oval office,

it does not follow from (12) and (13) that

> (14)   Hillary believes that the tallest man in the Oval office plays the saxophone,

even though it does follow from (11) and (13) that

(15)   The tallest man in the Oval office plays the saxophone.

The usual way of understanding Frege's treatment of all this is to reify sense and to suppose that Frege is committed to the following pair of theses:

Reification thesis I: The sense of a singular term is an entity associated with the term, and it is this entity that is its referent in oblique contexts.

And

Reification thesis II: The sense of a sentence is an entity, and it is this entity that a subject is related to when they entertain a belief.

Neither of these is required in order to preserve a Fregean account of reference.

The natural thing to say is that there is only one entity associated with a singular term, and that is its referent.[16] Similarly, there is only one entity that a subject is related to when entertaining a belief, and that is the world. If we say this, we can, however, still accommodate the basic Fregean insights. To insist that singular terms have sense is to insist that the use of them to express thoughts is a use with a rational power. The above pair of reification theses only come in if we then suppose that we need entities to explain this rational power. The alternative, which I recommend, is that instead of trying to explain the rational power of sentences by appealing to a configuration of reified entities, we should simply accept the rational power of sentences as a basic element of the behaviour of rational creatures.

The model that most people have in mind, which supports the above pair of reification theses, goes like this. Hillary Clinton thinks about Bill Clinton, and the idea of sense is employed to pick out the way she thinks about him. One feature of the way that Hillary Clinton thinks about Bill Clinton is that sentences impact upon her with a certain rational power. At the very least, this means that she is not committed rationally to endorsing (15) because she endorses (11). In short, Hillary Clinton has a pattern of sentence production and use that captures the rational organization of her behaviour. It is because her sentence production and use exhibit a pattern that makes rational sense of her behaviour that we take her to be a thinker. So far, this is just to remind ourselves of the data that everyone accepts. The contentious model that endorses the two reification theses is a model employed to explain Hillary Clinton's pattern of sentence production. It is this model that I think is unnecessary.

The contentious model tries to explain Hillary Clinton's behaviour by positing items the existence of which explains the rational pattern of her sentence production and use. There are two versions of this reified model of sense: the Platonic and the mental version. The Platonic version posits senses as items that exist within an abstract although objective realm. The mental version posits items that exist within the mind/brain and that are causally responsible for Hillary Clinton's pattern of sentence production and use. Historically, Frege has been associated with the Platonic version of reified senses. This captures his insistence that sense is objective and the currency of communication. The Platonic version suffers from a lack of a clear epistemology of sense. In the absence of a well-developed account of what it is to grasp Platonic entities, the benefit of a ready currency for communication is offset by the cost of the lack of an account of what it is to have holdings in such a currency. The Platonic version deals in uncashed metaphors. I shall consider only the mental version of the reified model of senses. The central flaw in the reified model of senses is common to both versions.

The mental version has intentional entities as the reified senses: the sense of the name 'Bill Clinton' and the composite sense that is the thought expressed by a sentence containing the name 'Bill Clinton'. On this model, sense is an extra entity associated with a name; it is an intentional entity.[17] This is an attractive model. It starts from the undisputed fact that linguistic behaviour exhibits a rational structure – the rational power of sentences. It then tries to explain this rational structure by positing entities that are causally responsible for it. In addition, the reified account of senses provides a literal reading of Frege's thesis that names in oblique contexts refer to their sense, not their reference, for in such cases the name stands for the reified intentional entity.[18]

This model is an exercise in the metaphysics of thought. The model is offered as a way of accommodating and explaining the undisputed fact that linguistic behaviour exhibits a rational structure. The metaphysical question that remains once you have accepted that linguistic behaviour exhibits such a structure concerns what this structure consists in. The attraction of the reified sense model is, I think, twofold. First, it accommodates the possibility of misrepresentation in the simplest and most obvious way possible. Second, in its mental version it offers to bring the phenomena of intentionality within the purview of causal explanations.

The possibility of misrepresentation (false thoughts) is constitutive of intentionality. The very idea of representation involves the idea of representations getting the world wrong. The capacity to think is the capacity to think thoughts that can be false as well as true. Any account of the metaphysics of thought must make room to accommodate the possibility of false thoughts. The reified sense model captures the possibility of misrepresentation in the way that a representationalist theory of thought does – the blueprint conception.[19] More specifically, the model allows the possibility of empty singular terms; for, in principle, you could possess the entity that constitutes the sense of a singular term regardless of the existence of the term's referent. On this model, senses are object-independent.

The idea that senses must be object-independent in order to accommodate false thoughts is common. It is also contentious. We need to distinguish at least two different concerns that prompt the need for object independence. One concern we express in terms of a general detachment of thought from how things stand in the world. What is distinctive of creatures with the capacity for thought is their ability to consider how things might be, to hypothesize and consider contrary-to-fact scenarios. Such a capacity would seem to inhere in a capacity to manipulate representations. In considering hypotheses about how things might be, we turn our attention from the world, and speculate by attending to our ideas. We manipulate our ideas; we consider how they might be rearranged to represent what is not presently the case, and, if we desire the outcome, then, other things being equal, we act so as to bring into being the state of affairs represented by our ideas. This description of what it is to be a thinker is platitudinous. Whether or not we should take it literally, the central idea that thought gives us a capacity to stand back from the world and not take it just as it is, is the idea of a capacity that is constitutive of being a rational subject and agent. This capacity to stand back from the world does not entail the blueprint conception of thought, the idea that the realm of thought is characterizable through and through, independently of the world. That is to say, the capacity does not entail either version of the reified model of sense. The capacity requires the possibility of false thoughts. It does not require the possibility of atomic error. This point is often missed.[20] The possibility of atomic error only seems natural if you have already endorsed a blueprint conception of false thought, for that then gets extended to cover thought components. The blueprint conception of thoughts is characteristic of Cartesianism, but common also in most contemporary theorizing about the mind.[21] This is not the place to examine such views, but it is important to note the foundations for such a metaphysics of the mind in the reified model of sense. Nevertheless, the general capacity for standing back from the world is compatible with a position that holds that the capacity for thought was in general world-dependent even if individual thoughts could be false. For example, if the best account of sense was an account of content that was not in general separable from an account of how the subject of thought was related to the world, then such an account of sense could not support the reified model of sense. It would be a theory of content in which the capacity for thought was world-dependent.[22]

The reified model of sense captures the phenomenon of misrepresentation, but does so in a very strong form, a form that endorses a metaphysics of thought that is Cartesian. Such an account of the separation of the realm of thought from the world is not necessary in order to make room for the possibility of misrepresentation.

The second feature of the reified model of sense is the idea of accommodating sense within a causal model of explanation. Many people assume that the only decent kind of explanation is a causal explanation. Causal explanations work by identifying entities or events as tokens of types, where the type features in a covering law. On a reified model of sense, in which thought concerns the manipulation of intentional entities, the prospect beckons of being able to treat the rational properties of thought in terms of the causal properties of the supposed entities. Indeed, in the standard representationalist model of thought, it becomes a condition of adequacy on the notion of content that content get identified with states that appear in regular causal chains of states. Once again, this is not the place to begin a study of the metaphysics of content causation or of the possibility for reducing the rational force of content to the causal power of states that could be identified with the contents of that-clauses. But we should note that such metaphysical matters turn on how we understand the core notion of content that flows from Frege's concept of sense.

Should we endorse the reified model of sense? Do we have to endorse the reified model of sense in order to make sense of Frege's theses regarding oblique contexts? The answer to both these questions is 'No'. The fundamental flaw with the reified model of sense is simple. The reified model of sense has thought as a configuration of entities. These entities are posited in order to explain the rational pattern of language use. Hillary Clinton believes that Bill Clinton is her husband. She also believes that Bill Clinton is President of the United States. Given these two beliefs, rationality demands that she ought also to believe that her husband is President of the United States. That is the data of rational ordering of sentence use. Hillary Clinton employs language in rational ways, and language impacts upon her actions in rational ways. Positing the reified configuration of sense is supposed to be required in order to explain the rational pattern of her language. But now, if we buy the story about sense as a configuration of reified items, those items will also have to exhibit a rational order. Indeed, if the explanation of the rational order of Hillary Clinton's language use is to be explained by the way sense is configured, then her realm of sense is going to have to exhibit just the same pattern as her linguistic units.

Hillary Clinton uses the name 'Bill Clinton' in various systematic ways. The systematicity of her use of this name is, in part, constitutive of her rationality. The reified model of sense posits a sense for the name in order to explain the systematicity of use of the name. But this means that the systematicity of use of the name that is constitutive of her rationality is duplicated in the systematicity of configuration of the sense of the name and the sense of other words that Hillary Clinton understands. In short, the reified model of sense seems to be saying this: We have a rational systematicity of language, a configuration of linguistic dealings that embodies our rationality. We are asked to understand this by positing a configuration of entities whose patterning is mimicked by the linguistic entities! This is no explanation at all. If the rational systematicity of language stands in need of explanation, nothing is gained by positing a realm configured by just the same rational systematicity. The hopelessness of such an explanation is further compounded by the ontological oddity of the realm that is supposed to serve as explanans. Neither the Platonic nor the mental versions of the reified model of sense deal in entities whose explanatory potential is very great. But the oddity of locating an explanation of rational power in either a Platonic structure or a mental structure is nothing compared to the sheer fatuousness of thinking that the rational power of one structure is explained by positing an isomorphic structure with just the same rational power! Of course, the escape from this is supposed to be that the rational power of sense (intentional entities) is reduced to the causal properties of the brain states with which these entities are identified. But, as we saw in chapter 7, the reductionist version of naturalism does not work. Furthermore, if you are going to try for such a reduction, why introduce sense at all? Why not reduce the rational power of linguistic input/output directly, in terms of causal behaviourism? The reason why people take the detour via sense as intentional entities is that they want to endorse intentional realism; but then, having done that, they want to return thought to the world by a reductionist naturalism.

The above criticism of the reified model of sense is, I think, fatal. Note that it does not affect theories of the mind that do not endorse intentional realism. The target of the above criticism is the idea that there is such a thing as a rational structure of intentional entities, the configuration of which explains the rational configuration of linguistic usage. The obvious target of the criticism is the idea of a Language of Thought; but any intentional realist who takes the rational-normative individuation of intentional states to pick out a configuration of entities is open to the above criticism. Not all versions of physicalism do this.

Dretske's physicalist model of mental causation is immune to the above criticism.[23] The reason is that Dretske's model assumes that causal explanation is the only viable form of explanation, and therefore takes it as a constraint on any account of content that the content of that-clauses should by identifiable with states that figure in causal processes. That is to say, Dretske's individuation of mental states with content is fundamentally causal, not rational-normative. Dretske is not, then, an intentional realist who believes in the realm of sense as something with rational-normative criteria of individuation. The difficulty for Fodor's position is that he *is* an intentional realist – belief states are individuated with the familiar rational criteria of individuation – but also believes that those very same states can be given a reductive analysis in terms of the causal power of physical states.

Notwithstanding the above differences, both Fodor and Dretske ultimately have to meet a challenge that, as we saw in chapter 7, looks to be unanswerable. The challenge is to capture the normative character of content with a causal analysis that deals, at most, with the notion of causal dispositions. This challenge arises in slightly different ways for Fodor and Dretske. For Fodor, it arises because of his intentional realism – his acceptance of the ordinary rationalizing individuation of content. For Fodor, that also amounts to a commitment to the Language of Thought hypothesis, and the causal-normative problem arises in trying to characterize a normatively individuated Language of Thought in causal vocabulary. For Dretske, the causal-normative problem arises in a subtly different form. As noted, Dretske starts with the restriction that contentful states be causally individuated, so he does not have the Language of Thought. Nevertheless, if Dretske's analysis is to be compelling, and if it is to capture the phenomena of agents acting for reasons, then at some point it will have to do justice to our ordinary rationalizing accounts of behaviour. In other words, the need to deliver the rational-normative out of the causal arises at a more general level for Dretske than it does for Fodor. But the problem still arises; for otherwise Dretske would be in danger of literally losing the subject – the rational subject who acts for a reason.

If we reject the reified model of sense but still endorse the idea of sense, there is, I think, only one alternative. I call the alternative conception of sense a quasi-behaviourist theory of content. Quasi-behaviourism holds that instead of trying to explain the rational power of sentences by appeal to a configuration of reified entities, we should simply accept the rational power of sentences as a basic element in the behaviour of rational creatures who think. This is behaviourist, for it takes the rational structure of behaviour as the locus of our rationality; content is individuated by the rational structure of our behaviour. It is only a 'quasi' behaviourism, however; for the behaviour appealed to is not behaviour characterized in terms of causal stimulus–response patterns, but behaviour characterized rationally. On a quasi-behaviourist account of sense, the notion of the way of thinking of an object is cashed out in terms of the way we are behaviourally oriented to an object. This is the idea I mentioned at the start of this chapter, of taking Frege's notion of a mode of presentation as a mode of orientation. All I am now suggesting is that we do not need to look for intentional entities in order to explain the rational structure of our orientation to the world. Rather, we understand the orientation of thought behaviourally, in terms of our rational patterns of orientation and response. We do not need to go beyond the data that most people appeal to – the data of rationally ordered behaviour – in order to locate our rationality and our cognitive capacities. These are things that are constituted by our rational patterns of orientation and response.

At the moment, quasi-behaviourism is a suggestion made in the place of the demise of the reified model of sense. But there are more important reasons for endorsing the quasi-behaviourist model of sense, which we need to start unpacking. Note this: that if we do not endorse the reified model of sense, then we cannot endorse a syntactic theory of content. If sense is not capable of reification, then there can be no fully codifiable account of content in which possession of content is modelled in terms of possession of linguistic or quasi-linguistic items. It is the pull of a syntactic theory of content that has driven most research into content over the last century, and it is this that lies behind the deep-seated appeal of a reified model of sense. If the reification of sense does not work, then content is going to be something that is in principle not capable of being fully specified linguistically. There will be senses that are not capable of individuation linguistically. Sense will outstrip linguistic meaning. The things that figure as reasons in our lives will not be susceptible to linguistic individuation. These are, for many people, radical suggestions. They are, however, claims that have become familiar in recent Fregean theory as Frege's sense/reference distinction has been applied to expressions like perceptual demonstratives, indexicals, token-reflexives, etc. As we see the way in which Frege's ideas can be applied to these categories of expression, we will see the deeper reasons for endorsing a quasi-behaviourist account of sense instead of a reified model of sense. We will also see the fundamental reason why sense is not descriptive. We pick these issues up in the next two chapters, especially in section 11.6f.[24]

Frege's thesis about *oratio obliqua* survives, but in a modified quasi-behaviourist form. To say that in (12) 'Bill Clinton' stands for its sense, not its reference, merely repeats the known data that we cannot assume that (13) is rationally linked with (11) and (12). But this failure of rational linkage is not explained by a failure of linkage between odd sense entities; it is no more than a failure of linkage within Hillary Clinton's rational behaviour.

9.5 Why Sense is not Descriptive

Most textbooks assume that Frege held a descriptive theory of sense, and that Frege's views about names are the same as Russell's. This is wrong. I have argued (section 9.3) that the sense of a singular term is a theoretical posit, that which is common to different whole thoughts. I have argued that the way you think of an object is as that which is triangulated by whole thoughts. You cannot think of an object without thinking molecular thoughts. Another way of expressing this fundamental claim of the theory of sense would be to say this:

Fregean: In thinking of an object, the object must be brought under molecular contents.

We might contrast this claim with two other claims that we can identify as the Cartesian and Kantian alternatives.

The Cartesian says:

Cartesian: In thinking of an object, the object must be brought under Ideas.

And the Kantian:

Kantian: In thinking of an object, the object must be brought under concepts.

The Cartesian alternative is, I assume, not a viable option, although it can be found in many classic authors, like Russell and Mill.[25] The Kantian alternative is an interesting one. If we assume, for the moment, that to bring an object under concepts is to bring it under descriptions, then the Kantian alternative amounts to a descriptive theory of sense. It is common to think of concepts as descriptive, although it is also mistaken.[26] But for the moment, the identification of conceptual content with descriptive content provides a contrast between the Fregean claim and the Kantian/descriptive alternative.

The Fregean claim demands that objects be brought under molecular contents, without restriction on what form those contents should take. The Kantian alternative is a restricted version of this, for it demands that the contents be descriptive. In contrast, the Fregean claim allows the possibility that the contents be non-descriptive, or singular. A singular content is one that is not specifiable in full linguistically; it requires an orientation to the object, for that is the only means of getting the individuation demanded by the constraint that we rationalize behaviour. A token singular sense is then one that is not susceptible to a syntactic or linguistic individuation. It cannot be party to a blueprint conception of sense. The idea of a singular sense is the idea that is left in need of exploration when we distinguish between the Fregean and Kantian positions. It is worth noting:

> A token singular sense is a sense that cannot be individuated syntactically.

If this is right, and if there are such things, then representationalism is false, for singular thoughts will only be capable of individuation relationally.[27]

Now, given that the Fregean position, as I have argued for it, is distinct from the Kantian/descriptive one, why do so many people think that Frege's notion of sense must be descriptive? Alternatively, why do most people fail to see the space for singular senses, senses that are not fully codifiable linguistically? I think there are two answers, one superficial and one that runs very deep.

The superficial answer is that whenever Frege gives an example of the sense of a name, he uses a description. This is, of course, rather feeble evidence on its own, although it points towards the deeper reason for thinking that sense must be descriptive. If you are to give an example of sense and to give it in writing rather than in speech, then you will have to be able to state the sense in a way that is fully expressible linguistically. This means that the content will have to be one that is context-insensitive. Descriptive content is such a form of content. It is a form of content the individuation of which can be achieved linguistically. We individuate descriptive contents by their syntactic shape, by the identity of the symbol strings used to express them. That is what Russell's theory of descriptions shows us how to do. So, if we are to be able to state the sense of a name in writing, we have to do so with a description.

If you are giving an example of sense in speech, and you are able to deploy contextual cues provided by perception, bodily orientation, etc., then matters are different. For example, I might show the way in which I am thinking of an object with a perceptual demonstrative, by pointing to the thing; I show the sense by employing information that is contextually sensitive. Of course, it is not possible to pin down the information fully in language, but that is the consequence of its being information that is not fully codable linguistically. This means that the sense of a perceptual demonstrative does not enjoy the sort of objective permanence that a descriptive sense enjoys. A sense that is characterizable descriptively is recoverable by re-employing the appropriate linguistic unit. This means that a descriptive thought is an objective content in the sense often associated with Frege; for it is not only sharable, but also permanently recoverable.[28] In contrast, the sense of a perceptual demonstrative is not objective in the same way. This does not mean that it is not sharable or that it is not a currency for communication; for the whole point of my showing you how I am thinking of the demonstrated object is that you come to share the perceptually supplied information that I enjoy. Such information is not, however, objective in the sense of being permanently recoverable. This means that demonstrative thoughts could never be candidates for entities within a Platonic realm of senses. This, however, is no problem; for a demonstrative thought is something the existence and continuance of which depend upon the contextual perceptual engagement with the environment. You cannot recover a perceptually based way of thinking merely by repeating a form of words; you need also to re-engage perceptually with the world. That sounds exactly right.[29]

Someone might object that, without a developed account of what a demonstrative sense is, the above observations cut no ice. For sure, a sense that is statable in writing will be descriptive, but without a theory of demonstrative senses, what is this notion of a sense that is shown by use of contextually sensitive information, as opposed to a sense that is stated using written language? This is a fair question, and one that will be answered in chapter 12. I suspect that the question is motivated by the deep reason for thinking that sense must be descriptive.

The deep reason for thinking that sense is descriptive is a metaphysical thesis about the mind and intentional content. Many people assume that intentional content (what is in the mind) is specifiable independently of the world. If there is such a thing as the layout of your intentionality, then it is characterizable independently of how things stand in the world. This is representationalism and its internalist conception of the mind. Internalism is broader than the representationalism of the reified model of sense, for plenty of people are internalists, whether or not they adopt a theory of sense.

Internalism is motivated by a number of different things. Fodor's version – he calls it methodological solipsism – is motivated by the methodological prescription of making content suitable for appearing in physicalistically respectable explanations of behaviour.[30] Some people think internalism is motivated by the need to capture the possibility of misrepresentation. As I have already suggested, this last motivation is unfounded.[31] And for some people internalism is motivated by the epistemological claim that nothing about the layout of the mind entails anything about the existence of the world.[32]

We will see in the next two chapters that there are many different responses to internalism, and that there are important differences between the kinds of externalism that now dominate most thinking about the mind and mental content. For the moment, though, just suppose that internalism were true. If internalism were true, then content would have to be definable in a way that was context-insensitive. If the layout of intentionality were world-independent, it would be possible to individuate content as something that could be carried from place to place, something that was indifferent to where you were. So, given internalism, content must be identifiable with linguistic meaning, for linguistic counters are just the sort of thing that you can take from place to place. But the only linguistic counters whose meaning is invariant across contexts are descriptive counters. As already noted, Russell's theory of descriptions shows us how we can individuate descriptive thoughts syntactically in terms of the arrangement of predicate letters and quantifiers. So, if you adopt internalism, you have to endorse a descriptive theory of sense, for it is the only way to get a notion of content that is invariant across contexts.

That is the deep reason why people are prone to think that sense is descriptive, because they either believe that internalism is true, or they at least assume that Fregeans are internalists. The Fregean theory of sense is not internalist. Indeed, contemporary Fregean theory offers the most radical form of externalism currently on offer. If this is right, then not only is there no good reason for thinking that Fregean theory is committed to a descriptive theory of sense, but Fregean theory offers the scope to exorcize internalism from our conception of the mind.

Sense, then, is not descriptive. This is just as well, for a descriptive theory of sense has many problems. Four problems are worth noting: (i) a descriptive theory of sense has no account of reference; (ii) a descriptive theory of sense entails a universalistic account of content; (iii) a descriptive theory of sense suggests a 'search and refer' epistemology for the operation of singular terms in language; (iv) names and descriptions behave differently in the context of modal operators. I shall comment briefly on the first three. The fourth problem is the starting-point for the causal theory of reference that I examine in the next chapter.

(i) *A descriptive theory of sense has no account of reference*   This sounds an odd charge to make to something that is generally thought to be a contribution to the theory of reference. If the sense of a name were a description, then the name's semantic role would be identical to that of a description. By Russell's theory we know that we can analyse sentences containing definite descriptions into an array of quantifiers and predicates. This means that the semantics of sentences containing terms with descriptive senses can be handled with the semantic concept of satisfaction only. If all the singular apparatus of natural language were subject to a descriptive theory of sense, then no reference would take place in natural language at all. There would be no need for a theory of reference; a theory of truth defined in terms of satisfaction would suffice. This observation is not critical as such, but it is puzzling that something that was supposed to be part of a theory of reference should have the upshot that there is no such thing as reference. The real force of this observation, however, comes in when we consider problem (ii).

(ii) *A descriptive theory of sense entails a universalistic account of content*   Given the point made under (i), if a descriptive theory of sense were right, all content would be universal. Again, this is because content would then be specifiable employing the resources of Russell's theory of descriptions. The content of sentences analysable by Russell's theory is a universal content, for it employs only universals. Put informally, if a descriptive theory of sense were true, all our thought would be thought about types of things. We would never have thoughts about particular things. There could never be a singular thought that was about a particular, rather than about a type of entity. Again, the universalism of a descriptive theory of content is a sign of the internalism of such a theory. It is because descriptive content is universalistic that it is a content that is specifiable independently of context, independently of how things actually are in the world. Although Russell held that names were disguised descriptions, he did not assume that all thoughts were universalistic.

(iii) *A descriptive theory of sense suggests a 'search and refer' epistemology for the operation of singular terms*   Frege frequently speaks of 'sense determining reference'; Dummett regularly uses this formulation too. The phrase can be misconstrued. All that it need mean is that an account of the sense of a sentence is sufficient to know the truth-conditions of the sentence. If you know the sense of a sentence, there is nothing more that you need to know in order to be in a position to know what it is for it to be true or false. On the assumption that to know the meaning of a sentence is to know its truth-conditions, then knowing the sense of a sentence suffices for knowing its meaning. It has sometimes been thought, however, that the thesis that 'sense determines reference' means that the sense of a term is a kind of search procedure whereby you calculate the term's reference. A descriptive theory of sense fits this reading, for it embodies the picture of sense as a contextually independent cache of information with which the thinker searches the environment in order to see if the singular term in question refers. Not only does this embody a dubious epistemology; it again means that the semantic role of the term is defined by satisfaction, not reference.

The fourth problem is the starting-point for the causal theory of reference in the next chapter. I shall conclude this chapter with a look at two further interpretations of Frege that are only slightly different from the reading that I have been defending.

9.6   Two Interpretations of Frege

Michael Dummett has done more than most to promote Fregean scholarship and theory. The account of the argument for drawing the sense/reference distinction that I have given owes much to Dummett's work. The central idea that Frege is not committed to a descriptive theory of sense, and that, therefore, there could be such things as singular senses, was promoted long ago in Dummett's first book on Frege.[33]

Dummett has always insisted that we should understand sense in terms of information that the thinker possesses. The sense of a term is something you know. He has also always insisted that this knowledge does not have to be verbalizable.[34] This is an important point. If sense were verbalizable, then it might also be thought to be verbalizable to the extent of being fully codable in language. And if it were fully codable in language, then, as noted in the previous section, it would be specifiable descriptively. By insisting that sense need not be verbalizable, Dummett ensures that sense cannot be descriptive.

I suspect that when Dummett says that sense need not be verbalizable, what he really means is that it need not be *fully* verbalizable. It would be odd to speak of a form of knowledge that was not verbalizable at all. Indeed, I take it that sense must be at least partially verbalizable. The reason for insisting on at least partial verbalizability is that sense is the thought expressed by a sentence. As such, the information that constitutes sense must be subject to some combinatorial structure, in order for the thoughts thereby expressed to be capable of truth or falsity. The only way that we have of telling that such combinatorial structure exists is by its marking by the repeatable component structure of language. Furthermore, our basic idea of content concerns the rational power of sentences. I am not denying that language is essential to being a thinker, only that possession of language exhaustively defines what it is to be a thinker. Written language was a late comer to the evolutionary scene. There is a real danger that from an evolutionarily late vantage point, we forget the exceptional character of written language, and ignore the obvious contextualization of the meaning of spoken language. When we speak, we do, much of time, fully express our thoughts. That, I hope, is banal.

The theoretically interesting question is whether the full expression is something that is extractable from the context of use and definable in terms of context-free language, like written language. That is the issue raised by asking whether there can be sense that is not fully codable linguistically. That is the interesting question.

Dummett's handling of this point is suggestive, although he never fully worked out what a theory of sense that was not fully codable might look like. That account had to wait for Gareth Evans's posthumous *The Varieties of Reference*.[35] Nevertheless, Dummett laid the foundations. Dummett's example of a non-vocalizable sense was that of a proper name the sense of which was to be construed in terms of a recognitional capacity. Consider a name with which you are competent. The sense of the name is something you know that makes you competent with it. What you know is who the name's bearer is; but perhaps you know this not because you associate a description with the name, but because you have a recognitional capacity for picking out the bearer.

This is how the epistemology of naming functions for most of us with most of the names with which we have a daily familiarity. It is often very difficult to put into words how we recognize someone as the bearer of a name. There is, however, a temptation to say that this is idle phenomenology, and should not be taken at face value. Although we might not notice how we recognize someone as the bearer of a name, it might be insisted that there must be some process of identification and satisfaction of features that prompts the otherwise phenomenologically spontaneous recognition.

It is not obvious how we should evaluate this response and its implicit appeal to unconscious inferences and recognition by satisfaction. On the one hand, the phenomenological immediacy of our recognition of an individual as the bearer of a name is familiar and uncontentious. Equally, the appeal to the notion of unconscious application of criteria of recognition serves the obvious need to see the recognition as a genuine cognitive achievement and, as such, something that is susceptible of justification if challenged. The idea of such justification is that an otherwise immediate recognition of so-and-so as the bearer of a name must be susceptible of defence if challenged. It does not, as such, support the idea of unconscious inference. What is required is a more developed model of what sort of cognitive achievement is being described by the appeal to recognitional capacities, and what makes them cognitive as opposed to, say, a pure stimulus response.

Dummett does not provide a more detailed explication of these matters. Nevertheless, a further device that he employs in his discussion of sense supports the case for non-descriptive senses. Dummett notes that Frege gives very few instances of the schema

The sense of _____ is . . . ,

253

for 'even when Frege is purporting to give the sense of a word or symbol, what he actually *states* is what its reference is'.[36] Dummett then employs Wittgenstein's *Tractatus* distinction between showing and saying to explain the lack of instances of the above schema. He continues:

> The sense of an expression is the mode of presentation of the referent: in saying what the referent is, we have to choose a particular way of saying this . . . we *say* what the referent of a word is, and thereby *show* what its sense is.[37]

This passage is important. It supports the view that sense is not an extra entity associated with a word in addition to its referent. There is only one entity associated with a word – its referent. The sense is just the way in which we refer to, the way in which we think about, the object. Dummett does not explain any further how a general metaphysics of thought is meant to develop from these suggestions. The only model that is compatible with these remarks is the quasi-behaviourist account for which I have already argued. On such an approach, the way in which we think about an object is shown by the rational structure of the molecular thoughts which we hold; it is shown by the way in which, given that '*a* is *F*' is true, we take '*a* is *G*' to be true, etc. Of course, if we state any of these further things, what we say is that the object *a* is such-and-such. There is only one thing that we talk about, the object; but we can choose to talk about it in ways that show how we are rationally oriented towards it. That is the sense, the way in which we think about it.

Dummett's idea that the showing/saying distinction helps us to understand Frege's theory was picked up by Evans and McDowell. I shall return to consider Evans's theory, especially the developed view of singular senses, in chapter 11, after we have reviewed the causal theory of reference. But a few foundational remarks are in order at this point, for Evans and McDowell have a distinctive development of Dummett's use of the showing/saying distinction.

Dummett's account of sense and reference does not permit us to state the sense of expressions; we state only their referent. This means that Dummett cannot expect a theory of senses, a theory that would allow us to generate instances of the schema above, or one that would generate accounts of what it is that you know if you know the sense of a name. The theory of sense, for Dummett, will only be a theory of, in general, the sort of thing you need to know if you understand a name. Given his use of the showing/saying distinction, he cannot expect a systematic explicit account of what we know for each expression that we understand. Evans and McDowell read Frege in a way that seems to permit a systematic theory of senses. I call their theory the austere theory of sense.[38]

On the austere theory of sense, there is a clear answer to the question, 'What does a speaker S know then they grasp the sense of a name "a"?' The answer is:

(16) S knows that '*a*' stands for *a*.

This is an answer that can be given systematically for all names, for it simply grafts a theory of sense on to the theory of semantic value, or reference. If the language for which we are constructing a general theory of meaning has names in it, and those are not reducible to descriptions, then a Tarskian-style truth theory for that language will need axioms of denotation for all the names. It will need axioms like

(17) 'Bill Clinton' stands for Bill Clinton.

The austere theory of sense then says that if Hillary grasps the sense of 'Bill Clinton', her knowledge is represented in

(18) Hillary knows that 'Bill Clinton' stands for Bill Clinton.

(18) shows the sense by stating the reference.

Note, the austere theory is not trivial, and the knowledge attributed to someone by such a theory is not extensional. The last point is seen by observing that in general, if

S knows that '*a*' stands for *a*

and

S knows that '*b*' stands for *b*,

and, furthermore, if

$a = b$,

this does not entail that

S knows that '*a*' stands for *b*.

The austere theory, then, is distinct from the object theory of reference, for it ascribes knowledge of an axiom of a T-theory in a sense-sensitive way. The theory does, however, share one important feature with the object theory: the austere theory is an object-dependent theory of reference. The austere theory has three important characteristics: (a) it has object-dependent senses; (b) it is not a descriptive theory; (c) the knowledge it attributes is not trivial, but substantial, knowledge.

The fact that it has object-dependent sense is an immediate consequence of the formal structure of the clauses used to state what someone knows when they know the sense of a name. You can only know something of the form '*a*' stands for *a*

if the object exists. On the austere theory, there can be no empty names.[39] Many people find the idea of object-dependent senses questionable, although most of the objections are founded on the general problem of accommodating misrepresentation and on an appeal to a phenomenology that assumes that the world and its objects are epistemologically problematic. There is also a specific objection regarding explanation. If perceptual error can prompt the same action as veridical perception, then the common explanandum (the action) requires a common explanans (the belief). But this means that the belief must have a content that is invariant across the veridical and illusory cases.[40]

To such arguments, the austere theorist can respond that misrepresentation does not exist at the level of singular terms. Genuine singular terms do not admit of misrepresentation. For sure, we might think that we are having a singular thought when we hallucinate a dagger before us. But the austere theorist can say that just as we are mistaken about the dagger, so too we can be mistaken about the kind of thought we are having. If there is no dagger, there is no singular thought; we must have been having a descriptive thought, not a genuinely singular one. With regard to the problem about explanation, there is a simple response: we deny that the actions are identical in the veridical and illusory cases.[41] This response, like the others, may seem counter-intuitive. But once we have a clear view of the resources available in neo-Fregean theory of singular thoughts, the whole business about false perceptual beliefs becomes much more tractable, and these responses get motivated within a rich structure of theory.[42]

The availability of such responses is extraordinarily interesting, for it shows up the deep connections between our theorizing about sense and reference and our metaphysics of the mind.[43] I have argued (section 9.4) that there is no such thing as atomic misrepresentation. This still leaves plenty of things for the neo-Fregean to say about the thoughts that are available in hallucinations and other forms of perceptual error. I cover some of this material in chapters 11 and 12. In turns out that the neo-Fregean has richer resources for handling these cases than the representationalist.

The austere theory is non-descriptive for the simple reason that it employs distinctive clauses of denotation in showing the sense of a name. The theory is non-trivial for just the same reason that a Davidsonian theory of meaning offers non-trivial axioms and theorems; indeed, the development of the austere theory owed as much to Davidson's work as to Frege's. Recall the distinction between knowing that *P* and knowing that '*P*' is a truth (sect. 4.6). The reason why the knowledge employed in the axioms of an austere theory of sense is not trivial, and hence non-extensional, is due to the difference between

(19) S knows that ' "*a*" stands for *a*' is a truth

and

(20) S knows that '*a*' stands for *a*.

(19) is trivial knowledge; it is something that anyone can know for any substitution for '*a*' given only that they know the general trick of disquotation for names. On the other hand, (20) constitutes a substantial piece of knowledge. You can only instantiate instances of (20) for names with which you are competent; recall the example of the little girl who does not understand what Vancouver is.[44] She knows that ' "Vancouver" stands for Vancouver' is a truth (instance of (21)), but she does not know that 'Vancouver' stands for Vancouver. It is because there is this difference between instances of (19) and (20) that the knowledge attributed in instances of (20) is not extensional knowledge, and the ascription of knowledge is sense-sensitive. Intuitively, it takes something to get into a state of knowledge reported as an instance of (20), and it takes more than it takes to get into a state reported as an instance of (19). Furthermore, there is no reason to suppose that just because two names '*a*' and '*b*' happen to be extensionally equivalent, it takes just the same to get from the instances of (19) for these two to the instances of (20).

The appeal to the distinction between (19) and (20) is, however, problematic for the austere theory. The distinction between instances of (19) and of (20) is a version of the more general distinction between knowing that *P* and knowing that '*P*' is a truth. As we saw before, this distinction is accounted for by saying that the latter, limited knowledge arises when the subject does not understand the sense of the embedded sentence. Furthermore, it is knowing the sense of the embedded sentence that takes you from knowing that '*P*' is a truth to knowing that *P*. If this is so, then the austere theory is left with the problem of having nothing in general to account for the difference between knowing that (19) and that (20). The difference should be that in (19) the embedded component is not understood – S does not know its sense – whereas in (20) the embedded component is understood. However, the embedded component is the name '*a*', and (20) is being offered as an account of what it is to understand the sense of the name!

As it stands, this leaves the ascription of knowledge in (20) obscure. We need an account of what the knowledge is that differentiates the knowledge ascriptions in (19) and (20); yet the knowledge we want to appeal to is precisely the knowledge ascribed in (20). This leaves us with sense-sensitive ascriptions, but without, as it were, an account of that to which these ascriptions are sensitive. We cannot factor out information, possession of which makes the difference between (19) and (20). This problem disappears when we look at the austere theory from a Davidsonian point of view. We then end up with an account that is equivalent to the quasi-behaviourist theory of sense defended in section 9.4.

Davidson would say that the ascription of knowledge in (20) only makes sense in the context of knowledge of an overall T-theory that makes best holistic sense of behaviour. But then the work is not done by (20) on its own. As a statement of what someone knows when they understand a name, it is only accurate in so far as it is part of an overall theory of behaviour. The knowledge in (20) cannot be factored out of an ascription of a holistic T-theory. (20) is not offered as part of a systematic theory of senses, for it is not a stand-alone statement of sense. (20) considered in isolation does not state the sense of '*a*' – the way that S thinks of *a*. The idea of 'the way that S thinks of *a*' makes sense only in the context of S's grasp of an overall theory. 'Thinking of *a*' is a theoretical posit within the context of an overall theory that makes best holistic sense of behaviour. If an overall T-theory fits S's behaviour, and that theory has

'*a*' stands for *a*

amongst its axioms, there will be such a thing as the way S thinks of *a*, and we can represent this fact by saying

S knows that '*a*' stands for *a*.

The work is done not by this single clause, but by the overall theory. Just as with Davidson's claim that reference is a theoretical posit, so too the sense of a singular term is a theoretical posit. And now the explanation for why the ascription of knowledge in axioms of an austere theory is sense-sensitive no longer requires curious sense items to account for this sensitivity. The sensitivity is a sensitivity to the overall holistic structure of the subject's behaviour, as mapped by the overall structure of the T-theory ascribed to the subject in order to understand their behaviour. The quasi-behaviourist account of sense is thus indistinguishable from the austere theory when that is seen in a Davidsonian light.

10

The Causal Theory of Reference and the Social Character of Meaning

10.1 Introduction

Kripke's *Naming and Necessity* changed the face of contemporary work on reference.[1] It gave what many now take as a definitive refutation of the descriptive theory of reference – the thesis that names are equivalent to descriptions, or bundles of descriptions. In addition, it provided an alternative picture of how reference worked. Although Kripke insisted that he was giving only a picture, not a developed theory, this positive contribution has become known as the causal theory of reference. Kripke's ideas also kick-started a resurgence of interest in the metaphysics of essence and the revival of broadly Aristotelian views about the distinction between essential and contingent properties. I shall have little to say about these matters here. Getting right the morals to be drawn from Kripke's book for the theory of reference is work enough for a single chapter.[2]

In this chapter I review the structure and consequences of Kripke's argument. I cover his critique of descriptive theories, his causal theory, the important idea of the social character of meaning that flows from the causal theory, the consequences of the above for a reformulated Fregean theory of reference, and, finally, how lessons drawn from Kripke's conception of the social character of meaning can help articulate a response to the problem concerning Frege's second thesis about sense – the idea that each singular term has a unique sense.

The idea of a causal theory of reference has attracted considerable attention. In the present chapter I shall only consider the idea in the light of Kripke's work. Kripke's concern was with understanding what determined the reference of proper names. His answer was that reference is determined by causal chain. For Kripke, the causal chain connects an object and a linguistic event, e.g. my use of the name 'Bill Clinton'. The central thought is that my use of this name refers to Bill Clinton just in case my use is causally related (in some appropriate way) to Bill Clinton. Much recent work employs a causal theory of reference that, although heavily influenced by Kripke, has the causal relation connecting different relata.

Putnam's development of a causal theory of reference has much in common with Kripke's, but a central concern of Putnam's has been to argue that 'meanings ain't in the head'. That is to say, Putnam believes that whatever notion of content could plausibly be thought of as something that was internal to the subject, that notion does not fully capture meaning, where meaning is defined in terms of truth-conditions. So, when Putnam says that 'meanings ain't in the head', he is defending an externalist conception of meaning. Kripke's work is not addressed to questions about internalism and externalism of meaning, where we think of meaning in terms of belief content. Indeed, Kripke insists that he is quite unsure what to say about belief ascription, and has himself produced a classic puzzle case that challenges all accounts of belief content.[3] Accordingly, we do well not to run together Kripke's causal theory about linguistic reference and Putnam's causal theory of belief content. In addition, there is another sense in which recent writers employ a causal theory of meaning.

In the light of Putnam's argument that what is in the head does not determine truth-conditions, many writers have tried to bifurcate the truth-conditional notion of meaning into two components: narrow content and broad content. Narrow content is content that can be characterized internalistically; that is, it is whatever notion of content that can be recovered from an account of in-the-head states. Broad content is the notion of content that is characterized by truth-conditions. On this approach, broad content is usually thought of as a function of narrow content + context. This is a dual-component conception of content; truth-conditional content is a function of in-the-head states plus context.[4] Now, regardless of whether you think you need only a notion of narrow content, or that you need narrow content + context, there needs to be an account of how the narrow content gets the content it has. In Fodor's hands, narrow content suffices for an account of content sufficient to play the fundamental role of explaining behaviour – it picks out cognitive significance.[5] But Fodor also has a causal theory of meaning, for he thinks that states with narrow content have their content in virtue of the causal relations they stand in to the environment.[6] In Fodor's theory, the causal relation connects internal states to the environment, in contrast to Kripke's theory, which relates linguistic utterances and the environment.

There are, then, a number of different issues to consider in evaluating causal theories of reference and of meaning in general. I propose to keep the above issues separate, by treating only Kripke's causal theory of linguistic reference in this chapter. Putnam's causal-theoretic externalism about belief will be saved until the next chapter, where it fits better with a more general treatment of indexicality. The debate between Putnam and Fodor with regard to externalism will also be discussed in the next chapter. I start with Kripke's negative arguments against a descriptive theory of reference. He has two such arguments.

10.2   Kripke's First Argument against Descriptivism

Kripke took himself to be offering criticisms of Frege's theory of sense and reference. In the light of the previous chapters, it should be clear that Kripke's criticisms have little to do with Frege's central concern. What Kripke explicitly says he is discussing is a theory of meaning which holds that a name refers to an object in virtue of the object satisfying a description, or set of descriptions. Neither Frege nor contemporary Fregeans hold such a view about reference. Russell held this view only with regard to expressions that he said were not genuine names. Searle has defended the thesis that names refer descriptively, and so has Strawson.[7] So the view is not a straw man, although it is not held by those most commonly thought to have held it.[8]

The descriptive theory of reference is committed to the following claim:

(1)   'NN' refers to O iff O satisfies the *F*,

where 'the *F*' is a description or cluster of descriptions. In order not to add to the considerable confusion that already exists in this area, I shall not speak of 'the *F*' as the sense of the name. I shall call it the meaning of the name. The import of the thesis that the meaning of a name is a description is that the semantic behaviour of names can be accounted for in terms of the semantic behaviour of descriptions. Kripke's first argument consists in observing that this is false, for names and definite descriptions behave differently in modal contexts. This observation is central to the formal direct theory of reference (FDRT).[9]

Consider the following example. Let the meaning of 'Benjamin Franklin' be given as

(2)   Benjamin Franklin is the man who invented bifocals.

Now compare the following two sentences:

(3)   ◊ Benjamin Franklin was not the first postmaster-general of the USA

and

(4)   ◊ The man who invented bifocals was not the first postmaster-general of the USA.

261

(3) and (4) make different claims. (3) says that a particular person, namely Benjamin Franklin, may not have been the first postmaster-general. In contrast, (4) makes a general claim; it is not specifically about Benjamin Franklin. This intuitive way of expressing the difference between (3) and (4) corresponds to a point that should by now be familiar. Descriptive sentences have a universal content; they are not about particulars. In contrast, (3) expresses a claim about a particular individual. This is the point that Kripke was making. The point can be expressed more accurately by invoking the notion of possible worlds.

The easiest way of understanding the modal operator '◊' is to read it as an existential quantifier that introduces a world at which that part of the sentence to the right of the quantifier is to be evaluated. So (3) reads as: There is a world in which Benjamin Franklin was not the first postmaster-general of the USA. Now, the heart of Kripke observations can be summed up by saying that in the case of (3), no ambiguity is introduced if we change the scope of the modal operator. Just the same claim is made by (3) as by

(3′)   Benjamin Franklin ◊ was not the first postmaster-general of the USA.

Informally, (3′) is read as: Benjamin Franklin is such that there is a world in which he is not the first postmaster-general of the USA. In either case the position of the name outside or inside the scope of '◊' makes no difference to the semantic value of the overall sentence.

The fact that (3) and (3′) make the same claim is summed up by saying that the semantic value of the name 'Benjamin Franklin' does not change as we change the world at which the sentence is evaluated. Given that the name is not empty, its semantic value (the object that is its referent) stays the same whatever possible world we consider. The name, as it were, holds fast to its semantic value across possible worlds. In contrast, although in the actual world the description 'the inventor of bifocals' picks out Benjamin Franklin, this is a contingent fact; it does not hold across possible worlds. This explains why (4) makes a different claim from either (3) or (3′). (4) says that there is a possible world in which the inventor of bifocals is not the first postmaster-general of the USA, and this has nothing to do with Benjamin Franklin. Indeed, (4) could be true at a world in which Benjamin Franklin does not exist.

Some have responded to Kripke's argument by noting that there is a way of reading (4) in which the first description has wide scope; that is,

(4′)   The inventor of bifocals ◊ was not the first postmaster-general of the USA.

The force of placing the description outside the scope of the modal operator is to ensure that the description gets evaluated at the actual world and then, having secured whatever semantic value it has there, that value is then held constant as we consider it at the world in which it (the actual world inventor of bifocals) is not the first postmaster-general of the USA. This manoeuvre, of giving the description wide scope, ensures that (4′) is about Benjamin Franklin, for he is the semantic value of the description at the actual world. Some have then responded to Kripke's argument by saying that it shows, at best, that if the meaning of a name is a description, it has to be a description with wide scope.[10]

Kripke can respond that this manoeuvre misses the point, for there is still a difference in behaviour between names and descriptions. Names do not have a narrow-scope reading: there is no difference between (3) and (3′). I expressed this point before by saying that the name holds fast to its semantic value across possible worlds. This is an important idea. It is Kripke's thesis that names are rigid designators:

> **Rigid designation:** A name is a rigid designator iff it refers to the same individual in all possible worlds in which that individual exists.

It is important to be clear that the thesis that names are rigid designators is a thesis about the stability of reference across possible worlds; it is not a thesis about how names get their reference in the actual world. That is to say, rigidity has nothing to do with 'directness' of contact between name and object. It has nothing to do with the name/object connection in the actual world. It says that howsoever a name is attached to an object, once attached, it stays attached to that object in all possible worlds. The rigidity thesis has the negative consequence that the attachment between name and object cannot be descriptive. If the attachment were descriptive, it would not survive across possible worlds, because what descriptions pick out in different possible worlds depends on whether they have wide or narrow scope.[11]

The idea that names are rigid designators already carries considerable metaphysical baggage. The thesis requires that we can identify individuals across possible worlds. For example, (3) is not true, because we can consider a world in which the person named 'Benjamin Franklin' is not the first postmaster-general of the USA. That is to say, (3) is not rendered true simply because there is a possible world in which Mr and Mrs Franklin have no offspring but, suppose, their neighbour, who just happens also to be called 'Franklin', has a son whom they baptize 'Benjamin'. That is not the sort of world you need to consider to see that (3) is true. (3) is true because failing to become first postmaster-general of the USA is something that might have been true of, as it were, *our* Benjamin Franklin. The notion of rigidity requires, then, that we be able to keep track of individuals across possible worlds. That is the point of insisting that there is a difference between names and descriptions. In order to be able to track individuals across possible worlds, something must remain constant about them, in order that we can say that it is the same person. The features of an individual that remain constant across all possible worlds in which it exists are its essential properties. The thesis of the rigidity of names entails essentialism. This is a contentious metaphysical issue: What constitute the essential properties of an individual? A favourite candidate for the essential properties of an individual person is that person's origin. This means that Benjamin Franklin exists in all possible worlds in which the actual zygote formed by egg and sperm also exists, regardless of what else is true or false of that zygote.

Leaving aside the metaphysical consequences of all this, the rigidity thesis means that names are indexed to the actual world. The reason that there is no ambiguity between (3) and (3') is because, in effect, they both say:

> The object that is actually Benjamin Franklin might not have been the first postmaster-general of the USA.

It might still be objected that this indexing to the actual world has just the same effect as fixing the meaning of the name with a description with wide scope, as in (4'). This objection, however, misses the key point that Kripke is making.

Kripke's central point is that with descriptions there is an ambiguity, for we have to know with respect to which world we are supposed to evaluate them. This is not the case with names, for their rigidity means that they are always indexed to the actual world. Descriptions are not automatically indexed in this way. We can use descriptions in a way that indexes their evaluation to the actual world, but note two points about this phenomenon. First, it is not the most natural way of reading a descriptive sentence with a modal operator. Second, and more importantly, the fact that the use of a description with wide scope is not the most common reading suggests that the wide-scope evaluation is forced upon us by the pragmatics of sentence use, rather than being a semantic fact. Recall Kripke's response to Donnellan's idea of referential uses of descriptions.[12] Kripke argued that Donnellan's referential use of descriptions should be seen as a feature of the pragmatics of use, and not as introducing a genuine ambiguity in the semantics of descriptions. A similar point applies to the attempt to rescue a descriptive theory of meaning by appeal to descriptions with wide scope.

The upshot is that names are rigid, descriptions are not. Descriptions can be used in a way that has the same effect as if they were rigid, but this use is plausibly a feature of the pragmatics of use of descriptions, not part of an account of the semantics of descriptions. This means that Kripke's first argument against a descriptive theory of meaning is successful. It is important, however, to note how little this argument shows.

First, it shows nothing about the viability of a Fregean distinction between sense and reference. Second, the rigidity of proper names says nothing about what it is for a name to stand for an object. If the name 'Benjamin Franklin' is rigid, this just means that whatever object is assigned to it as its semantic value in the actual world, we should employ that semantic value in calculating the truth-value of modal sentences in which the name occurs. In other words, the thesis that names are rigid designators only gives us a rule for calculating the semantic contribution of a name to various complex expressions (sentences with modal operators) *given* an assignment of a semantic value to the name in the actual world. The thesis tells us nothing about what it is for a name to have an object as its assigned semantic value, other than that this is not fixed descriptively.

The significance of this result is twofold. The argument shows that names are different from descriptions. In addition, if you are writing a semantic theory for a language and want to know how to write rules for computing the semantic value of sentences containing modal operators, Kripke's argument shows that you must expect different rules governing names and descriptions. Neither of these points bears upon the task in which we are currently engaged of understanding what it is for a name to refer, where an answer to this is required to illuminate what it is to think about an object. We could express this last observation by saying that our interest is in the nature of the reference relation as it exists between names and objects in the actual world. Kripke has an answer to this issue of actual world name/object relation; it is his causal theory of reference. For the moment I want to insist that we keep separate the negative and positive aspects of Kripke's position.

One last remark on Kripke's first negative argument. I have insisted that the thesis that names are rigid designators is a thesis about the behaviour of names in modal contexts, and that it has nothing to do with the name/object relation in the actual world. In the preface to the book version of the 'Naming and Necessity' lectures, Kripke says that rigidity is not just about modal contexts. He says that the name Aristotle is rigid in the simple sentence

Aristotle was fond of dogs.

Kripke's explanation of this is as follows:

the thesis that names are rigid in simple sentences is, however, equivalent to the thesis that if a modal operator governs a simple sentence containing a name, the 2 readings, with large and small scope, are equivalent.[13]

So rigidity is about modal contexts after all! This passage is, to say the least, odd. There is, however, an important point that perhaps explains Kripke's insistence that rigidity is not *just* about modal contexts, despite the fact that his explication of this point says plainly that it *is* about modal contexts. Recall the observation

265

I made above, that although rigidity is a thesis about the behaviour of names in modal contexts, it has bearing upon our account of the reference relation, for it rules out a descriptive account of reference. If you assume that reference is either descriptive or direct, then rigidity, by default, entails a direct theory of reference. It is likely that Kripke is making the assumption that reference must be either descriptive or direct; for, like many people, he sees no space for the idea of a singular sense. If so, this might explain this otherwise puzzling passage in which, contrary to what he says elsewhere, Kripke claims that rigidity applies to simple sentences.

10.3 Kripke's Second Argument against Descriptivism

The form of Kripke's first argument went like this: Assume 'the *F*' is the meaning of the name 'NN'. This assumption cannot be correct, for the name and the description embed differently in modal contexts. Kripke's second argument is simpler. It consists in a challenge to the initial assumption that 'the *F*' is the meaning of the name 'NN'. The form of the challenge goes like this: For any description 'the *F*' that is offered as giving the meaning of the name, it always makes sense to say

(5)   ◊ NN is not the *F*.

For example, if 'the inventor of bifocals' really did give the meaning of 'Benjamin Franklin', then how do we understand the thought that Benjamin Franklin might not have invented bifocals?

The heroic response to this would be to protest that we make sense of (5) only because 'the inventor of bifocals' is not the real meaning of the name; something else must be the meaning. This response does not work, and the example that Kripke employs shows why. It also reveals the central idea underpinning this second negative argument.

Kripke's example for this second argument concerns the name 'Gödel'. About the only thing that most people know about Gödel is that he proved the first incompleteness theorem for arithmetic. So, if any description constituted the meaning of the name, the description 'the person who proved the first incompleteness theorem for arithmetic' must be the prime candidate. Call this 'the *F*'. Nevertheless, even if you are one of those for whom the most you know about Gödel is that

(6)   Gödel is the *F*,

it still seems to make sense to suppose that

(7)   ◊ Gödel is not the F.

You cannot respond to this by saying that you understand (7) because some other description fixes the meaning of the name; for, by hypothesis, no other description is available – (6) exhausts your knowledge of Gödel. Neither does it seem an adequate response to try to insist that, given that (6) exhausts your knowledge of Gödel, then you do not understand (7). Again, that seems a heroic response that is at odds with the data concerning ordinary use. Even if (6) exhausts your knowledge of Gödel, it is relatively easy to fill out a story in terms of which (7) not only makes sense, but you come to believe that

(8)   Gödel is not the F!

For example, suppose that your logic tutor informs you one day that recent research has shown that the incompleteness theorem associated with Gödel's name was in fact proved by Schmidt, from whom Gödel pinched it. In the light of this information, not only is it likely that you will come to believe (8), it is also the rational thing to believe. Yet, by hypothesis, you have learnt nothing new about Gödel to replace your previous solitary bit of information. But now, if you believe (8), 'the F' cannot possibly constitute the meaning of 'Gödel', for then (8) would have a contradictory content. In the circumstances, however, (8) not only does not have a contradictory content, it is the reasonable thing to believe.

What moral are we meant to draw from these considerations? First, once again, we seem to be presented with a cogent argument against a descriptive theory of meaning for names. More importantly, the examples at work in this second argument draw attention to a key insight in Kripke's work on reference. The insight can be summed up with the phrase 'the social character of meaning'. The Gödel example shows the extent to which our capacity for referring to individuals draws upon the social character of naming. We might, individually, know nothing about Gödel, but still successfully use the name and refer to him. If so, we do this by trading upon the social character of meaning; we defer to other speakers.

The idea that the mechanism of reference is, in some way, socially constituted is one of Kripke's central insights. It picks up on a feature of our naming practices that it would be difficult to deny. We can lock into a name-using practice on the basis of the slightest conversational encounter with a name. Most of us have taken part in conversations at social gatherings where an unfamiliar name is employed. The following is a coherent situation. You are at a crowded party. You start the evening on one side of the room and overhear a conversation at which the exploits of 'NN' are recounted in limited detail. On the basis of this limited conversational fragment, you move across the room and, on repeating a few exchanged remarks about 'NN', establish a new set of initiates into the 'NN' practice. You are all talking about NN, and you succeed in doing so by deferring in your practice to the original speaker who introduced the first conversation about NN.

This is an attractive picture. It rings true to the way in which we deal in proper names.[14] It is, however, for the moment a picture. We do not yet have an account of how this social character of meaning works. We need some account of what binds people in a name-using practice and what constitute entry and exit criteria to the practice. Kripke's positive suggestion is that what binds speakers together in a name-using practice is a web of causal relations. I shall consider this shortly. Whatever account we give of a name-using practice, it must capture the ease with which we can be initiated into such practices. Consider the following example.

In chapter 8 I introduced the intuitive appeal of the Fregean theory with the example of a name with which you are unfamiliar, in the sentence

> (9)   RM is a historian.

The intuition was that in order to be a competent user of this name, you would require some information to control your use, and that information is sense. But now consider the following scenario. As things stand, the sentence in (9) has no use for you. The intuition that you do not really know what you are saying if you utter (9) looks plausible. But suppose you were in a group who had been reading this chapter, and you decided to see what you had all remembered. Suppose someone says, 'Well, I remember that RM is a historian', and that the rest of you agree. 'Oh yes,' someone says, 'RM is a historian all right.' Now, do you or do you not now constitute a name-using practice. You might be several thousands of miles away from where RM lives and have no means of identifying him. But this is true of lots of people to whom you regularly refer. Your inability to identify Kripke on sight is irrelevant to your ability to refer to him, so why should this matter in the case of RM? Spatial proximity is clearly irrelevant to reference, as is temporal proximity, or else we would not be able to treat 'Gödel' and 'Aristotle' as names.

You might think that in the imagined scenario you constitute a name-using practice with 'RM', for your practice defers to me. I have offered this name to you, and although there is little you can do with it other than repeat (9) and produce sentences like

> (10)   I learnt of RM from Luntley's book

and

(11)   RM is a historian of Michael Luntley's acquaintance,

why should not this limited linguistic display constitute a name-using practice? Indeed, if it does, why does it need a group of you to establish it? Why could it not be the case that merely by reading the original sentence in chapter 8 you became initiated into the 'RM' name-using practice? 'People's intuitions about such cases are not, by themselves, reliable, and I do not think we should rely on intuitions. Nevertheless, it is an important ingredient of the idea of a name-using practice that it is the sort of thing that you can get into with ease. Whatever account we offer of the constitution of a name-using practice, it must accommodate this. For the moment, bear in mind the possibility that, contrary to the suggestion in chapter 8, you have become a participant in the 'RM' name-using practice merely by reading this book. Accommodating this possibility will serve as a useful marker of how we define name-using practices.

One further important point about the idea of name-using practices needs noting. The idea of a name-using practice puts pressure on Frege's second thesis about names: the thesis that each name has a unique sense. I have arguedthat Kripke's arguments against a descriptive theory of meaning do not touch the Fregean conception of sense. But I have also repeatedly deferred a defence of Frege's second thesis about sense, and have only defended the first thesis. If I am right in thinking that the first thesis that names have sense is so far intact, the idea that each name has a unique sense looks to be on shakier ground. Because the idea of a name-using practice is such an indispensable tool in our understanding of language use, it is worth getting clear the precise point at which this part of Kripke's work bears upon Frege's ideas. I do this in the next section. I shall then return to consider Kripke's positive suggestions about what constitutes a name-using practice.

10.4   Putting the Pressure on Frege

Frege's thesis II – that each name has a unique sense – is required to capture the role that sense plays as the currency of communication. The Platonic version of the reified model of sense has no difficulty in positing unique senses for each name. It faces insuperable difficulties, however, in formulating a credible epistemology of our grasp of sense, and therefore gives no real content to the idea that sense is the currency of communication. The idea of a name-using practice appears to put pressure upon Fregean theory in two different ways.

It is tempting to think that, despite his Platonism, Frege endorsed an idiolectic model of sense. The temptation arises in part from the mistake of identifying sense with descriptive content. If you do that, you cannot help but note that, for any given name, we seem to associate different descriptions with that name. This then suggests a model in which, if we agree that names have sense (thesis I), we are left only with a model of senses as private caches of information. This has the consequence that we speak private idiolects.

This is a hopeless model for communication, and is clearly at odds with Frege's repeated insistence that sense is objective, and is not to be confused with subjective ideas. The best that you could expect from an idiolectic theory would be that communication occurs by virtue of overlap of idiolects; that despite our differing caches of information for the name 'Bill Clinton', there is sufficient in common to allow us to communicate.

The overlapping idiolects model of language use raises just as many problems as it attempts to solve. The critical problem concerns the degree of overlap of private caches of information that is necessary for communication to occur. In the light of Kripke's Gödel/Schmidt example, there is good reason for thinking that no overlap of information is required, for the simple reason that communication might occur when both parties know nothing about the individual.

We cannot defend a Fregean theory of sense and reference, however, by repeatedly invoking the disclaimer that sense is not descriptive. Even without the mistaken assumption that sense is descriptive, there is still a presumption that the argument for sense that I defended in the previous chapter is individualistic. The idea of a name-using practice impinges not only upon the discredited descriptivist model of sense, but upon the core notion of sense that I have defended. The core notion of sense is under pressure from Kripke's work, because of the fundamental role that the idea of rationalizing explanations of behaviour plays in the account of sense. This is because it is tempting to think that the information that is individuated by rationalizing explanations of behaviour must be individualistic rather than social. The information is individualistic, because it is information that characterizes the individual's point of view. Note that it does not follow from this idea of capturing the individual's point of view that the information is, in any useful sense, in the head.[15] I have already indicated that the fundamental individuation of sense requires a radically externalist account of content, even though it characterizes the thinker's point of view. This is the distinctive mark of the neo-Fregean programme: cognitive significance is externalist. For the moment, however, it is important to observe that the pressure that Kripke's insights place upon Fregean theory cannot be dodged simply by disavowing descriptivism. There is a genuine insight that fuels the idea of a name-using practice. We need some account of what constitutes such a practice. Before investigating this issue, we should note that there is a presumption that Fregean theory favours an individualistic (non-social) account of content. It is here that Kripke puts pressure on Frege. There is a presumption that Fregean theory is poorly placed to provide an account of what constitutes a name-using practice. Kripke's work, then, raises a genuine and serious challenge to the Fregean. Before we see whether the Fregean can meet this challenge, I turn to look at Kripke's own positive account of name-using practices.

10.5   The Causal Theory of Reference

The causal theory of reference is Kripke's positive account of the name/object relation. It is distinct from the thesis that names are rigid designators, for that thesis is concerned only with the stability of the name/object relation across possible worlds. It is to the causal theory that we must look for Kripke's account of what the relation is that retains the modal constancy of rigidity. It is not, however, easy to say what the causal theory is.

Part of the problem with identifying the causal theory is that Kripke has always insisted that he was not giving a theory as such, but more a new picture that should inform our thinking about reference. This is a fair point, but there is a danger of confusing the notion of a causal theory with the picture comprised simply by the idea of the social character of meaning. The idea of the social character of meaning is captured with the concept of a name-using practice. That is a picture that illuminates important aspects of naming, but it is not in itself a statement of a causal theory. The idea of a name-using practice is neutral until we have an account of what constitutes such a practice. So, if the causal theory of reference is just a picture that is meant to inform our theorizing about reference, it must nevertheless offer some account of what constitutes a name-using practice.

So the causal theory is more than the idea that meaning is social; it is an explanation of how meaning is social. I start with a crude statement of a causal theory of linguistic reference:

> **CT**: 'Aristotle' as used by speaker S refers to Aristotle iff S's use of 'Aristotle' is causally related to the initial baptism of Aristotle.

The central thought is that use of the name refers via causal link, rather than descriptive fit. Kripke repeatedly stresses that descriptions may *fix* a reference of a name, but they do not *determine* the reference.[16] That is to say, a description may serve the pragmatic role of fixing the reference, but it does not serve the semantic role of determining the reference of a name. Reference is determined by the use of the name being causally related to baptism.

CT has three distinctive features. First, CT captures the social character of meaning and the idea of a name-using practice. A name-using practice will be constituted by all those speakers whose use of a given name is causally related to the bearer's baptism. We constitute socially relevant groups of referrers in virtue of the causal links we share with objects. Second, the causal constitution of a name-

271

using practice accounts for the ease with which we can be initiated into a practice. Participation in name-using practices turns on the simple matter of the causal encounters experienced in language use. Causal exposure to language is ubiquitous. It is no wonder, then, that we end up with a facility for referring to so many different people of whom we appear to know nothing virtually nothing. This means that, according to CT, you are initiated into the 'RM' name-using practice, for the name has causally impacted upon you. Note that even if your intuitions incline you to think that you are a member of the 'RM' name-using practice, this is not evidence in favour of the causal theory, for it may turn out that a non-causal account of the constitution of name-using practices would give the same result.

The third feature of CT is that it is a non-cognitive account of name use. The constitution and participation in a name-using practice are not, according to CT, sensitive to information, let alone to information that the speaker possesses. CT provides an account of name-using practices defined in terms of causal relations. To be a participant in a given name-using practice, you need to have causal links to the bearer. There is no requirement that you have information links. This last point is central to the causal theory. Kripke is clear about the informational insensitivity of his proposal. To see this, consider an example that Kripke uses to make just this point.[17]

Suppose that S picks up the name 'Cicero' from Smith and others, who use it to refer to the famous Roman orator. Suppose that S later forgets that he got the name from Smith, and comes to believe he got it from Jones, who, unknown to S, uses the name for one of Jones's contemporaries. According to Kripke, it is not 'how the speaker thinks he got the reference, but the actual chain of communication, which is relevant'.[18] So, according to the causal theory, S still uses 'Cicero' as a name of the Roman orator in this case, and if S utters

(12)   Cicero weighed 240 pounds,

this is true just in case the Roman orator weighed 240 pounds. This example makes clear that Kripke thinks that a name-using practice is supposed to be constituted in a way that is information-independent. But the example has a number of features that make this claim dubious.

First, there are not clear intuitions about these kind of cases. If S utters (12), then, other things being equal, it is likely that the correct answer to the question, 'Who is S speaking of?' must be Cicero, the Roman orator. Is it so clear, however, that if we ask 'Who is S thinking of?', we get the same answer? The correct reply to the latter question is much less obvious. One reason for this difference turns on the fact that the example employs a famous name.

With names like 'Cicero', 'Bill Clinton', etc., there is always a presumption that, in the absence of a clear indication to the contrary, we take the speaker as speaking of, and thinking about, the famous bearer of the name. This is a reflection of the social character of meaning. It would, for example, be misleading to announce in front of massed TV cameras at a Democratic Convention that Bill Clinton was a crook and a liar, even if it were the case that a petty criminal of that name had just been convicted at the county court of theft and perjury. I shall call the presumption at operation that explains this the 'famous name convention'.

So, ordinarily we would take S to be referring to the Roman orator and also thinking about the same individual. In the case, as Kripke describes it, in which S erroneously believes he got the name from someone who had never heard of the Roman orator, the famous name convention is less powerful with regard to the question, 'Who is S thinking of?' This is because we would ordinarily expect the issue of who you are thinking of to be informationally sensitive, and in this case we know that the only information that S has with regard to this name has nothing to do with the Roman orator. Nevertheless, this is hardly persuasive as a response to Kripke, for Kripke officially expects reference to be determined in an informationally insensitive way. We need further analysis of the matter to see what is really going on.

Let us vary the example slightly. Suppose that S not only believes that he got the name from Jones, but believes some of the information that Jones believes about Cicero. S now believes that Cicero was born in Orange County. Now, who is S referring to and thinking of? The answer, surely, cannot be the Roman orator. Note that the information involved need not be descriptive. Imagine the case in which S simply believes he got the name from Jones, and then hears Jones say,

There's Cicero now

as a figure enters the room. S's information at this point is perceptual information that need not be descriptively coded; perhaps Cicero is too far off for S to spot any distinguishing features that he could formulate; he simply keeps perceptual track of the person entering the room. In this case I take it that it is clear that in uttering (12) S is both referring to and thinking about Jones's friend and not the Roman orator.

The above variation on the example strengthens the claim that it is the famous name convention that is doing the work in Kripke's example as he formulates it. And although this emphasizes the social character of meaning and the idea that there are name-using practices governing the use of names, it does nothing to force the idea that the practice is defined causally rather than informationally.

The fact that the variation on the example prompts a different result from the one Kripke claims in the original example suggests that more than mere causal connection is at work in determining reference. Of course, Kripke is right to insist that it is, as it were, very easy to get into a thought about someone and to get into the relevant name-using practice. Even in the variation I described, it seems clear that, on the basis of little information, S is not thinking about Cicero, but about Jones's contemporary. Nevertheless, the thoughts about *that* Cicero are still what we might term elastic – they are easy to get into. It does not take much information to get into a Cicero-directed thought. The question that needs answering is whether being in a causal chain is sufficient.[19]

Once you begin to scrutinize Kripke's example, a number of features become salient: (a) the chain that Kripke speaks of is a chain of *communication*; (b) the account looks more like an account of 'deferred reference' than reference; (c) Kripke's formulations frequently employ informationally sensitive characterizations of the causal chains despite his earlier claim with the Cicero example that S's beliefs are irrelevant to the reference of 'Cicero'. Let me explain these points in turn.

(a)   Kripke contrasts his account with Strawson's. He says that what the speaker thinks is irrelevant, for it is 'the actual chain of communication' that is relevant. If this means that it is more than merely standing in a sequence of sound productions that are causally traceable back to Cicero that matters, we need to be told what more is involved. Clearly, there are causal chains that connect name use with ancient bearers of names, where those causal chains are not chains of communication. Indeed, given the complexity of the causal nexus within which we are all located, there are doubtless innumerably many causal chains connecting my use of the name 'Cicero' and the Roman orator. In addition, there are probably a good few chains connecting my use to the use of a long-forgotten neighbour who named his dog 'Cicero'.

Surely, then, it cannot be merely causal connections that determine reference, for the simple reason that the causal connections are too numerous and too complex. If this means that to speak of 'chains of communication' is to speak of something more than mere causal chains, we must be told what. The obvious thought is that a chain of communication is defined by the information that it carries, not by the causal trace of the signals. But if this is the notion that is at work, the causal theory is not a theory that is insensitive to information. Indeed, it is an informationally sensitive account of reference, and it is the informational links which you have, not the causal links, that do the work.

There is a problem in subjecting Kripke's remarks to scrutiny, in so far as he says that he is presenting only a picture, not a developed theory. It is worth noting, however, that at the point where he makes this disclaimer, he reverts, as so often, to emphasizing the negative value of his position as a critique of the descriptive theory of reference.[20] Now that, I suggest, is simply beside the point. We are agreed that reference is not descriptive. The issue that we want addressed is the issue of what constitutes a name-using practice, given that we know that it is not a practice governed by descriptive content. At this point, it is relevant to remind ourselves of what should be banal – that Frege's theory of sense is not descriptive. The options before us are a theory in which reference is determined causally and a theory in which reference is determined informationally. The Fregean favours the latter. The Fregean also has the pressing problem of giving an account of an informationally determined account of reference in which we can make sense of Frege's thesis II: each name has a unique sense. The choice is not, however, between causal and descriptive theories.[21]

(b)   Kripke's Cicero example is in danger of begging the key question about reference. As Kripke formulates the example, S picks up the name from 'Smith and others, who use the name to refer to a famous Roman orator'. So S's mastery of the name is derivative of the mastery of Smith and others; S's referring defers to Smith and friends. What, then, is it for Smith and others to use the name to refer to a famous Roman orator? We appear to be offered a two-stage account of reference. One stage involves what we might call the primary reference achieved by the primary thinkers of the object; the other involves those whose thought involves secondary reference, secondary thinkers. If this is so, then the causal theory is not giving an account of reference at all; it is not giving an account of what it is for a name to have a particular object as its semantic value, where this account illuminates thought about objects. Instead, the theory provides a mechanism to account for the sharing of thoughts, how we get into thinking about the object by making our thinking (referring) dependent on that of the primary thinkers (referrers).

The thesis that names are rigid designators has nothing to say to the fundamental question of what it is for a name to have an object as its semantic value. It speaks only of the stability of that relation across possible worlds once it is established. I am now suggesting that the causal theory of reference is really no such thing; it is a causal theory of deferred reference. It is a theory of how reference can be deferred by secondary thinkers to the achievements of primary thinkers. The model then looks like this:

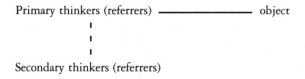

The vertical line is a causal link, but what is the nature of the horizontal line? On the current analysis, the causal theory does not address this issue and the horizontal line can be analysed informationally as a relation characterized by sense. If so, the model would be a composite model. We would then have a version of the causal theory that was compatible with Fregean theory. Devitt and Sterelny employ a distinction between primary and secondary reference, but they claim that both lines in the above diagram signify causal relations.[22] This, however, is merely a claim on their part; they offer no argument in favour of construing both lines causally. Indeed, their description of the connections between primary thinkers and objects is, just as much as their description of the connection between secondary and primary thinkers, a richly informational description. Like Kripke, they speak of chains of communication in the latter case. In the case of the primary link, they say that it is established perceptually, and that this is a causal relation. This remark is true but irrelevant. Perception is a causal process, as is, I assume, every other relation in which we stand to the environment. But that observation is no more than the platitude that there is no magic in this universe; the place is wired together causally. Having got that out of the way, acceptance of the underlying physical character of the universe and the relations that obtain within it does nothing to characterize what makes a perceptual relation important in an account of reference. I take it that it is the information that perception gives us of the world that makes it significant in characterizing the relation of primary thinkers to objects. If so, the account is still richly informational. The only point worth noting about this is that to say it is informational is not to say that it is descriptive; but it should, by now, be getting a trifle wearisome to keep on having to be reminded of that.

There is still a major problem with the Fregean theory; it is the problem of accounting for thesis II – each name has a unique sense. This is the problem of getting an account of sense that provides the currency for communication. Kripke's insights, whether or not they sustain a real alternative to the Fregean theory, put enormous pressure on Frege's thesis II, because of the way they reveal what I have called the elasticity of thought. Thoughts about objects are easy to get into; we can share thoughts about objects, we can come to talk about them and have intentional relations to them, on quite limited contacts with name-using practices. That much is right about Kripke's picture, I suspect. But it still leaves us with only a picture, and we need to pin down what makes the picture work.

(c) I do not think that the last suggestion of a composite model with sense characterizing primary reference and causality characterizing secondary reference is tenable. The reason for this is that it is unclear how it could be that the way into thinking about and referring to an object is solely via causal links. The composite model is inherently unstable. It has primary thinkers getting into a thought via sense and secondary thinkers getting into a thought via causality. How could they get into just the same thought via these two quite different routes, the former of which is an informationally sensitive account of thought and reference, the latter not?

As I formulated it, CT is informationally insensitive, and that, officially, is how Kripke wants it to be. Nevertheless, that bald formulation is clearly wrong, for causal links pick out too much. Evans's example of 'Madagascar' gives a clear statement of the problems. Our name-using practice with this name derives causally from Marco Polo, who got the name from the natives he encountered on visiting the island. The natives, however, used the name to refer to a part of the African mainland. Marco Polo mistook their intention, and took it as the name of the island. If we trace our use of the name via causal links, we must be referring to the African mainland; for our name-using practice would be defined causally, and would therefore be continuous with that of the original natives. That, however, is ridiculous. We refer to the island, and our name-using practice is distinct from that of the original natives; it begins with Marco Polo. But if that is so, the characterization of our 'Madagascar' name-using practice cannot be achieved purely in causal terms.

The problem generated by this example and others like it goes like this.[23] For any given name, there are all sorts of causal connections that link it to various entities, amongst which will be the object we take to be its bearer. The causal chains connecting the name use to that object will constitute the name-using practice. However, in order to filter out the erroneous causal connections, we require some principled way of collecting together the correct causal links in order to define the name-using practice. But the notion of 'correct causal links' is not itself a causal concept. Causal links simply are; they bear in themselves no normative property of being correct or incorrect. If this is right, the fact that we can describe different causal chains in disambiguating problem cases like the 'Madagascar' story is neither here nor there. We can describe these different causal chains only in so far as we appeal to non-causal concepts in order to differentiate the correct and incorrect causal chains for the name. The point at issue here goes back to something we have run into repeatedly; it concerns the irreducibly normative character of content. It is what we noted Charles Taylor referring to as the 'irreducible rightness of meaning' in chapter 7.[24] It is also, of course, a point that we noted Kripke emphasizing in his discussion of Wittgenstein's rule-following argument, in which he insists that a dispositional account of meaning rules cannot capture the normative force of meaning.[25]

In his treatment of names, Kripke is curiously indifferent to this problem. In the book version of the lectures he mentions it, but treats it as a technical problem, something to be ironed out in the details of a causal theory. What he says in response to Evans's example is, however, illuminating. He says:

> a name refers to an object if there exists a chain of communication, stretching back to baptism, at each stage of which there was a successful intention to preserve reference.[26]

This is a richly cognitive account of reference, and the historical links that it requires are informational links. The passage refers to 'chains of communication'; it is transfers of information that matter, not mere causal contact. This is contrary to the earlier official line on the Cicero example. The passage also speaks of an 'intention to preserve reference'. This requires the thinker to possess certain information, for how else could they form the relevant intention? Furthermore, the intention to preserve reference has to be 'successful', so the thinker must have the right information.

All this means that the composite model I suggested above must be wrong. The vertical line cannot be a mere causal connection; it must be an informational link. Once again, part of the diagnosis of why so many people seem to miss the relevance of non-causal concepts in describing what is supposed to be a causal story must turn on two points that I have repeatedly emphasized. One point is the ongoing confusion between constructing a refutation of descriptive theories of reference and constructing a refutation of Fregean, informationally characterized theories of reference. The other point concerns what I called the famous name convention. The examples employed in discussions of reference often use famous names. This is in part a mere reflection of everyone's general erudition and classical learning. More importantly, famous names get employed so that everyone will know what the example is about! In other words, writers use a famous name to ensure that we are party to a name-using practice before the discussion of what constitutes a name-using practice gets under way. This means that most of what constitutes a name-using practice goes unnoticed, because we are asked to consider an example with which we are familiar. This is not, once more, to doubt the cogency of using such examples in a refutation of a descriptive theory of reference; but we know now that that is not the point.

Kripke is aware of the above difficulty with a causal theory. It is a difficulty that I think is fatal if a causal theory is supposed to be a genuine alternative to an informationally based theory. In Kripke's case, I think we have to conclude that, despite the passage in which he contrasts his account with Strawson's, he does not see the causal theory as an alternative to an informationally based theory. As ever, the evidence for this turns on Kripke's preoccupation with providing a picture to replace the descriptive theory. He notes the possibility of deviant causal chains, and acknowledges that other conditions – non-causal conditions – 'must be satisfied in order to make this into a really rigorous theory of reference'.[27]

Furthermore, in offering an example very like my case of 'RM', he again leaves room for much non-causal apparatus in the account of reference. Suppose, he suggests, that a teacher tells children that 'George Smith first squared the circle' and that 'George Smith' is the name of the teacher's neighbour. The teacher just picks out the first name that comes into his head, for all he wants to inculcate is 'the belief that there was a man who squared the circle'.[28] Kripke then says that it 'doesn't seem clear in that case that the students have a false belief about the neighbour, even though there is a causal chain going back to the neighbour . . . more refinements need to be added to make . . . a set of necessary and sufficient conditions'. The moral to be drawn from this is that what makes the causal theory look good in the cases used to set up the picture is that in such cases causal links are employed that happen also to be informational links. Of course, as already noted, I am not denying that informational links are causal links. What matters is that not all causal links are informational links. So, if an example is employed in which the causal link appealed to is obviously an information-carrying link (and the appeal to 'intention to refer', 'chains of communication', etc. guarantees this), then it is the informational character of the link that does the work, not its causal realization. In contrast, the 'George Smith' example, the 'RM' example and cases of mixed causal chains – 'Madagascar' – are cases in which the existence of a mere causal link is not sufficient for reference, because the link in question is not an information-carrying link.

The upshot of all this is that the composite picture is no good. The real picture that captures Kripke's insights about the social character of meaning and the idea of name-using practice must be like this:

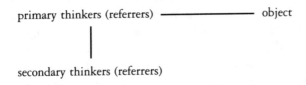

In this picture both links are informational links. Such links are realized in causal connections ('No magic in this universe, please!'); but what gives them the role they play in determining reference is the information carried in the links, not their causal realization.

10.6   The Social Character of Sense

The above picture is compatible with a Fregean theory of sense and reference in which sense is not descriptive information, but includes information that is not fully codable linguistically. The Fregean can then accommodate the insights concerning the social character of meaning and the idea of name-using practices. This means, however, that grasping a thought will amount to membership of a name-using practice. If you are a member of the 'RM'-using practice, you will be able to think about RM. On the face of it, this amounts to a serious reconstruction of basic Fregean claims. The appearance, however, is illusory.

Regardless of allegiance to Fregean theory, many people are attracted to internalism. Internalism can arise from adoption of the mental version of the reified model of sense. It also arises from the general intuition that thoughts are in-the-head kind of things. On an internalist account of thought, thinking about RM

279

amounts to something going on inside you skull: having a token of an RM symbol running in your language of thought, having a Lockean Idea of RM flashing across the Cartesian theatre of your introspective consciousness, having a neuronal sequence firing that is functionally identifiable as a state apt to cause talk employing the name 'RM', etc. If we adapt Kripke's insights into the framework of the theory of sense, we cannot endorse an internalist model of thought. The capacity to think about RM will turn, in the first instance, on participation in the 'RM'-using practice. For this still to be a Fregean account of thought, it would then have to make sense of the idea that what such participation granted you was possession of information. Furthermore, the model must have some account of how Frege's thesis II – that each name has a unique sense – could be true. I believe a social model of sense can satisfy both these demands.

Consider the following example. There exists a body of information that we call 'the theory of relativity'. Few people know all the information that constitutes this theory, indeed perhaps no one does. Most of us know a little about the theory and can formulate some of its key ideas and consequences. Nevertheless, it seems uncontentious to speak of this theory as an objectively existing body of information. The objectivity of its existence is shown by the fact that you can get things wrong when telling someone what the theory is and what it says. There is such a thing as being correct or incorrect about the content of the theory of relativity.

To simplify matters, let us suppose that there is a group of people who know the theory of relativity in its entirety. Call these the primary knowers. The rest of us stand to these primary knowers as secondary knowers. We are in possession of information that enables us to access what the primary knowers know. Our epistemic situation *vis-à-vis* the theory of relativity is not unlike the relation between computer terminals linked to a central processor. The primary knowers know the theory, and we are party to this knowledge in so far as we have the information that enables us, as it were, to access the files held by the primary knowers.

The above apparatus gives us a picture of what it is for there to be knowledge that is common property, shared by a community most members of which only have a slight grip upon the knowledge. Nevertheless, the grip that everyone has upon the theory of relativity is an informational grip. We are all party to the information that constitutes the theory of relativity by virtue of the informational caches that grant us access to the information held by the primary knowers. I suggest that this model can apply as a solution to the problem of Frege's thesis II. Each name has a unique sense just in case it is intelligible to draw a distinction between primary knowers and secondary knowers within the name-using practice.

In the case of 'Bill Clinton', I take it that there is a good case for saying that Hillary Clinton counts among the primary knowers. It is to Hillary that we defer in our use of the name. She's the person we turn to for guidance if confronted with a Bill Clinton look-alike. She can spot the difference. On this model, holding a preliminary cache of information about Bill Clinton enables you to think about him, because it immerses you in a web of information that is directed at him. And remember, there is no reason to suppose that this web is descriptive information. Indeed, most of the important information held at the centre will not be descriptive, but perceptually supplied information like, 'That's my Bill'.

This model for sense is at odds with the internalism that informs most people's thinking about thoughts. It makes the content of a thought something that is 'out there' rather than in the head. Of course, some of the information is in the head in the trivial sense that without a processing unit like the brain you could not even have access to the preliminary caches of information. This is trivial, for even of the preliminary caches of information I would not want to suggest a model in which that information is theorized as an internal array that, suitably contextualized, provides access to something external. The preliminary cache is like a connection, not a plug, for, without its link to the primary information, it would not be the preliminary information that it is; it would be an isolated package of information leading nowhere.

So although the above model runs counter to internalist intuitions, I take that to be an advantage. The model of information as internal counters is deeply suspect. The above model of the social character of sense theorizes information in line with the account given in the last chapter. I there defended a quasi-behaviourist account of sense. The key feature of that position was the idea that, instead of reifying content into a configuration of entities held to be causally responsible for behaviour, we instead theorize content as *the way that our behaviour is rationally structured*. We accept *sui generis* the rational structure of behaviour. The same point applies to the social character of sense, for the rational structure of my 'Bill Clinton' behaviour reaches out, as it were, to include the rationality of my responses towards the likes of Hillary Clinton and other close associates. The rational impact of the name 'Bill Clinton' upon my behaviour is open-ended, and reaches as far as the informational trail may take me.

If the above model of the social character of sense is anywhere near right, it means definitively that the theory of sense cannot aspire to be a theory of senses. Because of the open-endedness of the sense of a name, we will not be able to write a theory that completes the axiom

The sense of 'Bill Clinton' is _____.

The most we can get is a theory of sense that outlines the general structure of our intentionality, and describes the differences between the different varieties of reference available to us in thought and talk.

Another consequence of the above model is that it makes the sense of a name

281

contextual, for it depends on the social context quite what the shape and extent of the relevant information is. This means that the theory of sense cannot be a theory of language, where we think of language as a context-independent configuration of signs. The theory of sense is a theory of the context-sensitive use of signs to express our intentionality. That, I suspect, is not a problem, but merely a reflection of the deeply contextual character of all intentionality. It is the consequence of the move taken in chapter 2 to treat semantics as concerned with the properties not of symbols, but of their standard uses. The important insight that I am taking from Kripke is that 'standard use' is, in part, socially constrained. In the next chapter I turn to examine those features of language use that everyone acknowledges to be contextually sensitive. By the final chapter, we shall see that the above sketch of an account of the social character of sense fills out to a general prescription for sense for singular terms.

11

Content and Context

11.1 Introduction

Language is a context-independent set of symbols, counters that can be carried from place to place and used many times over. Much of our language has a meaning that is also context-independent. That is the great power of language; it serves as a record of what has happened, what could happen, what is planned to happen. It is possession of language that gives us the sense of history and culture distinctive of human civilization. Notwithstanding the dominance that context-independent language and meaning have enjoyed in most of the theorizing about thought, I want to suggest that such language use is the exception. The use of language to express context-independent meaning, although essential for the activity of writing books, doing mathematics, or keeping historical records is not the theoretically most interesting or basic form of language use. Indeed, I believe that a powerful leitmotif throughout this century's philosophy of thought has been an insight due to Russell. It is an insight that challenges the idea that meaning is context-independent.

A lot of recent work has explored the phenomenon of context-sensitive meanings. Much of this has seen the phenomenon in terms of anomalies that stand in need of special treatment.[1] My own view is that the context-sensitivity of meaning is ubiquitous, and is the grounding for the semantic power of all language and thought, including the context-independent portions of language which, on my account, turn out to be the exceptions. Despite Russell's position as a key theorist of context-independent language use (his theory of descriptions), his principal position was as a defender of the idea that the semantic power to represent enters language via context-sensitive expressions.

Russell held that the semantic power of language to represent was founded on the context-dependent parts of language. Russell's insight is often missed, in part because of his important contribution to the study of context-independent language use and in part because of the naïve way in which he accounted for his insight. Nevertheless, despite the fact that it is context-sensitive language use that has predominantly been seen as problematic, I think the force of Russell's insight is gradually being recognized and theorized in a more promising manner.

In this chapter I shall review some of the different ways in which contemporary theorists have explored the context-sensitive components of language use and context-sensitive thoughts. Our topic is linguistic expressions whose semantic value is a function, in part, of their use in a context; the determination of their semantic value is indexed to a context. Such expressions include natural kind terms, perceptual demonstratives, indexicals of person, place and time ('I', 'You', 'here', 'there', 'now', 'then', etc.).

I start with Russell's insight, followed by Putnam on natural kind terms and Fodor's critique of Putnam's arguments. I shall then turn to indexicals proper and to the theories offered by such writers as Kaplan and Perry. The emphasis is on the metaphysics of thought. It is only in the final chapter that I shall sketch what I think is the correct account of context-sensitive contents derived from Evans.[2] In that chapter I shall review some of the profound consequences for our self-conception of giving indexicals a key place in our theory of thought.

11.2   Russell's Insight

The orthodox view of Russell's contribution to the theory of thought goes like this. Russell, like Frege and numerous writers since, wanted to construct an ideal language fit for science and mathematics.[3] His concept of logical grammar and his theory of descriptions illustrate his acceptance of the idea that natural language is an imperfect instrument for science and philosophy, an instrument that can systematically mislead, as it originally misled Russell's ontology prior to his development of the theory of descriptions.[4] Now, scientific-mathematical language is the paradigm case of a language with context-independent meaning. It is therefore tempting to think of Russell as an exponent of the view that meaning is fundamentally context-independent. The chief consequence of this view is the idea that the job for the philosopher of meaning is to construct a systematic theory of meaning, a formal theory that will apply to a language adequate for science and mathematics. Such a conception of the philosopher's task then leaves the study of semantics divorced from a theory of thought. It breaks the connection between content or meaning and the role that content plays in the explanation of behaviour. Semantics becomes a formal study of formal languages that have little or no bearing upon behaviour.

If this becomes our model for semantics, it is tempting to try to force other aspects of language use into this mould, and to expect to be able to give an adequate account of the whole of natural language within a formal semantic theory. On one reading, Davidson's original project was construed as a manual-theory of meaning – although I argued in section 4.4 that Davidson should be read as offering a different conception of theorizing – what I called the theory-theory of meaning.

I do not believe that Russell subscribed to this formal model of semantics, for his key insight is incompatible with such an approach. Russell's insight was:

> **Russell's insight:** The semantic power of language to represent derives from the semantic power of context-sensitive expressions.

If this insight is correct, the representational power of language is not fully codifiable, for the meaning of context-sensitive expressions is not fully codifiable. Such meaning cannot be theorized in the representationalist manner. A formal theory of language could then, at best, only tell half the story. It would describe a structure that, without the anchorage provided by context-sensitive expressions, bore no content. Content, *contra* the representationalist, is not characterizable independently of that which it represents. Russell's insight captures the intuitively plausible idea that language, as it were, touches home with the world at those points where its use is governed by contextual features – the perceptual demonstratives.

Russell's insight raises an obvious problem concerning the possibility of misrepresentation. The possibility of misrepresentation is essential to the idea of thought and content.[5] Russell's insight entails object-dependence for singular contents. Therefore, the content of context-sensitive expressions is not characterizable independently of what they represent. Singular contents (e.g. singular senses) cannot misrepresent. There is no such thing as atomic error. Allowing that singular senses are object-dependent is compatible with the possibility of misrepresentation as long as that is cashed out in terms of the falsity of whole thoughts. In section 9.3 I claimed that the idea of atomic error can play no role in the connectivity of thought. Let me expand on this claim and show why the idea of object-dependence is not only unproblematic, but necessary. I call this the semantic argument for object-dependency.[6]

The reason why atomic error (empty names) plays no role in the connectivity of thought is because thoughts bear on one another inferentially in terms of their truth and falsity. Suppose we had a thought with an empty component. Consider the thought expressed by the sentence

Bill is bald,

where the name picks out no one. Now, if 'Bill' picks out no one, it is unclear what thought you are supposed to be considering. The fact that it is unclear is due to the fact that the putative thought has no bearing on other thoughts. The putative thought does not even stand in a relation of contradicting the putative thought expressed by

Bill is hairy,

for we have no conception of the conditions under which either would be true or false.[7] We can have no conception of the truth-conditions of these putative thoughts, for the simple reason that they are, in effect, incomplete. Because the name is empty, we do not know what is being said, what thought is being expressed, with these sentences. This means that there is no argument for empty names from the phenomenon of error that does not beg the question in favour of a blueprint conception of content. It is only because people assume a blueprint conception, and take for granted the idea that singular thought components have the capacity to represent, that they think that the possibility of empty names is coherent. But we lack any notion of what it would be for names to represent independent of their semantic power in contributing to the truth/falsity of whole thoughts. Putative empty names make no contribution to the truth/falsity of whole thoughts, for they lack a semantic value. The thesis of object-dependence, then, is merely a consequence of the central Fregean idea that truth is more primitive than reference, and that our account of the reference of a name is not independent of an account of its grammar in the production of sentences that are true or false. It is curious that the supposed problem with empty names is often seen as a recherché feature of contemporary neo-Fregean theories. Russell had just the same thesis of object-dependence, but it is rarely, if ever, commented on.

Russell did not permit the idea of atomic error. Genuine singular terms and predicate expressions were guaranteed a semantic value via the relation of acquaintance. His account of the latter relation is problematic, given its atomic character. Nevertheless, all error, for Russell, is molecular. This point is sometimes missed, for people assume a blueprint model of content according to which content is thought of in terms of possession of signs. Russell does allow a notion of error which consists in possession of signs, but only for descriptions. It is a mistake to think that this is an example of a blueprint conception, for when a description is empty, the notion of error involved is falsity. A description is, despite superficial grammatical appearances, a sentence. An empty description is not an empty sign; it is a false sentence. The apparently empty sign 'The King of France' is really the false sentence

$$\exists x \, (Fx \, \& \, \forall y(Fy \rightarrow x = y)).$$

That is the point of Russell's theory of descriptions.

That Russell's insight characterizes Russell's own theorizing is evident in two related respects. First, Russell's theory of reference is a context-sensitive theory of reference. The semantic power of demonstratives is a function of the mind's capacity to fix upon a patch of sense-data and bestow a demonstrative upon it. Second, all other linguistic expressions of reference are analysable by the theory of descriptions and the thesis that names are truncated descriptions into first-order quantification theory. The strings produced by such analyses comprise quantifiers and predicate letters. The semantic power of these strings resides in the semantic notion of satisfaction as applied to predicates. Russell's view about the semantic power of predicates was of a kind with his view about demonstratives. According to his principle of acquaintance, to understand an expression, you must be acquainted with its semantic value.[8] For Russell, understanding a predicate required acquaintance with the universal for which it stood.

In short, for Russell, language connects with the world at two points: universals and the particulars (patches of sense-data) picked out by demonstratives. The whole of the semantic power of language is built upon these two kinds of acquaintance. On this basis, a formal semantic theory might reveal the way in which the semantic value of complex expressions was compositionally computable from the semantic value of primitives; but the semantic value of primitives is a function of the subject's acquaintance with patches of sense-data and with universals. The semantic power of language thus resides in the relation of acquaintance.

In the case of acquaintance with universals there is no reason to suppose that the satisfaction of predicates is context-sensitive. Nevertheless, the fact that a predicate, e.g. '. . . is red', has a context-independent meaning can only consist in the thinker's capacity to retain an acquaintance with the universal redness. I do not know what a developed theory of acquaintance with universals would be like, but the best way of understanding the idea of retaining an acquaintance with universals would be in terms of a recognitional ability that allows us to demonstratively pick out a property. If this is right, then even the semantic power of predicates is based on context-sensitive language use, for it is a use based upon the contextually sensitive ability to recognize a universal. 'Context-sensitive' here just means that the ability is not mediated descriptively, so the content of a universal expression is not individuated linguistically, but requires the recognitional ability that *relates* us to things – objects and universals.

In the case of demonstratives, acquaintance with sense-data patches constitutes a reference relation that is obviously context-sensitive. Therefore, with regard to reference, the semantic power of language derives from the semantic power of context-sensitive expressions. If the above hypothesis about the nature of the acquaintance relation with universals is correct, then the semantic power of the whole of language derives from semantic power of context-sensitive expressions. In the remainder of this chapter I shall show how, with respect to reference, Russell's insight has been repeatedly revisited for different kinds of expressions. In the hands of the neo-Fregean theory of singular thoughts, it comes to be recognized as a key truth about the nature of content.

The chief difference between the neo-Fregean and Russell lies in the account of acquaintance. Russell understood this atomically, whereas for the neo-Fregean it cannot be understood independently of the 'grammar' of acquaintance. Either way, the role played by the concept of acquaintance means that the knowledge that constitutes sense must be a form of practical knowledge, not theoretical knowledge, for acquaintance has to be understood relationally. This means that knowledge by acquaintance cannot be abstracted from the encounter with the object/property and treated as a piece of theoretical knowledge. Being acquainted with something is practical knowledge: knowing how to attend to an object, touch it, manipulate it, etc. Russell saw this, but the insight was buried in his otherwise old-fashioned Cartesian epistemology. We will not get to a proper appreciation of these points until the next and final chapter.

If Russell's insight is granted this much significance, the following must be true:

(a)   There can be no account of content in which knowledge of content is fully codifiable as theoretical knowledge – knowledge of propositions that codify meaning;

(b)   language mastery must be theorized as a practical skill grounded in practical 'knowledge how' – knowing how to pick out things, although not in the atomistic manner of Russell;

(c)   the concept of logical grammar will not be exhausted in terms of an account of the structure of a language (a syntactic structure), it will be at root the structure of a practice;[9]

(d)   the emphasis on practical skills need not threaten the objectivity of linguistic mastery if the skills are seen as subject to a compositional analysis; the point is only that the analysis is not completable in, or grounded in, the structure of a language or quasi-linguistic system;[10]

(e)   our practical abilities to pick things out is our point of contact with the world, and is defined in terms of that contact.

There is much at stake in giving Russell's insight a central role in the theory of reference. The emphasis on a conception of practical knowledge that it brings has consequences across a broad metaphysical and epistemological front. A theory of reference that accommodates Russell's insight will be a theory in which the thinking subject is an embodied subject, embedded in its environment, with a practical sense of its location and orientation.[11] Stripped of the epistemology that drove Russell's way of explaining the semantic power of context-sensitive expressions, accommodating Russell's insight provides a radical refutation of the Cartesianism that has been latent in most theorizing about the mind and content.[12]

11.3   Natural Kinds

Putnam claims the meaning of natural kind terms is indexical. He says that the meaning of a natural kind term like 'water' is indexed to *that stuff roundabouts whatever its nature may be*. Like Kripke's account of proper names, Putnam says that natural kind terms do not pick out a stuff descriptively; they are indexed to the actual stuff, however it may be exhibited to our senses. The term 'water' is indexed to the H_2O stuff, regardless of what this stuff looks like, tastes like, or feels like. The indexing is achieved via the causal connection between our use of the term and the stuff.

Putnam comes to this account of natural kind terms by considering the following thought-experiment.[13] Consider a place called Twin-Earth. Twin-Earth has a colourless tasteless liquid that fills its oceans and rivers and is used by its inhabitants for making coffee, extinguishing fires, washing clothes, etc. Suppose that we all have *doppelgängers* on Twin-Earth leading twin lives to ourselves. The stuff that our *doppelgängers* use to make coffee with, etc. has a molecular structure not of two hydrogen atoms plus one oxygen atom, but of XYZ. Now, answer the following question: Is this Twin-Earth stuff water? Putnam's intuition is that we would not call such stuff water, despite its similarity to water. We would say that our *doppelgängers* made coffee with something that looked like water, tasted like water, and so on, but not that they made coffee with water.[14] Suppose that the Twin-Earthians had a word for the XYZ stuff, and the word was 'water'. Nevertheless, the meaning of their word would be different from our word 'water'. To avoid confusion, I will mark their word thus: twater. Water is not twater; it just looks like it.

On Putnam's model the meaning of 'water' and 'twater' is indexed to the actual stuff with which the users of the word causally interact. It may be that some people in the respective communities know the nature of this stuff: Earth chemists know that water is H_2O; Twin-Earth chemists know that twater is XYZ. If so, this reflects the phenomenon we met with Kripke's theory of names – the social character of meaning, for our use of 'water' defers to the chemists. For example, if on being presented with a sample of twater we were to say, 'This is water', then despite the fact that we may be unable to tell the difference between water and twater, our utterance would still be false, because it is not water. That might be the sort of thing that only a chemist could tell. The truth-conditions of our utterance are such that we speak truly only if the stuff before us is H_2O, not XYZ.

Putnam's thought-experiment has generated an enormous literature, which cannot be covered here.[15] I shall concentrate only on capturing the assumptions at play that generate the notion of context-sensitivity for which Putnam argues. The first point to be noted about Putnam's claims is that he is speaking of the 'meaning' of natural kind terms. The catchy slogan that he employs to sum up his position is that 'meanings ain't in the head'. What is at stake with these remarks? One of the things that Putnam originally took himself to be challenging was the idea that there was a notion of meaning that could be thought of as internal to the subject and that determined the reference of terms used by the subject. This sounds like a descriptivist version of Frege's theory that Putnam has in his sights, and, for sure, Putnam's argument is opposed to a descriptivist account of the meaning of natural kind.

So the claim is that the meaning of natural kind terms is not descriptive. It is indexed to the stuff in the environment of the language-user. This means that the meaning of 'water' is approximately 'That stuff' as used in the perceptual presence of a water sample, or otherwise a meaning causally traceable to such a demonstrative. The demonstrative signals the fact that the meaning of the term is singular, not descriptive. The word 'stuff' signals that the meaning picks out a kind rather than any particular instance of the kind.

Now, because Putnam is claiming that the meaning of 'water' is not descriptive, he must be opposed to an internalist account of the content of natural kind terms. The reason for this goes back to the discussion in section 9.5. Internalism entails that content can be specified independently of how things stand in the environment. The only kind of content for which internalism looks plausible is descriptive content. The idea of a singular meaning is necessarily the idea of an externalist conception of meaning – hence the claim that meanings ain't in the head. So far, so good; but the initial plausibility of Putnam's claims is based on a number of assumptions that we need to bring into the open.

There are a number of distinctions that need to be noted and that affect our assessment of Putnam's externalism and the other varieties I consider later. First, we need to distinguish between a truth-conditional conception of the meaning of a natural kind term and a conceptual-role conception. On the former, the meaning of 'water' is whatever we need to appeal to in order to get an account of the truth-conditions of sentences employing the term. On the latter, first explored by Field, the meaning of the term is a function of its systematic connectedness within a language.[16] To speak of meaning in terms of the conceptual role of a word is not necessarily to endorse internalism – that only follows if the systematic connectedness within a language is something that can be studied independently of the environment. If 'language' is understood as a symbolic structure, then this would be the case, and the conceptual role of 'water' would then be an internalist conception of its meaning. Putnam is plainly endorsing a truth-conditional account of the meaning of 'water'.

Second, we need to distinguish between a theory of meaning of natural kind terms whose main function is to capture the notion of meaning that figures in the explanation of behaviour and a theory that does not so constrain its account of meaning. I shall speak of a theory of the former kind as a 'B-explanatory' account of meaning. Third, we need to distinguish amongst B-explanatory theories of meaning those that employ causal explanation (instantiation of regularities) as the model of explanation and those that employ non-causal models of explanation. An example of the latter kind would be a theory that used meaning to explain behaviour, but took the form of explanation to be teleological. Fourth, we need to distinguish between theories that assume that psychological states are internal states and those that allow that psychological states are externally individuated. I shall speak here of psychological internalism and psychological externalism.

We can summarize the permutations available with these four distinctions in a chart:

1 Meaning is	(a) truth-conditional	/	(b) conceptual role
2 Meaning is	(a) B-explanatory	/	(b) not B-explanatory
3 Explanation is	(a) causal	/	(b) teleological
4 Psychological states are	(a) internal	/	(b) external

At first sight you might think that Putnam's position could be characterized as (1a) and (4b), with no evidence yet given for classifying him on either option for (2) and (3). This, however, is mistaken. The temptation to think that Putnam endorses (4b) arises from his claim that meanings ain't in the head. Putnam is not, however, an externalist about psychological states; he is only an externalist about truth-conditional meaning. Indeed, as Putnam makes clear in setting up his Twin-Earth story, he assumes the truth of psychological internalism in order to make the story work.

The only thing that is uncontentious about Putnam's position is his classification on (1a): Putnam's conception of meaning is truth-conditional. To see why Putnam is a psychological internalist, consider this aspect of his Twin-Earth example. Putnam asks us to consider Oscar and his Twin-Earth *doppelgänger* Twin-Oscar. Both Oscar and Twin-Oscar use the word 'water' to refer to the stuff with which they make their coffee. Oscar uses the word to refer to H_2O, Twin-Oscar to refer to XYZ. It is central to Putnam's critique of a descriptivist theory of natural kind terms that the reference that each achieves with the term is not determined descriptively. The point of the thought-experiment that is used to force this claim is the supposition that both Oscar and Twin-Oscar, when confronted with a glass of what each calls 'water', are in *identical internal states*. Putnam also says that the stuff before each of the Oscars looks the same, is experientially identical. As far as the phenomenal qualities of the two stuffs go, you cannot tell them apart.[17] The whole point of the thought-experiment is that Oscar and Twin-Oscar are psychologically identical.

Putnam, then, endorses (4a); he is a psychological internalist. Note that Putnam's reasons for endorsing psychological internalism are contentious, and rest on two important epistemological assumptions. First, he makes an epistemological assumption about what I shall call the *range* of experience. By 'range of experience', I mean how far out into the world our experiences reach. Putnam believes that Oscar's experiences and Twin-Oscar's experiences have the same experiential reach, for he believes that Oscar can never have an experience the content of which is of H_2O. Similarly, Twin-Oscar can never have an experience the content of which is that it is of XYZ. This is not to deny that Oscar has an experience of H_2O; it is only to say that the content of Oscar's experience when confronted with water is restricted to the phenomenal properties – the wetness, colourlessness, etc. This, however, begs the question; for why should we assume that the phenomenal qualities that characterize experiential content have to be restricted to descriptive content?

We have to be careful here not to confuse experiential content with what Putnam calls 'meaning'. Meaning is truth-conditional. Experiential content is the level of psychological content that Putnam claims is identical for both Oscar and Twin-Oscar. The present point is the observation that Putnam's claim that experiential content for Oscar and Twin-Oscar is identical depends on the epistemological assumption that experiential content is restricted to that which is characterizable independently of the environment (internalism) because the range of our experience is restricted to phenomenal properties that can be, as it were, stripped off the environment. As we have learned from previous chapters, the notion of content that is environmentally independent like this is descriptive content. So, Putnam's claim that truth-conditional meaning is externalist depends on the claim that experiential content is internalist and descriptive! And this turns on the epistemological assumption that the range of experience reaches just as far as a level of phenomenal awareness that is environmentally independent.

The second epistemological assumption that I want to identify in Putnam's position is not explicitly endorsed by him, but it is an assumption that would ground the first assumption about the range of experience. Putnam's assumption about the range of experience is common, and therefore may not look contentious. If, however, we ask on what basis we should make such a restriction about the range of experience, it is difficult to formulate a reason other than to say: The range of experience is restricted to descriptive content because that is the sort of thing you can be sure of. That is to say, it is possible to doubt that the liquid before you is water, but it is not possible to doubt that it appears colourless, odourless, tasteless, etc. This means that the issue about the range of experience turns on a further epistemological assumption: The reach of experience goes no further than that about which it is not possible to doubt. Contrariwise, if it is possible to doubt that something is F, then that it is F cannot be an experiential content. This is the idea of the *transparency* of experience. The transparent is that which is, as it were, too close to doubt, and experience reaches no further than that. The assumption that experiential content is transparent goes back to Descartes. It gives a conception of experience that is disengaged from the world and thus characterizable independently of how things are. It produces the familiar predicament in which we are, epistemologically, cut off from the world.

Now, it is part of Putnam's position to claim that meaning is environmentally dependent. Furthermore, Putnam uses this claim to defend an objection to scepticism. Putnam thinks he can defeat brain-in-a-vat scepticism via considerations about the meaning of natural kind terms. The idea is that because the meaning of 'water' is causally indexed to H_2O, then if we were brains in vats, we would not be able to refer to water. But we do refer to water, and so, because meaning is externalist, we cannot be brains in vats, for our use of 'water' is indexed to H_2O.[18] The central idea is that because of our ability to refer with 'water', we must be causally hooked up to H_2O. We cannot be detached from the world, as the sceptic suggests. This, however, is not incompatible with the identification that I have made of the epistemological assumptions about the range and transparency of experience in Putnam's work. Putnam wants to say that we are causally hooked up to the world, for that is his account of how the reference of natural kind terms is determined. However, in order to convince us of a causal hook-up to the world, he assumes that we are experientially disengaged – that we are psychologically detached from the world.

This means that Putnam's concept of meaning is wholly unconnected with any epistemological notions; it is a concept of meaning that is invariant across our epistemological situatedness. Once we have learned 'water', it refers to H_2O, regardless of whether we are then confronted with a sample of XYZ. I conclude, then, that Putnam holds (1a), but is a psychological internalist, (4a), for psychological internalism is necessary in order to set up the Twin-Earth thought-experiment. I sum this up by saying that although Putnam is not a psychological externalist, he is a causal-theoretic externalist. His conception is, at heart, a conception of internal psychological states the experiential content of which is invariant across environmental change. It is such invariance of experiential content that provides the identity between Oscar and Twin-Oscar as we 'spin the possible worlds'. The reference of their internal states is fixed by their causal anchorage. Causal-theoretic externalism is then an option characterized by the claim that there are internal states with an environmentally independent content, and that the meaning of such states is determined by causal anchorage.

Where does this leave Putnam with regard to (2) and (3)? With regard to explanation, although Putnam does not explicitly consider the point, I take it that the model of explanation he works with is causal. We should note, however, that the meaning of 'water' does not, of itself, have any clear explanatory role. Putnam thinks that reference is determined by causal link, so it is reasonable to assume that he generally has a causal model of explanation. He does not, however, have a clear explanatory role for meaning. It is not possible, then, to classify Putnam with respect to (2). This fact points the way to a response to Putnam's account of the meaning of natural kind terms that renders the whole theory irrelevant.

11.4   Fodor – Putting Meaning Back in the Head

The above analysis of Putnam's position on natural kind terms leads naturally to the response to Putnam that lies at the heart of Fodor's work.[19] It also develops into what has become an orthodoxy regarding indexicality. Suppose Putnam is right, and that the truth-conditions of sentences employing natural kind terms are externalist. What role, if any, does this concept of meaning have to play in the explanation of behaviour? On the face of it, Putnam's causal-theoretic variety of truth-conditional meaning has no role to play in the explanation of behaviour. Fodor, like many theorists, takes it as constitutive of our interest in meaning that our account of content should be linked to that which figures in our ordinary rationalizing explanations of behaviour. That, of course, is the position that I have adopted throughout this book. If, however, Putnam's conception of meaning provides no explanatory leverage on behaviour, we might concede that his account of the truth-conditions of sentences containing natural kind terms is correct, but look to an alternative conception of content in order to gain explanatory purchase on behaviour. This is what Fodor does.

   The explanatory irrelevance of Putnam's conception of truth-conditions is apparent from the following consideration. Suppose Oscar and Twin-Oscar are both confronted by a glass of colourless, tasteless liquid that they call 'water'. Oscar and Twin-Oscar have beliefs that they both express with the words

   (1)   Water is thirst-quenching,

although when Oscar uses (1) he refers to H_2O, and when Twin-Oscar uses (1) he refers to XYZ. The pair of them also have a belief expressed by the following sentence:

   (2)   The glass in front of me contains water,

and have a desire to drink some water. For the moment, we should not assume that the belief they have when using (2) is the same belief. We know that (2) has different truth-conditions when uttered by Oscar and his twin, but we should not beg the question in Putnam's favour by assuming that the only notion of belief content that we want is truth-conditional. Similar remarks apply to the desire(s) they each express with the sentence

(3)   I want a glass of water.

Now, in the light of the beliefs/desires expressed by (1)–(3), what do Oscar and his twin do? Surely, they do the same thing, and, as such, the explanation of their action should appeal to something in common. Indeed, were Oscar and his twin instantaneously switched as they sat before their respective glasses of liquid, this would have no bearing on their subsequent action. They would both reach out in identical fashion and drink from the glass before them.[20]

The common explanandum demands a common explanans, and this is available in terms of the notion of content that Putnam already appeals to in setting up the thought-experiment: the notion of experiential content. Let us call this notion of content 'narrow content'. Narrow content does not determine truth-conditions, for we are assuming that Putnam has the account of the truth-conditions right for (1)–(3). Narrow content is the content that is invariant across Oscar and his twin's psychological states; but it is precisely that notion of content that is explanatorily salient. Hence, if we restrict content to that which figures in our ordinary rationalizing explanations of behaviour, we do not need Putnam's externalist truth-conditional concept of meaning. Such a conception of meaning plays no role in the explanation of behaviour.

Furthermore, although the above argument appeals to our ordinary rationalizing explanations of behaviour, because the states picked out by the notion of narrow content are invariant across contexts, they are states characterizable in terms that pick out types of states. As such, narrow-content states are states suitable for figuring in causal generalizations. Indeed, the above considerations implicitly appeal to the relevant generalization: namely, states of the kind that Oscar and his twin are in are apt to produce glass-picking-up behaviour. The very fact that narrow-content states are invariant across environmental changes makes them just the sorts of thing to figure in causal explanations. This is a happy result, for it suggests a way in which our ordinary rationalizing explanations are reducible to the familiar model of causal explanation by instantiation of regularities, just so long as we stick with the concept of narrow content and not truth-conditional content.

The above position can be summed up by saying that there are two distinct notions of content at play in contemporary discussions of indexicality. There is narrow content, which suffices for an account of content as it figures in psychological explanation. In addition, there is a notion of broad truth-conditional content that is explanatorily inert. If you want to construct a truth-conditional theory of meaning for a natural language, then you will need the notion of broad content. If, however, you want a theory of content rooted in an explanation of behaviour, narrow content will suffice. Fodor wants content to be tied to the explanation of behaviour, so he concludes that, although Putnam may have the truth-conditions of (1)–(3) correct, the only notion of belief/desire content that we need to explain what agents do is narrow content. This theoretical structure is often referred to as a dual-component theory of content: truth-conditional content has a dual-component structure in which truth-conditions are determined by narrow content plus context.[21]

On the matter of Putnam versus Fodor, Fodor looks to have it right; for Putnam's causal-theoretic externalism produces a concept of meaning and a meaning state that have no role to play in a characterization of our lives. It is simply unclear what kind of state the broad-belief state is when Oscar believes (1). Clearly, there is a state picked out by the broad-belief state; it is the narrow state (roughly equivalent to Oscar having the sentence 'Water is thirst-quenching' running through his head) plus this state standing in a relation of causal anchorage to H_2O. But the bit about causal anchorage plays no role in our understanding of what Oscar does.

Furthermore, because Oscar's narrow-content state for (1) is identical with his twin's narrow-content state for (1), the causal anchorage of Oscar's narrow content is contingent. The narrow-content state as such could just as well be anchored in XYZ rather than H_2O, as indeed it is for Twin Oscar. So, whatever it is that makes narrow content explanatorily salient, it is nothing that makes it a content about water rather than, say, twater. This last remark is nothing less than the official line on narrow content. It is, however, indicative of a number of problems that run deep in the very idea of narrow content. Before turning to those problems, let me complete the review of how Fodor proposes that we should respond to Putnam's account of indexicality.

It is important to realize that just as Putnam, like Kripke, proposes a causal theory of reference, so too does Fodor. In Fodor's case, however, the theory plays a subtly different role. Putnam thinks that meaning is determined causally, in virtue of the causal anchorage of that which is invariant between Oscar and Twin Oscar. What is invariant is narrow content.[22] Narrow content is definable in terms of that which is in the head, but it takes narrow content plus its causal anchorage to determine truth-conditions. Now, it does no harm to think of narrow content in terms of conceptual role. What differentiates one narrow content from another is, of course, its role in explaining behaviour. But the idea of narrow content is the idea of something specifiable independently of context, so it must be possible to model narrow content in linguistic terms, for linguistic strings are context-independent entities. As such, we can think of narrow content as definable over the configuration of linguistic entities within the head of the subject. Such entities are discriminable in virtue of their syntax, their shape. So narrow content is a notion of content that is identifiable syntactically. One narrow content is differentiable from another just in case it is syntactically discriminable. The thought that Oscar and his twin have the same narrow content when they utter (1) is then the thought that they have the same syntactic configuration running through their heads. Indeed, the simplest way of putting this is just to say that they have the same sentence running through their heads. The upshot of all this, then, is to say that to be in possession of the narrow content expressed by

> Water is wet

is to have the sentence 'Water is wet' running through your head! The causal part of Fodor's theory is required in order to explain the semantic power of these internal expressions and the sentences that they form. It is problematic whether a causal theory can be the basis of an account of semantic aboutness. In addition, the positing of inner sentential-like structures suggests that we have made little headway in our understanding of content. The position is now open to the central problem that beset the reified model of sense discussed in section 9.4.

11.5   Problems with Bifurcationism

The real weakness in Fodor's position is a structural weakness that arises from the bifurcation of content into broad and narrow kinds. To see the sorts of problems that accrue to this distinction, consider first the following point. Narrow content is invariant across contexts. Many writers take this to be the advantage of the concept of narrow content, for it provides a causally respectable notion of content. If narrow contents are identifiable as symbol strings, then their semantic properties are potentially reducible to, or at least supervene upon, their shape or syntax. The shape or syntax of a symbol string is the sort of thing that can account for its causal properties, the way it interacts with other strings (conceptual role), and the way it interacts with other items – for example, inducing behaviour by stimulating muscle cells, etc.

If we take as basic the requirement that contents have, as it were, a causal handle to them, then the notion of narrow content is well suited for meeting this requirement. The cost of this benefit, however, is the worry that the notion of narrow content fails to marry with our ordinary rationalizing concept of belief content. For some writers the price is insignificant, and the conclusion is drawn that our ordinary concept of belief must be allowed to wither away in the face of the scientifically respectable notion of narrow content.[23] Fodor is not willing to let go of the ordinary rationalizing concept of belief content, but this means that although the concept of narrow content is not a truth-conditional concept of content, it must be possible to capture the ordinary rationalizing force of truth-conditional content. It is for this reason that Fodor requires a causal theory of reference for narrow contents; for it is the causal theory that is supposed to supply the 'aboutness' to narrow contents. Supplying the 'aboutness' for narrow contents is no mean task. It is this that reveals the deep structural flaws in the bifurcationism about content of the broad/narrow content distinction.

There are three competing intuitions at play in Fodor's bifurcated theory of content: intuitions about phenomenology, rationalization and physicalism. The first of these arises from Fodor's appeal to the way things are for the subject; for he thinks that it is only such an appeal that gives us our ordinary explanatory handle upon people's actions.[24] The appeal to the way things are for the subject is an appeal to phenomenology. It is this that constitutes the individualism that applies to Fregean theory; it is the notion of the subject's point of view. Second, the notion of content that characterizes this phenomenology must drive rationalizing explanations of behaviour; so it must be a notion of content that captures the normative force of why, in the face of a set of beliefs and desires, the rational thing to do is, for example, to pick up and drink from a glass of water. Third, for Fodor, the rationalizing notion of content must also be physicalistically respectable and amenable to characterization in a way that instantiates causal regularities. Fodor's third requirement is met by the idea that narrow content is syntactically definable.

It is not clear that any single notion of content can satisfy these three intuitions, hence the bifurcation into broad and narrow content. Once the bifurcation is made, however, it leaves the important properties of content disconnected from one another and the very idea that narrow content has any representational power a mystery. The phenomenological appeal would seem harmless, for unless we have a notion of content that picks out states of the subject, we cannot begin to get explanations of the subject's actions as opposed to things that happen to the subject. The problematic intuition concerns the rationalizing force of content.

The obvious way of capturing the rationalizing force of content is via a truth-conditional account of content. The reason why one ought, in the face of beliefs and desires (1)–(3), to pick up the glass is because these beliefs and desires are *about* water. These are contents that are about that stuff, and it is the aboutness of these states that provides you with a rational orientation to the stuff. It is the aboutness of the desire content that, as it were, points you in the direction of water, given your belief that the stuff before you is water. Fodor believes, as many do, that a state that enjoys semantic aboutness should be characterizable independently of that which it is about; our belief states should be characterized in a way that is semantically inert.[25] The intuition about semantic inertness is, however, ill formed. The correct point is that an account of belief content should not presuppose that all your beliefs are true, for you can believe that a stuff is water when in fact it is not. The intuition that drives the idea of the semantic inertness of belief characterization is simply the intuition that where there is representational content, there is scope for misrepresentation. This intuition alone does not force internalism. Furthermore, Fodor is left with a conception of states whose possession of content, let alone the right content, must be in doubt. The following argument derives from Evans's argument that narrow content is not really content, but a schema for content.[26]

Narrow content is context-invariant. The narrow content of 'water' or 'twater' is the conceptual role of the words. This means that the only thing these narrow states (words) are intrinsically about is stuff that is a colourless, tasteless, odourless liquid. This means that narrow content is descriptive content, or, if indexical, it is the linguistic meaning of the indexical, e.g. the descriptive content for 'I' – 'the speaker'. This should not be surprising, for descriptive content is everyone's familiar notion of content that is context-independent. As noted previously, however, this means that there is nothing about Oscar's narrow contents that makes them about water rather than twater. The aboutness all resides in the story about context. This, however, is puzzling. If context provides the aboutness, then it is context that provides the semantic power to narrow content, for narrow content represents no particular thing and no particular kind of thing until it is placed in a context. This is an odd conclusion, for the whole point about the distinction between broad and narrow content is that broad content is a function of content plus context, but why call the former component 'content' if it has no aboutness? Similarly, why call the latter component 'context' if it is the component that provides the semantic power?

One explanation of this odd conclusion would be to say that advocates of a dual-component theory are taking for granted the notion of descriptive aboutness. If that were so, then the idea would be that, given an unproblematic status for descriptive aboutness, the broad truth-conditional content that arises when a descriptive narrow content is placed in a context is of a kind with the notion of descriptive aboutness. That, however, is incoherent, for the aboutness of a contextually sensitive term is quite different from the aboutness of a contextually insensitive term. Contextually insensitive terms enjoy a descriptive aboutness; they are about kinds of things – their representational power is predicative. The whole point of contextually sensitive terms is that the kind of aboutness they enjoy is indexed to a particular; their representational power is singular. Nevertheless, I suspect that most people see no problem here, because they take for granted the idea that descriptive contents enjoy semantic aboutness.

What we are up against is a deep-seated problem with bifurcationism. The position gains plausibility only at the price of taking the aboutness of descriptive contents for granted and then thinking that indexical aboutness is much the same except that it varies from context to context. That, of course, means that indexical aboutness cannot possibly be 'much the same'! But what is involved in taking for granted the aboutness of descriptive content? The answer is representationalism.

What is assumed within the orthodoxy of birfurcationism is the idea that descriptive narrow content unproblematically represents or stands for kinds of things. The notion of descriptive content being satisfied by kinds of things is taken as primitive. We have to be careful how we express the assumption that I believe lies at the root of bifurcationism. As noted, given the context-invariance of narrow content, the only thing that Earth 'water' and Twin-Earth 'twater' are intrinsically about is a stuff that is tasteless, colourless, odourless, etc. That is to say, the idea of narrow content presupposes a level of descriptive content that picks out types of stuff in terms of their perceptible qualities. The level of descriptive aboutness of narrow content is not, of course, sufficient to pick out water; that part of the story is supposed to come from an account of the causal anchorage of the narrow content within a context. Nevertheless, there is a level of description that picks out not natural kinds like water, but perceptible kinds. It is the aboutness that accrues to descriptive content about perceptible kinds that is taken for granted by bifurcationism. This amounts to an advocacy of internalism premised on an epistemological priority given to perceptible kinds over natural kinds. The internalism is a blueprint model of content – there is a level of content that can be characterized independently of the environment and that, as it were, is offered to the environment by the mind for satisfaction or not. The level of description available within this blueprint conception is a level characterized by perceptible kinds. I shall call this the perceptible blueprint conception of narrow content. The perceptible blueprint conception of narrow content supports the idea of a level of content that can be thought of as a talismanic array within the mind – a language of thought, a configuration of ideas, etc.

This privileging of perceptible kinds over natural kinds is problematic in two respects, epistemologically and semantically. The privileging of perceptible kinds might be thought to be harmless and understandable, for it is such things that are salient to the human perceptual systems. It is via the properties picked out by these perceptible kinds that we make contact with the world, so why is it an objection to note the privileged role such properties play within an account of content? Epistemologically the problem is this: bifurcationism assumes that our epistemological contact with the world is characterizable in terms of a primitive vocabulary – an observation language. This means that experience reaches out no further than contact with perceptible types. For consider this, the perceptible types represented by narrow content only get their semantic aboutness via their causal contextual embedding, so the official story goes. But if it is the causal theory of reference that is supposed to provide semantic aboutness, why not appeal to the causal story to pick out perceptible types? That is to say, the perceptible types of narrow content are taken from a standard empiricist epistemological framework. It is just assumed that such types are the types that are salient to the human perceptual systems. But why assume this? What if it were the case that our perceptual systems were built to respond to H_2O rather than wetness, tastelessness, etc.? Indeed, given our evolution within an environment that contains water and not the XYZ stuff, it does not seem so extraordinary to suppose that our perceptual systems have evolved a sensitivity to the stuff that is roundabouts, rather than merely a sensitivity to stuff that looks like that which is roundabouts.

The move that needs questioning is the move that takes us from sensitivity to water to sensitivity to water-looking stuff. Without the backdrop of a contentious although familiar empiricist epistemology, the above move is questionable. The backdrop is the idea of a level of content characterizable in terms of a sense-data array. Indeed, if the bifurcationist thinks that truth-conditional content gets into the mind only via the story about the contextual causal embedding of narrow content, would it not save a lot of time and effort to have the perceptible properties defined in terms of the causal sensitivity of our perceptual systems, rather than the phenomenal account that is normally given? This objection does not deny that an account of the causal sensitivity of our perceptual systems will pick out properties or kinds, for causal sensitivity will be defined by the causal capacities of our perceptual systems. And an account of the causal capacities of our perceptual systems will have to pick out features of our systems that instantiate generalities, so the causal capacities will be defined in terms of general properties that the systems are responsive to. All that I am currently questioning is the assumption that the appropriate properties should be those that are epistemologically salient rather than causally salient. The notion of perceptible kinds is the notion of properties that can be epistemologically stripped off the world and that then characterize our observational reports, our sense-data or whatever.

Note that the account of perceptible kinds that is at work in bifurcationism is not motivated simply by the phenomenological assumption that I said was part of Fodor's background set of assumptions. The phenomenological assumption was that we should individuate content from the subject's point of view, for only then do we get an account of content that gives us explanatory purchase on the subject's actions. That assumption is, I believe, correct. The notion of 'point of view' that is invoked in the phenomenological assumption is not, however, the same as a notion of point of view picked out by perceptible kinds. This point is generally missed, but it is of enormous importance. The basic phenomenological idea of a point of view is that of the way the subject is orientated with respect to the environment, where the 'way the subject is orientated' figures in ordinary rationalizing explanations of behaviour. That idea is distinct from the idea that the subject is orientated to the environment in terms of perceptible kinds defined via a traditional empiricist epistemology. In short, we do not have to treat the idea of a point of view epistemologically.[27]

The semantic problem with privileging perceptible kinds is more general, and is, I believe, fatal to the bifurcationist enterprise. If the account so far is correct, the assumption on which bifurcationism depends is that the capacity of a restricted category of general terms to represent is primitive. As noted, the restriction that defines this privileged category is normally understood epistemologically, but even if that were not so, bifurcationism posits a category of predicate terms whose power to represent certain kinds of things is basic. Whatever this category of predicates amounts to, for these terms we are back to a reified model of content. The position is basically Platonistic.

Suppose the privileged category is simple perceptible universals like colour and shape. The bifurcationist is then committed to the idea that contents about such kinds of things (red circular things) can be defined in terms of configurations of entities whose capacity to represent redness and roundness is primitive. What could such entities be? There appear to be only two types of answer to this question. Either the entities in question are arbitrary, and only conventionally related to redness, roundness, etc.; or they are essentially related to redness, roundness, etc. Surely, the latter option is the only viable one for a theory that takes the capacity to represent such properties as primitive, for otherwise we are no better off than the claim that the symbol 'red' stands for redness, and that cannot be an adequate foundation for a theory of content. But if we take this second option, there appears to be nothing that is intrinsically related to redness *in the appropriate way*. Of course, red sense-data, if such things exist, are intrinsically related to redness, for they look red; but that is not to say that a red sense-datum *represents* redness. One can have a red sense-datum, an after-image for example, without representing anything at all.

Neither of the two options before us is satisfactory. Either way, the notion of narrow content is a blueprint model of content in which content is defined over a configuration of entities that enjoys the aboutness of predicate satisfaction. The options concern the characterization of the blueprint. One option is to treat the blueprint as a configuration of entities conventionally related to properties in the environment. That option explains nothing. It is the option that says that the symbol '. . . is red' has content because of an inner symbol '. . . is red' that has content! The alternative option is to treat the blueprint as a configuration of entities, like sense-data, that *look like* what they represent. This option is to ground the representational power of narrow content in the pictorial representational power of patches of sense-data. I do not believe that any current writer would endorse this option, although I suspect that something like it probably lies deep within the assumption that narrow states have content. The problem is really very simple. Once narrow states are thought of as configurations that can be exhaustively characterized independently of that which they are supposed to represent, there is nothing about these states that makes them stand for anything. This problem becomes invisible only because people are prone to take for granted the idea of predicate representation and assume that there is a level of such representation that is primitive. But to assume that is either to give in to a crass reliance on pictorial representation or to give no account at all of what it is to be in a state with representational content. The threat is that we are left with the claim that representing redness and roundness consists in no more than being in possession of a configuration of internal entities that are red and round!

Whichever way the blueprint is understood, the idea of narrow content captures a central Platonistic image, the idea of content definable in terms of an abstract structure of entities, a structure that has absolute truth-values. I argued against the idea of a reified model of content in section 9.4 when considering Frege's sense/reference distinction. Before looking at another kind of bifurcationist model of content, it would be helpful to return to the problem of reified theories of content. We need to unpack the key assumptions that motivate the impulse to treat content as definable as a configuration of entities.

11.6   Concept and Content

We need to clarify a distinction that has been implicit in much of the discussion in earlier chapters of this book. The distinction is between fully codifiable and non-fully codifiable content, although I shall frequently leave out the 'fully'. This should not be misconstrued, for if it is not already obvious, the idea of content that is not codifiable at all is simply not an option. The idea that needs exploring is the idea of a content that is not fully codifiable. There is a powerful set of assumptions that supports the view that all content, or, more accurately, all conceptual content, is fully codifiable. If all conceptual content is fully codifiable, then our model of content will be a blueprint model of content that is capable of supporting internalism. If content is fully codifiable, it is characterizable in terms of the systematic arrangement of the symbols that encode it, and such an arrangement is in principle characterizable independently of the environment. In this section I want to disarm the assumptions that support this view.

Whatever else we think about content, the kind of content that we are interested in is content that stands in rational relations of support to other contents and to actions. We are interested in the content of beliefs. Call these thoughts, as Frege did. Thoughts are structured parcels of information composed of caches of information the reoccurrence of which in different thoughts accounts for the rational connections between those thoughts. So much by way of recap of things that are familiar.

The notion of content that stands in rational relations of support to other contents and to actions is the notion of conceptual content. I take that as definitive of conceptual content.[28] The idea of conceptual content is neutral with respect to the issue of whether or not conceptual content is fully codifiable, despite the fact that many writers employ the label 'conceptual content' for content that *is* fully codifiable. More to the point, such writers introduce the label 'non-conceptual content' in order to capture contents that are not fully expressible with the linguistic resources of the subject, usually because the subject's experience has a content that is more fine-grained than the words the subject has to label that content.[29] This is a mistake, but one that is easily made by confusing the bearer of content with the content itself. For example, the predicate expression

> . . . is red

is the bearer of a conceptual content, but is not itself that content. That, of course, should be obvious, for the expression is only a conventional sign for the content. It is a sign that bears the same conceptual content as the French expression

> . . . est rouge.

Notwithstanding the above point, many writers fall prey to assuming that where there is conceptual content, there must be a bearer of the content that fully encodes it. The disposition to make this assumption is aided by the temptation to use the word 'concept' both for the bearer of content (the sign) and the content itself.[30] I want to clarify the options here once and for all. So let us consider the bare desiderata that characterize a subject in possession of conceptual content.

Call such a subject a thinker. I suggest that the following features are a minimum set of characteristics of thinkers. I list these features in a way that suggests a reification of content entities. I do this for two reasons: ease of expression and in order not to beg the question in favour of the non-reified model of content that I endorse. It should be remembered, however, that when I speak of the rational impact of contents, I mean only that a thinker is subject to the rational impact of sentences, for contents are not entities. I explain the reason for this shortly, but for the moment let us try to consider neutrally a minimum set of characteristics for being a thinker.

If T is a thinker,

(i) T is subject to the rational impact of content.
(ii) The rational impact of a given content C is manifest in T's normative requirement to hold other contents or to undertake action, given C.

(iii)   The normative requirements under (ii) are accounted for in terms of the compositional structure of contents.

(iv)   *T* has the capacity for holding false contents.

(v)   Contents have absolute truth-values.

I take the above five features of what it is to be a thinker as characteristic of the notion of conceptual content. Features (i)–(iii) merely characterize the rational systematicity of content, and are, I take it, as uncontentious as anything I have claimed so far in this book. Features (i)–(iii) ensure that conceptual content is content that figures in reasons for belief or action to which the subject of thought is susceptible. This rules out treating the information processed by sub-personal states that do not figure within the subject's rationality as conceptual content. Features (i)–(iii) ensure that any distinction between conceptual and non-conceptual content must be between contents that figure in the subject's system of reasons and those that do not. This has the effect of ensuring that the individuation of conceptual content is achieved in the context of our account of the subject's rationality, but it demands nothing more than that.[31] The thinker's conceptual capacities are capacities for responsiveness to, and propensity to employ, reasons.

One bad reason for identifying conceptual content with content that is fully codifiable is avoided by the above account of conceptual content. The bad reason would be to think that conceptual content is content composed of concepts; concepts are the content of predicate letters, and, according to Russell's theory of descriptions, we know how to individuate the content of sentences composed of predicates and quantifiers by their syntactic structure. The error in this line of reasoning is the supposition that concepts are the content of predicate letters. The basic notion of concept that flows from (i)–(v) is that of a content component that features in items that can be reasons for belief or action. This will, of course, include predicate contents, but it is not restricted to that. Note that the identification of concept with the idea of predicate content has the consequence, without further argument, that the conceptual content of a demonstrative identification of a colour shade can apply only to the colour word, not to the demonstrative. So, for example, if I think about and refer to

That blue,

the conceptual component would be restricted to the contribution made by the word 'blue' and not that made by the demonstrative. This rules out the possibility that thinking about a shade of blue in this manner might be the exercise of a conceptual capacity. I shall return to this example shortly. For the moment let us note that we should not prejudge the issue about this case in the absence of an account of the individuation of demonstrative contents.

305

It is features (iv) and (v) that prompt the idea that conceptual content ought to be fully codifiable, and that where there is conceptual content, there should be a bearer of that content that fully codes it. Feature (iv), the possibility of misrepresentation, we have noted on many occasions. I have also suggested that the need to acknowledge this does not entail representationalism and the idea that contents can be characterized independently of the environment. This suggestion runs counter to most people's intuitions; for, just as the need for a representative theory of perception is often thought to flow uncontroversially from the need to accommodate the possibility of illusion and hallucination, so it is common to think that a blueprint model of content is required to capture the possibility of misrepresentation. There are, however, alternative theories of perception that accommodate misperceptions without the need for reified representative entities; similarly, there are alternative accounts of thought content that accommodate misrepresentation without the need for blueprints. It all depends on what our final principles of individuation are for conceptual contents. I want to continue to defer defence of an account of content that accommodates misrepresentation without the need for a blueprint theory, because I want to note the way that feature (v) appears to push us in the direction of a blueprint account of conceptual content. For the moment, then, I shall note that feature (iv) is commonly thought to push us in the direction of a blueprint account of conceptual content. I want to show how, in tandem with (v), this pressure can seem irresistible.[32]

Conceptual contents have to be bearers of absolute semantic values, otherwise we get no account of the validity of argument. So, for molecular, whole thought contents, they must possess absolute truth-values. Whole thoughts will have absolute truth-values in virtue of their component contents having absolute semantic values: singular contents will have an absolute assignment of objects, while predicate expressions will have an absolute assignment of extensions. Suppose this possession of absolute semantic values did not hold. It that were so, then if some given content C had the value true on some occasions and false on others, we would have no way of evaluating the validity of arguments in which C figured. To have any account of the validity of argument, we need the notion of repeatable components that recur in premises and conclusion in systematic ways. If a molecular content lacked an absolute truth-value, then it might change value half-way through an argument, rendering the argument invalid.

Now, the need to talk of contents, rather than sentences, having truth-values arises for the familiar reason that sentences, *qua* strings of words, have only a conventional connection with what they represent. It is what is said with the sentence that is true or false, not the sentence itself. This is why we can say just the same thing with different sentences, e.g. 'Snow is white' and 'Der Schnee ist weiss'. Nevertheless, I shall take it that it is constitutive of being a thinker that rational sensitivity to content be manifested in some degree of symbolic manipulation.

It is only by noting a creature's sensitivity to repeated sentential entities (and their sub-sentential components) that we have any evidence that they are creatures with a capacity for argument. I assume, then, that a creature can only be in possession of conceptual capacities if it is in possession of capacities for systematically manipulating symbols. This is why I said earlier that where there is content, there must be some degree of content codifiability. The idea of a conceptual content that was not codifiable at all does not, I am assuming, make sense. The issue that I want to explore is the reason for thinking that content must be fully codifiable.

There are many trivial examples that show that what matters in the construction of a valid argument is that there should be repeatable components that bear absolute values, and that it is the content identified with the repeatable symbolic component that matters. For example,

> Argument 1:
> Bill Clinton is President of the United States of America.
> Bill Clinton is a thief.
> ──
> The President of the United States of America is a thief.

This is not a valid argument if we are using different names in the two premisses. This is, of course, a real possibility, due to the ubiquitous nature of most personal names. The validity of an argument is a matter of syntactic form. Where there is the appropriate formal syntactic structure, there is a valid argument. This requires that we have a well-defined account of the identity-conditions for the items that recur throughout the formal structure of a valid argument. The above example shows that the identity-conditions of the repeatable argument components may not themselves be something definable symbolically, for symbolically we have the same recurrent item 'Bill Clinton', even though it may be instances of two different names. The example looks trivial, but here are two more.
Consider the following:

> Argument 2:
> Water is good to drink.
> The stuff in the glass is water.
> ──────────────────────────────
> The stuff in the glass is good to drink.

For this to be a valid argument, we need to know that the term 'water' in the two premisses recurs with a stable, absolute semantic value. If Putnam is right, we cannot know this without knowing the world on which the premisses are employed. For suppose someone were espousing argument 2 but, after announcing the first premiss, were instantly transported to Twin-Earth. In this case, on Putnam's account, premiss 2 would be false, although the conclusion would remain true.

Furthermore, despite the fact that the conclusion does not now follow from the premises, the thinker would believe that it did and would, as far as she could tell, believe that she had enunciated a valid argument. Here is a more familiar version of the same phenomenon.

Consider this:

> Argument 3:
>   This is good to drink.
>   This is water.
>   Water is good to drink.

For this to be an instance of a valid argument, we need to know that the demonstratives introduce a common bearer of absolute semantic value in both premisses. There are, however, plenty of circumstances in which this would not be the case. Suppose our subject asserts the first premiss after tasting the stuff in a glass perceptually present. Suppose our thinker then loses interest in the glass and goes off to look at other things. Suppose then that premiss 2 is uttered as she faces a different water sample to that which prompted premiss 1. Clearly, it would not then be valid to draw the conclusion on that basis. Indeed, even if she returned to the original glass before uttering premiss 2 and uttered it in full perceptual contact with the original glass, it would not necessarily be enough to render argument 3 valid. To render the argument valid, we need to know that the contribution of the demonstrative is the same in each premiss, and even under the last supposition this is not guaranteed. It all depends on our principles for individuating the content-bearing contribution of perceptual demonstratives.

On the face of it, the above three arguments are cases in which the content required to define the repeatable component necessary to count an argument as valid is not fully codifiable. In each case, the relevant common component is not definable in terms of the symbols employed. Most writers, however, treat these cases as different. The case of argument 1 is normally considered trivial, and the scope for ambiguity regarding shared proper names is thought to be avoidable by the simple expedient of distinguishing different names by some arbitrary device. For example, for purposes of logical analysis we could mark the names 'Bill Clinton$_1$', 'Bill Clinton$_2$', and so on. The phenomenon exploited in argument 2 has not, to my knowledge, been used to raise the issue about validity in this way before, although Dennett considers a similar issue about the constancy of belief in cases of similar switches, and concludes that the ordinary rationalizing notion of belief does not survive the existence of such scenarios.[33] Note, Dennett's response to an argument 2-type case is effectively to give up on the notion of conceptual content as something that has its home in rationalizing explanations of what we do and say. The case of argument 3 is well known, and everyone thinks that demonstratives are problematic. My current interest is in unearthing the reasons that prompt the idea that demonstratives are problematic.

I do not think that demonstratives deserve being cast as the 'bad guys' in reference. Indeed, I suspect that all three cases tell the same story; but to see that, we first have to shake off the impulse to treat all conceptual content as fully codifiable. Part of this impulse stems from the need for recurrent content components. For the above argument schema to have instances that are valid arguments, we need a recurrent component in the appropriate position in the two premises. It is tempting to think that this requirement should be met by positing entities that reappear in the two premises. But this reification is not required. It is one way of securing (v) – that entities bear absolute truth-values – but there is another way. If the idea of a conceptual capacity is tied to content that figures in reasons for belief and action, then, returning to the earlier example of a demonstrative thought about a shade of blue, the conceptual content is well defined without the need for reification. For example, suppose I am looking through colour charts for paint for my home. I fix on a sample and think,

(4)　That blue is fine for me.

I call the shop assistant and tell him that I want a can of that blue as I again pick out the shade in question demonstratively. In this case, my thinking about 'that blue' recurs in my second identification and thought about the colour. There is nothing mysterious about this. It is the most natural and ordinary rationalizing explanation of my beliefs and actions in this situation to see my reference to that blue as the exercise of a conceptual capacity, for it is the exercise of a capacity to recognize and think about that colour in a rational systematic way.

To the above argument it may be objected, 'But what is this conceptual content that recurs in the demonstrative thinking?', and 'How do we individuate it?' The answer, of course, is that I have just individuated it by locating it within the rationalizing explanation of my behaviour. What this reveals is the quasi-behaviourism of the neo-Fregean approach to content. Content is individuated by no more and no less than our best rationalizing explanations of behaviour. But content is not an entity that explains the structure of our behaviour. To say that a subject is in possession of a given content is to say that their behaviour is understandable in a certain rationalizing way that exhibits a rationalizing systematicity to its component structure. At this point, the neo-Fregean account of content is indistinguishable from Davidson's position.[34] To attribute content to a subject is not to attribute possession of a configuration of entities that is then supposed to explain their behaviour. To attribute content to a subject is to say no more than that the best interpretation of their action is one that employs a Tarski-style truth theory employing biconditionals the right-hand side of which involves the ascription of beliefs that makes best overall sense of what the subject is doing. Apply a Tarskian truth theory in the services of interpretation, and you get the best account of what they are about. The singular mode of presentation of a perceptual demonstrative is a posit made in the context of ascription of thoughts that make best overall sense of behaviour.

Generalizing the above considerations provides us with a definitive statement of why conceptual content should not be identified with content that is fully codifiable symbolically. I characterized a thinker in term's of rational sensitivity to contents, but warned that the apparent reification should not be taken literally. Wherever we say that a subject is responsive to the rational impact of content, this has to be understood in terms of their sensitivity to the rational impact of sentences. However, sentences do not, *qua* symbol strings, have rational power. With the exception of sentences that figure in formal languages, such as mathematics, when their rational power is definable in terms of their syntactic structure, sentences *qua* symbol strings are rationally impotent. Of course, if our concern was only with the provision of a semantic theory for a formal language, there would be no problem about the individuation of content, content components, and the identification of the recurrent entities that render symbol strings instances of valid argument schemata. In a formal language, that could be defined in terms of the syntactic arrangement of the symbol strings. But this can only be achieved in the restricted and atypical case of a formal language. Such cases have dominated most of the formal developments in logic and semantics, and I have no doubt that many philosophers have, in the grip of the ease with which formal semantic theories can be constructed, remained blind to the difficulties that arise in the individuation of content once we turn our attention to empirical contents that bear directly upon action and empirical belief. So, it is definitive of a language being a non-formal language that its symbol strings do not, *qua* symbol strings, have rational power.[35]

If sentences *qua* symbol strings do not have rational power, and if we take conceptual content as defined by its being the notion of informational content that is located within the rational systematicity of belief and action, then conceptual content cannot be definable as something that is fully codifiable. If that were possible, it would make sense to say that sentences *qua* symbol strings (in the case of those that fully code conceptual, content) have rational power. It must then follow that in the above minimal characterization of what it is to be a thinker, the idea of being subject to the rational impact of content cannot be fully definable in terms of sensitivity to the rational impact of sentences, for sentences as such lack rational power. The very notion of conceptual content must be definable in terms of the thinker's sensitivity to the rational impact of sentences in a context of use. If sentences as symbols strings do not possess rational power, there is no alternative but to see their rational power as a function of the way they are used, and not merely as a function of their syntactic structure.[36] But this then explains quite simply and naturally what is going on in the case of arguments 1–3 above. Construed as symbol strings, 1–3 provide argument *schemata*; they do not provide arguments. Anything that is an instance of 1–3 will be a valid argument. In all three cases, however, the idea of an instance of the schema is not itself symbolically definable. The idea of *same name* – we must have the same 'Bill Clinton' in premises 1 and 2 of argument 1 – is not a symbolically definable idea, any more than the idea of *same demonstrative* is symbolically definable. But this means that the conceptual content components carried in these cases by the symbols cannot be fully codifiable. In the first example, the rational impact of the symbol string 'Bill Clinton' is not just a function of the string *qua* string of symbols, but of the string *in the context of a socially accepted use*. In the second example the rational impact of the symbol 'water' is not just a function of the letters *qua* symbols, but of the symbols *in the context of use indexed to a particular planet*. In the third example, the rational impact of the demonstrative is a function of the symbols *in the context of use in a perceptually stable engagement with the environment*. In each case we see what I called Russell's insight in operation. The semantic power of symbols (rational power) is grounded in the semantic power of context-sensitive expressions. In the above three cases, the type of context involved is different, ranging from a context defined by social conventions to a context defined by the perceptual presence of objects. The general point, however, is the same. Conceptual content is not fully codifiable. Russell was right.

The above general argument explains the hopelessness of the representational theory of mind and content. Sentences as such lack rational power. The proponent of a representationalist theory of mind tries to find an account of what gives sentences their rational power in terms of the structure of the language of thought, the configuration of the representational entities posited in a representationalist theory of mind. Alternatively, the representationalist who is not an intentional realist tries to account for the rational power of sentences in terms of the causal structure of states responsible for behaviour. Either way, if public sentences as such lack rational power, nothing is gained by turning our attention to the sentences within the inner language of thought, or states individuated by causal role. Both types of representationalist will have to either replicate or reduce the public normative rational power of sentences. Reduction does not work, and replication goes nowhere. Despite this, a representationalist theory of mind of one type or another is the standard option. This is because most writers see no other way of capturing both the ordinary rationalizing explanations of behaviour and the idea that content can figure in ordinary physicalist explanations. It is the attempt to capture both rationalizing and physicalist causal explanations with one type of entity/state that prompts the reification of content which marks a representationalist theory of mind. No wonder, then, that for many writers the option is seen as either following Fodor or following the eliminativist strategy which denies that our ordinary rationalizing form of explanation picks out a genuine form of explanation. There is, however, another option. It is the option of intentional realism without the reification of content – intentional realism without representationalism. Content is not a queer sort of thing that needs to be squeezed into causal regularities. Content is the *way* we causally interact with things. That is the option taken both by Davidson and by neo-Fregean writers after Evans. It is, I believe, the only option that saves the full-blooded truth-conditional idea of content as that which figures in reasons for belief and action. Such an idea of content is not, it seems to me, an option; it is constitutive of our deepest self-conception. It is also an idea of content that, as I have now argued, is ineliminably context-sensitive. It is the idea of conceptual content as not fully codifiable.

11.7 Perry on Indexicals

I close this chapter by briefly remarking on an important and influential attempt to treat indexical contents due to Perry and Kaplan. I discuss Perry's work, but it should be borne in mind, as Perry himself acknowledges, that his account of indexicals is both influenced by and similar to Kaplan's work. Perry and Kaplan have a version of a dual-component theory of truth-conditional content, but they arrive at this model from a study of referring expressions that everyone admits to be context-sensitive: the demonstratives, the token-reflexives of person, place and time. The general picture that they want to endorse goes like this.[37]

Consider a context-sensitive referring expression like the perceptual demonstrative 'this' or 'that', or the token-reflexive for first-person reference, 'I'. These expressions clearly have a linguistic meaning, by which is meant a content that is invariant across contexts. The demonstrative 'this' has a linguistic meaning roughly equal to 'the object perceptually present to the speaker and in close proximity to the speaker'. The first-personal pronoun has a linguistic meaning roughly equal to 'the speaker of this expression'. This linguistic meaning in each case is what Kaplan called the 'character' of the expression. The dual-component nature of the Kaplan/Perry theory of indexicals comes out in the idea that belief content (truth-conditional content) is a function of character plus context. The abstract structure of the account is then the same as that of the dual-component theories of Fodor and Putnam, even if the motivation and categories of expressions are different. I shall not say any more about Kaplan's theory here, for two reasons. First, Kaplan's theory was explicitly developed as part of the attempt to construct a formal semantic theory for a language containing demonstratives. His goal was to regiment and codify the concept of valid inference for such a language. Hence Kaplan was never as explicit as Perry about the connection between doing semantics and explaining behaviour. This is something that, as I have noted on a number of occasions, Perry has always insisted on. Second, Kaplan's theory requires the idea of singular truth-conditions, and this is something that the neo-Fregean requires too. I shall return to the idea of singular truth-conditions in the next chapter; suffice it to remark for now that it is the idea that is central to the neo-Fregean account of thought and reference. In contrast, not only has Perry always insisted that the point of doing semantics was to give an account of content that figures in the explanation of action; he has also continued to attempt to pin down content in a way that implicitly assumes that conceptual content, if not directly fully codifiable, is nevertheless definable via fully codifiable rules for manipulation of codifiable contents. His latest position is to treat the truth-conditional content expressed by a sentence employing an indexical as a function of linguistic meaning plus context, where the context can be specified in terms of rules for applied linguistic usage. In short, truth-conditional content for sentences with indexicals can be defined in terms of the meaning of symbol strings plus rules for the applied usage of symbol strings. Albeit indirectly, this amounts to endorsement of the idea that conceptual content is fully codifiable.

I start with a brief account of one of Perry's seminal papers that prompted work in this field.[38] Perry shows the impossibility of capturing indexical truth-conditional content in a fully codifiable way, although that is not how Perry himself saw the significance of the paper. He starts by outlining what he calls the traditional theory of the proposition. By 'proposition' he means thoughts as Fregeans understand them. So I'll use 'thought'. Thoughts are (i) objects picked out by 'that-clauses' – e.g. when we say 'Sally believes that Harry is embarrassed', the clause 'that Harry is embarrassed' stands for a thought; (ii) thoughts have absolute truth-values; and (iii) we individuate thoughts with a degree of fine-grainedness sufficient to provide rationalizing explanations of behaviour. The idea of content involved here is that of conceptual content as I have defined it. Next Perry considers the following situation.

Perry is shopping in his local supermarket and spots a trail of sugar leading around the shop floor. He thinks that someone has a leaking bag of sugar in their supermarket trolley. Now suppose that it is Perry's trolley that contains the leaking bag of sugar. Perry's central observation is that if he is to recognize that it is he who is making the mess in a way that gives him a reason for attending to the bag in his trolley, it is essential that he comes to think about himself with the indexical 'I'. He must come to think, 'I am making the mess'. It would not, for example, be sufficient to think 'The bearded Californian philosopher is making the mess', unless he also thinks 'I am the bearded Californian philosopher'. Similar thoughts apply to any descriptive way of thinking about the person who is making the mess. Whatever description '*d*' comes to Perry's mind, if he is to have a reason for reaching into his trolley, he must think 'I am *d*'. The need to think of yourself indexically in order to have reason to act is, I believe, correct. It captures the intuitive idea that being an agent, as opposed to being something acted upon, is to have a point of view or perspective upon how things are. Having a point of view requires the capacity to think indexical thoughts, for they characterize your point of view.[39]

If the indexical way of thinking is essential for agency, however, Perry's worry is that 'the essential indexical is a problem for the doctrine of propositions'.[40] Perry expresses this worry by saying:

> The sentence 'I am making a mess' does not identify a proposition. For this sentence is not true or false absolutely, but only as said by one person or another. . . . So the sentence by which I identify what I came to believe does not identify, by itself, a proposition. There is a *missing conceptual ingredient.*[41]

In the light of the discussion of the previous section, this is a revealing quotation. Perry's worry is that he cannot individuate the proposition sententially; the sentence has, he thinks, a missing ingredient. Furthermore, he calls the bit that he thinks is missing a conceptual ingredient. He assumes that a conceptual ingredient is something that ought to be fully codifiable within the sentence. If that were so, the sentence would suffice to individuate the proposition. That it cannot do so is, so Perry thinks, the problem with the essential indexical. To sum up, indexical thoughts are essential for an understanding of action, but they are not identifiable sententially.

The second part of Perry's claim is, in light of the previous section, simply not a problem. It is only because Perry is implicitly assuming that conceptual content must be fully codifiable that he sees a problem with the essential indexical. The diagnosis that I offered in the last section of why people think that conceptual content should be fully codifiable applies to Perry. The second characteristic of the traditional theory of propositions is, he says, that they have absolute truth-values, and that is one of the characteristics of thought that I identified as prompting the assumption that conceptual content must be fully codifiable. This is a mistake. Perry's problem in this paper is structurally identical to the problem which many people have with demonstratives.

In the previous section I argued that thinking about a demonstrated shade of blue can be the exercise of a demonstrative conceptual capacity just in case the thinking plays the standard role within rationalizing explanations of behaviour. The same point could be made in the case of Perry's example in the supermarket. Perry thinks that if we concentrate on the sentence

(5) I am making a mess,

we will conclude that there is a missing conceptual ingredient. But if the use of 'I' to refer to self plays the systematic role within the subject's own rationalizing explanations of what they are doing, should we not conclude that the use of 'I' is, just like the use of the demonstrative in 'that shade of blue', the exercise of a conceptual capacity? The key thought that makes this option available is simply the idea that conceptual content individuation should be anchored in our rationalizing explanations of behaviour; and, so anchored, it does not require that the systematicity of reasons has to be mirrored in the systematicity of a language. The space of reasons is not a linguistic or a linguistically identifiable space.

Many writers find the idea that we might disconnect the idea of the systematicity of reasons from the systematicity of a linguistic system as mysterious and methodologically problematic. It looks to be mysterious, for it requires that we understand the systematicity of reasons (the rational power of content) *sui generis*. No explanation is given or can be given of rationality. This looks methodologically suspicious, for it appears to leave no constraint on how we describe the systematicity of reasons. The last worry draws attention to the idea that the systematicity of reasons is not constrained by language to the degree that it is fully describable in language; but it does not follow from this that it is unconstrained. And anyway, the systematicity of reasons is constrained in a way that just about everyone ultimately acknowledges; it is constrained by our ongoing attempts to make sense of ourselves and others.

The above concerns are legitimate, but I think they are defused by the following thought. As writers like Perry attempt to individuate conceptual content linguistically, what they are attempting to do is to provide an individuation based on linguistic meaning plus rules for applied linguistic usage that will capture the pre-theoretic idea of content that is located within our rationalizing explanations of behaviour. To repeat, Perry is emphatic that the idea of belief content is the idea of that notion of content that figures in rationalizing explanations of behaviour. So Perry accepts that the idea of conceptual content that I have been outlining is a legitimate idea. His task is to try to capture that idea as a function of linguistic meaning. The central problem for Perry then amounts to whether he can write rules of applied linguistic usage that are capable of capturing the rationalizing notion of belief content without presupposing that very notion. At the end of the day, I believe that this is not possible. Furthermore, without endorsing a representationalist theory of the mind, it becomes unclear what is lost by giving up on the aspiration to treat conceptual content as fully codifiable. Let me conclude this chapter with a brief account of why I think Perry's project must fail. I develop the point in more detail in the next chapter.

Perry's strategy is to adopt a dual-component theory of truth-conditional content in which he distinguishes between belief states (what is characterized by linguistic meaning) and beliefs. The former are what we have in common if we all use the sentence 'I am making a mess' to think something about ourselves. Perry captures this by saying that we are in the same belief state. However, we all express different beliefs when in this belief state. So 'belief state' is like Kaplan's idea of character. Perry's task is to define belief as a function of belief state plus rules for applied linguistic usage. This enterprise becomes problematic when we consider dynamic thoughts. Dynamic thoughts are thoughts that persist through time as we keep track of objects and ourselves and, they are beliefs that persist through changes in linguistic expression. For example, we can keep track of a meeting in the sequence of beliefs:

(6)   The meeting will begin,

(7)   The meeting is beginning

to

(8)   The meeting has begun.

A simpler example would be a whole belief of a perceptually present object towards which we are moving that remains constant and that is variously expressed by

(9)   That is my coat

and

(10)   This is my coat.

In both cases we have a sequence of linguistic expressions that, pre-theoretically, we take to be expressive of a common belief/common belief component. The need for a common content flows from the need to see the agent's behaviour as rationally organized. The behaviour has a rational unity through time. Perry's task is to define rules for the modulation of belief states (the linguistic expressions of belief) that capture the constancy of content through time and/or spatial movement. Such rules need to pick out sequences of belief states that hang together rationally. Perry's problem is that there would appear to be no general rules for collecting together sequences of such states that do not appeal to the very idea of belief content that he is trying to define. The reason for this is that bare rules of applied linguistic usage covering modulation of tense or modulation of demonstrative expression from 'this' to 'that', or vice versa, must not be so coarse-grained that they end up attributing to us an idealized rationality. If you are in the belief state expressed by (6) at time t_1 where the meeting is due to start at $t_1 + 10$ minutes, then it is a rule of applied linguistic usage that the correct way to express a thought about the same meeting in 11 minutes' time will be with the belief-state (8). It does not follow as a matter of rationality that someone who had the belief expressed by (6) at time t_1 will have the belief at $t_1 + 11$ minutes, for they may have simply lost track of the time, or forgotten which meeting they were in, etc. The rules of applied linguistic usage must, then, be more fine-grained than simply encoding the grammatically correct principles for modulation of belief expression through time and spatial movement. There must, however, be some such modulation, or else our beliefs would never survive beyond the moment of their first articulation, and we could then make no rational sense of our behaviour through time or spatial movement. In the absence of an appeal to the grammatically correct principles for modulation of belief expression, any attempt to specify rules of applied linguistic usage will have to appeal to our pre-theoretic idea of belief and the way we take our behaviour to hang together in rational segments across time and space. But this means that Perry will have to employ the very rationalizing concept of belief content that he is supposed to be trying to define in a codified way. If this is right, the worry that divorcing conceptual content from linguistic meaning looks mysterious and methodologically suspect evaporates. There is no alternative to employing the idea of conceptual content that I have been defending if we are to fit content to the project of rational self- and other-understanding.[42]

12

Contextual Content

12.1   Introduction

The obvious objection to the account of conceptual content that I have defended throughout this book is to say that it amounts to no more than a lazy description of our pre-theoretical concept of belief content. The divorcing of the individuation of content from linguistic principles of individuation might capture our ordinary rationalizing explanations of behaviour, but because this is merely descriptive of our common-sense habits of belief description and behaviour explanation, it cannot amount to a theory of content. Furthermore, whatever difficulties beset the representationalist theory of content in particular, and the attempt to codify conceptual content in general, at least such accounts offer a theoretical regimentation of our ordinary practices of content ascription and behaviour explanation. At best, the account that I have been defending amounts to a descriptive phenomenology of our intentionality. It does not amount to a theory of intentionality, let alone one ripe for bringing our intentionality within the purview of a naturalistic account of ourselves and our cognitive abilities.

This is a powerful objection. It demands a response. In this final chapter I meet this objection and, along the way, provide some detail of the structure of a neo-Fregean account of content. My response to this objection is twofold. First, although the neo-Fregean approach endorses a kind of phenomenological description of our intentionality that, of itself, is not a problem. As I indicated in chapter 1, before we can offer a theory of content that shows how content can be found a place within a broadly naturalistic world-view, we need an accurate description of the phenomena in which we are interested. Second, the descriptive enterprise engaged in by a neo-Fregean account of content is no 'mere' description. If it looks as if it can offer no more than homely reminders of something very familiar from our common-sense understanding of belief ascription and explanation and behaviour, that is a mistake. Once we get right the underlying principles of the neo-Fregean approach, it becomes evident that the metaphysical picture needed to make sense of the approach has profound consequences for how we understand what it is to be a creature possessed of intentionality and the capacity for conceptual thought. The neo-Fregean account is a radically externalist account of content. It is an account that has the subject of thought as essentially an embodied subject with an orientation to its environment.

The underlying metaphysical image of the Cartesian subject was an image of the subject of thought as a *spectator*, an entity with the power to survey the configuration of inner symbols possession of which constituted its intentionality. That image is barely changed when the configuration of inner symbols changes from a spectral array of ideas to entities within the language of thought, or states within a neurophysiology. The most up-to-date physicalist has a large Cartesian inheritance.[1] The underlying metaphysical image that replaces the Cartesian spectator model of the subject of thought is the image of the embodied *agent*, a subject whose intentionality consists not in its capacity for surveying and rearranging its inner symbols, but in its capacity for acting in and manipulating the world. This is the move from the idea that possession of content amounts to possession of inner symbols to the idea that possession of content amounts to possession of the world. The way we possess the world is by being embodied agents responsive to the world's impacts upon us and with the ability to impact on it.

The shift in metaphysical imagery here is not idle; neither is it a shift that leaves our descriptive phenomenology of content divorced from the prospects of a naturalized account of intentionality. This shift provides novel options for naturalizing content. It is a shift that brings thought and content into the world, not by the convenience of causal chains that connect inner entities/states to the outside, but by giving a phenomenology of content that has content constitutively in the world.

I start by reviewing the basic Fregean principle for the individuation of content, and show why this has to be understood in a way that is ineliminably context-sensitive, such that the contents that it individuates are contextualized contents. I then cover the account of demonstrative thoughts provided by neo-Fregean theory, before examining the question as to whether singular thoughts are object-dependent. Having done this, I will then be in a position to show how a contextualized treatment of singular thoughts can provide a nuanced account of perceptual misrepresentation. In the final section of the chapter I show how the neo-Fregean account, far from closing off further avenues of theoretical enquiry because of its alleged descriptive character, offers a rich vein of ideas to be explored in understanding our intentionality and consciousness in general.

12.2   The Intuitive Criterion of Difference

The basic principle for individuating content that Frege repeatedly appeals to is what Evans calls the intuitive criterion of difference. It took Evans's work for people to realize that the Fregean criterion was applicable to context-sensitive singular terms, like perceptual demonstratives. What I now want to argue is that this criterion was always employed in a context-sensitive way. The criterion is:

> **Intuitive criterion of difference:** Sentences S_1 and S_2 express different contents iff it is rationally possible for a subject to understand both and assent to one and dissent to the other.

There are two aspects of this criterion that need amplifying. First, the criterion gives no indication of the temporal boundaries of the test of rational possibility of differential assent/dissent disposition. Second, the criterion leaves implicit our grasp on the non-temporal boundaries of what constitutes a rationally possible pattern of assent and dissent to sentences. These omissions make the test appear simpler to apply than it really is.

The first omission concerns the temporal boundaries to the idea of rational possibility. Evans formulates the criterion with an indexing to a time.[2] That, however, fails to provide a marker for the boundaries of rational possibility that apply to the persistence of content through time. There are two separate points about the temporal boundaries of rational possibility. The first is that without some indication of time, the criterion would not permit counting

(1)   Hesperus is bright

and

(2)   Hesperus is bright

as expressing different thoughts if the sentences were considered by the subject at different times. It is, however, rationally possible to assent to this sentence when considered in your youth and, many years later, dissent to it simply because you have lost track of what Hesperus is, or have mistakenly remembered what it is, etc. It is not a demand of rationality that once you have assented to a sentence, you should always do so. To insist that the criterion applies to the possibility of differential assent/dissent to sentences *at a time* removes this problem about the temporal boundaries of rational possibility. A temporal indicator is required in order that the individuation of content across time is not too broad, for without it the limits of rational possibility would be fixed merely by the individuation of the sentence as a type of symbol string. If, however, we leave the test indexed to a time, we run the danger of making the individuation of content too narrow.

The relativization to a time means that the criterion does not allow that differential assent/dissent is measured across time insensitive to changes in the subject's informational matrix across time. By indexing the test to a time, we remove that problem. The second point about the temporal boundaries of rational possibility is untouched by this, however; for we need some marker to indicate the rational persistence of assent/dissent, without which we run the risk of having thoughts with no temporal persistence at all.

The problem is sharpest with singular thoughts employing perceptual demonstratives that persist through time and through systematic change of expression. Suppose a subject is visiting an art gallery and, on entering a room, assents to

(3) That's a Canaletto,

and then, keeping their eye on the work, proceeds to move quickly across the room to study the picture close up. On arriving in front of the picture, the subject assents to

(4) This is a Canaletto.

In such circumstances, it is not rationally possible for the subject to have differential assent/dissent with respect to these two sentences. If, on reaching the painting, they had discovered that it was a Guardi, then that would mean that they had been mistaken with their assent to (3) on entering the room. This means that there is a single thought that persists through time and through the change in linguistic expression. This is a dynamic thought. It is an example of an important class of thoughts that is central to our actions and conception of ourselves as creatures occupying space and time with a capacity to move through space keeping a track of ourselves and the objects that surround us.[3] Without further information about the temporal boundaries of rational possibility, we have no way of individuating such contents.

There is need to consider how we measure the persistence of contents through time and individuate them in a way that is neither too broad nor too fine. I shall leave this problem of the temporal boundaries of rational possibility until later, for we can get some purchase on it only after addressing the issues about the non-temporal boundaries of rational possibility. For the moment, bear in mind that the temporal boundaries of rational possibility need to catch our intuitive idea of the way our behaviour falls into rationally cohesive sequences. For example, the visitor's movement across the room in the art gallery forms a unified sequence; there is a rational narrative unity to their actions. The bottom line on content is that it is that which figures in the rational explanation of behaviour. Therefore, when our behaviour exhibits a rational unity across time, so too must the contents that rationally explain the behaviour. It is because there is a persisting content that the behaviour hangs together through time as a rational unity.

The second class of indicators that are absent from the intuitive criterion of difference are non-temporal indicators. For example, much like the case of (1) and (2), it is rationally possible to assent to

(5) Bill Clinton is a thief,

and dissent to

(6) Bill Clinton is a thief,

just in case one of these sentences employs the name of the President of the USA and the other employs the name of someone else. Because of the ubiquitous character of personal names, there is always going to be a problem about how we measure rational differential assent/dissent to sentences employing proper names. What constitute the boundaries of rational possibility in such cases? I suggest that the answer here can be no more than to say that it is social convention that provides a contextual indicator of name, and hence of thought boundaries. In chapter 10 I remarked on the existence of what I call the famous name convention, whereby, in the absence of other contextual indicators, the use of a name borne by a famous person is always taken to be a use of that famous person's name. In other words, if in assenting to (5) you were not making reference to the President of the USA, then to fail to provide some indication of this fact is misleading. Note, however, that there are plenty of circumstances in which an explicit indication is not required. Suppose you are drinking in an establishment frequented by the other Bill Clinton and are reviewing his character with a bunch of his cronies. In such circumstances it is not necessary to do anything other than assent to (5) to make your point.

It might be objected that the above contextualization of the boundaries of rational possibility of assent/dissent for sentences employing names is guilty of confusing the tasks of semantics and pragmatics. In chapter 2 I suggested that Strawson's and Donnellan's criticisms of Russell's theory of descriptions confused pragmatic and semantic issues, and the point could now be applied to the current suggestion. The case, however, is different. For sure, the contextualization of name identity, and thereby also thought identity, is not semantic if by 'semantic' you mean something capturable within a formal theory of the properties of signs. But, as I remarked in discussing this matter in chapter 2, Russell's notion of meaning is not of 'sign meaning', but of the meaning of a sign in its *standard pattern of use*. The contrast between semantics and pragmatics as it arose in chapter 2 was the contrast between the standard use of signs and those uses that override standard patterns of use.[4] The idea of semantics that I have repeatedly appealed to and defended is the idea of the theory of that which figures in rational explanations of behaviour. The idea of sign meaning, if there is such a thing, is not the appropriate notion of meaning for semantics as I have defended the business. Signs as such have no rational power. It is only in the context of standard patterns of use that signs have a rational power. Therefore, the contextualization of the boundaries of possibility of assent/dissent for sentences employing names does not confuse semantics and pragmatics. The contextualization is required in order to get the appropriate notion of semantics off the ground.

I summarize the above by saying that the boundaries of rational possibility for sentences involving proper names are marked by the boundaries of a *conversational context*. The point about drinking with the other Bill Clinton's cronies is that it is your participation in a conversation that renders the need for explicit indicators that the President is not being talked about redundant. Of course, when the conversation ends and you go out in the street, some explicit indication is required in order to avoid a dangerous ambiguity. I expressed this before by saying that there is a famous name convention. The point of that convention can now be expressed by saying that, with famous names, it is implicitly assumed that we are all, in principle, party to an ongoing name-using practice. In the absence of an indication to the contrary, the use of a name borne by a famous person is taken as a naming of that person. Conversations are datable uses of name-using practices. Conversations about the famous bearers of a given name are always taken as the default conversation. If you want to talk about someone else who bears the same name, you have to signal that you are starting a different conversation. Such signalling can be stated explicitly, or it can as often involve the deployment of further contextual information – a nod of the head indicating the reprobate Bill Clinton slumped boozily in a chair in the corner of the bar.

The idea of a conversation to which I am appealing is not something that is definable explicitly. If that were the case, then sentences as such would possess rational power, and there would be no need to use the idea of a conversation in the way I have just suggested. The idea of a conversation is essentially the idea of a contextually sensitive item. Conversations are datable exchanges between particular people engaged in rational activities. Conversations are things that are identified in part by the name-using practices involved (cf. sect. 10.6), but this does not mean that we can identify a name-using practice independently of the conversations in which it appears. The reason why there is no priority between the concepts of conversation and name-using practice is because neither concept is definable explicitly, let alone definable in terms of sequences or patterns of symbol use. A conversation is a contextually defined item, as is a name-using practice. Conversations are contextualized things because they are ultimately grounded in the demonstrative use of language, which anchors both the use of the names employed and also the participation in the conversation.

The first kind of anchoring is something that most writers acknowledge. For example, causal theorists want a notion of communication chains, in order to characterize the observed division of linguistic labour – recall the discussion of Kripke and also of Devitt and Sterelny in section 10.5. Such division of labour is grounded in the reference of primary speakers, those to whom everyone else party to a conversation about Bill Clinton defers. It seems uncontentious to add that the relationship in which primary speakers stand to the referred object is a perceptual one; that is what gives such speakers primacy. But, as I argued in chapter 10, the perceptual relation must itself be understood as an informational relation, and not merely as a causal one. The information made available by perceptual contact with an object is fundamentally contextual; it is the kind of information conveyed in perceptual demonstrative utterances. Our conversations about Bill Clinton defer to the person who is prone to say 'That's my Bill'! The point is obvious. It does, however, draw out deep metaphysical implications for our conception of what it is to think of an object. The point could be rephrased by saying that our capacity to think of an object is grounded in our capacity to think of it as the sort of thing of which we could say 'That's it'. Reference to a particular is grounded in the capacity to refer demonstratively.

The last way of expressing the contextualized character of conversations is due to Strawson, who stressed the way in which our capacity for thinking about a material object depends on our capacity to locate it within the single uniform spatial environment that spreads out from the environment of demonstratively presented objects roundabouts.[5] Singular reference is grounded ultimately in our capacity to have demonstrative thoughts about things. It is demonstrative reference that provides the particularity to a singular reference. If our reference were not grounded demonstratively, it would be subject to massive duplication. This is characteristic of descriptive thinking in which we think of a kind of thing, something that could be multiply instantiated. In singular thought, however, we think of a particular. Demonstratives also provide the second kind of anchorage that conversations require, an anchorage of participation.

If you are at a party in which a large number of people are engaged in linguistic exchanges, some of those exchanges constitute conversations, and some constitute background noise. Which is which is not a function of the symbol sequences employed, for another group may be using the name 'Bill Clinton' but not be party to your conversation about the President – same name-using practice, but a different conversation. Similarly, a group of people who are also talking about the President (like your group, they defer to the demonstrative references of Hillary Clinton) are not thereby party to your conversation. Indeed, even if another group are at time *t* agreeing on some point about Bill Clinton (e.g. the number of states he won in the 1996 presidential election), that would be of interest to your conversation at *t* as you and your group disagree about this matter; again there are still two conversations at play, not one. Nothing changes even if we assume that both groups are at the same precise point of dispute about the size of Clinton's 1996 victory. What distinguishes the two groups, regardless of the similarity, relevance or otherwise of the information about Clinton with which they are dealing, is simply the fact that the exchanges of one group have no rational bearing upon those of the other. In a conversation, you adjust your linguistic outputs to the rational power of the outputs of others. If there is a group of people at the party whose outputs have no rational power over your own, then they are not participants in your conversation, even if they are dealing in information that is relevant to your conversation. The participation in the conversation is determined demonstratively by the perceptual fix you have upon those whose outputs rationally bear upon your own.

Of course, others can rapidly enter your conversation, and whole conversations can merge by the simple expedient of the recognition by participants in one conversation that another is dealing in the same information. But even in that case, the merging of conversations is contextually circumscribed. For even if you over-hear a salient bit of information about Bill Clinton and bring its producer into your conversation, you still have to ascertain that they were talking about the right Bill Clinton. That, of course, is something we ordinarily do not bother with in the case of famous names, but that is because with famous names we work with the convention that we are all, in principle, party to the same name-using practice. If the name involved is not a famous name, the need to check that the other people are talking about the same person is obvious. What that check amounts to is a check that the other people defer to the same stock of demonstrative thoughts held by the primary thinkers/referrers.

Even in the case of proper names, the boundaries of rational possibility invoked in our use of the intuitive criterion of difference are contextualized boundaries governed by demonstratives. The intuitive criterion of difference for proper names could then be rewritten as.

> **Intuitive criterion of difference for proper names:** Sentences S_1 and S_2 that are constituents of a single conversation express different contents iff it is rationally possible for a subject who is party to that conversation to understand both and assent to one and dissent to the other.

The test of rational possibility is contextualized to a social entity, a conversation. That entity is itself a contextualized entity, because of the way it is fundamentally shaped by the use of demonstrative reference, both to ground the name-using practice and to identify participants in the conversation. That being so, we need an account of what constitute the boundaries of rational possibility in the case of sentences employing demonstrative reference.[6]

12.3   Egocentric and Objective Conceptions of Objects

The account of demonstrative thought individuation that I want to sketch is taken from Evans.[7] The structure of the account is fundamentally of a piece with the above account of the individuation of thoughts expressed with proper names, but it makes explicit one feature of the above account that normally goes unnoticed. I shall start by drawing out the feature in question from the previous section.

The idea of a conversation in section 12.2 was the idea of that which controls the subjective use of a proper name. Amplifying further the previous discussion of the social character of sense given in section 10.6, we need to distinguish between the preliminary dossiers of information that participants in a conversation bring to their thinking about the named person and the information that the primary thinkers possess that governs the constitution of a conversation. We could say that the distinction is between the thinker's egocentric conception of the object and the controlling objective conception provided by participation in the conversation. Recall that the preliminary dossiers of information are to be thought of not so much as packages identifiable independently of the conversation, but as the *way in which you are connected to a conversation.*[8]

In the absence of the egocentric conception, we would not be dealing with a thought that characterized the way a subject was oriented towards the object, the subject's point of view. That is to say, we would not have something whose basic role lay in its position within the subject's rational economy. Recall the moral shared with Fodor, that we want the idea of the subject's point of view in order to get a rational handle on how things are for the subject. This is what the egocentric conception of the object does. Without the objective conception of the object, however, we would not have a conception of the object that provided the conception of what it would be for a thought to be objectively true/false. To see this we need to return to the generality constraint first discussed in section 1.5.

The generality constraint flows from a basic idea of what it is to think a thought, where the idea of a thought is the idea of something susceptible for evaluation as true or false. If you are thinking

Fa,

your thinking about *a* must exhibit a generality such that you understand what it would be for other predicates to be true of *a*: you must understand what it would be for *Ga, Ha*, etc. to be true. Similarly, your thinking about *F*-ness must admit a generality such that you understand what it would be for other things, *b, c, d* . . . to be *F*. In both cases, the requirement of generality flows from the idea of what it is for the original thought to be true. Let us concentrate on the case of thinking about the object.

The requirement that your conception of *a* admits a generality is the requirement that your egocentric conception of *a*, as it were, latches on to an objective conception of *a*. Your egocentric conception must acknowledge a controlling idea of the object, a way that allows that, as it were, you could hold the object still in thought and vary the predicates true of it. If you are really thinking that *a* is *F*, then you are thinking about an objective entity and thinking of it that it is *F*. But then you should, in principle, be able to separate it in thought from your thinking that it is *F*, for only then have you genuinely got a conception of the thought being objectively true or false.[9] If you can single out your thinking about it independently of your thinking that it is *F*, then your conception of the object can be thought of as something that can recur in other thoughts you have, and this means that we then have a grasp of what it would be for your thinking of *a* to occur in arguments. By 'single out', I do not mean 'factor out', where that entails an atomistic conception of the sense of '*a*'. On the contrary, to single out an object in thought is to have the capacity to think other things of it than that it is *F*. Singling out is a grammatical notion concerned with the normative systematicity of thought; it is not an atomistic representationalist idea.[10] It is by your thinking about the object being the sort of thing that can feature in arguments that we get the basic form of semantic control upon thought. What I am thinking at any point is determined by the inferential systematicity of its connections with other thoughts.

Now, unless your egocentric conception of the object gives you the ability to think of the object under an objective conception, you will not have the capacity to single out the thinking about the object that is required for an objective evaluation of a thought as true/false. We need the egocentric conception in order to capture the subject's phenomenology – the idea of the subject's point of view. We need the objective conception in order that the subject's thought be a thought about an objective item – a thought subject to truth and falsity. The egocentric conception and the objective conception are not, however, alternative conceptions. It is not that you could have an egocentric conception without having an objective conception, or vice versa. The point is that the egocentric conception is a special way of thinking of the object, the way that characterizes the subject's phenomenology. It is, nevertheless, a way that must be controlled by an objective conception, or else it is not subject to semantic evaluation. The objective conception provides the fundamental idea of the object; it is the idea that fundamentally individuates the object concerned and provides the conception of what it is to hold the object constant while varying the predicates that might apply to it.[11]

In the case of personal proper names, the above structure applies in the following way. A subject's egocentric conception of an object is their preliminary dossier of information that characterizes the way in which they are part of a conversation. The objective conception of the object is the idea of the object that the primary thinker possesses. This means that the fundamental idea of the object is the individuation of the object by the primary thinker. The fundamental idea of Bill Clinton is Hillary Clinton's idea of him. For personal proper names, the distinction between egocentric and objective ways of thinking of the named object has intuitive appeal. It is less clear that the machinery of distinctions currently in play fits other examples of proper names. For example, in the case of proper names of countries, towns and cities, it is unclear that the notion of a fundamental idea of the object can be clearly defined. This does not mean that there is no such thing as an objective way of thinking of a town; it simply means that there is no well-defined general conception of what such a fundamental idea of a town is. The objective way of thinking of a town is something that can evolve during the course of a conversation, and a conversation can last a very long time!

For other cases, the concept of a fundamental idea and its role in separating the egocentric conception from the objective conception of an object is clear. Take the case of numbers and our names for them. An egocentric conception of a number will be the way that a given subject thinks about it in virtue of their preliminary dossiers of information. The objective conception of a number, which the egocentric conception must be answerable to if it is to be a thinking of something that can be singled out of the information contained in the egocentric conception, is controlled by the fundamental idea of a number. The fundamental idea of a number is the idea of a number's position in the number line, something definable in terms of the basic axioms for the generation of numbers.

The reason we picked on the idea of primary thinkers in the case of personal proper names was that such people have direct perceptual contact with named object. It is their capacity for demonstrative thinking about the object that controls the conversation and provides the objective framework for individuating the object. The short answer to why the referential apparatus of proper names is context-sensitive, then, is that the apparatus of proper names is grounded in the demonstrative reference of the primary users of the names. This model then presupposes an account of demonstrative reference. Such an account will have to say what the use of perceptual demonstratives is grounded in. To summarize, an egocentric conception of a named object is grounded by the thinker being in a conversation, where that in turn is grounded in the demonstrative thinking of the primary thinkers. We now need to know in what the egocentric conception of a demonstrative thinking is grounded. The answer that I believe is not only correct, but of enormous significance, is that the egocentric demonstrative conception of an object is grounded by the thinker being in the world. We have to be in conversations to use names, but we have to be in the world to use demonstratives. This marks the radical externalism at the root of the neo-Fregean conception of reference.

12.4 Demonstrative Thoughts

Evans's account of demonstrative thoughts bears close study. The broad outline of his conception is relatively easy to state, although I note some of the areas for disagreement as we proceed. One area of contention is the object-dependency of Evans's account of singular senses. Many people find this counter-intuitive. Now I have already argued in section 11.6, that object-dependency is required in order to give singular terms a role to play in the fundamental notion of semantic evaluation – the truth and falsity of whole thoughts. I called that argument the semantic argument for object-dependency. I think it is correct. Nevertheless, many people think that the idea of object-dependency conflicts with the best account of perceptual error and the sorts of thoughts that perceptual error sustains. The idea of empty singular terms is thought to be shown possible by the existence of illusions and other forms of perceptual error. So, despite the semantic argument for object-dependency, there is a need to show that the neo-Fregean has something worthwhile to say about perceptual error and the thoughts that it sustains. I shall show that the neo-Fregean not only has something worthwhile to say about such cases, but that the object-dependent theory provides rich resources for giving a complete and sophisticated account of the thoughts that perceptual error sustains.[12]

The account of demonstrative thoughts fits the model of the previous section. In demonstrative thought about a material object there is both the egocentric conception of the object and the objective conception in virtue of which the former offers a way of thinking of the object subject to objective truth and falsity. Evans's notion of the egocentric conception of the object is handled by his idea of the subject's *informational link* with the object.[13] There are aspects of the idea that are contentious, so let me first state its general role.

The idea of an information link with an object marks the fundamental difference between a demonstrative thought and a descriptive thought. In a demonstrative thought, the way you think of the object is determined by the way you are in perceptual contact with it; your thought is controlled by your perceptual experiences. A demonstrative thought is one which is determined by your perceptual states, and not by your reflective cognitive states. The latter might suffice for an account of descriptive thoughts, but not for demonstratives. So far, then, the idea of an information link marks the perceptual dependency of demonstrative thoughts. The egocentric conception of an object in a demonstrative thought is a perceptual conception.

For Evans the perceptual dependency of the information link guarantees that demonstrative thoughts are object-dependent, for you cannot have a link to something that is not there. Evans does not see this as problematic, for he holds that all sense is object-dependent. As he puts it:

> It is really not clear how there can be a mode of presentation associated with some term when there is no object to be presented.[14]

This means that there cannot be thoughts that are perceptually dependent, yet empty. It is this aspect of the object-dependency thesis that strikes people as wrong. Why couldn't you have an illusory demonstrative thought, just as Macbeth has when he refers to the dagger before him?[15] Nevertheless, Evans's point is stronger than it seems. Macbeth has a thought that is perceptually dependent in the sense that it is determined by the state of his perceptual system. However, because his thought is illusory, it is tempting to think that you could characterize the informational state of his perceptual system independently of the environment. If this is possible, then such an informational state will be a descriptive state. That is to say, in the case of an illusory demonstration of an object, although the subject may think that he is having a demonstrative thought, he is not. He is really having a descriptive thought of the form 'There is a dagger before me', rather than the demonstrative 'This is a dagger'. This means that the neo-Fregean will treat the putative empty demonstrative thought as belonging to a different category of thoughts – the descriptive. This looks to be a striking consequence of the neo-Fregean theory, although it is a feature of a number of forms of externalism. Because the singular demonstrative thought is object-dependent, the subject's authoritative knowledge of what thoughts he or she has is as fallible as the knowledge of the objects the thoughts are about. The mind is no longer transparent, but opaque. It is as opaque as the world that the mind thinks about.[16]

The idea of an information link thus introduces into the neo-Fregean conception of the mind two features that superficially look puzzling. First, it renders the mind opaque and places the neo-Fregean under some obligation to account for the phenomenology of the apparently authoritative character of self-knowledge. It makes knowledge of the world appear easy, but at the price of making self-knowledge problematic. In such thoughts we gain the world, but stand to lose our minds. You might think that this reversal of fortunes from the traditional Cartesian framework is a bonus. Second, the information link, as Evans understands it, means that demonstrative thoughts are object-dependent.

To say that Evans holds that demonstrative senses are object-dependent is not to say that he thinks that the demonstrated object is a constituent of the thought. His conception of thought is still Fregean; it is not like the idea of propositional content employed by Kaplan. Evans's concept of thought is anchored in the idea of how things are for the subject, where that picks out the subject's phenomenology. The point is that it is a condition of the phenomenology being the way it is in a demonstrative thought that the object exist. The configuration of your mental layout depends upon the world having an object at the right place. Thus the perceptual dependency of demonstrative thoughts means that they must be understood relationally. The perceptual contribution to the thought cannot be peeled off the world and treated independently of the world. A demonstrative thought is, according to Evans, one in which we are perceptually orientated in the world. This externalism is brought in by the objective conception of the object.

For the egocentric conception to amount to a thinking, it must enable the subject to exploit the generative capacity of thought. The egocentric location of an object must locate the object in a way that enables you to single out the object in thought and be able to think things about it other than just that it is present before you. As Evans puts the point, if I am having a demonstrative thought about an X, I must be able to make sense of the idea that that X is the same one that I saw yesterday. But to do that, I must be able to conceive of what it would be for just that X to be the one that I saw yesterday. My thinking of an object as 'That one' must bear inferentially upon other thoughts. But for this to be so, I must know how the 'that' picks out something that is relevant to the semantic evaluation of those other thoughts. My 'that' must give me an ability to single out the object and think other things about it. To do this, my 'that' must be grounded in an objective conception. So, an egocentric location of an object is only a location of an object if it is possible to impose an objective way of thinking upon the egocentric location. The objective conception provides the fundamental idea, the fundamental ground of difference, for material objects. Now, the fundamental ground of difference for material objects is spatial location at a time. No two objects of the same kind can occupy the same place at the same time. What fundamentally distinguishes two identical chairs, even if they are alike in all observable respects, is their distinct spatial paths through time. If you are thinking of one particular object rather than merely an object of a kind (and to think of a particular is to have a singular thought about it, e.g. a perceptual demonstrative thought), then to think of that object, rather than merely of one that looks the same, is to have your thinking controlled by your conception of what it is for the object to occupy a unique spatio-temporal track.

For Russell, a demonstrative thought was constituted solely by its egocentric element, the way things looked to the subject. Russell's demonstrative thoughts were constituted by the arrangement of inner items within a Cartesian theatre model of the mind. This is problematic in two respects. First, it means that Russell has to take for granted that his egocentric conception of the object is a conception that has content, that it stands for something. Taking that for granted is constitutive of what I called Russell's semantic Cartesianism. Second, the primitiveness of Russell's idea that such an egocentric conception succeeds in standing for things turns on the atomic character of his egocentric conception. It is because Russell's conception of the egocentric conception is atomistic (piecemeal) that it has no grammar, no role to play in the systematic connectedness of thought. In contrast, it is because, for Evans's neo-Fregean account, truth is taken as the primitive semantic concept, that reference is understood in terms of the role singular terms play in thoughts that are true/false. Evans's account of demonstrative thoughts is an account similar to Russell's in broad structure, save for the denial of the atomism. Demonstrative thoughts are grounded in our grammatical conception of that which is independent of will – the egocentric conception is grounded in the objective because the type of acquaintance involved in the former is a notion of acquaintance that is not disengageable from the truth-orientated structure (grammar) of whole thoughts. That structure is the structure of the way we are in the world.

For Evans, the egocentric conception of the object is grounded in the metaphysics of our conception of the world as extending around us in space and time, with objects possessing unique spatial paths through time. It is by having a conception of an object as occupying a unique spatial path through time that you can single it out in your thinking and understand what it would be for the object to satisfy predicates other than the ones that currently apply to it.

Evans's account can be summed up by saying that a demonstrative thought about an object requires an egocentric conception (perceptual dependency) that picks out an object the fundamental idea of which invokes our conception of the world of items whose spatial occupancy at a time provides their fundamental ground of difference. Evans says:

> One has an adequate idea in virtue of the existence of an information-link between oneself and the object, which enables you to locate that object in egocentric space. (That the idea is adequate depends on your ability to relate egocentric space to public space.)[17]

Note that egocentric space is not a different space to objective public space. Talk of egocentric space is talk of the way that we perceptually engage objective space. Note also that objective space is not the same thing as absolute space. There is no requirement that you be able to think in absolute terms about spatial location in order to have your thought controlled by an objective conception. The point of the objective conception is that it gives you the conception of what it is to single out the demonstrated object as something that exists independently of your perception of it. So the conception of objective space is not a conception framed in a special vocabulary that prescinds from the egocentric point of view. It is a conception of space that can be framed in just the same vocabulary with which we express the egocentric conception – the vocabulary of perceptual demonstratives and also token-reflexives of person, place and time.[18] All that is required is that the objective conception provide the resources to grasp what it is for the object to exist unperceived. The objective conception arises, then, when we grasp what it would be for a demonstrated object conceived of egocentrically as 'That object' to be the sort of thing that will still exist if we take our eyes off it, for it to be the sort of thing for which a variety of predicates could be true.

It might be objected that the above account shows only the need for an objective *conception* of space and the material objects that populate space in order for demonstrative reference to work, but that it does not need the actual existence of the spatio-temporal framework. This is wrong. To think that you could, as it were, give an account of demonstrative reference with a mere understanding of the objective conception of spatial relations between material objects, regardless of whether or not spatial relations exist, would be to assume that demonstrative reference is indexed to the availability of an account of the spatial world independent of the existence of the spatial world. But the idea of detaching a conception of objects existing in space and time in this manner is the idea of detaching a representation of objects in space and time independently of their existence. It is the idea of the conception of the spatial framework of objects as a meta-description that provides the ground for demonstrative reference. If this account made sense, the argument about the need for a fundamental Idea of an object as an objective conception of the object that controlled the egocentric conception would be no more than an argument for a complex kind of internalist model of demonstrative reference. On this account, it would be a *representation* of the spatial framework that is required for grounding egocentric location of objects, rather than the existence of the spatial framework.

The above looks to be a natural objection to make to the externalism of the neo-Fregean theory. It does not, however, work. The objection only seems to work by thinking of the objective conception of an object and the egocentric conception as separate conceptions, as if objective space and egocentric space were two different spaces. On the neo-Fregean account, the egocentric conception of objects never drops out of the picture, for it is the conception that ensures that the account is an account of thought. The egocentric conception is there to ensure that with demonstrative thoughts we are dealing with thoughts that are perceptually controlled. But it is this egocentric element of the demonstrative thought which shows that the thought cannot be individuated symbolically, and therefore that it cannot be individuated internalistically. It is the 'thatness' of a demonstrative thought that is captured by the egocentric conception of object location, thinking of an object as just there, that one, etc. It is the egocentric conception of object location that points outward. The objective conception, the idea that what you are pointing to in a demonstrative thought is genuinely an object, serves to ensure that the pointing is

333

anchored in the right sort of way. It is anchored in something that can be singled out of your thinking and re-emerge in other thoughts. This is the generality constraint that, in thinking that a demonstrated object is a blue pen, you must be able to make sense of the idea that the very same pen could be the one that you were given last Christmas by a favourite aunt. That conception exploits the idea that the demonstrated object has a continuous spatial path through time in virtue of which you make sense of the idea that the currently perceived item is the same as the one that came gift-wrapped last year.

To detach the objective conception as a mere representation, a theoretical structure that represents the spatio-temporal framework, would be to leave it unable to perform the role required of it: namely, that it underwrite the location achieved from within the egocentric conception. Detach the objective conception in the manner suggested, and it is incapable of integrating with the egocentric conception, for the latter is essentially something that is not definable symbolically. Furthermore, it is not possible to have a representation of objective location that is detachable from the egocentric location of perceptual demonstratives, for any such detached objective conception would be subject to the problem of massive duplication. The objective location in terms, say, of co-ordinates of eastings and northings as in maps, does not provide the particularity of reference required. It provides a general type of location that requires anchorage by the egocentric location of a perceptually controlled demonstrative thought. The objective conception of objects gives us the idea of particular objects only in so far as the objective conception is anchored by the egocentrically controlled demonstratives. But the egocentric conception on its own is also insufficient.[19] Detach the egocentric conception from an account of demonstrative thoughts, and we no longer get an account of thoughts that have the characteristic hallmark of perceptually dependent thoughts. The whole point to the neo-Fregean treatment of demonstratives is to resist the bifurcationism implicit in the objective canvassed. A demonstrative thought is not a dual-component entity. On the neo-Fregean account a demonstrative thought is, if you like, a two-sided beast. It is both something individuated by its place within a subject's rational economy and something the individuation of which is accomplished by reference to the spatio-temporal framework of the perceptually sampled environment. A demonstrative thought is a contextualized content, not an amalgam of a content plus context.

The boundaries of rational possibility at play in the intuitive criterion of difference when applied to demonstrative thoughts are boundaries drawn not by social entities as in the case of proper name thoughts. In the case of demonstratives, the boundaries of rational possibility are shaped by how things stand in the world. What is rationally possible with regard to patterns of assent/dissent to sentences employing perceptual demonstratives is a function of our grasp of how things are in the environment. This is why, in the example of the demonstrative sentences about the Canaletto (section 12.2), the test for the rational possibility for assent/ dissent turns on what is going on in the environment. The case would be different if, after assenting to (3) on entering the room, our subject took an indirect path to the painting, which involved her losing sight of it along the way. In such circumstances, it is rationally possible to dissent to (4) without it entailing a re-evaluation of the assent to (3) on entering the room, for it is possible that in the interval someone has switched the paintings or, more likely, that our subject has simply lost track of which painting it was she first spotted on entering the room. That is to say, it is consistent with the ground-floor conception of objects as things with unique spatio-temporal tracks that, on considering (4), our subject understand the thought that the demonstrated object lies on a track distinct from the one spied earlier. In the case where she keeps the object in perceptual contact, this is not possible.

The example shows the way in which the egocentric location of an object as 'that one' is controlled by the ground-floor conception of how the world works and of how it is basically a world of spatio-temporal particulars each with a unique spatio-temporal track. This provides a theoretical fine-tuning to cases that superficially look similar. The use of demonstratives when viewing objects over closed-circuit TV links, or the use of demonstratives to pick out the city you are in when, for example, you say, 'This is a fine city', are not genuine demonstratives. The first case – for example, the demonstration of an object located on a distant sea-bed by a remote-controlled camera – is not a genuine demonstrative, for the egocentric location is not integrated with an ability to objectively locate the object. The information link exists (there is an egocentric 'thisness' to your thinking), but the link does not provide you with a fundamental idea of the object unless you know how the space viewed by the camera is integrated with the space at the viewing screen. In this case, the apparent demonstrative reference to, say, a fish in the ocean depths, is really a disguised descriptive reference along the lines, 'The fish whose image is being presented to me . . .'. In the case of the apparent demonstrative reference to a city, it is the egocentric location that is absent.[20]

Both egocentric and objective conceptions of the object have to come together for there to be demonstrative thoughts. The former is indicative of the kind of mode of presentation at play (perceptually dependent in the case of a demonstrative); the latter is indicative of the fact that the thinking is answerable to semantic evaluation as true or false. It is because these two aspects are both required and cannot be separated from one another that the idea of demonstrative senses has been poorly understood. Most people assume that where there is content, there are representations, but without a separation of these two aspects of demonstrative senses, there is no scope to treat demonstrative content in a representationalist manner. Notwithstanding the lack of a representational talisman to bear the demonstrative content, the idea of a demonstrative sense is well-defined. What is well-defined is something that, by orthodox representationalist lights, looks a thoroughly queer sort of entity. The demonstrative thought is not a representation. It is something that combines the egocentric point of view of the subject and the objective location that controls the rational possibility of assent/dissent from that egocentric point of view. Nothing that is answerable to both sets of features can be individuated sententially. This means that you cannot conceive of demonstrative thoughts as representational items that stand between perceptual input and the output of action. The only way to conceive of such things is therefore in the quasi-behaviourist manner I employed earlier (cf. section 9.4). The idea of mode of presentation is not, then, definable as a set of sentences with which the subject confronts the world. The idea of mode of presentation must be understood as an *orientation*. The concept of orientation captures both the egocentric notion of the subject's point of view and the objective conception of the object's location in space and time.

Consider the case of a demonstrative thought that persists while you keep perceptual track of an object. Keeping track of a physical object is a matter of preserving an information link with the object in perception in such a way that it is not rationally possible to adopt different attitudes to your demonstratively expressed sentences about the object. For example, suppose I pick out an object perceptually and demonstrate it with a 'This'. If I keep perceptual contact with the object as we move apart, then although my demonstrative thought changes expression from a 'This' thought to a 'That' thought, it remains one and the same thought. Suppose I hang my coat on a peg and walk away from it but keeping my eyes on it. Although the sentences change from, for example,

(7)   This is my coat

to

(8)   That is my coat,

the thought remains constant, for under the supposed conditions it is not rationally possible to assent to one of these sentences and dissent from the other. If the circumstances were changed so that I took my eye off the coat as I moved, then it would be rationally possible to have different attitudes to the sentences and hence, by the standard Fregean test, there would then be two thoughts, not one.

The principles at work in the neo-Fregean treatment of such dynamic thoughts reflect the two-sided character of neo-Fregean theory. The intuitive criterion of difference is met with two complementary constraints. First, the notion of what is rationally possible is a notion of rational possibility from the thinker's point of view. This is a notion of how things are for the thinker; it is not merely an account of how things are.[21] The relativity to the thinker's point of view is essential to the neo-Fregean picture. That is the egocentric constraint. Second, the notion of rational possibility is constrained by our underlying metaphysics, the role that our ground-floor conception of objects and their causal powers plays in the explanation of experience. The continuity of experience as I walk away from my coat with my eyes fixed on it is explained by the continuing causal power of the coat. Short of positing magical coats, etc., there is no rational space for assenting to one sentence and dissenting from the other.

The individuation of the thought is both phenomenologically sensitive and responsive to our ground-floor conception of how the world is.[22] The responsiveness to our conception of how the world is, is a responsiveness to our 'best account so far' of how the world is. That is, it is still *our* account of the world that supplies the constraint here; it is not the world in itself. And because the account of the world is the 'best account so far', this allows for a dynamic thought to persist over small breaks in the information link. For example, my demonstrative thought about my coat will persist even if my line of sight of the coat is broken by someone walking across my perceptual field.[23]

On the neo-Fregean account, the mapping of the structure of thought is a mapping of a phenomenology. It is a phenomenology, however, that is mapped neither by introspection nor by the structure of language. The constraint imposed on the mapping of the thinker's point of view is the ground-floor metaphysical conception of the world. The structure of the thinker's point of view is a map of the cognitive import of their informational engagement with the world. The map of the informational engagement with the world is a map structured by a notion of a rational perspective upon the world constrained by the underlying metaphysics of the world thereby engaged. A neo-Fregean thought is something that characterizes our perspective upon the world; it has its roots in our egocentric point of view. This perspective is structured by a notion of what is rational within this point of view, where the notion of rational amounts to: rational with respect to the best ongoing account of how the world is. The rational structure of the thinker's perspective is not measured as 'rational with respect to linguistic meaning', for the collection of sentences with different linguistic meanings as expressions of a persisting dynamic thought is measured with respect to the ongoing egocentric point of view of the subject. It is because of this that a dynamic thought, like the thought about the perceptually demonstrated coat, has a principled individuation. The individuation is measured by the rational possibility of assent/dissent to various sentences; it is not individuated by the sentences themselves.

The intuitive criterion of difference for demonstratives will then have to go like this:

> **Intuitive criterion of difference:** Sentences S_1 and S_2 express different contents iff it is rationally possible for a subject who is perceptually in the world to understand both and assent to one and dissent from the other within that ongoing encounter.

The phrase 'perceptually in the world' is no metaphor. For the case of proper names, the boundaries of rational possibility were marked by the subject being in a conversation. In the case of demonstratives, the boundaries are marked by their being perceptually in the world. The integration of egocentric and objective frameworks that is required for demonstrative senses means that the idea of being perceptually in the world cannot be reduced to a notion of perceptual information that could be factored out of your engagement with the world and treated independently of the world's existence. It is because the idea of mode of presentation as orientation can only be understood relationally that the idea of being perceptually in the world has to be taken literally. The ability to think perceptual demonstrative thoughts requires the perceptual embedding of the subject in the world of spatio-temporal particulars. Such thoughts are not to be modelled as configurations within a language of thought, an inner system of representations that stands between perceptual input and action output. Such thoughts must be modelled as systems of orientations with respect to the environment. Evans says:

> A thought about a position in egocentric space . . . concerns a point or region of *public* space in virtue of the existence of certain indissolubly connected dispositions on the part of the subject, to direct his actions to that place, and to treat perceptions of that place as germane to the evaluation and appreciation of the consequences of thought.[24]

The systematicity of the connected dispositions directed to a place is the systematicity of our orientations. That is the systematicity of thought.

12.5 Singular Thoughts, Object-dependence and Perceptual Error

It is a consequence of Evans's treatment of singular thoughts that they are object-dependent. This means that it is possible for a subject to think that they are having a singular thought when in fact they are having a descriptive thought. This will always be the case when a subject hallucinates an object and attempts to have a perceptual demonstrative thought about it. I noted above that this consequence is not fatal to the overall theory, although many people find it surprising. Surprise is not an objection. In the light of the account sketched in the previous section of demonstrative and, especially, dynamic thoughts, we can now see some of the options available to the neo-Fregean for handling illusory cases.

For the representationalist, cases of perceptual error are all pretty much the same. You have the representation in mind that stands for the object, yet the object itself is absent. For the neo-Fregean, matters are more complicated, in a way that explains a number of features of thought in cases of perceptual error that for the representationalist remain puzzling. Consider, first, the simple case in which Macbeth hallucinates a dagger. On the basis of his perceptual experience, he says

(9)   That's a dagger,

but the demonstrative expression fails to pick out an object. He says (9) at time t_1. Suppose that the illusion vanishes almost immediately, and at t_2 Macbeth acknowledges that there is no dagger. Call this a level-1 illusion, for the putative demonstrative is only employed momentarily. So, at t_2, Macbeth agrees

(10)   There is no dagger.

Now, if the thought expressed by (9) contains an empty demonstrative, what bearing does his acknowledgement of (10) have upon (9)? It is not clear how the representationalist could answer this question. There are two problems here for the representationalist.

First, once the illusion has gone, what is left of the empty demonstrative thought that Macbeth supposedly had at t_1? If the empty demonstrative thought component is an entity, like the entity required by representative theories of perception to account for perceptual content, once it has gone, what could be left of the thought? If there is nothing left of the thought or, at least, not that part left, how does acknowledgement of (10) bear on his thinking at t_1, for that thinking has simply disappeared? Second, if the putative demonstrative component somehow survived the loss of perceptual experience so that the thought continued, there is no way that the putative thought expressed by (9) can be inferentially related to the thought entertained with (10). The putative demonstrative at (9) is supposedly empty. If it is empty, it provides no point of contact with the component structure of the thought expressed with (10). We want to be able to say that Macbeth's realization of the truth of (10) is what makes him realize that his thought at (9) was false. But this is not possible, for apart from anything else, the error involved in (9) is not falsity; it is atomic error. The supposed thought entertained at t_1 does not even make it to the stage of being true or false, for the demonstrative component lacks an object. (10) is the negative existential thought

(11) $\neg \exists x \, Fx$,

which contradicts any thought of the form

(12) Fa.

The trouble for the representationalist is that the supposed empty thought expressed by (9) at t_1 is not of the form of (12), for the supposed error in (9) on the representationalist view is not that the object a is not F; it is the idea of atomic error in which (9) fails because the demonstrative fails to pick anything out. Even if we grant the representationalist the assumption that the thought at t_1 can be individuated sententially, and so acknowledge that there is something of the form of (12) simply because there is an internal sentence of that form, this still does not help. For it remains the case that the idea of an empty demonstrative means that the error in that thought construed as internal sentence is still the wrong sort of error to be entailed by (10). Of course, if the demonstrative succeeded in picking something out, matters would be different.

Suppose Macbeth picks out a teaspoon, and calls it a dagger. If that is what he did at t_1 his thought then would be rendered false by the acknowledgement of (10) in the standard way. But in that case, he does not have an empty demonstrative; he has one that picks something out (the teaspoon), and he falsely applies the predicate '. . . is a dagger' to it. But that case is not an illusion at all. It is a case of perceptual error, not an illusory case. It is straightforward mistaken identity.

How does the neo-Fregean fare in these cases. Take the level-1 illusion. The neo-Fregean has to say that Macbeth does not have a demonstrative thought at t_1, even though he says he does. This means that he cannot be fully authoritative regarding his own thoughts, but that alone is not necessarily problematic. The obvious option is to say that the subject is having a descriptive thought rather than a singular one. The subject's report that they are having a singular thought is then treated disjunctively as a case either of having a singular thought or as having a descriptive thought. We still get the conclusion that the subject loses authority with respect to what thoughts they enjoy. Such a disjunctive account of thought would be compatible with the approach McDowell has taken in the treatment of perceptual experiences. But it is not the only option, for it all depends on the kind of descriptive thought we think is available to the subject in the illusory case.[25] For example, one option would be to say that the thought that Macbeth has at t_1 is descriptive, but with an embedded demonstrative reference to a place. So at t_1 he is thinking

(13)   There is a dagger *there.*

In effect, this option treats the level-1 illusion as a case of mistaken identity. Macbeth identifies a place and ascribes to it the property of having a dagger at it. There will be some types of illusion where this option is plausible, cases in which the subject's perceptual experience gives them an orientation to a particular place in front of them. In such cases, the suggestion offers a simple account of the connectedness of thinking at times t_1 and t_2, for at t_2 Macbeth thinks that there is no dagger there, so his error at t_1 is the simple falsity of a subject/predicate thought. What connects the thoughts over time is the common component of the demonstrative way of thinking of a place. At time t_1 he thinks that there is a dagger there, at t_2 he comes to realize that this is false.

Now consider more complex errors. Consider the case of illusions that support dynamic thoughts. Again, if it is an illusion and no object is present, the dynamic thought will still have to be about a place, not an object; but it introduces a theoretically distinct class of cases. Call these level-2 illusions. What distinguishes them is that they are perceptual experiences in which the subject's disposition to say (9) persists through some degree of both time and spatial movement. Some illusions can be like this; they can be resilient to a considerable degree of change of head position, etc. In such cases the subject keeps a fix on the place where the supposed object is perceived to be. The subject is tracking a place, not an object. Once again, the neo-Fregean can allow that the thought Macbeth really has from t_1 to the time when the illusion fades, and across movement from place to place, is a descriptive thought with a well-defined dynamic demonstrative identification of a place. As in the previous example, the error of the thinking, once light dawns, is easily explained in the ordinary sort of way. When Macbeth realizes he has been hallucinating, he does so because he thinks of the very same place that it is empty. Indeed, it will often be the case that one comes to this realization by extending one's dynamic thinking of the place to the point where, on passing one's hand through the space, one realizes it is empty. In such a case, in which the dynamic thought about the place persists through time from the onset of the illusion to veridical experience, the connectivity of one's thinking at the latter point to that at the former is the simplest kind of connectivity possible – that in which the two thoughts are connected by having a common component. At the later time one thinks

$$\neg Fa,$$

where during the former period one thought

$$Fa.$$

The difference between the level-1 and level-2 cases is the difference between cases where 'a' is a momentary demonstrative and cases where 'a' is an ongoing dynamic way of thinking about a place.

There are three lessons to be drawn from the above. First, the neo-Fregean has the apparatus to make discriminations between different categories of perceptual error that do justice to real phenomenological differences between different strengths of illusion.[26] Second, in having the resources to make these discriminations, the neo-Fregean is able to offer an account of the systematicity of thought over time, and to show how the thought available on realization of the perceptual error is inferentially connected to the thought ascribed to the subject when under the illusion. That is something the representationalist simply cannot do. Third, although the neo-Fregean has to acknowledge that the subject can get self-ascriptions of thought wrong, the mistake need not be so gross as to confuse a singular thought with a descriptive thought. The mistake need only be a mistake about whether the thought was singular with respect to a place or singular with respect to an object. Once that option is admitted, I think our intuitions about what Macbeth was really thinking at t_1 become less clear. The claim that he was really having a demonstrative thought about a place does not seem to me to involve such a fundamental correction to his own self-ascription. The fact that there is some redescription of the subject's self-ascription merely shows that the kind of phenomenology (the account of how things are for the subject) involved in the neo-Fregean position is not driven by introspection. It is a content-driven phenomenology. It is not concerned with qualia or with how things authoritatively seem to the inner gaze of the subject. There is, for the neo-Fregean theory of content, no such thing as the inner gaze. There is only the outward orientation to the world. And that is the sort of thing about which subjects can, at times, be mistaken.

12.6   Agency and the Practical Turn

If perceptual error can support dynamic demonstrative thoughts about places, because the subject is orientated to a place even if it is empty, is there anything more that we can say about what it is to have a demonstrative thought (or a dynamic one) about an object, other than that the place is non-empty? In other words, if the neo-Fregean can allow a sophisticated sort of thinking that looks close to object-directed thinking, what more is required to turn this into object-directed thinking? Obviously, the extra required is that there is an object at the place, but what does this amount to? It can sound like an odd question, for what else does there being an object at that place amount to other than that there is an object there? But recall, for the Fregean the idea of reference is not primitive; truth is. Reference is not explicable independently of our account of the role of singular terms in the formation of true thoughts. What, then, is the basic idea of the standard use of genuine singular terms?

For Russell, the answer to this question was that the standard use of a genuine singular term was the use in which the term was controlled by the ostensive attention of the mind upon an object. I called this semantic Cartesianism. It is not a plausible answer. The representationalist, in contrast, has no answer to this question; for the representationalist will either take for granted that singular terms have the ability to stand for things, or they will characterize what I am calling standard use in terms of causal connections between the singular term and object. The former option is the one that Brandom castigates when he says that representationalists give no account of the 'representingness of representings'.[27] I have repeatedly argued that the causal account fails to capture the normative idea of grammar, or standard use. If this is correct, we need an account of the distinctive grammar of demonstratives. What is the distinctive standard use of demonstratives?

I have argued that we should understand modes of presentation as *orientations*. This is a relational concept. It is the concept that makes explicit the radical externalism of neo-Fregean theory. But I have also allowed that we can have orientations to places in addition to objects, so we need an account of what makes the latter orientations distinctive. The latter type of orientation is the primitive variety, for I take it that an orientation to a place is possible only against the backdrop of orientations to objects. We triangulate places on the basis of our orientations to things. So we need an account of what an orientation to an object is. I think the answer to this question is deceptively simple. If it is correct, it marks a sea-change in our fundamental conception of what it is to be a thinking subject. The answer is this:

> The distinctive standard use of demonstratives is a use grounded in our capacity to act upon objects and, in turn, be acted upon by them.

This claim amounts to the idea that the standard use of demonstratives is a use in which their inferential role includes their role in thoughts about our capacity to touch objects, manipulate them, be obstructed by them, and so on. The idea is intuitively plausible; but, more than that, it is grounded in the foundations of our metaphysics.

The idea is plausible because the standard difference between an illusion of a dagger and a demonstrative thought about a dagger is that the former is revealed by the fact that the place to which our thinking is orientated offers no resistance to our movement. Or consider an example I first used in chapter 1 in articulating the idea of the canonical commitments of a judgement. What fundamentally distinguishes a thought about an object

(14)   There is a table there

and a thought about how things look,

(15)   It looks like there is a table there?

343

The difference is that the latter thought is not rendered false by the realization that the space is empty and that the appearance was generated by a hologram, whereas the former thought is. To engage the thought at (14) rather than merely the thought at (15) is to be committed to holding true various claims about how your movement will be impeded, how the movement of other objects will be impeded (coffee cups do not fall directly to earth when placed in this space), etc. The former impediments are the basic. The impediments to action are more basic than the impediments to other objects because of the fundamental role for the egocentric conception in the neo-Fregean account of thought. This is why the above thesis is not only plausible, but grounded in the heart of Fregean theory and metaphysics.

Objects are individuated in terms of their capacity to impede other things.[28] But in terms of thought, thoughts are always *our* way of engaging with the world. As I have noted on a number of occasions, in the Fregean account the subject of thought never drops out of the picture. It simply will not be an account of thought if the egocentric conception is not part of it, but it is not a part that is separable from the objective conception. The two are sides of the same thing, the way we are related to the objective world. This is why the fundamental structure of thought is a structure delimited by the structure of our actions upon the world and it upon us. The subject of thought is not, *contra* the Cartesian model that still informs representationalist thinking, a *spectator* of an inner theatre of ideas, representations, sentences in a language of thought, etc. The subject of thought is fundamentally an agent.

This means that the structure of intentionality is not a linguistic structure. Descartes thought that, and so have most people from the seventeenth century to the present day. In part this has been motivated by the idea that we must disengage thought from the world. That motivation is licit, but all it requires is the disengagement of molecular error – falsity. It does not require the disengagement of atomic error. Our demonstrative orientations are fundamentally distinguished by the way we orient to objects by acting upon them. The structure of intentionality is not, then, a linguistic structure; it is the structure of our orientations. Or, better, it is the structure of our practices. By 'practice' I do not mean anything specifically social. The concept of practice is simply the molecular analogue to the concept of orientation. Our orientations to objects, especially in dynamic thoughts, persist over time. They are integrated into other orientations. A practice is just the integration of orientations over time.

The shift represented above is the shift from what was called the linguistic turn in philosophy to what we might call the practical turn.[29] This shift changes the basic metaphysical categories in which we think about how we fit in the world. It is a change from the spectator to the agentual model of intentionality. One of the great benefits of this shift is the way that it makes visible a concept of practice and practical know-how that is not merely descriptive of socially constituted ways of doing things. It has been a recurrent theme in contemporary philosophy to try to retreat from an individualistic account of basic philosophical concepts – meaning, morals, truth, knowledge, etc. – to an account that emphasizes the practical understanding of these ideas. But so often this move collapses in a limp description of social behaviour that threatens to dissolve into an unstable relativism. Aside from the major metaphysical reorientation that the agentual account of content offers, it also offers a fresh way of understanding the practical and seeing how the practical is rooted not in the social, but in the way the individual relates in thought to the world.[30]

The chief benefit of the agentual turn, however, is the way that it thoroughly reshapes options in the philosophy of thought, the way it reshapes our approach to basic issues about the mind and intentionality. I have only indicated the outline of some of the options that need exploring. Explorations in this area are only just beginning.[31] The neo-Fregean approach offers a shape to contemporary philosophy of thought that, although sharing deep insights with founding figures like Russell and Frege, stands to close the twentieth century with a rebuttal of our Cartesian inheritance that is genuinely distinct. The agentual account of content brings thought into the world not via the device of causal connections, but because thought can occur only in creatures who find themselves in the world in their actions.

The agentual turn also offers a distinctive starting-point for the naturalization of content. If you adopt representationalism, the problem about naturalizing content is the problem of showing how physical entities can have normative properties. That problem looks insoluble, unless you invoke a special category of entities. That's what Descartes did, and no one wants to go back to Descartes. So how can physical entities have normative properties? The answer that is now visible from the agentual account of content is that they cannot! Physical *things* do not have normative properties; but that's all right, for thoughts are not entities according to the agentual approach. An orientation or practice is a way in which we act on the world. We act causally. How else could we do it? So for the agentual approach, our thinking lies in the pattern of our actions, where actions are causal encounters with the world. The normativity of thought is the normativity of the pattern/ structure of our causal encounters. So we do not need to say that physical things have irreducible normative properties. Nor do we need the extravagance of saying that queer non-physical things have these properties. We say that the patterns of our causal encounters with the world are irreducibly normative. This is a non-reductionist physicalism. There is only physical stuff connected together in standard causal ways. Some of the patterns that physical things, like us, get into are normative patterns. Normativity is a property of our patterns of causal encounters, not of queer non-physical things. That is a restatement of the quasi-behaviourism about sense that I first formulated in chapter 9. This is a form of naturalism; for, after all, what could be more natural than being a creature with the capacity to interact with the world causally?[32]

It might be thought that the agentual move of this last section involves a verificationist privileging of the sense of touch. The distinctive grammar of demonstratives is grounded in our capacity to act on things and them on us. But why this privileging of touch? For sure, we find out that a space is empty when it offers no resistance to touch, but is it not verificationism to take this as constitutive of the grammar of demonstrative reference? I think not. Touch is a privileged sense modality, but only for the simple, good reason that it is fundamentally through this modality that we act. We act causally, by pushing things around, and they push us back. When we push things around in patterns of pushes and shoves that are irreducibly normative, we are thinkers. That is what being a thinker comes to. At the fundamental level of thought, our thought cannot be detached from the way we manipulate the world. It cannot be treated as if we manipulate only symbols. The answer to our opening question, 'What is it to be a possessor of content?', is not, then, that we possess language; it is that we possess the world.

Notes

Chapter 1   Methodologies

1   There are at least two different problems of misrepresentation. I distinguish between them in ch. 7 and explore them in chs 9–11. A starting-point for contemporary discussion is Dretske, 1986.

2   Compare Fodor, 1985, 1987; Stich, 1992, for whom intentional realism includes a reification of belief. The reification occurs in order to meet a constraint that demands that beliefs figure in causal explanations of action and other beliefs. I prefer to keep these matters separate.

3   Fodor, 1987, introduction and ch. 1.

4   E.g. Fodor, 1987; Davidson's work, e.g. his 1984; Perry, 1988, which defends the individuation constraint against Wettstein, 1986. Bilgrami, 1992a, traces the individuation constraint back to Aristotle. The individuation constraint is central to Fregean theory, cf. below, chs 8–12.

5   As noted, the constraint that representations figure in causal explanations is central to Fodor's work, but see also Stich, 1992, for a clear statement of the role played by this constraint.

6   McGinn, 1989, p. 133: 'what happens at the causal nexus is local, proximate and intrinsic: the features of the cause that lead to the effect must be right there where the causal interaction takes place. Causation is the same with minds as it is with billiard balls. Their effects depend upon local properties of these entities.'

7   A causal powers account of the semantic properties of representations must then be representationalist in my sense, for it means that representations can be characterized independently of the environment; cf. Cynthia Macdonald's 'introduction' to the section on individualism in Macdonald and Macdonald, 1995, for a clear statement of this view.

8   Fodor's (1985) is still an excellent guide to literature on mental representation and the hotly contested distinctions between different kinds of physicalist theories of representation. All the fuss about whether to characterize psychological states linguistically or functionally is irrelevant to the way I set up the options. What matters is whether or

not, if you are an intentional realist, you are also a representationalist. That issue rarely gets raised, because virtually everyone is a representationalist of sorts, and most of the noise to date has been about what kind of representationalism is viable. I do not think any of them are viable.

9   Fodor, 1987, is still an excellent starting-point for Fodor's position, but see also Fodor, 1990, 1993.

10 Clark, 1988, calls these the descriptive and the engineering levels. I prefer 'constitutive', for 'descriptive' suggests an enterprise that ignores facts about the kind of creatures we are, biologically and psychologically. Although the constitutive task is descriptive, it need not be undertaken in complete disregard of scientific theory, and it need not be wholly a priori.

11 Cf. Quine, 1960; Dennett, 1987b, 1991a, 1993; Stich, 1983, 1990; P. M. Churchland, 1995; P. S. Churchland, 1986. Those who try to make the intentional work physicalistically include Fodor, 1987; Dretske, 1988, 1995a, 1995b, Jacob, 1997. Davidson is often classified as someone who has abandoned intentional realism, e.g. in Fodor, 1985. This is because he denies the reification of beliefs which I treat as a separate thesis that defines representationalism rather than intentional realism. There are deep affinities between Davidson's position and the neo-Fregean theory of content that I defend in the second half of this book. On my weaker account of intentional realism, Davidson is an intentional realist.

12 Millikan, 1984, is an excellent example of the naturalization of content in terms of biological categories. See also Millikan, 1986, 1989a, 1995 and note that she does not endorse the idea of a descriptive theory of content, for she does not see how that could be undertaken without endorsing Cartesian accounts the phenomenology. In this respect she is close to Dennett's instrumentalism (Dennett, 1987b, 1991a). I discuss Millikan's position in ch. 7.

13 *locus classicus* for this view is Quine, 1960, and Stich, 1983. See ch. 7 below.

14 E.g. Searle, 1990, 1993; Taylor, 1985, 1992; Dreyfus, 1992, are sceptical of the prospects of naturalizing content.

15 This is the eliminativist position; cf. P. S. Churchland, 1986; Stich, 1983; which is the inheritance of Quine's indeterminacy of translation argument (1960, ch. 2); see ch. 7 below for discussion.

16 Although cf. Stich, 1992, where he endorses a pluralist weak eliminativism rather than the older strong form.

17 Dennett, 1987b.

18 *locus classicus* Davidson, 1970.

19 See Evans, 1982; McDowell, 1986, 1994b; Peacocke, 1986, 1992b; Clark, 1991, 1993; Baker, 1994, 1995. See section 11.6 for discussion of the differences between McDowell and Peacocke.

20 Thanks to John Collins for this delightful slogan.

21 Jacob, 1997, calls this a 'bottom-up' methodology, although I reserve that label for a different idea.

22 Cp. Perry, 1988, who agrees that we do semantics in order to explain behaviour, *contra* Wettstein, 1986, who thinks that, so construed, semantics is impossible.

23 Recall that the definition of representationalism requires only states characterizable independently of the world; it does not require a linguistic individuation of them.

24 See Brandom, 1994, ch. 1, for the problem of what he calls the representingness of representings, also McDowell, 1986, esp. sect. 5, and 1994b, for the related idea that a Cartesian account of representations leaves the mind empty of content.

25 We have to be careful how we express the lack of dependence on science. For Frege, the investigations into semantics are a priori, abstract and formal. Contemporary Fregean work is informed by scientific accounts of the mechanisms that underpin conceptual mastery. That does not mean that the constitutive account of concept possession must defer completely to the science of psychological mechanisms. There can be a constitutive account of concept possession even if it is not fully completable independently of some knowledge of psychological mechanisms. For the delicate working of this interplay between conceptual and empirical investigations cf. Eilan et al., 1993; Campbell, 1994; Peacocke, 1995.

26 On the general issues concerning reductionism and explanation, cf. Charles and Lennon, 1992.

27 Cf. Peacocke's (1992b) notion of canonical commitments in characterizing the meaning of a concept. Also Brandom, 1994, and what he calls the inferentialist approach.

28 Frege, 1884.

29 Cf. Luntley, 1995b, for further discussion of the epistemological consequences (mostly harmless) of this point and the argument against thinking that scepticism in its various forms, including the melodrama of postmodernism, follows from it.

30 Wittgenstein, 1953, sect. 38.

31 It is debatable whether there is such a thing as a formal study of grammar. Cf. Dummett, 1973, ch. 4, for an attempt to give a purely linguistic criterion for something being a proper name.

32 The creativity of linguistic understanding was a key idea in Chomsky's development of the notion of generative grammar; see Chomsky, 1965. It was also an important part of Davidson's early arguments about the idea of a theory of meaning being based on a recursive theory of truth; see Davidson, 1967b, and also ch. 4 below for much more detail on Davidson. See Schiffer, 1987, for criticism of the idea that the phenomenon of creativity entails the idea of a compositional semantics.

33 See Davidson, 1977b, for his rejection of a bottom-up 'building-block' approach.

34 Russell is the classic example; cf. his 1911 and 1918. As we shall see in the next chapter, for all his importance in defining many of the key philosophical tasks of the twentieth century, Russell is a philosopher with one foot firmly rooted in an older, Cartesian tradition. Frege defines the twentieth-century approach to thought and language, whereas Russell straddles the old and the new. Many contemporary philosophers are still caught astride the fence. I return to contemporary work on reference in ch. 8 below.

35 Evans, 1982, pp. 100ff. The argument can be traced back from Evans to Strawson, 1959.

36 I shall speak of judgements, rather than assertions. I use the term 'judgement' to cover both those things that are said and those things that are thought. I do not want, at this

stage, to prejudge the issue of whether thought is prior to language or whether all thoughts are fully expressible in language.

37   Evans argues for the generality constraint in terms of thoughts, rather than assertions. I agree that thought is more basic, but for present purposes nothing hangs on the difference. I shall return to the issue of the priority of thought over language later, in chs 9 and 11.

38   Davidson, 1973.

39   This is an issue which affects the constraints the philosophy of thought places upon our psychological theorizing about cognition. Fodor, for one, is someone who has taken the structure of thought to be an empirical phenomenon and something thereby to be captured in empirical models of cognitive processes. The status of such claims is, however, contentious and turns, in part, on why we hold thought to be structured. See Fodor, 1987, esp. the appendix, 'Why there still has to be a language of thought'.

40   Cp. Wittgenstein, 1961, proposition 7.

41   The example about events is, of course, at the heart of Davidson's philosophy of language. Davidson argues that the logical grammar of judgements about actions reveals a commitment to the existence of events. An event ontology is required in order to provide judgements about actions with the grammar necessary that they be truth-evaluable judgements; see Davidson, 1967a, 1969.

42   Contrast the account of analysis provided by ordinary language philosophers like Austin – cf. Austin, 1970 – and compare Wittgenstein's defence of ordinary language and his thesis that philosophy can only describe, not improve upon, linguistic structure; e.g. Wittgenstein, 1953, sect. 124.

43   This is the point that we should not assume that semantics as the study of content which rationalizes behaviour can be reduced to a formal semantic theory. The idea that the study of grammar cannot be a purely formal or linguistic study becomes visible in ch. 2 in my account of Russell and Mill. It acquires central importance in later chapters of this book (8ff), although I return to discuss the point briefly in section 1.7.

44   Despite this, Davidson has claimed the priority of our theory of truth over our metaphysics (1977a), and Dummett has been prepared to take the priority of the study of language to the study of metaphysics as definitive of analytic philosophy (1993). Neither of these extreme positions is, I believe, tenable.

45   Cf. Peacocke, 1986, 1992b.

46   See below, chs 9, 11, 12.

47   Brandom, 1994, esp. ch. 2.

48   See Dummett's (1973, ch. 4) efforts on Frege's behalf to find purely formal criteria for something being a name. At the end of the chapter Dummett has to appeal to the idea of 'criterion of identity' to get the right results, and that is a non-formal notion.

49   The idea of the space of reasons is from McDowell, 1994b. See my 1998a for a further overview of the metaphysical consequences of neo-Fregean externalism.

50   This is what Dennett is attacking when he writes of the 'myth of original intentionality' (1987a, 1990).

51 An obvious example of this is the claim pursued by Searle that current models of artificial intelligence necessarily fail to capture the phenomena of intentionality; see e.g. Searle, 1990, 1993.

52 Millikan, 1984.

53 This is the position of eliminative materialists who hold that our ordinary descriptions of intentionality – our folk-psychological explanations of behaviour – have no basis in scientific fact; *locus classicus* Quine, 1960; Stich, 1983; P. M. Churchland, 1995; P. S. Churchland, 1986. See ch. 7 below for discussion of Quine.

54 As I have characterized it, the Fregean methodology is committed to a description of our intentionality – there really is something that needs describing. Because I distinguish between this weak notion of intentional realism and representationalism, the former involves no commitment to reify the content involved in describing intentionality. Stripped of the reification of content that characterizes representationalism, the need to describe intentionality is common to lots of authors, many of whom are not normally counted as intentional realists because of their refusal to reify content. For example, Davidson's work – e.g. 1984 – is rich in descriptions of what it is to be a meaningful language user, despite his explicit disavowal of the theory of thought (1991). He is often classified as anti intentional realism – e.g. by Fodor, 1985. But that is only because he is opposed to what I call representationalism. We can gain considerable clarity in this project if we acknowledge the task of describing intentionality without assuming, at the outset, that the description has to be undertaken in a representationalist fashion. By keeping these matters separate, options become available that otherwise remain invisible. We also find that Searle, 1983, Putnam, 1975, Burge, 1979 and Baker, 1995, amongst many others, are all engaged in a project of describing intentionality despite their otherwise considerable differences. Indeed, it is only the eliminativists who fail to show up at our starting line for describing intentionality.

Chapter 2   Russell's Theory of Descriptions

1 Russell, 1905.

2 It has provided the resources for investigations into a wide range of ordinary language devices, from plural descriptions, possessives, to gerundive nominal constructions. For an excellent account of these developments, and a more detailed discussion of the theory in general, see Neale, 1990.

3 Neale, 1990, not only gives an excellent account of the developments of Russell's theory, but is one of the few treatments to take seriously the need to identify the philosophical and psychological underpinnings of the theory. I place emphases in slightly different places to Neale, but I am in considerable agreement with his treatment.

4 Variously labelled the naïve theory of reference, the direct theory of reference, the 'Fido'–Fido theory of reference. For contemporary defence of the object theory, see Salmon, 1986. Ryle, 1951, called it the 'Fido'–Fido theory.

5   Russell, 1903, p. 47.

6   Evans, 1982, pp. 22f; McDowell, 1982b.

7   Russell, 1918, p. 245.

8   The requirement of direct contact follows only if you assume that grasp of the meaning of the term equals grasp of the object. However, on a theory that distinguishes sense from reference, it would be possible to endorse the semantic value dependence thesis without proceeding to the requirement for direct contact as characterized in the text for Russell. Such a position captures both a Fregean identification of grasp of meaning with grasp of sense and the Russellian semantic value dependence thesis. This is the position of Evans, 1982; McDowell, 1977, 1984a. These options will be explored in chs 8ff.

9   Russell, 1918, pp. 225f.

10   Cf. Salmon, 1986, for defence of the object theory of reference from what he sees as the Fregean orthodoxy that denies the possibility of an extensional theory of judgement. See Recanati, 1993, for an attempt to square the Fregean sense/reference distinction with what is now known as 'direct reference theory'; see chs 8ff for more details on direct reference theory versus Fregean theory.

11   The label 'Millian', for a direct theory of names, is due to Kripke, 1972. Many writers have picked up this usage: e.g. Bach, 1987, p. 130.

12   Mill, 1875, bk 1, ch. 2, sect. 5, p. 22.

13   Thanks to Michael Dummett, who first pointed out to me that what Mill actually says bears little resemblance to the view known almost universally as 'Millian'. Mills says that names lack connotation. From a perspective informed by Carnap's systematic theory of denotations and connotations, if names lack connotation, all that is left is denotation. This perhaps explains why Mill has been adopted as emblematic for the direct reference theory. But Mill's notion of connotation is linguistic, not thought-theoretic. All he means when he says that proper names lack connotation is the thesis, which Russell would have resisted, that names are not equivalent to any other category of linguistic expression. Acknowledging that thesis does not, however, answer the question of how they stand for objects, to which, in the passage quoted, Mill appears to have a broadly Lockean model. Of course, if you assume a representationalist model of thought, then if names are not equivalent to, say, descriptions, and names are items within the representationalist model of thought, then they will represent directly. But that would be to assume that Mill is party to a contemporary debate in a way that the quoted passage makes plain is illegitimate.

14   Cf. Russell, 1903, ch. 5.

15   Russell, 1912, p. 32; also 1911, p. 23.

16   See ch. 8 below for details of contemporary direct theories of reference, ch. 10 for the causal theory.

17   Russell, 1911, p. 16.

18   For a brief period Russell also allowed acquaintance with the self, thus admitting 'I' as a genuine singular term. See Sainsbury, 1979, pp. 26ff, for further discussion of Russell's conception of acquaintance.

19   In contrast, Mill does speak of ideas, and Mill is probably a semantic Cartesian, for that would explain why he says nothing about how ideas stand for objects; that they do so is a basic unexplained fact about the power of ideas.

20   Russell, 1918, p. 203.

21   Ibid.

22   The representation of logical grammar provided by the theory becomes complex when analysing sentences with multiple descriptions, but there is no reason why the theory need be represented in this particular formalism. Any formalism that captures the salient point that the descriptive phrase is a quantificational structure will do. Neale, 1990, is particularly clear on this point.

23   Russell, 1905, p. 48.

24   For the moment I ignore the issue of whether satisfying LEM is a legitimate test of whether or not a judgement is well formed – has expressed a definite claim about the world. This is a contested claim; cf. ch. 6 below.

25   It picks out what Blackburn, 1984, calls a universalist account of content.

26   Chs 8ff, esp. 11 and 12.

27   Other writers who have made similar points to Donnellan (1966, 1968, 1974) include Stalnaker, 1972, Peacocke, 1975, Hornsby, 1977, Kaplan, 1979, Recanati, 1986, 1989, Barwise and Perry, 1983. For a fuller discussion of these criticisms, cf. Neale, 1990, ch. 3.

28   Strawson, 1950a, p. 114.

29   See sect. 1.2 for the role of the locality of causation in substantiating representationalism.

30   Strawson, 1964.

31   If Strawson had Frege's concept of sense, he might then be able to say that the description's failure to achieve what it is designed for – viz. reference – does not entail that the sentence fails to express a judgement, merely that it fails to express a judgement with the semantic value true or false. However, Strawson's position is not like Frege's, and although Frege appeared to admit the possibility of sentences expressing judgements but which lacked a truth-value, this is distinct from the options available to Strawson, which are: either no judgement is expressed or one is expressed which is neither true nor false. It is important to note that the idea of a judgement that is neither true nor false is a much stronger thesis that the one Frege perhaps allows: viz. that of a judgement that fails to be either true or false. We shall investigate Frege's position in chs 8ff. On the distinction between being neither true nor false and failing to be either true or false, cf. ch. 6 below.

32   Cf. Neale, 1990, for a variety of examples like this.

33   See Strawson, 1964, for this admission.

34   Dummett, 1978a, p. xv and essay 2, complains that unless and until Strawson offers a systematic theory of inference that accommodates sentences that are neither true nor false, his critique of Russell must be rejected. Formal theories of presupposition have been developed, e.g. van Fraassen, 1966, 1968.

35   Strawson, 1964, takes presupposition in this way, in order to avoid the need to construct a three-valued logic.

36 Donnellan, 1966, 1968, 1974, and see the other works cited in n. 27 above.

37 Grice, 1969; see the example about Jones's butler at p. 141. It is structurally identical to the one about Smith's murderer.

38 Ibid., p. 143.

39 Kripke, 1977.

40 Ibid., p. 14, speaks of semantic reference as the 'conventional' reference of the word.

41 Dennett thinks that saying that signs only have meaning for us is equivalent to the myth of original intentionality – the idea that the intentionality of signs is derived from the original intentionality of our minds. The two things are, however, distinct. To say that signs only get content by being used by us is a much weaker thesis than the myth of original intentionality. The myth of original intentionality only comes into play if you assume that it takes a special 'inner reading' of signs to grant them meaning. The idea of a special 'inner reading' is semantic Cartesianism – the idea that there is an unexplained power of the mind to bestow meaning on signs. It is semantic Cartesianism that is the culprit. Dennett would, I think, agree, but does not seem to recognize that rejecting semantic Cartesianism is compatible with endorsing intentional realism in the weak form that I have defended it. In Dennett, 1990, he characterizes the 'myth' in two different ways: in terms of the Cartesian 'inner theatre' of special symbols and in terms of the concept of autonomous agency. The idea that there is a connection between intentional realism and the concept of autonomous agency is, I suspect, along the right lines; it is only the 'inner theatre' business that is metaphysically suspect. See ch. 12 below for the connection with agency.

42 Wittgenstein's later work is often taken to incorporate a 'use theory' of meaning. Just as the appeal to the 'standard pattern of use' in elucidation of logical grammar should not be taken to signal an interest in the empirical study of actual usage, I believe we should be wary of assuming that Wittgenstein's talk of meaning-as-use commits him to anything less than a notion of normative usage. For more on Wittgenstein cf. ch. 7 below, also Brandom, 1994, for a reading of Wittgenstein's concept of use that stresses the idea of normative usage.

43 See sect. 2.7 for a physicalist theory applied to truth, ch. 10 for details on the causal theory of reference.

44 See chs 11 and 12 below for details of how the Fregean methodology supports this kind of externalism.

45 See ch. 7 below for discussion of Quine and Wittgenstein; chs 4 and 5 for Davidson; ch. 11 for Fodor; chs 8–12 for contemporary Fregean theory of thought.

Chapter 3   The Semantic Theory of Truth

1 To follow up any of the above positions, and many others besides, the best starting-point is Kirkham, 1992, which includes coverage of the redundancy theory of Ramsey, 1931, minimalist theories, e.g. Horwich, 1990; the pro-sentential theory of Grover et al., 1975.

2 See Kirkham, 1992, ch. 4, for details.

3   This means that Russell is the only classical correspondence theorist to count as such by my lights; cf. Russell, 1912. In contrast, Austin, 1950, Chisholm, 1977 and Bealer, 1982 would not count as correspondence theorists.

4   Kirkham, 1992, distinguishes between correspondence theories in which the relation is congruence and theories in which the relation is correlation. The latter (Austin, also Aristotle) take the relation to be purely 'conventional'. That fits my classification of not counting Austin as a true correspondence theorist, for the conventional character of the correspondence relation is evidence that he does not subscribe to representationalism.

5   Cp. Wittgenstein, 1961, 1.1: 'The world is the world of facts, not of things.' Wittgenstein has been paraded as a correspondence theorist who endorses the idea of isomorphism between true judgements and world; e.g. Haack, 1978. I think this gets Wittgenstein wrong, for Wittgenstein did not embrace representationalism. His position in the *Tractatus* is much more sophisticated than that. I discuss this in my *Wittgenstein and the Conditions for the Possibility of Judgement*, in preparation.

6   See below, sect. 3.7. This objection can be found in Strawson, 1950b, and Davidson, 1990, pp. 302–5.

7   For more on problems with correspondence theories, cf. Kirkham, 1992. Kirkham objects to the problem about facts because he thinks that 'facts can enter into causal relations' (p. 138). I think this is easily accommodated by saying that talk of facts entering causal relations can be paraphrased into talk of events entering causal relations. Similar thoughts apply to his other objections (ibid.).

8   See sect. 1.5.

9   E.g. see the approach in Cresswell, 1994.

10   Some have claimed that the language relativity is a problem for Tarski's theory: Blackburn, 1984, pp. 266–7; Putnam, 1985, p. 64. Language relativity is not a problem, although it does reveal the way that Tarski's theory presupposes our pre-theoretic notion of truth: Davidson, 1990, pp. 286–7; Bealer, 1982, pp. 200-2.

11   This point becomes significant in Davidson's use of Tarski to construct a general theory of meaning; cf. the next chapter, esp. sect. 4.6.

12   The physicalist representationalist complaint against Tarksi is discussed in sect. 3.7 below.

13   On the issue whether Tarksi was a correspondence theorist, cf. 'No': Haack, 1976; Mackie, 1973; 'Yes': Davidson, 1986, p. 309, although he changes his mind in 1990, p. 304; Popper, 1974; Platts, 1979; Field, 1974. See Kirkham, 1992, ch. 5, for further discussion.

14   Most famously Field's, 1972 physicalist objection to Tarski; cf. below, sect. 3.7.

15   The definition given of a predicate is Frege's; cf. Dummett, 1973, e.g. p. 31.

16   (10) does not accommodate sentences with multiple generality. Nothing of importance hangs on this technical complication, so I ignore it.

17   Field, 1972.

18   These two theses are characteristic of representationalist positions. See Devitt and Sterelny, 1987, for a clear endorsement of both physicalism and atomism.

19   But note that it is not Russell's atomism, for Russell's atoms were constitutively connected to things. Because of his semantic Cartesianism, they did not require a

theory of hook-up, for Russell's atoms were internally connected to objects, universals, etc.

20   In ch. 11 I shall suggest that although his Cartesianism is not viable, it expresses a key insight of Russell's that cannot be captured by a causal theory; cf. sect. 11.8.

21   Devitt and Sterelny, 1987, see their physicalist credentials as a boundary condition for any viable theory of content. The idea that truth, rather than reference, might be an explanatory primitive, they find 'obscure and unconvincing' (p. 36).

22   Mind the gap, first advertised in sect. 1.4, between semantics as the study of that which rationally explains behaviour and formal semantic theory.

23   Tarski himself advocated physicalism; cf. Kirkham, 1992, pp. 196f, for details.

24   Again, cp. Davidson, 1990.

25   Field, 1972, p. 95.

26   Recall the distinction in sect. 3.1 about correspondence as congruence (metaphysical) and correspondence as convention (banal and harmless).

27   The request for explanation is not explicit in Field, 1972; but cf. Field, 1986, p. 55.

28   Field, 1972, p. 97; also Kirkham, 1992, pp. 199ff.

29   Field, 1972, p. 96.

30   See Charles and Lennon, 1992, for a discussion of the viability of reductionism in a number of different cases.

31   See McDowell, 1994b, pp. 201ff, for the idea of different levels of explanation; Luntley, 1995b, for the idea of different explanatory spaces.

32   The following are willing to pay: P. M. Churchland, 1995, P. S. Churchland, 1986, Stich, 1983 and Quine, 1960.

Chapter 4   Truth and Meaning

1   Davidson, 1967a.

2   The notion of the 'cosmic exile' is taken from McDowell, 1987. McDowell uses the phrase to capture what he takes to be Dummett's over-demanding conception of what a theory of meaning should be like. His attribution of this ambition to Dummett is, I believe, correct, although it does not vitiate, as McDowell seems to think, all the anti-realist force of Dummett's critique of Davidson's enterprise. The anti-realist issue will be settled later; see ch. 6 below. The 'homely' modesty of Davidson's programme makes it quite different from Quine's account of meaning. See ch. 7 below for details on Quine, and also Hookway, 1988, ch. 9 for more details on the differences between Davidson and Quine.

3   See Davidson, 1991, for his disavowal of neo-Fregean theory of thought.

4   This identification is central also to Dummett – e.g. 1976. See Campbell, 1982; Fricker, 1982–3.

5   Dummett, 1978c, p. 1.

6   This response is given by a character in P. G. Wodehouse's novel *Ring for Jeeves*, from which Dummett took the example.

7   Cf. chs 11 and 12.

8   See Evans, 1981a, in response to Wright, 1981b. Martin Davies has developed Evans's treatment of tacit knowledge in a series of papers: Davies, 1987, 1989, 1995a, 1995b, also Davies and Stone, 1993.

9   The analysis given is subtly different from Evans's account. Evans treats tacit knowledge as involving a realism about internal states that are causally responsible for overt behaviour. Contrast this with Wright's behaviourist, 1981b. My account falls between the two. It is a kind of behaviourism, though a non-reductionist one that deploys rich intentional idioms in the description of behaviour. Once again, Baker, 1995, has a broadly similar version of behaviourism.

10 This is the analogue in a theory of action of the Fregean semantic claim that truth is prior to reference. The analysis does not deny that there are sub-actions, but it does deny that they are definable independently of their grammar in the combinatorial structure of whole actions. Similarly, the Fregean (and Davidsonian) view is that there is such a thing as reference, but it is defined with respect to truth. For Davidson's views on this, cf. sect. 5.6. Contrast Brandom's (1994) denial of the primacy of reference over an account of the grammar of expressions and his endorsement of the primacy of the inferentialist concept of grammar over that of reference. This misses the middle position that denies that there is any primacy one way or another between reference and grammar. The point is only that it is not possible to give an account of reference independently of an account of the grammar of the expression; see McDowell, 1997, for this response to Brandom.

11 See the argument for the generality constraint in sect. 1.4.

12 See items cited in n. 8 above.

13 For the argument that behaviour including a capacity for novelty is richer than behaviour as described in terms of its learning conditions, see ch. 7 below, esp. sect. 7.5 on Millikan.

14 See Evans, 1981a.

15 For caution on the relationship between folk-psychological categories and cognitive sub-personal psychology, see Brewer, 1993.

16 The manual-theory fits better with Quine's programme; see ch. 7 below.

17 For a general critique of the classical AI model of cognition, see Varela et al., 1991; also Clark, 1991.

18 The idea that the bottom-line justification for the appeal to truth as the central semantic concept amounts to no more than a series of platitudes concerning assertion is due to McDowell, 1976, also 1987. McDowell's argument is central to his contribution to the debate about realism in the theory of meaning. I defer discussion of that issue until ch. 6.

19 The metaphysical debate about realism and anti-realism was started by Dummett: esp. his 1976, but see also his 1977 and the essays in 1978b and 1991b. See also Wright, 1993. It is related to issues concerning the interpretation of Wittgenstein, raised not only by Wright, but also by Kripke (1982). My own contribution to this debate takes a different route: see Luntley, 1988, 1991a, 1996, also Tennant, 1987.

20 As noted, the idea that the role of truth in our theory of meaning is legitimized by no more than a set of platitudes was first elaborated by McDowell (1976). The idea is

implicit in Davidson's recent writings in his insistence that 'true' is one of our clearest concepts for which no further elucidation need – or can – be given; cf. Davidson, 1987a, 1990.

21   Cf. Luntley, 1996, for discussion of discipline in response to the failure of Crispin Wright's various attempts to construct a theory of meaning with something less than truth-conditions as the central semantic concept: Wright, 1992, 1993.

22   Davidson, 1967b, p. 25.

23   Ibid, p. 26.

24   In the terminology employed in ch. 1, Davidson's theory is a theory of the grammar of meaning. In contrast to Brandom's (1994) way of setting up options, it is not representationalist; but neither is it wholly inferentialist either. There are such things as truth, reference, etc., but these are not fixed independently of grammar.

25   The claim that we could determine this structure in the alien's vocalization involves assumptions that Quine famously denied. See ch. 7 for discussion of Quine. As previously noted, Quine's project is different from Davidson's. Davidson's project is homely, where Quine's is radically reductionist.

26   Evans and McDowell, 1976, 'Editors' Introduction', p. xi.

27   Recall the discussion in sect. 3.6.

28   Of course, they would say all this in Welsh; I leave the 'know that . . .' in English to make matters easier.

29   See Dummett, 1973, pp. 139f, for similar examples.

30   To keep things simple I pretend that the Welsh for the logical components is identical to the English.

31   Davidson, 1967a, p. 31.

32   See ch. 9 below, esp. sect. 9.4.

33   Start with Davidson, 1967a, 1969, and then try Bennett, 1988.

Chapter 5   Interpretation, Minimal Truth and the World

1   Davidson, 1974.

2   See McDowell, 1994b, p. 3.

3   Compare Davidson's analogy with organizing your closet (1974, p. 192). It is impossible to organize something that is not already within the reach of concepts.

4   The rejection of the idea of the given as a level of non-conceptual content is not a rejection of all uses of the idea of non-conceptual content. There is now a large literature on the distinction between conceptual and non-conceptual content, much of which is very confused and confusing; see e.g. Crane, 1992a, 1992b; Bermudez, 1994, 1995; Peacocke, 1992a, 1994; Jacob, 1997. Many writers use 'non-conceptual' as a label for content for which the subject of thought possesses no word, or even no descriptive word. Apart from the fact that this looks like an erroneous assimilation of conceptual content with content expressed by concept words (predicates), it is compatible with the idea that such content figures in rational considerations – i.e. it is capable of figuring in inference. It is, however, the idea of content that figures in inference that

is the hallmark of the notion of conceptual content, for it is the notion of content that satisfies the generality constraint. McDowell, 1994b, lecture 3, is particularly clear on this, and I follow him in taking conceptual content as that which figures in inference. This leaves the issue of perceptual experience having a content more fine-grained than that for which the subject has names or descriptions irrelevant in constructing a notion of non-conceptual content. This is not to rule out the idea of non-conceptual content; it is merely to stall the argument for it. See ch. 11 below for more on this; see Evans, 1982, esp. ch. 6, for Evans's notion of non-conceptual content, and McDowell, 1994b, for his response to Evans.

5   A start on the literature on Davidson would include Lepore, 1986; Lepore and McLaughlin, 1985; Vermazen and Hintikka, 1985; Follesdal, 1987; Putnam, 1987.

6   This is why the argument looks verificationist – what is allowed to exist is a function of our verifications; see Blackburn, 1984. It is this feature of the argument that suggests that Davidson is guilty of linguistic imperialism. There is a very clear account of this charge in Hacking, 1975; see also Rorty, 1986.

7   See last two paragraphs of Davidson, 1974, p. 198.

8   E.g. Davidson, 1973, p. 128.

9   It is the idea that holism is a constitutive claim that makes it such a problematic concept for those who assume that content must be reducible to a physicalist account: e.g. Fodor and Lepore, 1992.

10   As noted in the previous chapter, this is to make assumptions about what is observable – viz. patterns of usage – that Quine would deny; cf. ch. 7 below.

11   E.g. Davidson, 1977a, p. 200.

12   See Hurley, 1992.

13   E.g. Davidson, 1977a, p. 200.

14   Ibid.

15   Ibid.

16   Ibid. pp. 200–1.

17   The example of 'going native' amongst musicians is one that Blackburn, 1984, uses in his critique of Davidson.

18   See the discussion in Luntley, 1995b, and especially the collection Charles and Lennon, 1992.

19   It is a thesis that is central to Davidson's own anomalous monism in the philosophy of mind; cf. Davidson, 1970.

20   Wiggins has argued for the marks of truth in a variety of places: e.g. Wiggins, 1980, 1987. I take the latter as the definitive statement. There are important differences between these versions. The earlier account had six marks, and the sixth mark becomes significant in the next chapter. Also, the expression of the central third mark changes between the earlier and the later version. I shall indicate the importance of this change.

21   Wiggins, 1987, p. 146.

22   The present argument is, of course, the same as that for the generality constraint in ch. 1.

23   The point about the phrasing of Wiggins's third mark of truth is central to understanding Wright's discussion of Wiggins in Wright, 1992. Wright appeals only to

Wiggins's earlier (1980) formulation, in which Wiggins used the 'not consist in being believed by me' formulation, as opposed to the later more abstract 'not consist in being believed'. The formulation that Wright uses gives truth only an intersubjective character rather than an objective one. This, I believe, is inadequate to capture the central notion of a semantic mistake involved in the argument for the first mark. More on this below; cf. also Luntley, 1996.

24   The independence of truth from judgement that is provided by the third mark is the notion that Frege famously insisted upon in his 1918.

25   The metaphysics implicated by our account of content for such discourse will occupy us in later chapters, esp. 6 and 11.

26   This is minimal realism, for it falls short of metaphysical realism and a number of other varieties too. For more on different varieties of realism, see ch. 6.

27   Davidson, 1977b, p. 222.

28   Of the building-block approach Davidson says, 'It has often been tried. And it is hopeless' (ibid., p. 220). Brandom's (1994) hostility to representationalism is similarly motivated.

29   Further argument in support of this is given in ch. 7, where I look at Quine's naturalism and its failure to capture the normativity of meaning.

30   Devitt and Sterelny (1987) certainly think Davidson has things upside-down. But that is because they assume at the outset that semantics must be reducible to physical theory; hence, for them, the starting-point for semantics is a causal theory of reference.

31   Recall the point from ch. 3, that what appears on the right-hand side of the T-sentence is the world, because it is that which is independent of will.

32   My reading of Davidson is much influenced by McDowell, 1994b; see esp. Afterword, pt I, where he takes issue with the traces of causal theory in Davidson's coherentism. It is a delicate matter whether Davidson is guilty, as McDowell thinks, of reintroducing a causal notion of the given; but either way, the difference between McDowell and Davidson is slight. For Davidson's coherentism see his 1986.

33   Of course, most writers assume that the reductionist type of naturalization is the only one, hence the flurry of work in recent years on naturalization and normativity; see e.g. Boghossian, 1990, 1991a; also Peacocke, 1995; Villanueva, 1993.

34   This is how Wiggins handles the metaphysics of value, 1987.

35   Davidson, 1991.

Chapter 6   Meaning, Metaphysics and Logic

1   *locus classicus* for the debate with Davidson is Dummett, 1976, although his earlier writings, collected in Dummett, 1978b, had already formulated the general connection between truth, meaning and inference.

2   Devitt (1983) is one who really cannot see what all the fuss is about.

3   Brouwer's writings are not recommended for the faint-hearted, although his essay 'Consciousness, philosophy and mathematics', in Brouwer, 1975, is written for the general philosopher rather than for the mathematician. The serious student will need

to tackle Dummett, 1977. In addition, Prawitz's work (1974, 1977, 1987) is central to an informed view on the debate between classical and intuitionistic logic.

4 Cf. Dummett, 1978b, pp. xix ff, for a clear discussion of the significance of keeping these laws distinct; cf. also Luntley, 1988, ch. 4.

5 Care is required in formulating the modalities involved in treating not-A as 'provably not provable'. Even professed anti-realists sometimes get it wrong. See Luntley, 1988, pp. 125ff, for a criticism of Wright's (1981a) critical notice of Dummett's 1978b, in which Wright gets this point wrong.

6 The last sentence moves from Brouwer's way of expressing his anti-realism to the account I developed in my 1988.

7 The general formulation that truth gets replaced by knowable truth is open to a knock-down argument against the intelligibility of the anti-realist critique; see Edginton, 1985; Williamson, 1982, 1987a, 1987b; Wright, 1986; Melia, 1991; Mueller and Stein, 1996, for the debate. I discuss this argument in the final section of the present chapter. I believe it applies to only some of the variants of anti-realist argument that I want to distinguish.

8 Cf. Prawitz, 1974, 1977; Tennant, 1987; Dummett, 1991b.

9 Dummett has frequently endorsed this unintelligibility claim, so too have Prawitz, Tennant, Wright; cf. also Read, 1994, ch. 8, esp. summary pp. 234f. In response, many writers have taken the task of rebutting the anti-realist critique to be that of showing that the classical account of the constants is intelligible; e.g. Peacocke, 1986, 1988; also McDowell, 1976.

10 Luntley, 1988; Tennant, 1987.

11 There is a brief discussion of the issues involved in a proof-theoretic justification of deduction in Luntley, 1988, ch. 4, sect. 2. For more detail see items referred to in n. 8.

12 The requirement of harmony rules out 'tonk' as a logical constant; cf. Prior, 1960–1; Belnap, 1961–2.

13 The scope for dispute about conditional introduction that I have in mind is the dispute concerning relevance logic – should the introduction rule be constrained by a require-ment that A and B stand in a relevance relation governed by their content? Relevance logicians require such a constraint in order to avoid the paradoxes of material impli-cation. Cf. Read, 1988, for a defence of intuitionistic relevance logic that is also anti-realist.

14 See the debate between Tennant (1981, 1984, 1985) and Weir (1983, 1985, 1986). Tennant argued that DNE was an unjustifiable non-conservative extension of the basic set of self-evident rules for which only a viciously circular justification could be given. Weir's reply that such a procedure of justification is 'only circular from the absurd perspective of one trying to justify fundamental principles from independent ones' (1983, p. 178) illustrates the obvious central point: that everything hinges on how we demarcate the basic set. Furthermore, it illustrates the classical logicians' central complaint that DNE is constitutive of the meaning of negation. Weir thinks Tennant's basic set is 'independent' because it has left out negation!

15 The realism/anti-realism debate has spawned a large literature. The only book-length developments of Dummettian anti-realism available are due to Crispin Wright, Neil Tennant and Michael Luntley: Wright, 1993; Tennant, 1987; Luntley, 1988. In terms of the classification to follow, Wright's work is a reductionist kind of anti-realism; mine is firmly non-reductionist, and Tennant's is closer in spirit to mine, although sharing some central arguments with Wright. Defences of realism that engage with Dummett's arguments are primarily due to McDowell (1976, 1987), Peacocke (1986, 1988) and Campbell (1994, esp. chs 2, 4). Devitt (1983, 1991b) purports to defend realism and rebut Dummett's arguments, although I am sceptical that Devitt appreciates the underlying methodology that Dummett is employing. See also Devitt, 1991a, and Luntley, 1991b, for more debate with Devitt. My own view is that these responses are, for the main part, responses to the reductionist elements in Dummettian anti-realism, responses that I took account of in Luntley, 1988.

16 The classic statement of an anti-realism about both moral values and colours that sees our ordinary talk about such things as party to an error theory of value and colour is Mackie, 1977. There is now an enormous literature on both these cases, much of which draws comparisons between the two domains. Blackburn, 1988, is representative of a point of view that broadly follows Mackie; see also Gibbard, 1990, 1996, for a similar position. See Boghossian, 1991b; Campbell, 1993a; Johnston, 1989, 1992; Pettit, 1991; Pettit and Jackson, 1996; Wiggins, 1987; Wright, 1992, for a start to contemporary debates about the status of colours and values.

17 Cf. the essays in Charles and Lennon, 1992, for discussion of the metaphysical issues involved.

18 This is characteristic of both Mackie's and Blackburn's positions; see Mackie, 1977; Blackburn, 1988.

19 It might seem odd to stress the epistemological relativity of the idea of non-verifiability, but as I shall show below, there is need for what one might as well call a metaphysical concept of non-verifiability. See below, sects 6.7, 6.8 and 6.9.

20 The former challenge was more to the fore in Dummett, 1975; the latter challenge occupies much of the argument in Dummett, 1976, and much of his work since. The account of the manifestation challenge that I give in sect. 6.6 should not automatically be assumed to be Dummett's; it is meant to capture the way that Wright and others have taken Dummett's ideas. Dummett's own work is much more ambiguous, and there is some reason, though not conclusive, for thinking that Dummett's views are better represented by the sort of argument that I employ in sect. 6.8.

21 Wright is less hospitable to the criterial version of anti-realism than he used to be, but it is important to note its position within the anti-realist options. Wright's endorsement of the criterial strategy can be found in his 1980, 1982. His change of mind is in Wright, 1984. The approach is criticized in Luntley, 1988, ch. 5, sect. 2, and McDowell, 1982a.

22 McDowell, 1981; for the general idea of direct presence in the reading of Davidson's denial of the scheme/content distinction, see McDowell, 1994b.

23 See Wright, 1981a, and my response in Luntley, 1988, ch. 4, esp. sect. 8.

24 The argument sketched in the fourth objection is much influenced by Peacocke, 1986, 1988; see also Luntley, 1988, ch. 1.

25 Key texts: Luntley, 1988; Tennant, 1987; Wright, 1992, 1993.

26 E.g.: 'we cannot attach any sense to quantified statements by appealing to infinite sums and products that are supposed simply to *have* a value whether or not we have any means of arriving at it' (Dummett, 1978b, p. xxviii).

27 Ibid., pp. xxxiii ff.

28 This claim is central to Dummett, 1976.

29 McDowell, 1987.

30 Ibid.

31 Drawing this distinction lies at the heart of the anti-realist position I developed in my 1988. Tennant, 1987, acknowledges the distinction between recognition-transcendent truth-conditions and recognition-transcendent truth-values, although he endorses a version of the manifestation argument that I cannot distinguish from Wright's reductionist anti-realism. Wright, 1993, acknowledges the distinction I drew, but then makes nothing of it.

32 Cf. Luntley, 1988, for details of this approach, and Luntley, 1991a, for a shorter account.

33 In Luntley, 1988, I was less clear about the separability of the transcendental approach from an epistemic one, although most of the language in that book is formulated in the former way, and I took an explicit stance against Wright's epistemic approach.

34 I take this version of the argument from Mueller and Stein, 1996; see also Edginton, 1985; Williamson, 1982, 1987a, 1987b; Wright, 1986; Melia, 1991; for more on the debate around this argument. Thanks to Vincent Mueller for conversations that forced me to consider this argument more seriously, one result of which was to force me to acknowledge the extent to which my own version of anti-realism was not epistemically based.

Chapter 7   The Possibility of a Naturalized Theory of Meaning

1 See sect. 1.2.

2 On the idea that there are two fundamentally distinct modes of explanation, the causal regulatory and rationalizing, see McDowell, 1994b; Brandom, 1994. For a version of naturalism that accommodates irreducibly teleological explanations, see Stout, 1996.

3 The formulation in the text, that the fitness of our ordinary concept of belief turns on its having a place within a scientific account, does not distinguish between strong and weak forms of eliminativism. Strong eliminativism holds that if belief is not answerable to our best scientific theory of ourselves, then there is no such thing as belief. Weak eliminativism holds only that the concept of belief cannot be made scientifically acceptable if it is not answerable to our best scientific theory of ourselves. Stich (1992) draws this distinction, and notes that strong eliminativism looks implausible, for there are many concepts, e.g. 'the rate of inflation', that cannot be made answerable to basic physical theory , but one would hardly conclude from this that there was no such thing

as inflation – that makes economic management too easy! The distinction is not so clear-cut, however; for if the weak eliminativist does not deny the existence of beliefs, it is unclear what force there is supposed to be to the observation that the concept is not answerable to best scientific theory. Stich now advocates what he calls 'pluralism', but this is an ontological pluralism; he still favours explanatory monism – explanations to be decent must be physical. In which case, it is unclear what advantage there is to ontological pluralism if the categories thereby saved from elimination have no explanatory role to play. Contrast Stich's 1992 with his earlier strong eliminativist position (1983). Quine is the ancestor of strong eliminativism. Understanding the outline structure of Quine's arguments puts naturalist and eliminativist authors post-Quine into perspective.

4 Hume is often thought of as the first great naturalist, and Hume's problems are all problems with the normative concepts that are central to our self-conception – causation, morality, rational belief. From the resources of his naturalistic theory of ideas as entities that happen to be associated with one another but which bear no intrinsic normative properties, Hume finds that there is no such thing as what we should believe, what we should do, how things must be, etc. Hume's naturalistic response is to say that we are not creatures governed by reason; for he can find no reason to believe that things must be so, that we must behave so, that we should believe so, etc. Instead, Hume says that we are creatures governed by habit. I am not convinced that the historical Hume was a naturalist, but the point remains that his texts provide a familiar entry point to a naturalistic way of thinking. The naturalistic reading of Hume is best developed in Stroud, 1977, after Kemp-Smith, 1949.

5 Quine articulates this dilemma in his response to Brentano's claim that the irreducibility of intentional notions to physical ones refutes physicalistic accounts of the mind. Quine says: 'One may accept the Brentano thesis either as showing the indispensability of intentional idioms and the importance of an autonomous science of intention, or as showing the baselessness of intentional idioms and the emptiness of a science of intention. My attitude, unlike Brentano's, is the second' (1960, p. 221).

6 See Fodor, 1987, 1993, and see Cynthia Macdonald's 'Introduction' to the section on individualism in Macdonald and Macdonald, 1995.

7 Quine, 1960, p. 27.

8 Quine, 1979, p. 167.

9 Like any major systematic thinker, Quine has been met with an array of alternative accounts of what he really means. The emphasis that I place upon Quine's physicalism in differentiating between the underdetermination of theory by data and the indeterminacy of translation is also stressed in Hookway, 1988; but there is an enormous secondary literature on Quine that the reader is encouraged to sample: Kirk, 1986; Gibson, 1982; Romanos, 1983; and the collection Davidson and Hintikka, 1969. There is also a good collection of essays in a special number of *Synthese* for 1972, with papers by Dummett, Putnam, and Rorty. See Chomsky's paper in Davidson and Hintikka, 1969, and Rorty's in *Synthese*, 1972 for examples of early commentators who took Quine to be making an epistemological, rather than an ontological, point.

10 Quine et al., 1974, p. 495.

11 I skip over a fair bit of detail here, in which Quine outlines the basic categories of sentences that he thinks we can identify in the alien sound production: occasion sentences (whose truth varies from context to context), standing sentences (whose truth is not so variable), the class of stimuli analytic sentences, and others. See e.g. Hookway, 1988, ch. 8, for more detail on all this and, of course, Quine, 1960. The detail does not affect the general structure of Quine's argument as I present it.

12 Quine, 1981, p. 48.

13 Ibid., p. 50.

14 Quine, 1969, p. 46.

15 Ibid., p. 47.

16 Quine, 1981, p. 23.

17 Evans, 1975.

18 One difference between Evans and Davidson is that although the description for Evans is replete with intentional idioms, Evans takes a meaning theory to be empirically testable not only in terms of fitting the behaviour thus described, but also in terms of the cognitive architecture of the psychological mechanisms that produce language. Evans takes the ascription of knowledge of a truth theory to the speaker as embodying the realist assumption that the structure of axioms and rules in the truth theory will pick out identifiable modules in the cognitive mechanisms of the speakers. This is Evans's realist treatment of tacit knowledge; see Evans, 1981a. Davidson treats the empirical testability as residing only in fitting the behaviour. This is the issue first discussed in sect. 4.2.

19 See the argument for the generality constraint in sect. 1.5.

20 Hookway, 1988, ch. 9.

21 Millikan, 1984.

22 To get a proper understanding of Millikan's position, you need to read her 1984, 1986, 1989a. Millikan, 1989b, addresses the particular issue of her concept of 'proper function'; 1993 is a useful collection of her essays. See also Fodor's reply to Millikan in Loewer and Rey, 1991. A good introduction to Millikan's work is the section in Macdonald and Macdonald, 1995, which includes a debate between Millikan and Peacocke.

23 The problem raised by this example goes back to Dretske, 1986.

24 This is the locality of causation: McGinn, 1989, p. 133.

25 In addition to Dretske, 1986, see Fodor, 1984, 1993; Dennett, 1987b, 1996.

26 E.g. see Millikan, 1989a, p. 253.

27 Peacocke, 1995; this is a selection from Peacocke, 1992b.

28 Peacocke, 1995, p. 281.

29 Millikan, 1995, p. 289.

30 That is Fodor's position: see his response to Millikan in Loewer and Rey, 1991, also his argument against teleological accounts of content in 'A Theory of Content 1' in Fodor, 1990.

31 Essential reading on Wittgenstein's rule-following arguments includes Kripke, 1982; Pears, 1988, 1991; McDowell, 1984b; McGinn, 1984. Wright, 1981b, has a reading of Wittgenstein much like Kripke's, although his interpretation changes by 1989.

Also Baker and Hacker, 1984, 1988; Luntley, 1991b; Millikan, 1990; Williams, 1991; and Bloor, 1998.

32 Cf. Evans, 1982, pp. 100ff, for generality constraint, also sect. 1.5 above.

33 Kripke, 1982, pp. 22–3. Kripke's social account of Wittgenstein's response unfortunately ends up endorsing a kind of dispositional theory of meaning norms, the dispositions of the community, or of specialists in the community (e.g. p. 90, where he speaks of the answer the teacher 'would give', not 'should give'). This is one reason why Kripke's positive account is unsatisfactory.

34 Cf. McDowell, 1984b, for criticism of Kripke's reading of Wittgenstein that makes much of the point that Kripke presents Wittgenstein as assuming that all understanding is interpretative.

35 The idea that Wittgenstein's argument is a *reductio* is not held universally. Kripke takes him to be offering a sceptical challenge to a realist truth-conditional theory of meaning, and to be endorsing a response which holds that an anti-realist assertibility-conditions theory of meaning is immune to the sceptical challenge. Wright's version of Wittgenstein is similar. The Kripke/Wright reading has enormous currency, especially in disciplines other than philosophy, where Wittgenstein is often cited as advocating a broadly communitarian conception of meaning. I think this gets Wittgenstein seriously wrong. McDowell, 1984b; Pears, 1988, 1991; and Luntley, 1991b, all take Wittgenstein to be offering instead a *reductio*. They differ in various ways in their accounts of the target of the *reductio*, but hold much in common. Pears sees the *reductio* targeted at Platonism and the representationalist idea that grasp of meaning in modelled as possession of internal mental talismans. McDowell sees it as targeted at the idea that all meaning is based on interpretation. See also Brandom, 1994, for a *reductio* reading of Wittgenstein's argument.

36 Compare Wittgenstein's remarks about the arrow: 1953, sect. 454.

37 This is McDowell's way of putting the moral of Wittgenstein's argument. Curiously, Wright considered something very like this response in his 1989, where he says that the idea of an intentional state just is the idea of something with an intrinsic normative power to reach out and determine future cases; but then made nothing of this.

38 Wittgenstein, 1953, sect. 201.

39 See Thornton, 1998, for a discussion of Wittgenstein that engages him with contemporary work in the theory of content like Fodor. My *Wittgenstein on the Conditions for the Possibility of Judgment*, in preparation, contains extended discussion of individualist versus collectivist readings of Wittgenstein.

40 Cf. Dennett, 1987a, for the wandering two-bitser example of the vending machine. Dennett is hospitable to Millikan's approach; he just thinks that the biological norms she employs still fall short of capturing the ordinary full-blooded notion of belief – hence his instrumentalism about belief. This means that I am in close agreement with Dennett; I differ only by allowing that belief can survive if we jettison the representationalist assumption and treat belief relationally. For more on intrinsic/derived intentionality, see Dennett, 1990; Searle, 1990, 1993.

41 Dennett, 1990, characterizes original intentionality in two different ways. One is in terms of the inner Cartesian theatre of private ideas (bad idea), the other in

terms of autonomous agency. The latter is okay as long as it is kept clear from the first idea.

42   Cp. Davidson, 1991.

43   Dennett is instrumentalist about believers – e.g. 1988, p. 496: 'What it is to be a true believer, to have beliefs and desires, is to be an intentional system' – and ascriptivist about intentional systems. In contrast, I follow Clark (1993, pp. 214f) in thinking that Dennett's ascriptivism should be directed at beliefs, not believers. This amounts to intentional realism as I defined it in ch. 1, without the unnecessary reification of belief characteristic of representationalism.

44   E.g. Clark's work on connectionism (1991, 1993), Brooks's work on situated robotics (e.g. 1987, 1991), and see Varela et al., 1991, ch. 9.

Chapter 8   What is a Theory of Reference?

1   Kripke, 1972; Donnellan, 1966, 1968, 1974; Putnam, 1975; Kaplan, 1979, 1989. See Recanati, 1993, for a recent book-length treatment of the 'new theory'.

2   Although all of these, esp. Donnellan, see epistemological and metaphysical consequences of their rejection of Frege's theory. For Donnellan cf. sect. 2.7.

3   Recent Fregean-inspired work is replete with accounts of content that try to be phenomenologically responsive. Not all the following are explicit in their pursuit of phenomenology, but see Eilan et al., 1993, and Eilan forthcoming; Campbell, 1994; Hoerl, 1997; Luntley, 1997, 1998a; McDowell, 1994b; Martin, 1992, 1993a, 1993b.

4   E.g. Grayling, 1982; Haack, 1978; Devitt and Sterelny, 1987.

5   Rorty has repeatedly attacked metaphysical representationalism; e.g. Rorty, 1979.

6   The idea of specifying a non-semantic relation between word and object and then trying to define the semantic relation '. . . stands for _____' in terms of it is, of course, a strategy that Quine adopted and claimed could not succeed. That is the point of his argument for the indeterminacy of translation; cf. ch. 7 above. Although it is not an approach that I favour, the theory of formal semantics as practised in Cresswell, 1994, is significant in arguing that no reduction of the semantic facts about language to non-semantic facts can be achieved.

7   See sect. 1.2 for the definition of representationalism.

8   See Devitt and Sterelny, 1987, for a very clear expression of this point of view.

9   Charles Taylor has done much to explore how to acknowledge the constitutive role which language plays in our conception of reality without collapsing into idealism. See his 1992, where he distinguishes between descriptive and expressivist theories of language, in order to accommodate a notion of linguistic constitution of the real. I do not think Taylor's distinction is required in order to accommodate both the constitutive role which language can play, for example, in social and ethical discourse, and a worthwhile notion of objectivity. For some discussion of this see my 1998b.

10   Putnam has repeatedly argued against representationalism by appeal to the Lowenheim–Skolem theorem, which states (informally) that given any pair of systems there is always an infinite number of possible mappings of items from one domain to

the other that are internally consistent; e.g. Putnam, 1981. Once you separate language and world, à la representationalism, you will never get them back together. The only response seems then to see language as a natural part of the world (naturalism) or the world as part of language (linguistic idealism). The saner version of the latter response is not to see the world as part of language, but to see the world as that which is required in order for language to be the sort of thing it is: viz. a system with the semantic capacity for being correct/incorrect.

11   Cf. sect. 2.2 for details of Russell's object theory of reference.

12   E.g. see Crimmins, 1992, 1995; Salmon, 1986; also Recanati's mixed theory, 1993, 1995.

13   A very clear example of this, and one of Frege's clearest examples all round, is Frege, 1980, p. 80. The passage is quoted at length in Evans, 1982, ch. 1.

14   See sect. 1.2 for more details.

15   The possibility of misrepresentation that I invoke in the possibility of false thoughts is not the same as the possibility of empty singular terms. The two types of misrepresentation are connected. I discuss this issue in chs 9 and 12.

16   For just one example, see Bach, 1987, p. 12, where he lists the various ways of describing the attraction of direct reference theory accounts of thought that have accumulated in the literature: with direct reference thoughts we have the object 'in mind', or we are 'en rapport' with it, or in 'cognitive contact' or 'epistemically intimate' with it.

17   Recanati, 1993, calls them all neo-Russellians. I avoid this label, for Russell endorses direct reference only under the constraint of the principle of acquaintance, and that gives him a quite different motivation from contemporary theorists.

18   Searle (1958) held a descriptive theory of names, so Searle is threatened by FDRT.

19   Recanati, 1993, p. 1. Admittedly this is the vague opening shot, but it is meant to capture the idea abroad in the literature, and in that respect what he says is accurate.

20   Kaplan, 1989, p. 568, 'Afterthoughts'.

21   Ibid., p. 484.

22   Cf. chs 11 and 12 for discussion of the conceptual/non-conceptual content distinction, which has nothing to do with this more traditional identification of conceptual with predicative content.

23   Salmon, 1986, p. 6, however, says that Russellian propositions 'are the contents of thoughts and beliefs', although he does admit (p. 111) that such propositions do not, on their own, give an account of the rational patterns of assent/dissent to sentences.

24   I reserve the word 'proposition' for the notion of propositional content as used by Kaplan and others, and will only use 'thought' for the Fregean notion of content that is concerned with cognitive significance.

25   Kaplan, 1989, p. 532.

26   The character need not involve the idea of perceptual presence, for the 'his' may be working anaphorically, picking up a reference established earlier in the conversation.

27   Recanati, 1993, p. 37.

28   I discuss dual-component theories in ch. 11 below.

29   The indirectness of reference at the level of thought in 'direct reference theory' is

explicit in the endorsement of representationalism, an internalism about content. See Recanati, 1993, ch. 6, also chs 11 and 12 below. Or see Bach, 1987, p. 12, where he speaks of *de re* modes of presentation as 'mental indexicals'. Bach's model is internalist; singular senses are internal mental tokens that require a context in order to get a complete thought.

30   E.g. the symposium involving Crimmins and Recanati in Crimmins, 1995; Recanati, 1995.

31   This is the point that Wettstein, 1986, denied and Perry, 1988, defended. Perry's programme is to define sense in terms of formal rules of applied linguistic usage. See Perry, 1990, and ch. 11 below for more details.

32   Frege, 1892, p. 56.

33   Remember, that on this approach, belief is not an irritating puzzle to be ironed out in a formal semantic theory; its role is constitutive of content defined by its role in rationalizing explanations. See Bilgrami, 1992a, for a similar account of the basic constraint on content.

34   This is Evans' (1982) favoured locution for sense.

35   See Wiggins, 1984.

36   Frege, 1892, p. 59.

37   This introduces the possibility of a higher-order sense to explain how, in oblique contexts, the name stands for the sense – what is the mode of presentation of the sense in such contexts? See Dummett, 1981, ch. 6.

38   See sects 10.2, 10.3, for objections to the descriptive theory of sense.

39   See Dummett, 1981. The issue about objectivity in Frege is part of a larger debate about Frege's realism; see Dummett, 1982a, 1982b, 1991a, and Resnik, 1979, 1980, for an opposing view.

40   This is not necessarily to say that senses are causally real items. That would follow only if you thought that rationalizing explanations of action could be reduced to causal models. Fodor and Dretske provide the classic contemporary attempts to achieve this reduction: see e.g. Fodor, 1990, 1993; Dretske, 1988, 1995b; and Jacob, 1997, for a sympathetic treatment.

41   Cf. sect. 2.2 for the atomism of Russell's notion of acquaintance.

42   See Evans, 1981b, 1982; McDowell, 1977, 1986; Peacocke, 1981, 1992b; Campbell, 1988, 1993b; Luntley, 1995c, 1997; and McCulloch, 1989, for a start on the literature on singular modes of presentation. See Carruthers, 1987, 1988; Noonan, 1986, 1991, 1993; Segal, 1989a, 1989b, 1991, for objections.

43   Wettstein, 1986.

44   Perry, 1988.

45   E.g. Perry, 1990.

Chapter 9   Sense and Reference

1   See Frege, 1980, p. 80, for a clear expression of this point.

2   This is the central result in Kripke, 1972. See ch. 10 for detail on this.

3 See Luntley, 1984, for this way of putting it.

4 It is also a rejection of any approach that is 'representationalist' in Brandom's (1994) sense of that label. Cf. sect. 1.2 for discussion of Brandom.

5 Dummett, 1978a. Dummett's formulation is not altogether happy, for the idea of propositional knowledge is too suggestive of something characterizable in terms of linguistic meaning.

6 Russell, 1911.

7 Ibid., p. 22.

8 Recall the argument of sect. 2.2 that the object theory of reference entails what I there called the principle of contact. Russell's variation on this was to understand this contact epistemologically. See Bach, 1987, p. 12, for the different epistemological formulations of the principle of contact that abound in contemporary discussion.

9 The formulation is due to Evans, 1982, p. 18. See Frege's letter to Jourdain in Frege, 1980, p. 80, for one of the clearest examples of Frege's use of this test. In the same text he also voices his astonishment that anyone could countenance the possibility of an object theory of reference in which objects are constituents of thought. The passage is quoted at length in Evans, 1982, pp. 14–15.

10 See Bilgrami, 1992a, for clear endorsement of this bottom-line constraint on a theory of content. Bilgrami says that the constraint can be traced back to Aristotle.

11 This is the objection that lies behind Devitt and Sterelny's (1987, p. 36) astonishment that Davidson prioritizes truth over reference in e.g. Davidson, 1977b.

12 Luntley, 1998a, for more on this.

13 See sect. 1.4 for the generality constraint and Evans, 1982, pp. 100f.

14 The argument is developed below, sect. 11.2. see also Luntley, 1998a.

15 Compare Davidson's thesis that reference is a 'theoretical posit' within an overall theory of truth: Davidson, 1977b, p. 222.

16 Holding on to this reasonable view is one motivation for non-Fregean theories of belief ascription: e.g. Crimmins, 1992, 1995; Recanati, 1993, 1995; Salmon, 1986. Such theories do not take the rational power of sentences as their basic desideratum. I aim to have it both ways – to take the Fregean idea of the rational power of sentences as primary and hold on to the reasonable view.

17 For a physicalist, it will also turn out to be a physical entity.

18 The Platonic version captures this point too.

19 Compare the blueprint model for thought with the familiar representative model of perceptual experience, in which the existence of illusions and hallucinations is taken to show the existence of intermediary entities – sense-data – in perceptual experience. See Dancy, 1985, 1995, for an entry point to the literature on perception. See McDowell, 1982a, 1986, for a treatment that applies to both thought and perception. Snowdon's 1980–1 is important for formulating an approach to perceptual error – 'the disjunctive account of experience' – that renders error compatible with a direct theory of perception. This compatibility is generally missed. See Snowdon, 1990, 1992, for more on this.

20 Although his approach is very close to mine, Bilgrami, 1992a, misses this point, and seems to endorse a blueprint conception of thought.

21 The Cartesianism is most apparent in Fodor's work, most obviously in his classic 1980; but it is central to his defence of the language of thought hypothesis, e.g. the appendix to 1987. See Evans, 1982, appendix to ch. 6, for the charge of Cartesianism against Fodor. Garcia-Carpintero, 1995, like Fodor, is happy to acknowledge the Cartesian inheritance. The reified model of sense that endorses such separation of mind from the world is a pre-condition for setting up various familiar forms of scepticism. These general issues here are explored in McDowell, 1994b. As noted, Bilgrami, (1992a), although an externalist, seems to endorse a blueprint model. Part of the problem here is the ubiquity of the label 'externalist', which is often used to refer to causal-theoretic externalism, which endorses a dual-component theory of thought. The dual-component theory distinguishes between an internal component (blueprint model) that is then causally linked to the world in a context to determine truth-conditions. Such externalism is weaker than the form found in object-dependent singular thoughts. See ch. 11 below for more on dual-component theories. See Crane, 1991, and Jacob, 1993, for examples of recent work that run together talk about externalist theories of both causal-theoretic and neo-Fregean varieties.

22 This is the account of content that I favour. The argument develops in this direction through this and the next two chapters.

23 E.g. Dretske, 1995b.

24 The quasi-behaviourism that I am defending bears marked similarity to Lynne Rudder Baker's response to physicalist theories of content. She starts from a different point, but our conclusions are remarkably similar. See Baker, 1994, 1995. Thanks to Marc Slors for putting me on to the similarities between my way of understanding contemporary Fregean theory and Baker's work.

25 Recall the discussion of Mill in sect. 2.3 in which, contrary to popular belief, I showed that Mill subscribed to an Ideas-based theory of reference.

26 See McDowell, 1984a, in which he charges Burge, 1977, with failing to distinguish between concepts as content and concepts as bearers of content. The latter is the notion of a linguistic, or quasi-linguistic, item that bears content, and is usefully thought of as something that will carry a descriptive content. The reason for this is that only of descriptive content is it true to say that the contents can be individuated linguistically. In contrast, the notion of concept as content is not so restricted, for we may talk of a demonstrative concept and of the concept of 'I', both of which are clearly not descriptive. Working through the consequences of distinguishing between concept as content and concept as bearer of content will take us through to the end of the book. It is the same distinction as that in the text between the Fregean and the Kantian claims.

27 Recall the lesson from the previous chapter, that although contemporary 'direct reference theorists' acknowledge a notion of thought that is contextual, and so not definable syntactically, they also think that this is different from the idea of content captured by 'cognitive significance'. They cut 'cognitive significance' internally, in terms of a representationalist model of inner states. As I pointed out in the last chapter, the distinctive point about neo-Fregean theory is that it is sense as cognitive significance that is externally individuated. This is why the externalist account of thought on

neo-Fregean terms is both truth-conditional and thought-theoretic, where the latter means that it contributes to an account of the subject's point of view.

28 Hence the Platonistic version of reified senses.

29 The fact that demonstrative thoughts cannot be candidates for a Platonic realm of thought raises some interesting metaphysical puzzles, in addition to being the central insight that defines contemporary Fregean theory. On the former, cf. McGinn, 1983, for the observation that indexical thoughts pose a difficulty for the idea of God as a thinker. The perspectival character of such thoughts renders them unavailable to a mind that views the world *sub specie aeternitatis*. The latter point will occupy us further in chs 11 and 12; but it is the existence of demonstrative senses that blows the hole in the idea that Fregean senses are abstract entities and that the Fregean conception of content is that of linguistic meaning. Perry's classics, 1977, 1979, were thought by many to signal the end of the Fregean project; but they only signalled the end to that project understood in the reified model of sense. At the time Perry wrote, it was already becoming apparent that the Fregean concept of sense could pull apart from the notion of linguistic (i.e. descriptive) meaning, and hence that the reified model of sense, whether in its Platonic or mental version, did not apply to Fregean theory.

30 See Fodor, 1987, 1990, 1993.

31 See previous section.

32 A well-known version of externalism that takes issue with this is Putnam's response to brain-in-the vat scepticism on the basis of an anti-internalism about the meaning of natural kind terms. See Putnam, 1981.

33 Dummett, 1973.

34 Ibid., p. 225.

35 Evans, 1982.

36 Dummett, 1973, p. 227.

37 Ibid.

38 Key sources are McDowell, 1977; Evans, 1982.

39 Evans, 1982, pp. 22f, argues that the evidence that Frege allowed empty names is, at best, contentious. Also see McDowell, 1982b.

40 See Carruthers, 1987, 1988; Noonan, 1986, 1991, 1993; and Segal, 1989a, 1989b, 1991.

41 See Peacocke, 1993, for this response to the explanation problem.

42 See ch. 12, esp. sect. 12.5.

43 See McDowell's powerful essay, 1986, for further investigations in this area and the idea that the theory of singular senses prompts our disavowal of the fundamentally Cartesian imagery of the mind as a configuration that is transparent to introspection. McDowell's alternative is the suggestion that we should view the mind as potentially opaque to the subject, in just the same way that the world is. This raises difficulties in understanding what is nevertheless special about self-knowledge. The question of self-knowledge given externalism is a growing area of work: Bilgrami, 1992b, 1995; Cassam, 1994, 1996; Davidson, 1987b.

44 Sect. 4.6 above.

Chapter 10   The Causal Theory of Reference and
the Social Character of Meaning

1   Kripke, 1972.
2   The resurgence of interest in essentialist metaphysics owes as much to Putnam's work on natural kind terms, *locus classicus* Putnam, 1975. For a start on the metaphysics of essentialism, see Forbes, 1989.
3   Kripke, 1979.
4   For a classic statement of the dual-component theory of content, see McGinn, 1982.
5   The idea that narrow content picks out cognitive significance is shared by Kaplan, Perry, Bach and Recanati; see the discussion in sect. 8.4 above.
6   Fodor's use of a causal theory bears comparison with Field's idea of a causal theory of reference and satisfaction as an addendum to Tarski's theory of truth; see sect. 3.7 above.
7   Searle, 1958. Searle's later work is still informed by a view of intentionality that is best made sense of on a descriptivist theory of content. See Searle, 1983, in which even in his treatment of context-sensitive expressions like indexicals, he attempts to give a broadly descriptivist account of content.
8   It would be an interesting exercise in the history of ideas to trace exactly how this misconception arose about Frege. The view of Frege as a descriptivist is most common among American writers. One explanation for the different readings of Frege on either side of the Atlantic is that American students come to Frege through Carnap's account of him. Carnap's interests were in the development of formal model-theoretic semantics for language. For Carnap, the distinction between denotation and connotation was a distinction that took its place within a formal theory designed to capture the inferential structures at play in language, especially a language fit for scientific work. Apart from the fact that the term 'connotation' does not figure in Frege's writings, Carnap's idea has little if anything to do with the intentionality of thought; it is not part of a description of the structure of the way we think about objects. In British philosophy, the logico-empiricism of Carnap's enquiries never took firm root, and British philosophers were left to read Frege under an altogether different influence – that of Wittgenstein.
9   Cf. sect. 8.4.
10   This response was first made by Brody, 1977.
11   Amongst others, Devitt, 1981; Devitt and Sterelny, 1987; and Bach, 1987, use 'rigid' to mean direct reference in the sense of the Russellian object theory of reference.
12   Sect. 2.7.
13   Kripke, 1972, p. 12.
14   Putnam, 1975, has a similar theory about the social character of meaning of natural kind terms, in which he thinks that ordinary use of terms like 'water' and 'gold' defers to the scientific specialists who know the nature of the stuff.
15   A reason for endorsing the assumption that the content that figures in rationalizing explanations must be individualistic and in the head is the idea that rationalizing

explanations can be reduced to physical causal explanations, and that, therefore, the notion of content involved must be internalist. This is Fodor's reason for objecting to various forms of externalism: e.g. Fodor, 1987, ch. 2. More on this in the next chapter.

16 Kripke, 1972, pp. 15, 55, 57.

17 Ibid., p. 92.

18 Ibid., p. 93.

19 One response would be to see Kripke as merely making a point in favour of a direct reference theory, so that it is propositional content, the 'what is said' that is defined causally, leaving 'cognitive significance' to be filled out by some other means. This side-step does not work, for it is not compatible with the claimed informational insensitivity of reference. Furthermore, such a notion of linguistic reference, in not capturing cognitive significance, does not capture what matters about language use – viz. that we express thoughts with language. Perhaps Kripke, like many others, does not see the scope for a theory of thought that is not based on linguistic meaning, and so takes the linguistic result to have broader application than it really has.

20 E.g. Kripke, 1972, p. 95.

21 Contrast the way Devitt and Sterelny, 1987, see the options.

22 Ibid., pp. 49ff.

23 Evans gives an example of how mere causal chains get things wrong in the case of a switch of identical twins shortly after baptism (1973). See Devitt and Sterelny, 1987, p. 62, for their causal response to these problems. They blithely remark that we can distinguish different causal chains in these cases: e.g. the causal chain focused on Marco Polo and that focused on the original natives. That we can make such distinctions is besides the point. What matter are the principles according to which such distinctions are drawn, and I can see no way of drawing the distinctions correctly that does not appeal to informational links, rather than causal links. Indeed, the very idea of drawing the distinction correctly is constituted by the idea of informational links.

24 Taylor, 1992.

25 See discussion of Kripke, 1982, in ch. 7 above.

26 Kripke, 1972, p. 163.

27 Ibid., p. 93.

28 Ibid., p. 95.

Chapter 11   Content and Context

1 E.g. Kaplan, 1979, 1989; Perry, 1979, 1993; Barwise and Perry, 1983; Corazza and Dokic, 1994; Yourgrau, 1990.

2 Evans, 1982.

3 E.g. Field, 1980.

4 Cf. ch. 2 above for details.

5 E.g. Dretske, 1986; McGinn, 1982, pp. 212–13; also Recanati, 1993, pp. 213ff.

6   The argument for object-dependency in the light of cases of perceptual error is discussed in sect. 12.5.

7   Even adoption of a free logic is not going to help this particular problem. For a survey of options in free logic, cf. Read, 1994, ch. 5.

8   Cf. sect. 2.2 above for details.

9   This is not necessarily a social concept of practice.

10 Recall the argument against the reified model of sense and Fodor's language of thought hypothesis in sect. 9.4.

11 See the essays in Eilan et al., 1993, and Campbell, 1994.

12 Although the obvious consequence of accommodating Russell's insight lies with our conception of the mind, it has bearing on our account of judgement and reasoning in a number of key areas. One of these is the nature of moral judgement. The idea that the capacity for moral judgement might also be seen as a practical mastery of the way the subject is embedded in a moral world has been explored in Luntley, 1995a, 1995b, 1998b.

13 Putnam, 1975.

14 The fact that we would not call the XYZ stuff 'water' is indicative of the metaphysical necessity that water is H_2O; that is its essence.

15 The Twin-Earth thought-experiment has become stock-in-trade. Two collections that specifically address the broad issues concerning the environmental dependence of thought are Woodfield, 1982, and Pettit and McDowell, 1986. It is important to keep distinct Putnam's arguments for dependence of meaning on the natural environment and Burge's superficially similar arguments against what he calls 'individualism' that stress a dependence of meaning on the social environment in the case of *de dicto* beliefs. Burge's work is found in a string of important papers: 1979, 1986a, 1989. I have largely ignored Burge's arguments, not because I do not think them important, but because they do not fit easily into the dialectic I have been pursuing. My criticism of Putnam's form of externalism should not be thought transferable to Burge's. Indeed, Burge's anti-individualism is probably compatible with the more radical neo-Fregean externalism that I defend.

16 Field, 1977.

17 'XYZ is indistinguishable from water at normal temperatures and pressures' (Putnam, 1975, pp. 223).

18 This argument is in Putnam, 1981.

19 E.g. Fodor, 1987, ch. 2.

20 Dennett (1982) uses this sort of consideration to argue against the idea that there are adequate principles for the individuation of belief.

21 See McGinn, 1982.

22 Putnam does not use the term 'narrow content'; he is concerned only with meaning defined in terms of truth-conditions.

23 E.g. Dennett's instrumentalism, 1982, or the eliminativism of Stich, 1983, and P. M. Churchland, 1995, and P. S. Churchland, 1986. See also ch. 7 above.

24 This appeal is explicit in Fodor, 1980.

25 Fodor, 1987, esp. ch. 2.

26 Evans, 1982, pp. 206ff. Contrast Recanati, 1993, pp. 206ff, and his assumption that misrepresentation requires the possibility of empty names. I think the issue about empty names is a red herring; see sect. 12.5.

27 This point is central to much recent work in the philosophy of psychology on spatial representation and consciousness. It has been traditional to think of the idea of a point of view in terms of qualia – an epistemologically defined internal array. Recent work makes plain the option of treating the idea of a point of view not in terms of qualia, but in terms of the mode of presentation thought of as the orientation provided by e.g. the spatial representation of a place as 'here' or 'there', or as 'that place'. Cf. essays in Eilan et al., 1993.

28 See McDowell, 1994b, lecture 3.

29 E.g. Crane, 1992b; Bermudez, 1995; Jacob, 1997; Peacocke, 1992a, 1994.

30 McDowell, 1994b, accuses Burge, 1977, of this confusion.

31 The notion of informational content just alluded to is that found in much work in cognitive science. It is also the notion of non-conceptual content that Evans employs in his account of what he calls the 'information system' (1982, pp. 122ff). It is a different notion from the idea of non-conceptual content that is sometimes invoked in giving accounts of experience, where the content of the experience is finer-grained than is possible by reference to the linguistic resources of the subject of experience; see items referred in n. 29 above. I criticize this latter idea of non-conceptual content in the next chapter. The examples in the literature turn out, on the account defended, to be conceptual contents. I do not rule out the possibility, however, of there being an important notion of non-conceptual content.

32 For a defence of a direct theory of perception that accommodates misperceptions by defining 'looks' states disjunctively, see Snowdon, 1980–1, 1992.

33 Dennett, 1982.

34 For Davidson's opposition to the reification of content, cf. Davidson, 1991.

35 Indeed, even in the formal case I think it is a mistake to say that symbol strings have rational power. They have a formally defined power to prompt other symbol strings, but this is not rational power; it has nothing to do with reasons for belief, change in belief, or reasons for action. Cf. Harman, 1986, for the argument that the rational notion of change of belief is not the same as the logical notion of deductive entailment.

36 Herein lies the truth of Wittgenstein's dictum that 'meaning is use'. Recall also the point made in ch. 2 that Russell is not committed to the idea of 'sign semantics' – that symbols have semantic power *qua* symbols. All Russell needed to avoid Strawson's objection to his theory of descriptions was the idea that the semantic power of symbols was a function of normal use. The same point recurred in handling Kripke's analysis of why Russell's account of descriptions is not refuted by Donnellan's example; see sect. 2.7 for the contrast between semantic reference and speaker reference as a distinction between normal use and those cases where speaker's intentions override normal use. The idea that sentences as such do not possess rational power is, of course, the idea that sentences have only derived intentionality, not intrinsic intentionality. See Dennett, 1990, for critique of the idea that anything has intrinsic intentionality.

Fodor's language of thought hypothesis is the hypothesis that, for a favoured class of sentences (those within the language of thought), they do have intrinsic intentionality (rational power).

37   This is the model discussed briefly in sect. 8.4.
38   Perry, 1979.
39   The connection between agency and the capacity for indexical thinking has been noted by a number of writers – e.g. McGinn, 1983; Nagel, 1986.
40   Perry, 1979, p. 86.
41   Ibid.
42   For a fuller discussion of the phenomena of dynamic thoughts, see my 1997 and 1998a; Perry, 1990, 1993; Corazza and Dokic, 1994; Hoerl, 1997.

Chapter 12   Contextual Content

1   Evans was clear about this; cf. (his 1982), appendix to ch. 6. In contrast, Garcia-Carpintero (1995) does not see the Cartesianism of contemporary representationalist theories of the mind problematic.
2   Evans, 1982, p. 19.
3   Cf. Luntley, 1997, for more on dynamic thoughts.
4   Sect. 2.7 above.
5   Strawson, 1959, ch. 1.
6   Recanati (1993) treats proper names as indexical devices, for broadly similar reasons.
7   Evans, 1982, ch. 6.
8   Cf. sect. 10.6, where I said that the preliminary dossier should be thought of as the connection to, rather than the plug for, a name-using practice.
9   The notion of objective truth and falsity amounts, for present purposes, to the notion of minimal truth defended in ch. 5; it is the idea of things independent of will.
10   I use 'grammatical', rather than 'inferentialist', to contrast with Brandom's (1994) conception of inferentialist. The difference is that grammar includes a notion of normative patterns to thought that bring with them an ineliminable objectivity that is missing in the mere coherentism of an inferentialist conception of normativity. The objectivity of the normative patterns of demonstrative thought turns on their fundamental grounding in our 'hands-on' experience of objects. See sect. 12.6 below.
11   Evans, 1982, pp. 107ff.
12   For objections to object-dependency due to cases of perceptual illusion, see Noonan, 1986, 1991, 1993; Carruthers, 1987, 1988; Segal, 1989a, 1989b, 1991; Recanati, 1993. McDowell, 1994b, lecture 3, although in agreement with Evans on object-dependency, disagrees with Evans's use of the idea of the information link in Evans's epistemology of singular reference.
13   Evans, 1982, pp. 145ff.
14   Ibid., p. 22.
15   See Carruthers, 1987, 1988, for this sort of worry.

16 Other externalist theories have the same feature. It is not clear that the loss of mental transparency is a problem, although it does mean that any externalism that renders your own mind opaque owes you an account of the apparently privileged and authoritative character of self-knowledge. Bilgrami is one writer who has tackled this issue head-on: cf. Bilgrami, 1992a, 1992b, 1995. See also Davidson, 1987b; Cassam, 1996; and the essays in Cassam, 1994.

17 Evans, 1982, p. 173.

18 You have to be careful not to confuse the requirement for an objective conception with that for an absolute conception; cf. Luntley, 1989, for some general diagnosis of the philosophical errors that arise from confusing these. See Campbell, 1994, for use of the term 'absolute space' when discussing the difference between egocentric and allocentric locations of objects, in which, I take it, all he needs is a notion of objective space, not absolute space.

19 There is a sense, then, in which the very idea of a particular is understood only from the point of view of a thinking subject; for our very notion of what it is for something to be a particular is a notion such that the subject never drops out of the picture. Cf. Campbell, 1993a, for this point.

20 Evans, 1982, discusses these examples, esp. in ch. 6, sect. 3; see pp. 164f for the submarine example.

21 The latter would support the neo-Russellian notion of singular propositions familiar from the work of Kaplan and Perry; see discussion in sect. 8.4 above.

22 The modalities involved in the fundamental individuation of thoughts are not epistemic modalities. They would be better classified as transcendental modalities. Cf. Luntley, 1995c, for more on this.

23 See Evans, 1982, p. 176, for admission of this kind of possibility.

24 Ibid., p. 168.

25 McDowell endorses a disjunctive account of perceptual experience in 1982a, 1986. With regard to the thought that the subject has in illusory cases, McDowell has not explicitly taken the disjunctive approach that ascribes a descriptive thought when the object is absent. In his 1977 McDowell says that when the subject thinks they are having a singular thought when no object is present, what they are really having is a second-order thought that they think they are having a singular thought. This seems not to be true to the phenomenology. The option of a descriptive thought preserves more of the subject's phenomenal report, especially if it turns out to be a descriptive thought with an embedded singular mode of presentation of a place as I suggest.

26 Contrast Recanati's uniform treatment of perceptual error cases in 1993, pp. 206f.

27 Brandom, 1994, p. 6.

28 It is interesting to note that just as Descartes is often accused of having no adequate account of the individuation of minds, so he also lacks a credible account of the individuation of objects, for he thinks of them as fundamentally geometric entities. In contrast to Locke's account, objects for Descartes do not *occupy* space; they are merely a spatial shape. See Cottingham, 1986, for some discussion of this.

29 Luntley, 1998a.

30 Wittgenstein is often read as supporting a social concept of practice; for a recent defence of this, see Bloor, 1998. I think this is a mistaken reading of Wittgenstein (Luntley, 1991b). The worldly non-social concept of practice offers scope for a notion of objectivity in, say, ethical discourse, that does not collapse into mere social description; see Luntley, 1995a, 1995b, 1998b, and Wiggins, 1987. Others who seem to endorse a social concept of practice range from Brandom, 1994, and Wright, 1992, to Rorty, 1991, and Rouse, 1996.

31 For the importance of causal indexical thoughts, see Campbell, 1994. For work on spatial representation and consciousness, see Eilan et al., 1993; Eilan, forthcoming; on perception, see Brewer, 1993; Martin, 1992, 1993a, 1993b; McDowell, 1994a; see DeBellis, 1994, for a discussion of the conceptual/non-conceptual content distinction applied to the experience of music that draws upon elements of the neo-Fregean approach.

32 The prospect beckons of a naturalized theory of content that fits the Fregean description of intentionality into a detailed account of how we act in the world, an account that draws upon empirical work of developmental psychologists on attention, spatial and temporal thinking, etc. The Humanities Research Board Project on Consciousness and Self-Consciousness hosted at Warwick and directed by Naomi Eilan has as its brief just such an interdisciplinary approach. As I finished this book, the 27 March 1998 Workshop on Joint Attention was a paradigm of collaboration between philosophers and psychologists.

Bibliography

(Page references are to the last mentioned source.)

Austin, J. L. (1950): Truth. *Proceedings of the Aristotelian Society*, suppl. vol., 24, 111–28. Repr. in Austin, 1970, 117–33.

—— (1970): *Philosophical Papers*, ed. J. Urmson and G. Warnock Oxford: Clarendon Press.

Bach, K. (1987): *Thought and Reference*. Oxford: Oxford University Press.

Baker, G. and Hacker, P. M. S. (1984): *Scepticism, Rules and Language*. Oxford: Blackwell.

—— (1988): *Wittgenstein, Rules, Grammar, and Necessity (An Analytical Commentary on The Philosophical Investigations*, vol. 2). Oxford: Blackwell.

Baker, L. R. (1994): Attitudes as nonentities. *Philosophical Studies*, 76, 175–203.

—— (1995): *Explaining Attitudes: a practical approach to the mind*. Cambridge: Cambridge University Press.

Barwise, J. and Perry, J. (1983): *Situations and Attitudes*. Cambridge, Mass.: MIT Press.

Bealer, G. (1982): *Quality and Concept*. Oxford: Clarendon Press.

Belnap, N. (1961–2): Tonk, plonk and plink. *Analysis*, 22, 40–4.

Bennett, J. (1988): *Events and their Names*. Indianapolis: Hackett.

Bermudez, J. (1994): Peacocke's argument against the autonomy of nonconceptual representational content. *Mind and Language*, 9, 402–18.

—— (1995): Nonconceptual content: from perceptual experience to subpersonal computational states. *Mind and Language*, 10, 333–69.

Bilgrami, A. (1992a): *Belief and Meaning: the unity and locality of mental content*. Cambridge, Mass.: Blackwell.

—— (1992b): Can externalism be reconciled with self-knowledge? *Philosophical Topics*, 20, 233–67.

—— (1995): Self-knowledge and resentment. In P. K. Sen (ed.), *The Philosophy of P. F. Strawson*, New Delhi: Indian Council for Philosophical Research, 213–33.

Blackburn, S. (1984): *Spreading the Word: groundings in the philosophy of language*. Oxford: Clarendon Press.

—— (1988): How to be an ethical antirealist. In *Midwest Studies in Philosophy*, Minneapolis: University of Minnesota Press, vol. 12, 361–75.

Bloor, D. (1998): *Wittgenstein*. London: Routledge.

380

Boghossian, P. (1990): The status of content. *Philosophical Review*, 99, 157–84.

—— (1991a): Naturalizing content. In Barry Loewer (ed.), *Meaning in Mind: Fodor and his critics*, Oxford: Blackwell, 65–86.

—— (1991b): Physicalist theories of color. *Philosophical Review*, 100, 67–106.

Brandom, R. (1994): *Making It Explicit: reasoning, representing, and discursive commitment.* Cambridge, Mass.: Harvard Universily Press.

Brewer, B. (1993): The integration of spatial vision and action. In Eilan et al., 294–316.

Brody, B. (1977): Kripke on proper names. In E. French (ed.), *Midwest Studies in Philosophy*, Minneapolis: University of Minnesota Press, vol. 2, 64–9.

Brooks, R. (1987): *Intelligence without Representation.* Cambridge, Mass.: MIT Artificial Intelligence Report.

—— (1991): Intelligence without reason. In *Proceedings of the IJCAI*, Sydney.

Brouwer, L. E. J. (1975): Consciousness, philosophy and mathematics. In A. Heyting (ed.), *Collected Papers*, vol. 1, Amsterdam: Kluwer, 480–94.

Burge, T. (1977): Belief *de re. Journal of Philosophy*, 74, 338–62.

—— (1979): Individualism and the mental. In *Midwest Studies in Philosophy*, Minneapolis: Univesity of Minnesota Press, vol. 4, 73–121.

—— (1986a): Individualism and psychology. *Philosophical Review*, 95, 3–45.

—— (1986b): Intellectual norms and foundations of mind. *Journal of Philosophy*, 83, 697–720.

—— (1989): Individuation and causation in psychology. *Pacific Philosophical Quarterly*, 70, 303–22.

—— (1993): Mind–body causation and explanatory practice. In J. Heil and A. Mele (eds), *Mental Causation*, Oxford: Clarendon Press, 97–120.

Campbell, J. (1982): Knowledge and understanding. *Philosophical Quarterly*, 32, 17–34.

—— (1988): Is sense transparent? *Proceedings of the Aristotelian Society*, 88, 273–92.

—— (1993a): A simple view of colour. In J. Haldane (ed.), *Reality, Representation, and Projection*, Oxford: Oxford University Press, 257–68.

—— (1993b): The role of physical objects in spatial thinking. In Eilan et al., 65–96.

—— (1994): *Past, Space, and Self.* Cambridge, Mass.: MIT Press.

Carruthers, P. (1987): Russellian thoughts. *Mind*, 96, 18–35.

—— (1988): More faith than hope: Russellian thoughts attacked. *Analysis*, 48, 91–6.

Cassam, Q. (ed.) (1994): *Self-knowledge.* Oxford: Oxford University Press.

—— (1996): Self-reference, self-knowledge and the problem of misconception. *European Journal of Philosophy*, 4, 276–95.

Charles, D. and Lennon, K. (1992): *Realism, Explanation and Reduction.* Oxford: Clarendon Press.

Chisholm, R. (1977): *Theory of Knowledge*, 2nd edn. Englewood Cliffs, NJ: Prentice-Hall.

Chomsky, N. (1965): *Aspects of the Theory of Syntax.* Cambridge, Mass.: MIT Press.

Churchland, P. M. (1995): *The Engine of Reason, the Seat of the Soul: a philosophical journey into the brain.* Cambridge, Mass.: MIT Press.

Churchland, P. S. (1986): *Neurophilosophy: toward a unified science of the mind-brain.* Cambridge, Mass.: MIT Press.

Clark, A. (1988): Critical study of *Psychosemantics. Mind*, 97, 605–17.

—— (1991): *Microcognition: philosophy, cognitive science, and parallel distributed processing.* Cambridge, Mass.: MIT Press.

—— (1993): *Associative Engines: connectionism, concepts and representational change.* Cambridge, Mass.: MIT Press.

Corazza, E. and Dokic, J. (1994): On the cognitive significance of indexicals. *Philosophical Studies*, 66, 183–96.

Cottingham, J. (1986): Descartes. 'Sixth Meditation': the external world, 'Nature' and human experience. *Philosophy*, 20, 73–89.

Crane T. (1991): All the Difference in the World. *Philosophical Quarterly*, 4, 1–25.

Crane, T. (ed.) (1992a): *The Contents of Experience.* Cambridge: Cambridge University Press.

Crane, T. (ed.) (1992b): The nonconceptual content of experience. In Crane, 1992a, 136–57.

Cresswell, M. (1994): *Language in the World: a philosophical enquiry.* Cambridge: Cambridge University Press.

Crimmins, M. (1992): *Talk about Beliefs.* Cambridge, Mass.: MIT Press.

—— (1995): Quasi-singular propositions: the semantics of belief reports. *Proceedings of the Aristotelian Society*, suppl. vol. 69, 195–209.

Dancy, J. (1985): *Introduction to Contemporary Epistemology.* Oxford: Blackwell.

—— (1995): Arguments from illusion. *Philosophical Quarterly*, 45, 421–38.

Davidson, D. (1967a): The logical form of action sentences. In N. Rescher (ed.), *The Logic of Decision and Action*, Pittsburgh: University of Pittsburgh Press. Repr. in Davidson, 1980, 105–21.

—— (1967b): Truth and meaning. *Synthese*, 17, 304–23. Repr. in Davidson, 1984, 17–36.

—— (1969): The individuation of events. In N. Rescher (ed.), *Essays in Honor of Carl G. Hempel*, Dordrecht: Reidel, 216–34. Repr. in Davidson, 1980, 163–80.

—— (1970): Mental events. In L. Foster and J. Swanson (eds), *Experience and Theory*, Amherst: University of Massachusetts Press. Repr. in Davidson, 1980, 207–24.

—— (1973): Radical interpretation. *Dialectica*, 27, 313–18. Repr. in Davidson, 1984, 125–40.

—— (1974): On the very idea of a conceptual scheme. *Proceedings and Addresses of the American Philosophial Association*, 47. Repr. in Davidson, 1984, 183–98.

—— (1977a): The method of truth in metaphysics. In *Midwest Studies in Philosophy*, vol. 2: *Studies in the Philosophy of Language*, 244–54. Repr. in Davidson, 1984, 199–214.

—— (1977b): Reality without reference. *Dialectica*, 31, 247–53. Repr. in Davidson, 1984, 215–26.

—— (1980): *Essays on Actions and Events.* Oxford: Clarendon Press.

—— (1984): *Inquiries into Truth and Interpretation.* Oxford: Oxford University Press.

—— (1986): A coherence theory of truth and knowledge. In Lepore, 307–19.

—— (1987a): Afterthoughts 1987. Published with a reprint of Davidson's 1986 in A. Malachowski (ed.), *Reading Rorty*, 1991, 134–58.

—— (1987b): Knowing one's own mind. *Proceedings of the American Philosophical Association*, 60, 441–58.

—— (1990): The structure and content of truth. *Journal of Philosophy*, 87, 279–328.

—— (1991): What is present to the mind. In E. Villanueva (ed.), *Consciousness* (Philosophical Issues, vol. 6), Atascadero: Ridgeview, 197–214.

Davidson, D. and Hintikka, J. (eds) (1969): *Words and Objections*. Dordrecht: Reidel.

Davies, M. (1987): Tacit knowledge and semantic theory: can a five per cent difference matter? *Mind*, 96, 441–62.

—— (1989): Connectionism, modularity, and tacit knowledge. *British Journal for the Philosophy of Science*, 40, 541–55.

—— (1995a): Tacit knowledge and subdoxastic states. In Macdonald and Macdonald, 309–30.

—— (1995b): Two notions of implicit rules. In J. Tomberlin (ed.), *AI, Connectionism and Philosophical Psychology,* Atascadero: Ridgeview.

Davies, M. and Stone, T. (1993): Cognitive neuropsychology and the philosophy of mind. *British Journal for the Philosophy of Science*, 44, 589–622.

DeBellis, M. (1994): *Music and Conceptualization*. Cambridge: Cambridge University Press.

Dennett, D. (1982): Beyond belief. In Woodfield, 1–96.

—— (1987a): Evolution, error and intentionality. In Dennett, 1987b, 287–321.

—— (1987b): *The Intentional Stance*. Cambridge, Mass.: MIT Press.

—— (1988): Précis of *The Intentional Stance* and author's response. *Behavioural and Brain Sciences*, 2, 495–546.

—— (1990): The myth of original intentionality. In K. A. Mohyeldin Said, W. H. Newton-Smith, R. Viale and K. V. Wilkes (eds), *Modelling the Mind*, Oxford: Oxford University Press, 43–62.

—— (1991a): *Consciousness Explained*. London: Allen Lane.

—— (1991b): Real patterns. *Journal of Philosophy*, 88, 27–51.

—— (1993): The message is: there is no medium. *Philosophy and Phenomenological Research*, 53, 919–31.

—— (1996): Cow-sharks, magnets, and swampman. *Mind and Language*, 11, 76–7.

Devitt, M. (1981): *Designation*. New York: Columbia University Press.

—— (1983): Dummett's anti-realism. *Journal of Philosophy*, 80, 73–99.

—— (1991a): Aberrations of the realism debate. *Philosophical Studies*, 61, 43–63.

—— (1991b): *Realism and Truth*, 2nd edn. Oxford: Blackwell.

Devitt, M. and Sterelny, K. (1987): *Language and Reality: an introduction to the philosophy of language*. Cambridge, Mass.: MIT Press.

Donnellan, K. (1966): Reference and definite descriptions. *Philosophical Review*, 75, 281–304. Repr. in Martinich, 1985, 236–48.

—— (1968): Putting Humpty Dumpty together again. *Philosophical Review*, 77, 203–15.

—— (1974): Speaking of nothing. *Philosophical Review*, 83, 3–31.

Dretske, F. (1986): Misrepresentation. In Radu J. Bogdan (ed.), *Belief: form, content and function*, Oxford: Clarendon Press, 17–36.

—— (1988): *Explaining Behavior: reasons in a world of causes*. Cambridge, Mass.: MIT Press.

—— (1995a): Does meaning matter? In Macdonald and Macdonald, 107–20.

—— (1995b): *Naturalizing the Mind*. Cambridge, Mass.: MIT Press.

Dreyfus, H. (1992): *What Computers 'Still' Can't Do: a critique of artificial reason*, Rev. edn. Cambridge, Mass.: MIT Press.

Dummett, M. (1973): *Frege: philosophy of language*. London: Duckworth (2nd ed. 1981).

—— (1975): What is a theory of meaning? I. In S. Guttenplan (ed.), *Mind and Language*, Oxford: Clarendon Press, 97–138.

—— (1976): What is a theory of meaning? II. In Evans and McDowell, 67–137.

—— (1977): *Elements of Intuitionism*. Oxford: Clarendon Press.

—— (1978a): Frege's distinction between sense and reference. In *Truth and other Enigmas*, London: Duckworth, 116–44.

—— (1978b): *Truth and Other Enigmas*. London: Duckworth; Cambridge, Mass.: Harvard University Press.

—— (1978c): *What Do I Know when I Know a Language?* Lecture delivered at the Centenary Celebrations of Stockholm University, 24 May 1978, published by University of Stockholm.

—— (1981): *The Interpretation of Frege's Philosophy*. Cambridge, Mass.: Harvard University Press.

—— (1982a): Frege and Kant on geometry. *Inquiry*, 25, 233–54.

—— (1982b): Objectivity and reality in Lotze and Frege. *Inquiry*, 25, 95–114.

—— (1991a): *Frege: philosophy of mathematics*. Cambridge, Mass.: Harvard University Press.

—— (1991b): *The Logical Basis of Metaphysics*. Cambridge, Mass.: Harvard University Press.

—— (1993): *Origins of Analytical Philosophy*. Cambridge, Mass.: Harvard University Press.

Edginton, D. (1985): The paradox of knowability. *Mind*, 94, 557–68.

Eilan, N. (forthcoming): *Consciousness*. Oxford: Clarendon Press.

Eilan, N. McCarthy, R. and Brewer, B. (eds) (1993): *Spatial Representation*. Oxford: Blackwell.

Evans, G. (1973): The causal theory of names. *Proceedings of the Aristotelian Society*, suppl. vol. 47, 187–208.

—— (1975): Identity and predication. *Journal of Philosophy*, 72, 343–63.

—— (1981a): Semantic theory and tacit knowledge. In S. Holtzman and C. Leich (eds), *Wittgenstein: to follow a rule*, London: Routledge & Kegan Paul, 118–37.

—— (1981b): Understanding demonstratives. In H. Parret (ed.), *Meaning and Understanding*, Berlin: Gruyter, 280–304.

—— (1982): *The Varieties of Reference*, ed. J. McDowell. Oxford: Clarendon Press.

Evans, G. and McDowell, J. (1976): *Truth and Meaning: essays in semantics*. Oxford: Clarendon Press.

Field, H. (1972): Tarski's theory of truth. *Journal of Philosophy*, 69, 347–75. Repr. in M. Platts (ed.), *Reference, Truth and Reality*, London: Routledge & Kegan Paul, 1980, 83–110.

—— (1974): Quine and the correspondence theory. *Philosophical Review*, 83, 200–28.

—— (1977): Logic, meaning and conceptual role. *Journal of Philosophy*, 74, 379–409.

—— (1980): *Science without Numbers*. Oxford: Blackwell.

—— (1986): The deflationary conception of truth. In G. Macdonald and C. Wright (eds), *Fact, Science and Morality*, Oxford: Blackwell, 55–117.

Fodor, J. (1980): Methodological solipsism considered as a research strategy in cognitive psychology. *Behavioural and Brain Sciences*, 3, 63–73.

—— (1984): Semantics, Wisconsin style. *Synthese*, 59, 231–50. Repr. in Fodor, 1990, 31–49.

—— (1985): Fodor's guide to mental representation. *Mind*, 94, 55–97. Repr. in Fodor, 1990, 3–29.

—— (1986): Why paramecia don't have mental representations. In P. French (ed.), *Midwest Studies in Philosophy*, Minneapolis: University of Minnesota Press, 3–23.

—— (1987): *Psychosemantics*. Cambridge, Mass.: MIT Press.

—— (1990): *A Theory of Content and Other Essays*. Cambridge, Mass.: MIT Press.

—— (1991): A modal argument for narrow Content. *Journal of Philosophy*, 88, 5–26.

—— (1993): *The Elm and the Expert: Mentalese and its semantics*. Cambridge, Mass.: MIT Press.

Fodor, J. and Lepore, E. (1992): *Holism*. Oxford: Blackwell.

Follesdal, D. (1987): The status of rationality assumptions in interpretation and the explanation of Action. *Dialectica*, 36, 301–16.

Forbes, G. (1989): *Languages of Possibility*. Oxford: Blackwell.

Frege, G. (1884): *Die Grundlagen der Arithmetik*, trans. J. L. Austin as *The Foundations of Arithmetic*, 2nd rev. edn. Oxford: Blackwell, 1978.

—— (1892): Über Sinn und Bedeutung. *Zeitschrift für Philosophie und philosophische Kritik*, 100, 25–50. Trans. as 'On Sense and Reference', in P. Geach and M. Black, *Translations from the Philosophical Writings of Gottlob Frege*, Oxford: Blackwell, 1966, 56–78.

—— (1918): Der Gedanke. Trans. A. and M. by Quinton as 'The Thought', *Mind*, 65, 289–311. Repr. in P. Strawson (ed.), *Philosophical Logic*, Oxford: Oxford University Press, 1967, 17–38.

—— (1980): *Philosophical and Mathematical Correspondence*, English edn abridged by B. McGuinness, trans. H. Kaal. Oxford: Blackwell.

Fricker, E. (1982–3): Semantic structure and speakers understanding. *Proceedings of the Aristotelian Society*, 83, 49–66.

Garcia-Carpintero, M. (1995): The philosophical import of connectionism: a critical notice of Andy Clark's *Associative Engines*. *Mind and Language*, 10, 370–401.

Gibbard, A. (1990): *Wise Choices, Apt Feelings: a theory of normative judgment*. Cambridge, Mass.: Harvard University Press.

—— (1996): Projection, quasi-realism, and sophisticated realism. *Mind*, 105, 331–5.

Gibson, R. (1982): *The Philosophy of W. V. Quine*. Tampa: University Presses of Florida.

—— (1986): Translation, physics and facts of the matter. In L. Hahn and P. Schilpp (eds), *Philosophy of W. V. Quine*, La Salle, Ill.: Open Court, 139–54.

Grayling, A. C. (1982): *An Introduction to Philosophical Logic*. Brighton: Harvester.

Grice, P. (1969): Vacuous names. In Davidson and Hintikka, 118–45.

Grover, D., Camp, J. and Belnap, N. (1975): A prosentential theory of truth. *Philosophical Studies*, 27, 73–125.

Haack, S. (1976): Is it true what they say about Tarski? *British Journal for the Philosophy of Science*, 51, 323–36.

—— (1978): *Philosophy of Logics*. Cambridge: Cambridge University Press.

Hacking, I. (1975): *Why Does Language Matter to Philosophy?* Cambridge: Cambridge University Press.

Harman, G. (1986): *Change in View: principles of reasoning*. Cambridge, Mass.: MIT Press.

Hoerl, C. (1997): Changing your mind. In *European Review of Philosophy*, vol. 2: *Cognitive Dynamics*, Stanford, Calif: CSLI, 141–58.

Hookway, C. (1988): *Quine*. Cambridge: Polity Press.

Hornsby, J. (1977): Singular terms in contexts of propositional attitude. *Mind*, 86, 31–48.

Horwich, P. (1990): *Truth*, Oxford: Blackwell.

Hurley, S. L. (1992): Intelligibility, imperialism, and conceptual scheme. *Midwest Studies in Philosophy*, 17, 89–108.

Jacob, P. (1993): Externalism and the explanatory relevance of broad content. *Mind and Language*, 8, 131–56.

—— (1997): *What Minds Can Do*. Cambridge: Cambridge University Press.

Johnston, M. (1989): Dispositional theories of value. *Proceedings of the Aristotelian Society*, suppl. vol. 63, 139–74.

—— (1992): How to speak of the colors. *Philosophical Studies*, 68, 221–63.

Kaplan, D. (1979): Dthat. In P. French (ed.), *Contemporary Perspectives in the Philosophy of Language*, Minneapolis: University of Minnesota Press, 383–400.

—— (1989): Demonstratives: an essay on the semantics, logic, metaphysics, and epistemology of demonstratives. In J. Almog, J. Perry and H. Wettstein (eds), *Themes from Kaplan*, Oxford: Oxford University Press, 481–563.

Kemp-Smith, N. (1949): *The Philosophy of David Hume*, London: Macmillan.

Kirk, R. (1986): *Translation Determined*. Oxford: Oxford University Press.

Kirkham, R. (1992): *Theories of Truth: a critical introduction*. Cambridge, Mass.: MIT Press.

Kripke, S. (1972): Naming and necessity. In D. Davidson and G. Harman (eds), *Semantics of Natural Language*, Dordrecht: Reidel, 253–355. Published as *Naming and Necessity*, Oxford: Blackwell, 1980.

—— (1977): Speaker's reference and semantic reference. In P. French et al. (eds), *Midwest Studies in Philosophy*, vol. 2, 255–76.

—— (1979): A puzzle about belief. In A. Margalit (ed.), *Meaning and Use*, Dordrecht: Reidel, 239–83.

—— (1982): *Wittgenstein on Rules and Private Language*. Oxford: Blackwell.

Lepore, E. (ed.) (1986): *Truth and Interpretation: perspectives on the philosophy of Donald Davidson*. Oxford: Blackwell.

Lepore, E. and McLaughlin, B. (eds) (1985): *Actions and Events: perspectives on the philosophy of Donald Davidson*. Oxford: Blackwell.

Loewer, B. and Rey, G. (eds) (1991): *Meaning in Mind: Fodor and his critics*. Oxford: Blackwell.

Luntley, M. (1984): The sense of a name. *Philosophical Quarterly*, 34, 265–82.

—— (1988): *Language, Logic and Experience: the case for anti-realism*. London; Duckworth; La Salle, Ill.: Open Court.

—— (1989): On the way the world is independent of the way we take it to be. *Inquiry*, 32, 177–94.

—— (1991a): Aberrations of a sledgehammer: reply to Devitt. *Philosophical Studies*, 62, 315–23.

—— (1991b): The transcendental grounds of meaning and the place of silence. In K. Puhl (ed.), *Meaning Scepticism*, Berlin: De Gruyter, 170–88.

—— (1992): Practice makes knowledge?, *Inquiry*, 35, 447–61.

—— (1995a): Moral sentiments, and the difference they make. *Proceedings of the Aristotelian Society*, suppl vol. 69, 31–45.

—— (1995b): *Reason, Truth and Self: the postmodern reconditioned*. New York/London: Routledge.

—— (1995c): Thinking of individuals: a prolegomenon to any future theory of thought. In P. K. Sen (ed.), *The Philosophy of P. F. Strawson*, New Delhi: Indian Council of Philosophical Research, 179–212.

—— (1996): The disciplinary conception of truth. In F. L. Villegas (ed.), *Verdad: logica, representacion y mundo*, Santiago de Compostela: University of Santiago Compostela Press, 65–81.

—— (1997): Dynamic thoughts and empty minds. In J. Dokic (ed.), *European Review in Philosophy*, vol. 2: *Cognitive Dynamics*, Stanford, Calif.: CSLI, 77–103.

—— (1998a): The practical turn and the convergence of traditions. *Philosophical Explorations*, 1, 10–27.

—— (1998b): Towards an education of character. In T. McLaughlin and J. Halstead (eds), *Ethics and Education*, London: Routledge.

McCulloch, G. (1989): *The Game of the Name*. Oxford: Oxford University Press.

McDowell, J. (1976): Truth-conditions, bivalence and verificationism. In Evans and McDowell, 42–66.

—— (1977): The sense and reference of a proper name. *Mind*, 86, 159–85.

—— (1981): Anti-realism and the epistemology of understanding. In J. Bouveresse and H. Parret (eds), *Meaning and Understanding*, Berlin: De Grugter, 225–48.

—— (1982a): Criteria, defeasibility and knowledge, Henrietta Hertz lecture to the British Academy. *Proceedings of the British Academy*, 68, 455–79.

—— (1982b): Truth-value gaps. In *Proceedings of the Sixth International Congress of Logic, Methodology and the Philosophy of Science*, vol. 6, 299–313.

—— (1984a): De re, senses. *Philosophical Quarterly*, 34, 283–94.

—— (1984b): Wittgenstein following a rule. *Synthese*, 58, 325–63.

—— (1986): Singular thoughts and the extent of inner space. In J. McDowell and P. Pettit (eds), *Subject, Thought and Context*, Oxford: Clarendon Press, 137–68.

—— (1987): In defence of modesty. In B. Taylor (ed.), *Michael Dummett*, Dordrecht: Reidel, 59–80.

—— (1994a): The content of perceptual experience. *Philosophical Quarterly*, 44, 190–205.

—— (1994b): *Mind and World*. Cambridge, Mass.: Harvard University Press.

—— (1997): Brandom on representation and inference. *Philosophy and Phenomenological Research*, 57, 157–62.

McGinn, C. (1982): The structure of content. In Woodfield, 207–58.

—— (1983): *The Subjective View: secondary qualities and indexical thought*. Oxford: Clarendon Press.

—— (1984): *Wittgenstein on Meaning*. Oxford: Blackwell.

—— (1989): *Mental Content*. Oxford: Blackwell.

Macdonald, C. and Macdonald, G. (eds) (1995): *Philosophy of Psychology: debates on psychological explanation*. Oxford: Blackwell.

Mackie, J. L. (1973): *Truth, Probability and Paradox*. Oxford: Oxford University Press.

—— (1977): *Ethics: inventing right and wrong*. London: Penguin.

Martin, M. (1992): Sight and touch. In Crane, 196–215.

—— (1993a): The rational role of experience. *Proceedings of the Aristotelian Society*, 93, 71–88.

—— (1993b): Sense modalities and spatial properties. In Eilan et al., 206–18.

Martinich, A. P. (ed.) (1985): *The Philosophy of Language*. New York: Oxford University Press.

Melia, J. (1991): Anti-realism untouched. *Mind*, 100, 341–2.

Mill, J. S. (1875): *A System of Logic, Ratiocinative and Inductive*, 9th edn. London: Longman.

Millikan, R. G. (1984): *Language, Thought, and Other Biological Categories: new foundations for realism*. Cambridge, Mass.: MIT Press.

—— (1986): Thoughts without laws: cognitive science with content. *Philosophical Review*, 95, 47–80.

—— (1989a): Biosemantics. *Journal of Philosophy*, 86, 281–297. Repr. in Macdonald and Macdonald, 1995, 253–76.

—— (1989b): In defense of proper functions. *Philosophy of Science*, 56, 288–302.

—— (1990): Truth rules, hoverflies, and the Kripke–Wittgenstein paradox. *Philosophical Review*, 99, 323–53.

—— (1993): *White Queen Psychology and Other Essays for Alice*. Cambridge, Mass.: MIT Press.

—— (1995): Reply: a bet with Peacocke. In Macdonald and Macdonald, 285–92.

Mueller, V. and Stein, C. (1996): Epistemic theories of truth: the justifiability paradox investigated. In F. L. Villegas (ed.), *Verdad: logica, representacion y mundo*, Santiago de Compostela: University of Santiago Compostela Press, 95–104.

Nagel, T. (1986): *The View from Nowhere*. Oxford: Oxford University Press.

Neale, S. (1990): *Descriptions*, Cambridge, Mass.: MIT Press.

Noonan, H. (1986): Russellian thoughts and methodological solipsism. In J. Butterfield (ed.), *Language, Mind and Logic*, Cambridge: Cambridge University Press, 67–90.

—— (1991): Object-dependent thoughts and psychological redundancy. *Analysis*, 51, 1–9.

—— (1993): Object-dependent thoughts. In J. Heil (ed.), *Mental Causation*, Oxford: Clarendon Press, 283–308.

Peacocke, C. (1975): Proper names, reference and rigid designation. In S. Blackburn (ed.), *Meaning, Reference and Necessity*, Cambridge: Cambridge University Press, 109–32.

—— (1981): Demonstrative thought and psychological explanation. *Synthese*, 49, 187–217.

—— (1986): *Thoughts: an essay on content*. Oxford: Blackwell.

—— (1988): The limits of intelligibility: a post-verificationist proposal. *Philosophical Review*, 97, 463–96.

—— (1989): When is a grammar psychologically real? In A. George (ed.), *Reflections on Chomsky*, Oxford: Blackwell, 111–30.

—— (1992a): Scenarios, concepts and perception. In Crane, 105–35.

—— (1992b): *A Study of Concepts*, Cambridge, Mass.: MIT Press.

—— (1993): Externalist explanation. *Proceedings of the Aristotelian Society*, 93, 203–30.

—— (1994): Nonconceptual content: kinds, rationales and relations. *Mind and Language*, 9, 419–30.

—— (1995): Concepts and norms in a natural world. In Macdonald and Macdonald, 277–84.

Pears, D. (1988): *The False Prison: a study of the development of Wittgenstein's philosophy*, vol. 2. Oxford: Clarendon Press.

—— (1991): Wittgenstein's account of rule-following. *Synthese*, 71, 273–83.

Perry, J. (1977): Frege on demonstratives. *Philosophical Review*, 86, 474–97.

—— (1979): The problem of the essential indexical. *Nous*, 13, 3–21. Repr. in N. Salmon and S. Soames (eds), *Propositions and Attitudes*, Oxford: Oxford University Press, 1988, 83–101.

—— (1988): Cognitive significance and new theories of reference. *Nous*, 22, 1–18.

—— (1990): Individuals in informational and intentional content. In E. Villanueva (ed.), *Information, Semantics and Epistemology*, Cambridge, Mass.: Blackwell, 172–89.

—— (1993): *The Problem of the Essential Indexical and Other Essays*. Oxford: Oxford University Press.

Pettit, P. (1991): Realism and response-dependence. *Mind*, 100, 587–626.

Pettit, P. and Jackson, F. (1996): Moral functionalism, supervenience and reductionism. *Philosophical Quarterly*, 46, 82–6.

Pettit, P. and McDowell, J. (eds) (1986): *Subject, Thought and Context*. Oxford: Clarendon Press.

Platts, M. (1979): *Ways of Meaning*, London: Routledge & Kegan Paul.

Popper, K. (1974): Some philosophical comments on Tarski's theory of truth. In *Proceedings of the Tarski Symposium*, Providence, RI: American Mathematical Society, 400–2.

Prawitz, D. (1974): On the idea of a general proof theory. *Synthese*, 27, 63–77.

—— (1977): Meaning and proofs: on the conflict between classical and intuitionistic logic. *Theoria*, 43, 2–40.

—— (1987): Dummett on a theory of meaning and its impact on logic. In B. Taylor (ed.), *Michael Dummett: contributions to philosophy*, Dordrecht: Nijhoff, 117–65.

Prior, A. (1960–1): The runabout inference ticket. *Analysis*, 21, 8–39.

Putnam, H. (1975): The meaning of meaning. In *Mind, Language and Reality*, Cambridge: Cambridge University Press, 215–71.

—— (1981): *Reason, Truth and History*. Cambridge: Cambridge University Press.

—— (1985): A comparison of something with something else. *New Literary History*, 17, 61–79.

—— (1987): Truth and convention: on Davidson's refutation of conceptual relativism. *Dialectica*, 41, 69–78.

Quine, W. V. (1953): *From a Logical Point of View*. Cambridge, Mass.: Harvard University Press.

—— (1960): *Word and Object*. Cambridge, Mass.: MIT Press.

—— (1969): *Ontological Relativity and Other Essays*. New York: Columbia University Press.

—— (1972): On the reasons for the indeterminacy of translation. *Journal of Philosophy*, 79, 178–83.

—— (1975): On empirically equivalent systems of the world. *Erkenntnis*, 9, 313–28.

—— (1979): Facts of the matter. In E. Shahan (ed.), *Essays on the Philosophy of W V Quine*, Norman, Okla.: University of Oklahoma Press, 155–69.

—— (1981): *Theories and Things*. Cambridge, Mass.: Harvard University Press.

—— (1987): Indeterminacy of translation again. *Journal of Philosophy*, 84, 5–10.

—— (1995): Naturalism; or, living within one's means. *Dialectica*, 49, 251–61.

Quine, W. et al. (1974): First general discussion. *Synthese*, 27, 471–508.

Ramsey, F. (1931): Facts and propositions. *Proceedings of the Aristotelian Society*, suppl. vol. 7, 153–70.

Read, S. (1988): *Relevant Logic*. Oxford: Blackwell.

—— (1994): *Thinking about Logic: an introduction to the philosophy of logic*. Oxford: Oxford University Press.

Recanati, F. (1986): Contextual dependence and definite descriptions. *Proceedings of the Aristotelian Society*, 87, 57–73.

—— (1989): Referential/attributive: a contextualist proposal. *Philosophical Studies*, 56, 217–49.

—— (1990): Direct reference, meaning, and thought. *Nous*, 24, 697–722.

—— (1993): *Direct Reference*. Oxford: Blackwell.

—— (1995): Quasi-singular propositions: the semantics of belief reports. *Proceedings of the Aristotelian Society*, suppl. vol. 69, 175–93.

Resnik, M. (1979): Frege as idealist and then realist. *Inquiry*, 22, 359–78.

—— (1980): *Frege and the philosophy of mathematics*. Ithaca, NY: Cornell University Press.

Romanos, R. (1983): *Quine and Analytical Philosophy*. Cambridge, Mass.: MIT Press.

Rorty, R. (1972): Indeterminacy of translation and of truth. *Synthese*, 23, 443–62.

—— (1979): *Philosophy and the Mirror of Nature*. Princeton: Princeton University Press.

—— (1986): Pragmatism, Davidson and truth. In Lepore, 333–54.

—— (1991): *Philosophical Papers*, vol. 2: *Contingency, Irony and Solidarity*. Cambridge: Cambridge University Press.

Rouse, J. (1996): *Engaging Science: how to understand its practices philosophically*. Ithaca, NY: Cornell University Press.

Russell, B. (1903): *Principles of Mathematics*. London: George Allen & Unwin.

—— (1905): On denoting. *Mind*, 14, 479–93. Repr. in Russell, 1956, 41–56.

—— (1911): Knowledge by acquaintance, knowledge by description. *Proceedings of the Aristotelian Society*, 11. Repr. in Russell, 1953, 197–218, and in N. Salmon and S. Soames (eds), *Propositions and Attitudes*, Oxford: Oxford University Press, 1988, 16–32.

—— (1912): *Problems of Philosophy*. Oxford: Oxford University Press.

—— (1918): The Philosophy of Logical Atomism. In Russell, 1956, 175–283.

—— (1953): *Mysticism and Logic and Other Essays*. London: Penguin, Repr. of original edn of 1918.

—— (1956): *Logic and Knowledge: essays 1901–1950*, R. C. Marsh. ed. London: Allen & Unwin.

Ryle, G. (1951): The theory of meaning. In C. Mace (ed.), *British Philosophy in Mid-Century*, London: Allen & Unwin, 237–64.

Sainsbury, M. (1979): *Russell*. London: Routledge & Kegan Paul. Salmon, N. (1986): *Frege's Puzzle*. Cambridge, Mass.: MIT Press.

Schiffer, S. (1987): *Remnants of Meaning*. Cambridge, Mass.: MIT Press.

Searle, J. (1958): Proper names. *Mind*, 67, 166–73.

—— (1983): *Intentionality: an essay in the philosophy of mind*. Cambridge: Cambridge University Press.

—— (1990): Is the brain a digital computer? *Proceedings of the American Philosophical Association*, 64, 21–37.

—— (1993): *The Rediscovery of the Mind*. Cambridge, Mass.: MIT Press.

Segal, G. (1989a): The return of the individual. *Mind*, 98, 39–57.

—— (1989b): Seeing what is not there. *Philosophical Review*, 98, 189–214.

—— (1991): Defence of a reasonable individualism. *Mind*, 100, 485–94.

Snowdon, P. (1980–1): Perception, vision and causation. *Proceedings of the Aristotelian Society*, 81, 175–92.

—— (1990): The objects of perceptual experience. *Proceedings of the Aristotelian Society*, suppl. vol. 64, 121–50.

—— (1992): How to interpret direct perception. In Crane, 48–78.

Stalnaker, R. (1972): Pragmatics. In D. Davidson and G. Harman (eds), *Semantics of Natural Language*, Dordrecht: Reidel, 380–97.

Stich, S. (1983): *From Folk Psychology to Cogntivie Science: the case against belief*. Cambridge, Mass.: MIT Press.

—— (1990): *The Fragmentation of Reason*. Cambridge, Mass.: MIT Press.

—— (1992): What is a theory of mental representation? *Mind*, 101, 243–62. Repr. in S. Stich and S. Warfield, *Mental Representation*, Oxford: Blackwell, 347–64.

Stout, R. (1996): *Things that Happen because they Should: a teleological approach to action*. Oxford: Oxford University Press.

Strawson, P. F. (1950a): On referring. *Mind*, 59, 320–44. Repr. in I. Copi and J. Gould (eds), *Contemporary Readings in Logical Theory*, London: Macmillan, 1967, 105–27, and in numerous other collections.

—— (1950b): Truth. *Proceedings of the Aristotelian Society*, suppl. vol. 24, 129–56.

—— (1959): *Individuals: an essay in descriptive metaphysics*. London: Methuen.

—— (1964): Identifying reference and truth-values. *Theoria*, 30, 96–118. Repr. in Strawson, 1971, 75–95.

—— (1971): *Logico-Linguistic Papers*. London: Methuen.

Stroud, B. (1977): *Hume*. London: Routledge & Kegan Paul.

Taylor, C. (1985): *Human Agency and Language*. Cambridge: Cambridge University Press.

—— (1992): Heidegger, language, and ecology. In H. Dreyfus (ed.), *Heidegger: a critical reader*, Cambridge, Mass.: Blackwell, 247–69.

Tennant, N. (1981): Is this a proof I see before me? *Analysis*, 41, 115–19.

—— (1984): Were those disproofs I saw before me? *Analysis*, 44, 97–105.

—— (1985): Weir and those 'disproofs' I saw before me. *Analysis*, 45, 208–12.

—— (1987): *Anti-Realism and Logic*. Oxford: Clarendon Press.

Thornton, T. (1998): *Wittgenstein on Language and Thought*. Edinburgh: Edinburgh University Press.

van Fraassen, Bas C. (1966): Singular terms, truth-value gaps, and free logic. *Journal of Philosophy*, 63, 481–94.

—— (1968): Presupposition, implication, and self-reference. *Journal of Philosophy*, 65, 136–52.

Varela, F., Thompson, E. and Rosch, E. (1991): *The Embodied Mind*. Cambridge, Mass.: MIT Press.

Vermazen, B. and Hintikka, M. (eds) (1985): *Essays on Davidson: action and events*. Oxford: Clarendon Press.

Villanueva, E. (ed.) (1993): *Naturalism and Normativity*. Atascadero: Ridgeview.

Weir, A. (1983): Truth conditions and truth values. *Analysis*, 43, 176–80.

—— (1985): Rejoinder to Tennant's 'Were those "disproofs" I saw before me?' *Analysis*, 45, 68–72.

—— (1986): Dummett on meaning and classical logic. *Mind*, 95, 465–77.

Wettstein, H. (1986): Has semantics rested on a mistake? *Journal of Philosophy*, 83, 185–209. Repr. in Wettstein, 1991.

—— (1988): Cognitive significance without cognitive content. *Mind*, 97, 1–28.

—— (1991): *Has Semantics Rested on a Mistake?* Stanford, Calif.: Stanford University Press.

Wiggins, D. (1976): Truth, invention and the meaning of life, Henrietta Hertz Lecture to the British Academy. Repr. in *Needs, Values, Truth: essays on the philosophy of value*, Oxford: Blackwell, 1987, 87–138.

—— (1980): What would be a substantial theory of truth? In Z. van Straaten (ed.), *Philosophical Subject: essays presented to P. F. Strawson*, Oxford: Clarendon Press, 76–116.

—— (1984): The sense and reference of predicates: a running repair to Frege's doctrine and a plea for the copula. *Philosophical Quarterly*, 34, 311–28.

—— (1987): Truth as predicated of moral judgements. In *Needs, Values, Truth: essays on the philosophy of value*, Oxford: Blackwell, 139–84.

Williams, M. (1991): Blind obedience: rules, community and the individual. In K. Puhl (ed.), *Meaning Scepticism*, Berlin: De Gruyter, 93–125.

Williamson, T. (1982): Intuitionism disproved? *Analysis*, 42, 203–7.

—— (1987a): On knowledge of the unknowable. *Analysis*, 47, 154–8.

—— (1987b): On the paradox of knowability. *Mind*, 96, 256–61.

Wittgenstein, L. (1953): *Philosophical Investigations*, trans. G. E. M. Anscombe. Oxford: Blackwell.

—— (1961): *Tractatus Logico-Philosophicus*, trans. D. Pears and B. McGuinness. London: Routledge & Kegan Paul.

Woodfield, A. (ed.) (1982): *Thought and Object*. Oxford: Clarendon Press.

Wright, C. (1980): Realism, truth-value links, other minds and the past. *Ratio*, 22, 112–32.

—— (1981a): Dummett and revisionism: critical notice of *Truth and Other Enigmas*. *Philosophical Quarterly*, 31, 47–67.

—— (1981b): Rule-following: objectivity and the theory of meaning. In C. Hollzman and M. Leich (eds), *Wittgenstein: To Follow a Rule*, London: Routledge, 99–117.

—— (1982): Anti-realist semantics: the role of criteria. In G. Vesey (ed.), *Idealism: past and present*, Cambridge: Cambridge University Press, 225–48.

—— (1984): Second thoughts about criteria. *Synthese*, 58, 383–406.

—— (1986): Can a Davidsonian meaning-theory be constructed in terms of assertibility? *Mind and Language*, 1. Repr. in Wright, 1993, 403–32.

—— (1989): Wittgenstein's later philosophy of mind: sensation, privacy, and intention. *Journal of Philosophy*, 86, 622–34.

—— (1992): *Truth and Objectivity*. Cambridge, Mass.: Harvard University Press.

—— (1993): *Realism, Meaning, and Truth*, 2nd edn. Oxford: Blackwell.

Yourgrau, P. (ed.) (1990): *Demonstratives*, Oxford Readings in Philosophy. Oxford: Oxford University Press.

Index